Sailing Tours: The Yachtsman's Guide To The Cruising Waters Of The English Coast, Volume 4

Frank Cowper

SAILING TOURS.

Part IV.

LANDS END TO THE MULL OF GALLOWAY, INCLUDING THE EAST COAST OF IRELAND.

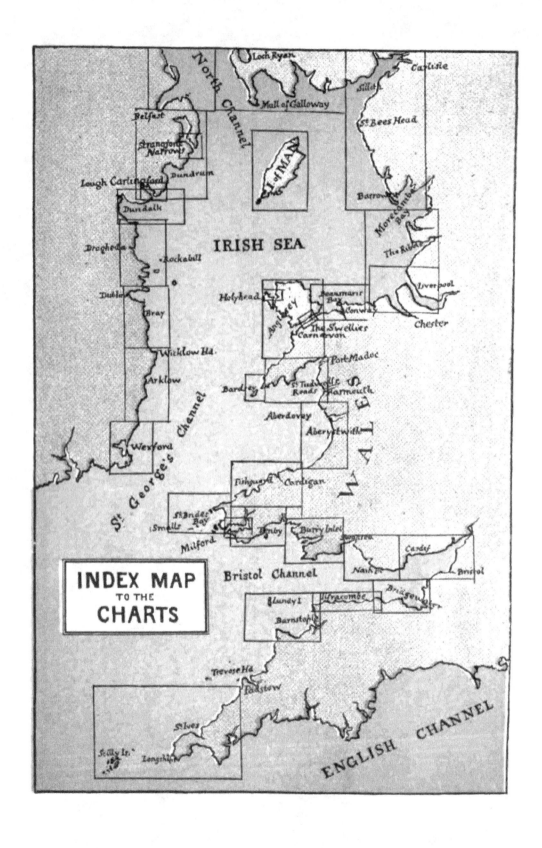

INDEX MAP
TO THE
CHARTS

Sailing Tours:

THE YACHTSMAN'S GUIDE TO THE CRUISING WATERS OF THE ENGLISH AND ADJACENT COASTS.

PART IV.

THE IRISH SEA AND THE BRISTOL CHANNEL, INCLUDING THE WESTERN COASTS OF ENGLAND AND WALES, THE SOUTH COAST OF SCOTLAND, THE EAST COAST OF IRELAND, AND THE ISLE OF MAN.

CONTAINING DESCRIPTIONS OF EVERY CREEK, HARBOUR, AND ROADSTEAD, SUITABLE FOR YACHTING PURPOSES, FROM

LANDS END TO THE MULL OF GALLOWAY, FROM BELFAST LOUGH TO WICKLOW, AND IN THE ISLE OF MAN.

By FRANK COWPER, M.A.

WITH NUMEROUS CHARTS.

LONDON:
L. UPCOTT GILL, 170, STRAND, W.C.

1895.

LONDON :
A. BRADLEY, LONDON AND COUNTY PRINTING WORKS,
DRURY LANE, W.C.

PREFACE.

———

At the beginning of my cruise last summer I happened to put
in at a little harbour where many yachts call on their way up
or down the Irish Sea.

When all was snugly stowed, and I had leisure to look about,
I found I was being greeted by a friendly "hail" from a smart
yacht close by, and at the same time a man in a dingey pushed
out round her stern, and came alongside with "the guv'nor's
compliments, sir, and will you go off and have a chat?"

"Why, certainly," I replied, and stepped into the boat.
Formalities being necessarily brief, for neither of us knew the
name of the other, the conversation turned naturally to subjects
"yachtical," and among other matters the number of hands
required to work vessels of various sizes was discussed.

I then discovered that I owed the civility by which I was
profiting to the fact that I .was regarded as a sort of curiosity
in a small way.

"She's a large craft for only one hand and a boy to
manage," remarked my host, looking at the poor old tub which
lay peacefully reflecting in the placid water. Poor old thing.
It is not for her beauty I admire my docile companion; it is for
her good qualities, and they are manifold. However, I will
refrain from writing a panegyric on my faithful friend and
continue, only I confess to a certain wistful feeling when I
see any "yachtical" person critically examining the lines of

my Argo. To tell the truth I don't think she possesses any "lines." But to the subject:

"If you go about as you appear to do with only that crew," added my friend, pointing to the small figure who was just appearing through the fore-hatch, "you must find it difficult going in and out of a strange port sometimes."

I confessed this was a weak spot in the comfortable enjoyment of my cruise, especially when it blew hard; but that hitherto I had managed without any hitch, and hoped my good luck would continue.

"You see," I added, deprecatingly, "I managed to pick up a good berth this morning"—I was told afterwards it was about the best in the harbour—"although this place is a little crowded."

"That is true, for we had to move from where we first brought up," commented my host; "but I do not understand how you manage it."

After a pause my new acquaintance took down a book, whose cover seemed to me familiar.

"By the way, since you go about as you do, and never employ any local help, this little volume ought to be of interest to you," he said, handing me the volume.

I took it and gravely turned over the leaves.

"Yes," I replied, "a very useful little publication. I have heard of it and seen it favourably reviewed, but I have never used it yet."

"Oh! my wife and I we swear by it. We always, when we came to a new place, said, 'Let's see what that fellow says about it.' You'll find it really useful. I advise you to get it. By the way, I don't know your name."

I told him; but that did not enlighten him much, as there are two ways of pronouncing my name, which, besides, is nearly as common as Jones.

"Yes," I said, "I will make a note of that book, 'Sailing Tours,' and get it as soon as I can. It does seem the sort of thing that is wanted."

"There is one thing you'll find. He makes all his geese swans. I think he lays it on pretty thick when he is describing some of the places. At least they read far more beautiful than they look."

"Ah! very likely; but that's the way with most specialists. Their views become distorted, no doubt," I commented, and then the conversation was interrupted by more visitors; but that afternoon I met another yacht owner, who also recommended me to get the books, and I decidedly agreed with him that they were very useful.

Next morning I left. Since then I have received Vol. III. of "Sailing Tours," but have not had occasion to use it, as I have not cruised S. of the Longships for the last two years.

This little incident seems to me a justification for my continuing to pursue the plan I first formed when I began this series. There only remains now the coast of Scotland to complete the work, which I venture to think will be in some way unique if I am enabled to bring it to a conclusion.

The coasts of Great Britain and Ireland have been surveyed many times, and Great Britain has been circumnavigated by amateurs before now, but I do not think they have been carefully studied by an amateur yachtsman for a definite purpose in the way I have been doing since I started from the Colne.

When I weighed anchor off Brightlingsea, in March, 1892, it was with the fixed intention of exploring every creek which, at low-water, could admit a vessel drawing 6ft., all round our coasts, and which I considered suitable for the purposes of amateur cruising. Such large and busy places as our great ports of commerce I did not consider fell within my scheme. Besides being well known they are places of business, not of pleasure, and my idea was to write a series of practical guides to those creeks and waters where the most pleasure could be obtained with the least risk and discomfort.

I have now in three years so far accomplished my scheme that, from Orford Ness to the Scilly Islands, from the Lands End to Inverary, and from the Tuskar to Rathlin Island, no place has been omitted which fell within the scope of my scheme, and I have besides explored minutely that part of the

Bay of Biscay, which forms the southern coasts of Brittany, from l'Abervrach to Noirmoutier.

So far in all this coasting I have never once employed a pilot, and up to the present I have had no real difficulty. The places where I incurred the greatest risk were in the Scilly Islands and off the coast of Wales. In the former place I was obliged to find my way in to St. Mary's Roads in the dark; and in the latter the shallow nature of the anchorages, combined with the strong tides, gave me some trouble.

Nowhere else have I had occasion even to be anxious, except in going through the Swellies in the Menai Straits.

The inlets and harbours of the East Coast of Ireland I found most delightful cruising grounds, and was surprised to see how few yachts there were enjoying such lovely sailing as Lough Carlingford can afford. This noble sheet of water, lying among the grand group of the Mourne Mountains and Carlingford Mountain, came upon me as a surprise, for it was also part of my scheme to look only at the chart, and find my way into these unknown waters with a perfectly unprejudiced mind. In this way the scenery presented itself in its true aspect—fresh and radiant, or bleak and gloomy, as was its actual nature. Afterwards I read what other people had to say of the places, and was often surprised to find how differently they spoke of them. I am not conscious of exaggerating the beauty of the scenes I have visited; but who can help writing enthusiastically when he remembers the joy with which, after a night of cheerless beating against a choppy sea and along a monotonous rock-bound coast, he saw soaring far above the gray mists ahead rugged peaks and lofty summits bathed in the pure light of early dawn and flushing with the lovely glow which flooded all the eastern sky?

I started with the deliberate intention of promoting as far as I could the taste for amateur cruising—of showing how easily and cheaply such a healthy amusement may be enjoyed, and, therefore, it was part of my scheme to do the work entirely alone, with the smallest number of hands. I have never had any other assistance in the management of my craft—which is a comfortable old cruiser, 50ft. long over all by 13ft. 6in. beam and drawing 6ft. of water, but with a very high free board—than that of a boy, whom I have picked up fresh for each cruise, and so far as regards the handling of the boat nothing could be easier.

I am now about to start on an exploration of the Western Islands of Scotland and the Orkneys. The difficulties I am told are very great. This is what I am always being told; but I can well imagine that the tidal currents of the Pentland Firth are very severe, and when I hear that in one gale the Island of Stroma was entirely swept by the sea, I can easily believe the waves are big. It will remain to be seen whether they are any worse than the seas off Ushant and the Iles de Sein.

The labour of preparing this present volume has been quite double what I incurred in gathering material for the previous parts, and I fairly own I am thankful to have brought it to a completion.

Owing to the length of coast to be described (over 1,200 miles) I have been obliged to curtail the gossiping part of the book. Business had first to be attended to, so that I fear this will be found much duller reading than any of the previous parts.

To those, however, who may use the book for practical purposes, this may not be a disadvantage.

With the object also of making this volume more readily useful, I have kept the description of the coast entirely apart from the running commentary which accompanied it in the preceding parts, and this will be found either in separate chapters or appended under a separate heading at the end of the sailing directions. This has been done partly of necessity in order to economise space, and also partly in deference to the suggestions of various friends. As I look back on the long line of coast which borders the seas described in these pages, I cannot help feeling that a great deal of it is too dangerous for an ordinary amateur. Coasting is almost

impossible from the Lands End to Milford Haven, unless the
journey is performed in a strong weatherly centre-board boat,
which can be hauled up on the beach at night. I have never
tried this way of sailing, and cannot recommend it; but no
doubt the coast might be explored this way, only the under
tow along the North Coasts of Devon and Cornwall is a little
against beaching in many places. The northern coasts adjacent
to the Lake District are not subject to this danger, and from the
Mersey to the Mull of Galloway a good, handy, sailing canoe
might be as good as anything for the work, especially about
Morecambe Bay and the Solway Firth.

From what I saw last season, I feel more than ever convinced that this delightful way of enjoying the summer holidays
will become increasingly popular. The ease with which such
favourite resorts as Barmouth, Llandudno, the Menai Straits,
Conway, the Isle of Man, and the beautiful Irish Loughs are
visited, combined with the extremely inexpensive way in which
such a holiday may be enjoyed, must render the sport popular,
for it appeals to all the sentiments which most influence a
vigorous manhood.

Adventure, sport, variety, lovely scenery, healthy exercise,
freedom from the trammels of an over-civilised age, artistic
tastes, the desire of seeing something new, all are provided for
or gratified by this delightful pastime. Above all, the joy of
accomplishing by one's own efforts what the products of the
most enlightened science of our age alone can procure for the
rest of mankind, who depend on others instead of themselves, is
immense.

Does no sense of pride and thankfulness steal over the hardy
Corinthian as he sits on the deck of his snug little craft and
watches the mail steamer come throbbing into the harbour
crowded with a load of miserable passengers, who are simply
like so many sheep herded on the deck? They are so many
incapables, depending entirely on the will or capacity of a set
of hirelings ; so many children conducted in a public peram-
bulator by nurses in gold-laced caps ; whereas you, O Corinthian, after the manner of your hardy forefathers, have guided

your own craft whithersoever your fancy listed, free as the winds, independent of others, a joyous vagabond in the world of waters.

In these western seas you are but following in the track of your forefathers. Wherever you go you will find traces of these hardy Norsemen who preceded you, and as you glide over the rippling sea, or skim the still waters of a placid lough, those lines, written more than two hundred years ago, will not seem inharmonious:

> A stirring courser now I sit,
>   A headstrong steed I ride,
> That champs and foams upon the bit
>   Which curbs his lofty pride.
> The softest whistling of the winds
>   Doth make him gallop fast,
> And as their breath increased, he finds
>   The more he maketh haste.

And if I add the sequel to old George Withers' stirring lines, I trust I shall not be accused of a lack of taste, for to me they are as beautiful as the first stanza:

> Take Thou, O Lord, the reins in hand,
>   Assume our Master's room;
> Vouchsafe Thou at our helm to stand,
>   And Pilot to become.
> Trim Thou the sails, and let good speed
>   Accompany our haste;
> Sound Thou the channels, at our need,
>   And anchor for us cast.

FRANK COWPER.

HOLM SOUND, ORKNEY ISLES.
  JULY, 1895.

CONTENTS.

___

INTRODUCTION.

CHAPTER I.

CHAPTER II.

CHAPTER III.

CHAPTER IV.

CHAPTER V.

CHAPTER VI.

CHAPTER VII.

b

CHAPTER XI.

CHAPTER XII.

CHAPTER XIII.

CHAPTER XIV.

CHAPTER XV.

CHAPTER XVI.

CHAPTER XVII.

CHAPTER XX.

CHAPTER XXI.

CHAPTER XXII.

CHAPTER XXIII.

CHAPTER XXIV.

CHAPTER XXV.

CHAPTER XXVI.

CHAPTER XXVII.

CHAPTER XXVIII.

CHAPTER XXIX.

CHAPTER XXX.

CHAPTER XXXI.

CHAPTER XXXII.

CHAPTER XXXV.

CHAPTER XXXVI.

LIST OF CHARTS.

NOTE.

THE Charts are coloured on the following principle :

Blue shows where there is **always**, at the very lowest spring-tide runs, 6ft. of water or upwards ; **Green**, where there is **less** than 6ft. of water at **low** tides ; **Yellow**, where the shore **dries** entirely at low water.

Both the **Green** and the **Yellow** limits *may* be passed at high water—the **Green** certainly ; the **Yellow** *perhaps*, depending upon the rise of the tide and the draught of the vessel.

ERRATA.

————

Page 205, line 5 from bottom, *for* N. side of Gored Goch *read* S. side.

Page 325, line 2 from top, *for* Astra *read* Ailsa.

SAILING TOURS.

PART IV.

THE LANDS END TO THE NORTH CHANNEL, COMPRISING THE IRISH SEA AND BRISTOL CHANNEL, WITH THE ADJACENT COASTS.

INTRODUCTION.

It has been my aim in this series of Yachting Guides for Amateurs, so to arrange the day's work that the skipper has always found a port under his lee wherein to spend a quiet night.

From the Thames to Aldborough, or from the Thames to the Scilly Islands, this is nearly always possible.

It is equally possible from Brest to the Loire, or even to Bordeaux. Once, however, Penzance is left behind, and the Longships are rounded, it will be very doubtful if the amateur cruiser will make any harbour before dark unless it be in the Scilly Isles.

Indeed, very few would attempt it, but would make up their minds to keep the sea and either make for Milford Haven, or, if bound for the Bristol Channel, would run for Padstow, or continue their voyage until they reached their port of destination.

B

The Bristol Channel is not, in my opinion, a suitable place wherein amateur sailors may practise cruising.

The tides are too strong, the coast too exposed, and the harbours of the poorest description, and few and far between.

When once Falmouth or Penzance are left behind, there is no really safe place, if caught in bad weather, until Milford Haven or Cardiff and Penarth Roads are reached, and these for small cruisers are none too comfortable in a gale of wind.

Padstow is the only approach to a safe harbour, and the entrance to that is so formidable in northerly or north-easterly gales that few masters would care to attempt it unless of necessity compelled.

There is no disguising the fact that the cruise which I am now about to describe is the most enterprising that an amateur—assisted only by amateurs, or depending on himself alone, with perhaps one boy as crew—could attempt.

Yet strangely enough when I contemplated this voyage for the first time under my usual conditions, no one thought it necessary to caution me against it, as so many did before I crossed the Channel to Ushant and explored the French coast.

Then no terms, expressive of rashness, were strong enough to stigmatise my undertaking ; but to round the Longships and thrash up the constant hurly-burly of the Bristol Channel, or run the gauntlet of the Irish Seas, needed no warning voice.

The reason was that coasters were constantly doing this voyage, whereas the other was a novelty.

However, I would willingly do the French cruise many times before I would encounter the prolonged buffeting of the western seas, with scanty ports and furious tides ; and a coasting voyage from Brest to the Loire is as a cruise from Chelsea to Richmond compared with the lengthy spells from the Longships to the Mull of Galloway, or Mew Island Lighthouse.

I do not write this to deter anyone from continuing his explorations of the English coasts, but simply to point out that none but those with perfect confidence in themselves and their craft should attempt this cruise.

I began gently. I took my Corinthian sailors to calm waters. They sailed in the mild streams of the Crouch, the Blackwater, the Colne, or the Orwell. If they did perchance get out of the channel, they could not come to much harm. Patience and a pipe would see them right eventually.

Then we grew bolder. From Essex marshes and Suffolk banks we sailed to the haunts of fashion and the head-quarters of the yachting world. We encountered the "chops" of the Channel, and the gaieties of Southsea and the Isle of Wight.

Grown bolder still we continued our voyage, until nothing remained but to leave the land and become in truth, as the French call them, "sailors of the long course."

Then we crossed to France, and explored the rocks and inlets of that pleasant coast, and so returned, become indeed by this time thorough seamen, inured to all the changes and chances of that hardy life, and fit to sail anywhere.

Now, in the cruise we are about to undertake, all our seamanship will be required. For however fine the weather may be when we start, the distances to be sailed from port to port are so great that there is no knowing what we may encounter on the way, or when we are making our harbour.

There is no use dissembling the fact; but from Falmouth to the North Channel there are only the harbours of Milford Haven, Holyhead, Kingstown, and the dubious shelter of Belfast Lough, wherein to take refuge in case of a really hard blow.

Not but what there are many minor shelters, such as Padstow, or even St. Ives with Hayle to run to at high-water, Bideford and Barnstaple, Ilfracombe, and the great commercial ports of Bristol, Cardiff, and Swansea; but none of these are to be compared with the easy entrances, quiet berths, and moderate tides of the south-coast harbours, that long series of "mouths" from Portsmouth to Falmouth, which, like the mouths of well-trained spaniels, hold you securely, but never maul you.

Then again there are the doubtful shelters of Aberdovey and Barmouth, St. Tudwall's and Pwllheli Roads. The former with tides which slue you in every direction, and banks and shoals of bewildering extent; the latter a refuge only for the destitute, worse almost than a Salvation Army shelter.

The Menai Straits look as if they should afford a perfect shelter, and so indeed they do when you get there. But the one really comfortable part—that lying between Carnarvon and Pwlfanog—can only be reached by threading the ever-changing sands of Carnarvon Bar, than which I have seldom navigated a more puzzling place; or else by encountering the terrible ordeal, for a stranger, of running the gauntlet of the Swellies, which has this certainty about it, that if you do strike nothing can possibly save you, as the natives say.

Beaumaris is fair, and Bangor Roads are resorted to; but the strength of the tides renders the latter a nasty place for anchoring, and the former is exposed to the E. and S.E., with little room for lying out of the tide. Conway, for small cruisers, is the only truly comfortable place I have found on the whole of the Welsh coast. It is little frequented because it is a bar harbour, but it deserves to be more widely known. Very little expense would make Conway a really excellent yachting resort, for there only can one lie afloat in perfect security and peace. As for Liverpool, the Dee, and the Mersey, those who live there do their utmost to get away as soon and as much, as possible. Sand banks, tides, and strong N.W. winds render navigation anything but a pastime in these places, and the Mersey has the additional disadvantage of being always crowded with shipping.

A disadvantage I mean merely from the amateur cruiser's point of view, for long may that crowd of shipping continue to mount with the flowing tide, and may the commerce of England never grow less.

From the Mersey to Solway Firth there are a succession of ports which do well enough, no doubt, for want of better. But Fleetwood and Barrow, Whitehaven and Workington, are poor places for an amateur yachtsman.

The Wigtonshire coast has indeed one harbour that, in this dearth of convenient shelter, is almost a blessing, for in Kirkcudbright Bay comfort may be found by those who know how to look for it ; but the amount is small and the tides are fierce. There is safety, perhaps, but that is all, unless a boat can take the ground.

The Isle of Man, to its great reproach be it said, does not possess a single harbour where a yacht can lie afloat and be in comfort or safety from every wind.

Douglas is the only harbour where a yacht can lie afloat at all, and there, if the weather chooses to blow a gale from the E. or N.E., things become pretty lively in that small pond, which calls itself a harbour.

Ramsey, the safest of all the harbours, is left dry at every tide, as are Peel and Castleton.

Many people make for Port Erin ; they lie afloat there, it is true, but it can hardly be called a harbour. There are the ruins of a costly breakwater, and that is all. One is entirely at the mercy of the wind, which sends in as much sea as it likes when it blows from the west.

The Irish harbours are a long way better than anything along the English or Welsh coasts.

Wexford—the worst of them, perhaps—would be a blessing in Cardigan Bay. Wicklow affords fair shelter. Kingstown is well known, but there might be better places in a N.E. wind.

The Boyne is a mistake, as I sadly found; but the noble shelters afforded by Loughs Carlingford and Strangford should be more appreciated. The latter, it is true, possesses a tide which is said to be the strongest in the United Kingdom ; but I entered it entirely unaided, and as a perfect stranger, and found no difficulty in picking up an excellent berth in that delightful anchorage, Audley Road.

I confess, to read about the dangers of Strangford Narrows, and to look at them on the chart, does make an intending explorer think a little sadly. But if the wind is anywhere off shore on the ebb-tide there is no trouble at the entrance when leaving, and an on-shore wind on the flood does not matter. As a rule, the wind is usually across the channel, not up and down it.

No doubt the race and overfalls at the entrance are bad with an on-shore wind and ebb-tide, especially at springs.

As for Lough Carlingford, it is simply a delightful place. There are many anchorages in the Lough, all are in very easy soundings, and out of the tide. The channel is admirably buoyed and well lighted.

In Belfast Lough there are really no comfortable anchorages in all weathers for small craft. Carrickfergus has a harbour, and it is safe enough inside, but the depth of water at low tide is scanty, and there is little room. Anchorage in Whitehouse, or Folly Roads, is fairly safe, unless is blows very strong, when one has to shift.

Bangor is memorable for the sad catastrophe in which Lord Cantelupe lost his life, and only affords secure anchorage in off-shore winds.

So much for the harbours in the Irish Sea. In the North Channel there are at the northern end of it two good shelters, Lough Larne on the W. side and Loch Ryan on the E. The former is a long way the safer.

Both are easy of access, but Loch Ryan is free from outlying dangers of any sort, whereas Lough Larne is, in a distant sort of way, encumbered with the Maidens and Hunter Rock.

When once the North Channel is passed, there are many good harbours within easy sail.

By far the best of all is Campbeltown. This harbour is a perfect model of a secure, land-locked anchorage. The depths are easy in it, for Scotch lochs at all events, and the tides mild.

Then comes Lamlash, in the Isle of Arran, a favourite yachting and coasting resort; after which there is a plethora of anchorage in the Firth of Clyde, but none hardly which in the winter affords perfect security without heavy moorings, far heavier than would be necessary in southern harbours, where there is not the weight of wind in the squalls, which come sweeping suddenly from the mountains of Argyle. Campbeltown and East Tarbert are the two safest shelters in the Firth of Clyde.

So much for a brief *resumé* of the places of shelter from Falmouth to the Clyde.

In the southern section they are few and far between, and what there are possess many doubtful qualities. In the northern section, however, there are many more, and most of very fair capacity.

I have now said enough to show that this cruise is going to afford plenty of sailing, and will give abundant opportunity for those who follow it to exhibit their seamanship and enterprise.

As I have pointed out in the other volumes of this series, my idea of the perfection of amateur cruising is for a party of four or five friends to set out entirely by themselves, with no paid hand, or at most a boy to do the dirty work, and if very luxuriously inclined, a cook.

In this way real sport is combined with amusement, and healthy work of a moderate quality adds a zest to the pastime.

I have done all these cruises with only myself and a boy, a different boy on each cruise, and who had to be taught everything, and whom I could never depend on for ten minutes together.

Only one boy out of the lot was good for anything, and he was a Plymouth lad. Naturally my work was considerable, as night work always fell to me, and most of the day's work, too.

When sailing down the English Channel this did not come hard, because there were very few nights in which one was out by reason of the many ports always handy; but on this cruise things were very different.

Not only were the distances much greater, but when I did make a harbour it was never a matter of certainty that I should not have to be on deck in the dark hours, owing to the strength of the tide and a wind getting up across it, which rendered it almost a certainty that the yacht would trip her anchor and get foul with something, or go ashore on a bank.

In such places as Aberdovey, or Glyn-y-Garth in the Menai Straits, never mind how well I moored, unless I had anchors out of all proportion to the craft, and allowed a scope of chain, not warp, on both anchors fit to ride in the Bay of Biscay, nothing held.

What I complain of in this western cruise is the absence of rest the amateur skipper gets. He is never free from a sense of responsibility. He can hardly ever turn in and feel sure he can take his fair snooze, leaving dull care behind.

Not until he reaches Irish or Scotch waters can he feel really comfortable. Such is my experience, and I think it will also be the experience of those who navigate these waters on their own responsibility.

Of course, it is not necessary to do the hard part of the voyage. There is such a thing as sending the little craft round and meeting her in the Mersey, or the Clyde, and thence enjoying the easy and lovely part of the cruise, for lovely this cruise is, and no mistake.

To one who starts from the Thames and finds himself one fine morning, as I did, looking upon mountains, rising ridge on ridge against the eastern sky, the morning mists lazily floating in the deep valley between, and the western sea washing merrily over the yellow sands of Wales, or dashing against the deep shores of Scotland, the change is marvellous.

And all the more delightful that one has accomplished it oneself.

CHAPTER I.

———

THE RUNDLE STONE TO CAPE CORNWALL.

IN the Introduction I took a gloomy view of things. There is always a certain sense of responsibility weighing on me when I write to induce others to cruise in strange waters.

It is as well, therefore, to begin by putting the difficulties and hazards first, as then my conscience will feel clear, and I can describe the delights of the cruise with an unhampered mind. For there are delights and joys before the hardy mariner in this western cruise which are altogether dissimilar to the attractions of the English Channel.

To some men the attractions of scenery are slight, the pleasures of sailing are everything ; others, again, enjoy yachting for the variety and healthy change it affords ; while to others, the charm of passing from the turbulent struggle of the open sea to the placid depths of land-locked waters, where, as they glide past the many coloured rocks and beetling cliffs, they can almost pluck the ferns or touch the overhanging crags, is an experience to be realised as often as may be.

Nowhere in the British Islands can this pleasure be enjoyed so amply as in Scotland, or the S.W. or W. of Ireland.

Cornwall, indeed, allows a slight foretaste of this novel way of yachting ; but the scenery is not to be compared to that of Scotland, although, to my mind, the greater comfort of the cruising far and away counterbalances the misty splendour of the rugged North.

It is the fashion to praise the rich colouring of Scotland ; but I have never seen anything to beat the glorious tints of the Fal, in October. Tregothnan Woods and King Harry's Reach are quite as gorgeous in autumn as anything I have seen in the Western Highlands, and they have this added pleasure to the tourist, that they can be seen for a modest sum.

But Cornwall cannot vie with Ireland, or Scotland, or Wales, in the romantic character of its scenery ; and it is the intimate approach which yachting allows to the very shrines of mountain solitudes and rugged grandeur which in this cruise is so delightful.

Sitting in your arm-chair at home and wondering where you will go next holiday, Snowdon and Cader Idris, the Mourne Mountains and Slieve Donard, Ben Lomond and Ben Nevis, seem distant possibilities ; but in your yacht you can move your house, your arm-chair, if you like, to the foot of all these, and be as near to them as if you were staying in the most expensive hotel, which is built expressly to exploit the tourist.

I do not think enough people realise where a yacht can take them, or how delightful a means of enjoying a holiday it is.

In this cruise the yachtsman will penetrate to all the most celebrated scenes of classic beauty, scenes which have been the theme of painters and poets for centuries ; or at least since painters tried to paint landscape, for poets have had the start of them in their admiration of that side of nature by many a century.

I do not know, of course, how others feel, but I do confess to a sense of placid pride when, without help from anyone, at a minimum of cost—in fact, at no more than that of living quietly in one's own house, if indeed so much—I find myself in my floating house within a walk of Snowdon, of Slieve Donard, or of Ben Nevis.

I do not think the Corinthian sailors, who flit about the Thames, or the Crouch, or the Orwell, realise what possibilities for unlimited roaming they possess, or how cheaply it may be done.

For this cruise, however, even more than for the French one, it is necessary to have a good, seaworthy boat.

I did all my work in the same old ship that had already helped to carry me from Harwich to the Scillies, and from Falmouth to St. Nazaire; but the work she has done in this cruise is equal to that of all the other cruises put together, and a lot over.

One thing I noticed many times, and that is, that the Bristol Channel serves as a gulf between the Corinthian sailors of the S. and E. coasts and those of the Clyde and the St. George's Channel, and I do not wonder at it.

To round the Longships always involves an element of risk for a small craft; one never knows what there is on the other side.

And now to begin suggesting how one is to get to that other side.

I will assume that you have put into Falmouth, and are starting from that excellent harbour.

As the coast from there to the Scilly Islands has been already minutely described in the second volume of this series ("Sailing Tours," Part 2—From the Thames to the Scilly Islands), I will not go over the same ground. No difficulties are likely to occur, for all is plain sailing if you give the Manacles and the rocks off the Lizard a wide berth, and you are not likely to start on this lengthy cruise without a probability of fair weather, at all events. Whether you will get it when you have reached the Longships is another matter.

Some people, perhaps, would put into Penzance, and make that the point of departure. If you are there, well and good, you are so many miles nearer the turning. But I do not myself like Penzance, and see no need to pay the heaviest harbour dues in the English Channel, except Ramsgate, which are the same, unless I am compelled by stress of weather.

I remember once being very glad to get in there; but I also remember more often the pleasure with which I got out of the harbour, where I had the main-sail cover stolen off the deck, and never had a day's rest from being shifted round and round the dock.

I have since met others who said they enjoyed their stay in Penzance. Possibly, if one is the owner of a large yacht and has a crew who will do all the shifting necessary, there is not much to complain of. I was told that in the early summer there was less coal dust, and that yachts were allowed to lie in peace sometimes. I can only speak of the place as I found it, and I believe that chief of amateur seamen, Mr. MacMullen, found it very much as I did.

From Penzance—or, rather, from the **Rundle Stone**, or **Runnel-stone**—then, I will take up the duties of pilot and cicerone, for the navigation now requires attention.

We are now passing the **black bell buoy** moored 70yds. **S.W. ½ W.** of this very dangerous rock, which is **steep-to** on its **outer** side. The rock is **very small**, being not more than **4yds. long** by **2yds. broad**; but it dries 7ft. at low water, and is a most pernicious stone, against which I nearly had the misfortune to bump one dark night in the end of October, when beating back from the Scillies in half a gale of wind from the E., after having tried to run into Tol-Pedn-Penwith, or Guethenbras Point, a little beyond it.

From this rock the **Longships Lighthouse** bears **N.W. by N. ¾ N.**, about **four miles away**.

It is possible to go between the Rundle Stone and the mainland, but as there are several rocks, and not much is gained by doing so, it is better to keep outside of it.

Observe, by the way, the **two beacons** erected at Porthgwarra near Tol-Pedn-Penwith. The **outer beacon** is red and conical. The **northern** or **inner** one is **black**, with a **white band just above the base**. When in one they bear **N. by E.**, and are in line with the **Rundle Stone**.

To pass **outside** the Rundle Stone, we must be **careful not to bring these beacons in line until the base of the northern one is entirely seen above the land**, which it will be **when the Longships bear N. by W.** A **vessel** then may **pass** to the **southward** in safety, and steer a course for the Longships.

To pass **inside** the **Rundle Stone**, the **white band** on the **northern beacon** must be **entirely hidden**, and the **Longships just open of the land**; but, as I have said above, it is **better not to do this** unless obliged.

The **Longships Light shows red** over the Rundle Stone and to the land.

We are now steering N.W. by N. to pass just outside the Longships. **We might pass inside.** There is **a channel**, and we should save something by it. The **leading marks**, which are a **good way off**, are the **highest part** of the **northern Brison, open westward** of the **highest part** of the **southern or lowest Brison, bearing N.N.E.**

This channel leads between **Ketel Boton Rock** and **Peal Point** in eight to eleven fathoms, and the **average width is half a mile.**

The **Brison Rocks** are two **rocky islets**, 90ft. and 71ft. high **above high-water, lying W. ½ S. half a mile** from Cape Cornwall, and **N.E. ¾ N.** three miles and a half from the **Longships,** so that they are fully five miles off when we use them as a guide.

The **rocks** which **lie off** Lands End make it dangerous taking the **coast** too closely, as there are **several small heads close to the large rock** at the S.W. corner of **Peal Point (the extreme point of Lands End),** and **Ketel Boton lies E. by S. five cables and a half** from the lighthouse, drying at **one-quarter** ebb. **Sharks-fin** lies six cables and a half N.E. by E. from the Longships Light, drying at one-third ebb. It is steep-to, except at the S.W. side. Between these two rocks lies the Fe-les, a dangerous rock, which uncovers at three-quarters ebb, with deep water round it.

Mill Bay is an open cove, bounded on the N. by Peal Point, otherwise Lands End, and Guethenbras on the S.

By **keeping at a distance of half a mile** from the shore until the **leading marks for passing between Ketel Boton and Peal Point come in sight, all dangers will be averted, when, as soon as the Brisons are visible, steer as directed N.N.E.**

The Longships are a group of rocks from 20ft. to 44ft. above high-water and distant from **Lands End** about a mile. **Ketel Boton, Sharks-fin,** and **Fe-les** may be considered part of the group.

Sunken rocks also extend about **two cables S.E.** of the **southern rock of the Longships.**

Longships Light.—On the highest rock is a circular gray tower, 110ft. above high-water, exhibiting an intermittent light of the first order, suddenly eclipsed for 3sec. every minute. The light is white, seaward, between the bearings of S.S.W. ½ W. and N. by W. ¼ W.   Red between the bearings of S.S.W. ½ W. and S.W. ¼ S., and also between the bearings of N.S.W. ¼ W. and N.W. by N.   Towards the land a red light of less power is shown.

The bearing S.S.W. ½ W. leads half a mile W. of the Brisons, and the bearing N. by W. ¼ W. leads three-quarters of a mile W. of the Rundle Stone.

The white light in clear weather should be visible sixteen miles.

Fog-signal. — In thick weather a fog-signal, giving two reports like the discharge of a gun, is fired every 10min. The interval between the two reports is about 5sec.   A bell is sounded twice in quick succession every quarter of a minute when the fog-signal is not available.

Tides.—It is high-water, full and change, at 4hr. 35min. local time, and 4hr. 58min. Greenwich time. Springs rise 20ft ; neaps, 14ft.

At the Seven Stones Light-vessel the tide turns to the N.E., within a few minutes of high- and low-water at Dover, which is nearly the same as at Liverpool, i.e., at 11hrs. full and change ; at Trevose Head a few minutes later ; and so on into the Bristol Channel.

Between the Lizard and the Scilly Islands the tide on the ebb runs S.E., S., and S.W., from the Wolf Rock, whilst the flood-tide sets N.W., N., and N.E., or towards the Wolf Rock.

I have been told that the N.E. tide sets for nearly 9hrs. through the Longships channel, but hesitate to give this as a fact, as I cannot find it corroborated, although I believe it to be true.

The Wolf Rock Light is distant from the Longships seven miles and three quarters, bearing S.W. ½ S., and from Tol-Pedn-Penwith it is seven miles and a quarter, bearing S.W. by W. ¼ W.   It is a circular gray granite tower, 135ft. above high-water-mark. The lantern and gallery are painted black. It is built on the Wolf Rock, awash at high-water neaps.

From this tower is exhibited, at an elevation of 110ft., a revolving red and white light, taking 1min to complete the revolution, being alternately white and red every half-minute. It is visible sixteen miles.

There is a fog-bell, giving three strokes in quick succession every quarter of a minute.

This lighthouse was built with the greatest difficulty, as the rock is only 56yds. long by 38yds. wide at low-water, and entirely covered at high-water springs. It is steep-to all round, rising from a depth of thirty to forty fathoms, being a mere pinnacle, 240ft. high, rising in the ocean from that depth to the surface.

In the first year (1864) of the attempt at building the light-house, only eighty-one working hours out of the whole year could be obtained.

The Seven Stones Light-vessel is moored in thirty-nine fathoms, about two miles E. ¼ N. from Pollard Rock—the Longships bearing S. 71deg. E., distant twelve miles and eight-tenths ; the Wolf Rock, S. 35deg. E., distant twelve miles and a half ; and St. Martin's day-mark S. 73deg. W., distant nine miles and three-tenths—in latitude 50deg. 3min. 40sec. N., and longtitude 6deg. 4min., 30sec. W.

The light-vessel shows one white light, giving three flashes in quick succession, followed by 36sec. darkness every minute, visible eleven miles.

There are three lights on the Scilly Islands, two of which are of assistance when navigating in the neighbourhood of Lands End.

St. Agnes Light shows, at an elevation of 138ft. above high-water, from a white tower a revolving white light, attaining its greatest brilliancy every half-minute, visible eighteen miles ; bearing W. ¼ S., distant twenty-five miles and a half from the Longships, and from the Wolf Rock bearing W. ¾ N. northerly, distant twenty-one miles.

This light is obscured N.E. of the group on certain bearings by the northern islands.

Round Island.—On the **N.** side of the **Scilly Islands,** at a height of 180ft. above high-water, **a flashing red light of 5sec. duration every half-minute** is shown, **visible twenty miles.**

Southward of the **Scilly group** the light is **obscured on certain bearings** by the **islands.**

The Bishop's Rock Light, although not visible while passing the **Longships** at any reasonable distance, is of the first importance to vessels homeward bound, and making either for the English or Bristol Channels.

On a rock at the **extreme W.** of the **Scilly Islands** is a gray granite circular tower, showing at an elevation of 143ft. above high-water a double-flashing white light every minute, visible eighteen miles. The two successive flashes are of 4sec. duration each, followed by an eclipse of 4sec. Northward of the group the light is obscured by the islands on certain bearings.

Fog-signal.—During fogs an explosive fog-signal gives one report every 5min., similar to the report of a gun.

The Scilly Islands are minutely described in the second volume of this series ("Sailing Tours," Part II.—The Nore to the Scilly Islands), but it is as well to mention now that in case of being caught in a strong easterly wind when off the Lands End, and not liking to stand up against it, there is **excellent shelter** in the **anchorage** off the Scilly Islands.

The **safest entrance** for a **stranger** from the **S. and E.** is to steer **for St. Agnes Light,** and **when St. Mary's Sound** comes open and the leading marks bearing N.W. by N. (N.E. part of Mincarlo in line with the highest part of Great Minalto), are seen, **to steer through** on that **course** between the **Spanish** and **Bartholomew Ledges** on the **W.** and the **Woolpack Beacon on the E.,** until **St. Martin's day-mark** comes in line with the **Greeb Rock** open of St. Mary's, bearing N.E. by E. ½ E., when steer for **Tresco,** and bring up with **Nut Rock,** distant four cables, and in line with Hangman's Island (off Bryher) in five fathoms, or even nearer in if of light draught.

The safest harbour is **New Grimsby,** which may be entered at any time from the N., and at high-water, or a little before, from **St. Mary's Road.** (See directions, Part II., "Sailing Tours.")

Crow Sound can only be taken at from half flood to half ebb, and with great caution at this latter state of tide. The E. going tide runs through Crow Sound for nearly 8hrs., and is stronger than the W. or ebb-tide.

In entering New Grimsby from the N. steer for Shipman Head, the N. headland of Bryher Island. This bold cliff is steep-to and can be kept well on board. When Hangman's Island, off Bryher, is in line with St. Mary's Castle, it clears all dangers on the E. or Tresco side of the channel. Sail boldly on, and anchor close to Hangman's Island in four or five fathoms, or S. of it close to Bryher. This is the safest anchorage in the Scilly Islands.

Round Island Lighthouse serves as a guide to New Grimsby. It is only about a mile and half to the E. of Shipman Head, which must be kept well open of Round Island to clear the dangers off White Island at the N.W. end of St. Martin's.

To return now to the navigation about the Lands End.

After Peal Point is passed, the coast recedes and forms White-sand Bay, with Sennen Cove at its southern end, where there is a good anchorage in easterly winds, in ten or twelve fathoms, with Cape Cornwall bearing N.N.E. ¼ E., half a mile off the Bounder Rock, on which there is three fathoms and three quarters at low water, Mathew's House in line with Sennen Church bearing S. ¼ W., distant half a mile from the shore.

Sennen Cove is protected by Bo Colloe and Bo Col Rocks, awash only at high-water springs. The Little Bo dries at half ebb, and is the easternmost rock, lying at a third of a mile from the shore.

Light.—There is a small fixed white light for the use of fishermen, visible between the bearings of N.W. by W. ½ W. through N. to N.E. ½ E.

There is a rocket and lifeboat station here.

From the N. end of Whitesand Bay the coast trends N. to Cape Cornwall, with cliffs varying from 190ft. to 300ft. after Gwynver Sands, in Whitesand Bay, are passed.

Cape Cornwall is 197ft. high, and is a far bolder headland than the Lands End. Off it lie the Brisons, two rocky islets,

C

90ft. and 71ft. high above high-water, lying **W. ½ S.** from **Cape Cornwall**, distant **half a mile**, and **N.E. ¾ N.**, **three miles and a half** from the Longships.   The **northern island is the higher** of the two.   **Between these islands and Polpry Point** is **Pornanyon Cove**, girdled by reefs and ledges which dry at the last quarter of the ebb. There is **shoal water** for nearly **one cable S.W. by W.** from the **S. Brison,** and at the **same distance W. ½ N.** is a patch of 16ft. least water.   The Brisons in line lead **westward** of the Greeb patches off Polpry Point.

The **Vyneck** is a group of **detached rocks** lying **one-third of a mile N.N.W. ½ W.** of Cape Cornwall.   They **dry at three-quarters ebb.**   A line from the **Longships Light,** touching the **E. shoulder of the small Brison,** passes over them.

There are **two shoals** which lie off **Cape Cornwall.**   Although there is plenty of water over them, eight fathoms being the least known depth, yet the sea in bad weather is so heavy on them, particularly in N.W. gales, that they should be avoided by small or heavily-laden vessels.

They are **Bann Shoal,** lying **five miles N.E.** of **Cape Cornwall,** and **Cape Cornwall shoal,** a **rocky ridge,** with its **N. end bearing** from the **Longships N. ½ E.** and **Battery Point bearing S.E. by E. ¼ E.**   It is nearly **three miles** long, and **extends** in a **N.N.E.** and **S.S.W.** direction, and is only **half a mile broad,** with **twelve fathoms** least water at its S. end.

Bann Shoal has its least **depth (eight fathoms) when Cape Cornwall** and Sennen Church are in line, bearing S. by W. and Battery Point S.E. ½ S., distant twelve miles and three quarters.

To clear these banks in proceeding N. from Lands End, the Longships kept bearing S. ¼ E. will lead one mile W. of Cape Cornwall Bank.   The **Brison islets in line lead between** the shoals, and Cape Cornwall bearing S. by W. ¾ W. leads one mile E. of Bann Shoal.

Remarks on the appearance of the coast—Objects of interest visible from the sea—Mousehole to Cape Cornwall.—The coast, after passing Mousehole, is mostly rugged and precipitous. The cliffs are interspersed here and there with gulleys, and there are one or two coves where a landing could be effected,

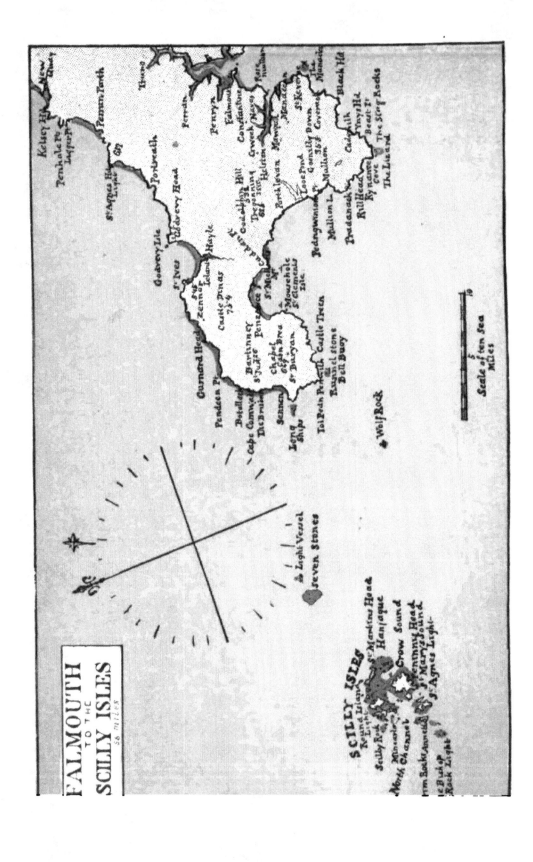

FALMOUTH
TO THE
SCILLY ISLES
56 miles

SCILLY ISLES

Scale of ten Sea Miles

especially at Lamorna Cove, about two miles S.W. of Mouse-hole ; Penberth and Porthcwrnow, little coves to the E. and W. of the singular headland of Castle Treryn, or Treen, at the end of which is the celebrated Logan Stone. If it were a calm day, and the yacht were making little progress, it would be well worth while to land in the dingey on either side of this bold peninsula, and visit both the Logan Stone and Castle Treen, or Treryn an Dinas, as it is called in Cornish, meaning the "fort of fight." A triple ditch and mound guarded the only approach to the promontory. Passing through this the path leads to the Logan Stone at the end. The position is remarkable and beautiful, as the rock juts out 600ft. into the sea and descends in abrupt cliffs on each side.

Lieutenant Goldsmith, commanding a revenue cutter, and nephew of Oliver Goldsmith, upset the Logan Stone to confute the statement of Mr. Borlase, the Cornish antiquarian, to the effect that the stone could not be moved by any mechanical force.

However gratified the lieutenant must have been to see the huge mass, weighing six y-five tons and a half, go rolling and bounding down the cliff, it must have been with consider-able astonishment he received the order from the Admiralty to put it up again. The legend of Humpty Dumpty had not been well considered by the reckless naval officer.

The stone was put up again, but it has never rocked so easily since, and Lieutenant Goldsmith became Smith without the gold before the operation was completed, for he was nearly ruined.

St. Levan's Church is visible up the romantic ravine which leads from the little cove of Porthchapel, and beyond it to the W. is Porthgwarra, a fishing-village, also at the head of a deep ravine. Here are the beacons for avoiding the Rundle Stone. All this coast scenery offers countless attractions for exploration, and a day's cruise along here in settled fine weather, with the dingey towing astern to go ashore where one liked, would be well worth enjoying. Excellent shell-fish are to be obtained off here, and Porthgwarra lobsters are supposed

C 2

to be the finest-flavoured of any. St. Levan used to live here
and fish.   He never caught more than one fish a day however much he tried.   He tried very hard once because his
sister and her son came to see him, but he only caught one
just the same—it was a wretched chad.   So he threw it back
and tried again, but he only caught the same chad, and had
to take it home, with the result that the nephew was choked
eating the bones, for there was nothing else.   And they say
St. Levan reproached himself with the death, for he ought to
have been satisfied with the gift of Providence.   Saints see
more than other people.

Tol-Pedn-Penwith comes next.   It is a fine headland, and
takes its name from the strange hollow or hole in the headland.   A chasm 100ft. deep, and only 8ft. in diameter, cut quite
smooth, descends from the cliff to the sea

Guethenbras is the S.W. point of this headland.

I have some reason to know this spot, for I suppose few
people have had a narrower escape from shipwreck than I had
here.

I was returning from the Scilly Islands in the last week of
October.   The day had been calm with a falling glass.   I only
made the Seven Stones by nightfall, the wind, such as there
was, being E.   After dark it freshened considerably, and came
on to rain in torrents.   By the time I judged it right to go on
the next starboard tack, from about two miles N. of the Wolf
Rock, it was blowing very hard, with heavy squalls and
blinding rain.   I only had a boy with me, and he was below.
After thrashing through the nasty sea for some time I thought I
would go below to see how things were down there, for we had
encountered one or two very heavy shakes-up, and I knew the
boy would never see to stowing anything that might get adrift.   I
called him up therefore, told him to let me know directly the Longships Light—which was under our lee and hidden by the main-
sail—changed from white to red, and went down.   As I thought,
the cabin was in a pretty mess.   The sea had driven in under
the skylight, and there was more water about the floor than
I had ever seen on scrubbing day, and many books, charts, &c.,

had got adrift, and were soaking in the wet. After I put this right I went into the forecastle and tidied up a bit there. Then I thought I would look out, so I pushed back the fore-hatch and looked up.

For a second I hardly realised what I saw. There was an intensely black mass looming against the darkness of the night. It seemed almost over my head. It was right in front. I scrambled up as smartly as I could, and saw the gleam of the sea as it spouted over a rock close under our lee bow. I yelled to the boy to put down the helm, and I let go the jib-sheet at the same time. The old boat came up to the sea marvellously, and as we flew round I saw we were all but on the rocks, and above us were the beetling cliffs, awful in their blackness. It was the little rock lying close in to the S.W. of Guethenbras, which nearly did our business. Another minute's delay in tidying up the cabin and it would have been all over, nothing could have saved us.

Then we thrashed away on the other tack and listened for the Rundle Stone Bell Buoy. I heard it give one toll, and then we were in the white light of the Longships, and I knew we were so far safe.

But I had a bad time of it afterwards. It blew harder, and the sea grew heavier, until in the gray dawn I saw the breakers foaming over the rocks off Tetter-du Point, and had to stand out to weather Carn-du and St. Clement's Isle. It was then I was glad to get into Penzance.

Lands End is an insignificant looking headland, only 60ft. high. A hotel stands near it, and further back on the Sennen road is a house on which used to be written on one end "The First House in England," and on the other "The Last House in England," and the inscription may be there now, only it is no longer true since the hotel has been built.

Sennen Cove is the best place from which to see Lands End, and in quiet weather, or even in rough weather with the wind easterly, one could remain safely anchored there. I have anchored in worse places off the Breton coast many times.

Sennen Church is worth seeing ; it possesses an ancient fresco of New Jerusalem, and a fourteenth-century monument with an early font. It has been well restored.

This church and that of St. Buryan, about three miles inland, stand conspicuously, Sennen being 387ft. above the sea, and St. Buryan 409ft. above it.

Along Whitesand Bay there are many sandy carns. Some of the names of these carns are pretty : Pedn-men-du has at its base an off-lying rock, called the Irish Lady ; there is Carn Leskez, the carn of light ; and Carn Creeb, the cockscomb carn.

People go a long way to see Lands End, but I must say it is a greatly overrated piece of scenery. Cape Cornwall is finer by far, and so is Tol-Pedn-Penwith ; but none of this part can compare with either the Lizard, or what is less known but a long way more striking, Strumble Head, and the cliffs round Fishguard, in Pembrokeshire.

CHAPTER II.

———

CAPE CORNWALL TO GODREVY HEAD.

Bearings from Cape Cornwall.—St. Ann's Light, Milford Haven, bears N.E. by N. northerly, distant ninety-five miles. Saltee's Lightship, N. ¼ E., distant one hundred and twenty miles and a half. Cork Harbour, N N.W. westerly, one hundred and forty miles. Lundy Island Lighthouse, N.E. ½ E. easterly, seventy-three miles. Trevose Head, E.N.E., thirty-six miles. The Smalls Light, N.N.E. northerly, ninety-six miles.

Dangers between Cape Cornwall and Battery Point, W. side of St. Ives Bay.—The coast trends N.E. to Pendeen Point, two miles and a half from Cape Cornwall, and is much indented, the cliffs varying from 20ft. to 100ft.

On Pendeen Point, which juts out like Castle Treryn, there is a watch-house. Three rocks lie off this point, called The Wra, or Three Stone Oar. They are always above water and are steep-to. Between Cape Cornwall and these rocks there is **Manver Rock**, dry at half ebb, two-thirds of a cable from Botallack Head. Cokle Marney Rock is dry at half ebb, and lies one cable in a northerly direction from Botallack Head. **N.W. of Pendeen Point** are the Skinvynecks, distant one cable and a half. The two inner ones dry at one-third ebb, and the outer one is awash at low-water. The Three Stone Oar Rocks are one-third of a mile N.E. of the watch-hill, Pendeen Point, and are only just above ordinary spring tides. Avarrack

Rock, lying S.W. by W. three-quarters of a mile from the
Three Stone Oar Rocks, is dry at half ebb.

There is a cove one mile E. of Pendeen Point, with a coastguard station and rocket apparatus. Off the cove, N.E., at two
cables from the shore, lie the Mozen Rocks, which dry at
three-quarters ebb.

Gurnard Head is three miles E. of Pendeen Cove, off which
lie several detached rocks. The Ebal is the largest of them,
and is covered at high-water springs. It is one cable from the
shore. Gurnard Head is a singularly striking jagged headland,
185ft. high. There is a deeply-recessed cove on its E. side.

From this headland to Carn Naun Point, or Trefalgen Point, is
about two miles and a half, with several coves and rocks in
between, all of which can be cleared by keeping half a mile off
the shore, none of the dangers lying out farther than two cables
and a half. From Carn Naun, or Trefalgen Point, the coast
bears E. by S. ½ S. to Battery or St. Ives Point, distant two
miles and a half. The Caraks lie half a mile W. of Carn Naun,
and are two cables off shore. The highest part is 25ft. above
high-water. The rest of the rocks uncover at the last quarter
ebb.

The land behind Carn Naun is high and rugged.

St. Ives Bay lies between Battery or St. Ives Point and
Godrevy Head, and is three miles and a half across from E. to
W., and is two miles deep.

Battery Point is 104ft. high, with a pilot watch-house and a
three-gun battery on it. As the coast recedes little of St. Ives
can be seen until quite round the point, which is fairly steep-to.

When well to the eastward of this point the town will appear
rising up the side of the hill, with Tregenna Castle on a hill
to the S. of the town, while on a hill further S. is Knill's
Monument (an obelisk), behind which will be seen Trecroben
Hill (590ft.).

The bay is entirely open to northerly winds, the best
anchorage being in eight or nine fathoms stiff clay, with Battery
Point bearing N.W. ½ W., and Knill's Monument open E. of a
farm bearing S.W. ½ W. But this is an impossible anchorage

with N. or even W. winds, and is not very comfortable with a strong E. one.   As a matter of fact, St. Ives is not a place which offers any shelter except with off-shore winds.

The harbour dries nearly 6ft. above low-water springs.   There is 14ft. at high-water springs and 8ft. at neaps.   At the pier-head there is 20ft. at high-water.   A stone pier, 166yds. long, was built in 1770, and an addition of 100yds. has since been added. There is a breakwater, 200yds. long, but the outer end of piles and rubbish have been destroyed by gales to the extent of 140ft., and the ruins of it form a half-tide reef, called **Fisherman's Reef.**

The bottom of the harbour is sand covered with shingle.   The fishing-boats moor to iron posts fixed above high-water-mark for bow-posts, and to two buoys for stern-fasts.   They often come adrift owing to the heavy ground swell.   It will at once be seen that this is no place for a yacht.

Light.—On the inner pier a **fixed light is shown** at the height of 28ft. above high-water, showing **red** through an arc of 60deg. between the bearings of S. 17deg. W. and S. 83deg. W., covering the breakwater ; and **white** S. of the **red sector**, where there is 10ft. or more at the pier-head, and **green** when there is less than 10ft.   Visible nine miles.

There is an old light-tower standing inshore of this light, but it is disused.

Directions.—St. Ives is easy to enter as regards absence of dangers other than those arising from the sea.   It goes without saying that with on-shore gales it had better be avoided.   Merran Rock, lying between Battery Point and the outer pier, covers when there is a depth of 12ft. in the harbour.   Keep Knill's Monument open E. of the outer pier or breakwater and round up to the stone pier, to which it will be well to make fast as far in as possible if there is room, otherwise a vessel must use legs unless she can take the ground easily.   The W. pier is constructing, meanwhile two red lights are shown on it vertically.

Tides.—It is high-water, full and change, at 4hr. 44min. local time, or 5hr. 6min. Greenwich time.   Springs rise 21ft.; neaps, 15ft.

Hayle Estuary.—At the head, or S., of St. Ives Bay lies the entrance to Hayle Creek, the outlet of several small streams. As the whole isthmus across to Marazion on Mounts Bay is not more than five miles there is not much room for a large river.

The whole coast from **Carbis Bay** to **Godrevy Head** is bordered by wide sands. A channel is **kept open** to allow of vessels drawing 14ft. to enter at high-water by sluicing the estuary from reservoirs, and a **half-tide dyke, 643yds.** long, extends from **Chapel Anjou Point** on the **W. side of the entrance,** on which are **five perches or warping posts,** and **two black buoys mark the continuation of the sand bank seaward.** **Square red buoys,** with rings for warping, **mark the E. side. The outer red buoy is a can buoy.**

The bar, marked by a black nun buoy, has a depth of 20ft. at high-water springs, and 14ft. high-water neaps, and is dry at low-water; but vessels drawing 6ft. can get up as far as Lelant at three-quarters flood.

Tide Lights.—On the **W. side,** at **Chapel Anjou Point, two fixed white lights are shown when there is 12ft. on the bar.** The **high light is painted red and stands on three legs.** The low lighthouse is placed on four legs and **painted black.** They are **92yds. apart, and are 81ft.** and **59ft. above high-water.** The lights are **visible six miles.** The lights are shifted as the bar changes.

Lelant Church is a good mark to steer for over the W. point of Hayle entrance until the **bar buoy** is seen.

At **Lelant Quay,** opposite Hayle on the W. side. a **red light** is shown.

The coast from Hayle Bar Buoy is bordered with sand, stretching out nearly a quarter of a mile from the shore as far as **Godrevy Head.** Towans, or sand hills, fringe the coast as far as Gwythian, where the shore becomes steep, with rocks showing through the sand.

Bassack Rock lies S.W. by S. of **Godrevy Island,** four cables. from the shore. **It dries at two-thirds ebb.** Lelant Church open of **Black Cliff, S.W.,** clears it to **the N.W.**

Godrevy Head is 228ft. high, and is bold, but with ledges **extending** off it one cable and a half.

Godrevy Island lies off the head. **It is 80ft. high,** with an islet off its N.W. side. The **S.E. side is foul with rocks, drying at half ebb.** On the **S.W.** is a reef awash at low-water, half-a-cable off, called **Shore Lanner.**

There is a **channel,** with **6ft. low-water, one cable wide,** between the island and the head.

Godrevy Lighthouse.—In an octagonal tower, 86ft. high, is shown a flashing **white light** from a height of **120ft. above high-water,** giving a flash every 10sec., visible fifteen miles.

To point out The Stones, a fixed **red light** is shown from the **same** tower, 27ft. below the flashing light. The **red** light is only visible between the bearings of S. by E. ¼ E. to S.E. ¼ E.

Fog-signal.—A bell is sounded every 5sec.

The Stones.—These dangers lie one mile and a tenth from Godrevy Lighthouse, bearing N.W. ½ N. **Hevah Rock** is the outermost of these rocks, and **uncovers** at low-water springs, and the rocky bank is one cable and a half in extent to the three-fathoms depth. Between it and the eastern group of rocks, extending nearly half a mile, is a deep-water channel, with a strong tide setting through it. The eastern rocks, which show at low-water, are four, uncovering from one-third to three-quarters ebb.

A black buoy with **staff and ball** is moored in ten fathoms, a quarter of a mile N.E. of the **Hevah Rock,** but it is often washed away.

Clearing Marks.—**Gurnard Head,** open of Carn Naun, W. by S., leads one-third of a mile N. of The Stones. **Gwinear Church** (behind Gwythian) in line with the E. side of **Godrevy Island,** S. ¼ W., leads E. of The Stones ; and Gwinear Church, in line with the old engine chimney, bearing S. by E. ¼ E., leads to the W. of them.

The Sound between **The Stones** and **Godrevy Island** is nearly half-a-mile wide, with four fathoms and three quarters depth. **Trecobben Hill** (590ft.) between **Carrack Gladdon Farm** and **Fishery Beacon House,** bearing S.W. ¼ W., leads through.

Remarks on the appearance of the coast and objects of interest visible from the sea, or worth visiting from St. Ives, between Cape Cornwall and Godrevy Head. — The coast is very rugged and forbidding-looking after Cape Cornwall is passed. The celebrated Botallack mine lies just beyond the Cape. This mine goes down to the depth of 1050ft., and some of its galleries extend 1200ft. or more under the sea. The roar of the waves is said to be heard distinctly down below when the Atlantic is tumbling home before a howling N.W. or W. gale. The Prince of Wales visited this mine with the Princess when he took his bride to make the acquaintance of her new Duchy. Behind **Botallack**, St. Just, in Penarth, is seen. The church is very interesting, with a tomb to one Silus, said to date from the sixth century. There is some quaint Celtic tracery, and the columns have unique capitals. In the village there is what is called a British amphitheatre, and several ancient prehistoric monuments are in the neighbourhood.

It was St. Just who behaved so badly to St. Keverne when he dined with him. He stole his spoons. St. Keverne did not actually know this, but he knew "St. Joost." So after dinner he said he would see him home part of the way, anyhow. It was only a walk of about thirty miles, but Cornish saints thought nothing of that. On the way he picked up some stones; they did not weigh more than half-a-ton or so each. He was able to conceal these about his person, as saints did not wear trousers, only loose frocks.

When they reached Breage, nearly half-way to St. Just, St. Keverne said he must be going back, but would like to take his spoons with him if St. Just did not mind. St. Just did mind, however, and was very indignant. However, St. Keverne, after listening politely for a short time, produced his stones, with which he proceeded to bombard the person of his saintly brother, whereupon St. Just dropped the spoons and ran.

The stones are there at Tremen Keverne, near Breage, to this day, and there are no others like them, except at Crousa-down, where St. Keverne picked them up. So there is no doubt about the story.

Sailing E. we see Pendeen Point.   Behind it is a new church built in imitation of the cathedral of Iona, at the expense of Mr. Aitken, the vicar.   Pendeen House dates from the seventeenth century, and there is an ancient cave-dwelling near it.   Lanyon Cromlech, or the Giant's Quoit, lies inland, from the centre of the bay, between Pendeen Point and Gurnard Head, about two miles as the crow flies.   The upper slab is 18ft. long by 8ft. broad, and three stones about 5ft. high support it.   There is another cromlech close by on Lanyon Farm; and the Men-an-Tol, or Holed Stone, with the Men Scryfa, or stone inscribed with the words "Rialobran Cunova Fil" encised on it, are a few yards farther on.   These prehistoric remains precisely resemble the menhirs and dolmens of Brittany, and were evidently erected by the same or kindred people.

Conspicuous behind the rugged headland of Gurnard is Mulfra Quoit, a high hill crowned by a ruined cromlech, from which there is a magnificent view over Mounts Bay and the Bristol Channel.

• The picturesque village of Zennor lies below, with its fishing-cove and old church.

Behind Carn Naun the hills rise steeply, and the scenery is wild—Zennor lying in a deep valley shut out from the rest of the world by rugged steeps and moorland.   The contrast between the N. and S. coasts is very conspicuous when ashore. All here is bleak and barren, whereas at Gulval, only six miles away, tropical plants grow in the open air.

St. Ives is built on the steep slopes of hills, to its considerable discomfort sometimes after heavy rains, as the water pours down through the steep streets, flooding the shops and houses. The rains of December, 1894, were remarkable for the destruction they caused.

The old name of the town was Porth-Ia, from the name of an Irish virgin who travelled with St. Piran when he came over as a missionary in 460.   Here she died and was buried. It is curious to note how in the fourth and fifth centuries everybody was busy converting some one else.   The Bretons say the Welsh or British saints came over and converted them; the Cornishmen say Irish saints converted them; the Irish say that they were converted by the Scotch; and the Scotch by the Gauls. But they were all doing it about the same time, and no one seems to have thought of converting their own people. However, St. Ia gave her name to St. Ives.

The town suffered during the Cornish revolt in 1549, when so much landed property changed hands, passing from the old families into the possession of the new courtiers; and again in the civil wars of Charles I.

The population is 6445, and there is a very comfortable hotel, Tregenna Castle, standing in beautiful grounds. The railway station is the terminus of the branch line of the Great Western Railway from St. Erth.

The quay is very busy in the pilchard season, from July to October, and the fishing-luggers are smart, handsome craft. They have to moor stoutly in the harbour owing to the scour of the sea in westerly and northerly gales.

The church is a fifteenth-century building with a Norman font, and the bones of St. Ia—so they say.

Battery Point is at the end of what is called the island.

Boat-building is carried on here and at Hayle; but the chief support of the place is the pilchard fishery, the fish being exported to Italy.

The monument which has been referred to as a sea-mark is a granite pyramid erected by John Knill, collector of customs, in 1782, at St. Ives, in memory of himself. He died in 1791, and established a quinquennial festival to his own memory. By his will he left property to provide for the following items of expenditure: £10 for a dinner for the mayor, the vicar, and the collector of customs, who may each invite three guests; £5 to be divided among ten little girls, born in the borough, who are to dance round his grave; £1 to the fiddler to play to the girls; £2 to two widows who are to act as chaperons; £1 for ribbons; £1 for an account-book and a marriage-portion for a St. Ives woman selected for good conduct; £5 as a prize for knitting nets; £5 for curing pilchards; and £5 to two "follower boys."

The date of the festival is July 25.

At Carbis Bay there is a watering-place, and it is becoming a favourite bathing-place.

Lelant is an old fishing village, and a great resort of the pilchard boats. It has a quay, and might be a good place to lay up small yachts; it is opposite **Hayle**. At Hayle there is a fair amount of foreign and coasting trade. The wharves accommodate a good many vessels. There are building slips and machinery works, and there is a steam tug to assist vessels in and out.

If only there were a little more water always in the river Hayle would be a convenient shelter to stop at in coasting up the Bristol Channel.

The coast is bordered by sand hills, some 100ft. high, between Phillack, on the E. side of Hayle estuary, and Gwythian, which is the last village before Godrevy Head is reached.

Inland the country rises to high hills, lying between Camborne, Penrhyn, and Helston, but the view offers nothing of a remarkable nature.

CHAPTER III.

FROM GODREVY HEAD TO TREVOSE HEAD.

Trevose Head bears from **Godrevy Light N.E. by E. ½ E.**, distant twenty-three miles and a half, and from **Cape Cornwall E.N.E.**, thirty-six miles. **St. Agnes Head** bears from **Godrevy Light E. by N. ¼ N.**, distant eight miles.

The coast is fairly clear of dangers, what there are being mostly visible, and none farther out than about one cable and a half from the shore.

The **cliffs** from **Godrevy** to **Portreath** are about 250ft. high, and there are many sand hills along the bays.

Navax Point lies close E. of **Godrevy Head**, off which are the **Lethegga Rocks**. The shore recedes in a cove here, and on the E. of the large bay are the **Samphire Islands**, 91ft. and 148ft. above high-water   One-third of a mile N.E. are the Crane Islands, 121ft. and 126ft. high, and near **Portreath** are the Horse and Basset, 86ft. and 100ft. high. **Portreath** is about four miles **E. ½ S.** of **Godrevy Head**. It is a **tidal harbour**, with two **tidal basins, 300ft. by 100ft.** and **200ft. by 100ft.**, respectively, with entrance **26ft. wide**, protected by booms. There is a depth on the sills of 15½ft. and 9½ft. at high-water. springs and neaps, respectively. The tide rises 18ft. at high-water springs.

The population in 1881 was 785. The Great Western Railway has a mineral railway to the harbour, but Portreath is not a place I should advise any one to make for in bad weather, or, in fact, at any time. There is a heavy ground swell usually.

Tide Lights and Signals.—Flags are exhibited at the long pier or the Eastern Hill by day. A red one is shown when to enter, and a white one when to keep off. At night a red light shows when to approach, and a green one when to keep off.

The entrance is easily known by a white tower, 122ft. above high-water, on the E. side. The pier runs out N., and is on the W. side.

The harbour is only used by coasters discharging coal or pit props, and taking in copper or tin.

St. Agnes Head is four miles to the E. It is a bold headland, with St. Agnes Hill, crowned by a beacon, 617ft. above high-water, behind it. On the N.E. side of the hill are mine buildings and chimneys.

The coast between Portreath and St. Agnes Head is mostly high cliff, varying from 150ft. to 200ft., bordered by sands, with coves here and there.

From St. Agnes Head to Trevose Head the course is N.E. ½ E., distant sixteen miles and a half. Off St. Agnes Head, bearing N.N.E. ¾ E., distant one mile, are the Boden Rocks; also called the Man and his Mate. They always show above high-water. Between these and the shore there is a clear channel, with seven fathoms and a half.

Opposite the rocks, in the bight of the bay, is Porth Trevaunance, one mile and a half E. of St. Agnes Head, with a small harbour pier 200ft. long. The breadth of the harbour is 90ft., the entrance 24ft., rather narrow to steer for in a heavy ground swell.

Tide Signals.—White flag by day and two white lights at night when there is no water. Red flag by day and one white light at night when the port is accessible.

The coast continues high to Porth Perran, three miles and a half to the E., whence the coast becomes sandy, Ligger, or Perran, Bay being a wide extent of sand, with sand hills behind.

D

Holywell Head, or Penhale Point, is a conspicuous promontory at the N.E. of Ligger Bay, with a deeply recessed bay to the E. of it. There are several mine buildings on Penhale Point, and the Carters Rocks, always above high-water, lie off it. On the N. of Holywell Bay are the Chick Rocks, lying off Kelsey Head, with a rock 16ft. below low-water.

There is another deeply recessed cove to the E. of Kelsey Head, and then comes the entrance to what looks like a convenient and safe creek. Unfortunately the Gunnel, or Cranstock, Creek dries right out, and is a shallow tract of sand. Coasters only can get in at high-water springs. The entrance is close under E. Pentire Point on the N.E. side.

All these bays and coves are encumbered with sand.

Towan Head is on the E. of Fishtal Bay, and round it on the E. side is New Quay, or Towan. The little town is not seen until Towan Head is well opened to the E. A coastguard flagstaff and beacon stand on a hill, half-a-mile inland of Towan Head, which is 100ft. high.

The ground off Towan Head is foul to more than a quarter of a mile out.

A branch of the Great Western Railway runs to New Quay from Par, and is continued to the S. pier, 140yds. long. The N. pier is 70yds. long. The entrance between is 80ft., with a depth of 17ft. high-water springs, and 12ft. high-water neaps. N.E. gales clear away the sand often to the depth of 2ft.

Northerly gales send in a heavy sea, causing vessels to strike heavily on the hard bottom of the harbour, which dries out.

The population of New Quay is 1600. It exports china-clay and grain.

The little place is a rising watering-place, and in the pilchard season is busy.

From New Quay to Trevose Head is eight miles. The coast is high and bold, with deep indentations. The course is N.E. ½ N. About mid-way lies Park Head, with foul ground off it to the extent of three cables.

Watergate Bay lies between it and New Quay, with a long sandy beach fronting it, lying out to one cable and a half from the cliffs.

Trevose Head looks like a round island from this bay.

Two little coves lie in Watergate Bay—St. Columb Porth to the S.W., and Mawgan Porth to the N.E., distant two miles and a half from each other.

North of **Park Head** is **Trevose Head**, one of the most important promontories in the Bristol Channel. When first seen from the sea it has the appearance of an island, as the land falls behind it. The headland is 232ft. high. The white lighthouse on its N.W. side, the coastguard station behind, and the **Quies** inlets, one mile off to the W., all serve to make this headland unmistakable.

Trevose Light.—At an **elevation of 204ft. above high-water, an occulting white light** is shown, **visible twenty miles.** The **light is occulted, or obscured, three times in quick succession every minute, each period of darkness and light occupying 3sec.**

The lighthouse is **white and circular.**

There is no fog-signal.

The **Quies Rocks** are nearly a quarter of a mile in extent, and lie nine cables off **Dinas Point**, the **W. extreme of Trevose Head.** One rock called the Moor Quies lies close to Dinas Point. A passage with deep water half-a-mile wide lies between this rock and the outer Quies. The outer **Quies,** sometimes called the **Cow and Calf, are high islets, black and jagged.** The **S.E.** rock is the **highest.** They form a con-spicuous feature in this wild coast, and are a good **day-mark to know** when a vessel is approaching **Trevose Head** and **Padstow,** the only possible harbour to make for between Penzance and Bristol in heavy winds.

Remarks on the appearance of the coast, and objects of interest visible from the sea between Godrevy Head and Trevose Head.—The coast has a dreary and monotonous appearance from the sea. It is all the more gloomy-looking as it suggests the many wrecks, accompanied almost always with the total loss of life of the ship's company. Off Portreath only last January, 1895, a steamer sank, two hands only being saved after terrible sufferings. It is not the rocks or the coast, however, that cause this great mortality from Gurnard Head eastward. It is the sea. The vessels that are lost nearly always founder, and no winter passes without many brave fellows looking their last on this rock-bound shore.

I well remember the first time I pounded along here. I had left Fowey at nine o'clock the morning before. It had been calm until four o'clock. After drifting only as far as the Dodman, a fresh little breeze sprang up westerly, and away I bowled for Beast Head, as near as I could get the old tub's head to lie.

By the time I passed the Lizard there was a fine breeze, of course, right ahead—when is it ever otherwise going west?—and I thrashed through the turmoil of a heady ebb. There were some thirty other craft, coasters mostly, doing all they could to churn up the sea. It was a pretty sight as we all pounded into it together, and tacked and luffed to weather those treacherous rocks, which, to my mind, are as dangerous as any in the whole Channel. People talk of the Manacles, but the Stags and Man-o'-War Rock are far worse, and have no beacon or buoy to mark them, although they lie right in the course of all the Channel route.

When once Mounts Bay was opened the breeze came off the land, and away we all scudded for the Rundle Stone Buoy.

It was dark by the time I opened the Longships Light, and then the wind came ahead and the tide set against me. By midnight, however, I was standing close into the Brisons and off again. Before I left the helm to look up the chart and get some food I was abreast of Cape Cornwall, and the sea was growing lumpy.

By sunrise I had made no more than some ten miles to the N. of Gurnard Head, and the old boat was putting her nose into it. I wanted to get to Milford Haven, but at this rate it looked as if I should be some time doing the ninety odd miles to St. Ann's Head.

The sea, too, was getting up with the freshening northerly wind. However, I put the old thing as close as her nose would go, and thrashed on. At last I opened up St. Ives Bay and the low land through which the Great Western Railway runs down to Marazion.

I looked round for my companions of the night before. The whole covey was almost hull down astern, pounding away on the other tack; two only were keeping in my wake.

When I came abreast of Godrevy Head the wind freshened to quite a strong breeze, and I made up my mind to go for Padstow, as I had no wish to pound along, and only make some thirty miles of my direct course after sailing some sixty all through the day.

Then it was I had a good look at the coast, for with eased-off sheets and almost a beam wind the little craft slipped easily along, allowing me time to enjoy myself and take life easily.

Carnbrae Monument, 75ft. high, caught my eye after passing Godrevy Head. It stands between Camborne and Redruth, and serves·to show where the richest mines of Cornwall lie. Dolcoath yields tin and copper, but the workings are now so deep (nearly 2500ft.) that the expense of raising the ore is doing away with the dividends.

Gwennap is another celebrated mine, and here it was John Wesley preached so earnestly that the Cornish miner became a changed man; and instead of indulging in swearing, drinking, and other vices, he now prays, reads his Bible, and indulges in some of the other vices, too, if those who know him best tell the truth.

Neither the allurements to repose offered by **Portreath** or **New Quay** tempted me to visit them, and I flew along this wild shore unmindful of its attractions.

There is, however, much to be said for the neighbourhood of **New Quay**, and those who cruise in very small craft, and have no objection to taking the ground, could do worse than turn in there for a spell. The "town" boasts of two hotels, and lies beautifully under the shelter of high and fantastic cliffs of limestone. There are even rocks of **blown** sand, which harden under the action of wind, sun, and water until it becomes a good building stone, and when burnt forms an excellent cement.

They have built a church at Cranstock of this blown sand-stone, and it has quite a "terra-cottery" effect ; besides, there is inside an old font and outside a Holy Well, which gives name to the point and bay.

In the limestone cliffs there are many fossils to be found, and from the hill above Towan Head the "Huers" watch for the pilchard shoals as they come up channel, saluting their appearance with the cry that sounds almost Bacchic, "Heva, Heva," reminding one strangely of "Evoé, Evoé," as "Ja" does of "Jah." In fact, there are many things to make one reflect on Semitic themes in Cornwall.

Behind Columb Porth is the village of St. Columb Minor, with the scanty remains of one of the most modern of Mediæval Priories. Railton Priory was founded in 1500 by Prior Vivian of Bodmin, Bishop of Megara, "in unbelieving parts," but the foundation was very soon suppressed. From which it is clear the worthy Bishop did not see the signs of the times.

There is a blow-hole at Colomb Porth which delights the children of the place as well as tourists. The pent-up air drives out the water as the tide rises, after the manner of a spouting whale.

Watergate, however, possesses some really interesting places, which might be visited from Padstow most easily.

In the centre of the bay, and standing back a little way from the shore, is Mawgan, about three miles from its little cove of Porth Mawgan. The village lies in a pretty valley, and possesses an old church with a fine pinnacled tower, of the fifteenth century. What gives this old church its peculiar interest is the number of monuments it possesses to that ancient Cornish family, the Arundells of Lanherne. There were three principal branches from the original stock, but those of Lanherne and Trerice are the most known to fame. The present Lord Arundell of Wardour is the head of the family now, and his grandfather bestowed the ancestral manor-house of Lanherne on a Society of Nuns of St. Theresa, driven from Antwerp by the French Republican troops. They had been settled in Antwerp since 1619, and must have found the change from the

precincts of that splendid cathedral to the quiet of this secluded
Cornish village very great.   However, as their rules are so
strict that no one, not even their Father Confessor, or their
servants, ever see their faces, this tranquility is hardly likely to
affect minds so utterly abstracted from the world.   Their food
is served them on a turn-table, so that no one need enter this
sacred seclusion, and here the sisters live, "the world forgetting,
by the world forgot." They never leave the convent.   No one
ever hears them speak except the Father Confessor, who never
sees their faces. The medical man is the only one so privileged,
and then only in cases of extreme necessity. Their very burying-
place is screened from all observation.   The lay-sisters are
the only intermediaries between these living dead and the life
outside their walls.   Large estates belong to the foundation, and
the sisters are said to be very charitable. It would, indeed, be
a pity if they did not do some good in the world, considering
the trouble they take to keep themselves good, if such a life
can be considered by anyone approaching "goodness," which
after all may be to some as much a puzzle as was "Truth to
Mocking Pilate."

This manor-house of Lanherne has been the seat of the
Arundells since 1231. There are some brasses in the church
to their memory, and other monuments, but the bow of a boat
is perhaps the most weird memorial of the "departed dead."
It belonged to a fishing-boat which drove ashore one winter's
night in Beacon Cove with ten ghastly bodies.   The poor
fellows were frozen to death, and so came ashore grimly to
their burial.

There is a quaintly-carved cross in the churchyard, and a
Norman font in the church.

The Arundells took different sides in the Civil Wars. Stout old
Sir John, of Trerice, held Pendennis Castle for the king, and had
the honour in his eighty-second year of marching out with bag
and baggage, matches alight, and banner displayed, to surrender
to the Parliament the last fortress that held out for the king.

His kinsman, Humphrey Arundell, of Lanherne, after helping
to defend St. Michael's Mount against the Roundheads, turned

traitor and was executed. There is some explanation for this supposed treachery, in the fact that Sir Francis Basset was appointed governor of a stronghold which had belonged to the Arundells for some time.

A third branch of the family were the Arundells of Tolvarne, one of whom interceded for that strong-minded woman, Lady Kiligrew, after her piratical escapade in Falmouth Harbour, which was accompanied by murder and plunder after the true buccaneer fashion.

In spite of all these memories my mind wanders more especially to that gray old house in the wind-shorn country. As the sea dances by and the sails draw taut and full with the fresh breeze ; while all the earth, and sea, and sky, seem full of life, and motion, and freedom ; I think of those desolate lives— those women immured against all the promptings of Nature in that living tomb, never to speak, never to see or be seen, never to know or wish to know aught that goes on in the life of their fellows. A mystery hangs over that old gray house in the brown and yellow landscape—a mystery of strangely warped imaginings.

Beyond Mawgan Porth, but still in the N.E. part of Water-gate Bay and S. of Park Head, are Redruthan Steps, a tangled mass of chaos, where rocks lie piled on rocks, and all is wildly beautiful in the glowing light of the western sun as it streams over the wide Atlantic. One of the rocks is called Queen Bess, for seen in one way it has a sort of look of that "lion-like" woman, as Henry of Navarre called her, with ruff, and farthingale, and crown.

After Park Head is passed, Trevose Head seems close by. The geological formation of this noble headland is a little mixed. It is composed partly of trap-rock, sandstone, and argillaceous slate.

In the bay and close to the shore on the S.W. side is the ruined church of St. Constantine, half smothered in sand, and some little distance inland is the interesting old church of St. Mervyn.

The Quies Rocks are striking objects, perhaps too much so sometimes, for the impression they would make, assisted by the heavy ground swell nearly always running on the shore here would be lasting.

Once to the N. of Trevose Head and the way into Padstow becomes open.

I was very glad when I saw it, for the weather had come on nasty, and the sea was getting heavy with the N. by E. wind and the flood-tide ; besides, it was a good long way from Fowey, which I had left at nine the morning before.

CHAPTER IV.

———

TREVOSE HEAD TO HARTLAND POINT.

Sailing Directions.—From Trevose Head, Stepper Point, the E. headland of Padstow Bay, bears E. ¼ S., distant about three miles. Tintagel Head bears E. by N. twelve miles and a half, and Hartland Point N.E. by E. thirty-four miles.

There are two fine islets marking the entrance to Padstow —the Gull, or Gulland, and the Newland; the former 93ft. high, the latter 114ft. The passage lies between these two.

The Gulland is one mile and a quarter from the shore; within it are Gurley and Chimney Rocks, with a depth on them of 11ft. at low-water. There are three other rocks, lying from two to three cables from the E. side of Trevose Head. The channel between the Gulland and the Gurley Shoal is three-quarters of a mile wide, but a stranger should always pass to the N. and E. of the Gulland.

There is anchorage in Padstow Bay in six or seven fathoms, with mild tides, a little S. of a line joining Trevose Head and Stepper Point, in the centre of the bay; but the heavy ground swell nearly always prevailing makes it an uncomfortable berth.

Stepper Point is easily known by its conspicuous day-mark, a tower 40ft. high and 272ft. above high-water. The dangers on the E. side of the bay are the off-lying rocks of the Newland Islet. On the W., distant one cable, are the Rainer Rocks, dry at half ebb. On the E. are the **King Philip** and **Villiers Rocks,** with 3ft. and 6ft. over them at **low-water** springs. In the trough of a heavy ground swell these rocks show.

Off **Pentire Head** is a sunken danger with 9ft. over it, **except** when there is a **low tide and heavy ground swell,** when it **shows.** It is called the **Roscarrack,** lying N.W. ¼ W. distant a quarter of a mile from **Rumps Point,** the N.E. point of Pentire Head. The **Rumps Rocks** lie close to the point, and **Mouls Islet** lies one cable and a half E. of the Rumps; it is conical and 154ft. high.

South of Pentire Point is **Trebetherick Point,** with **Hell Bay** between. Off **Trebetherick Point** stretch the **Doom Sands** to within a cable of **Stepper Point;** the channel, therefore, is **extremely narrow.**

When coming from the W., the Quies, the Gulland, and the Newland may appear as one rock, as they are all in line. They soon open out, however, and being so high are excellent marks. The **second of the Quies rocks,** in line with **Trevose Head;** leads through the S. channel; the **Villiers Rock** on the **E. side** is in line with the **Newland** and the **Mouls Islet;** while **Trebetherick Point** just opening of **Pentire Head** and the **Quies,** seen S. of the **Gulland,** clears it; but a stranger would do far better to **keep** to the open and **central channel.**

Directions.—To **enter Padstow Harbour** is **easy** with **winds** from N. by W. to E.S.E. round northerly, but the sea breaking on the **Doom Bar** is somewhat alarming if there is much wind, and as the channel is so narrow there is a heavy roll and broken water for some little distance inside. Stepper Point is steep-to and must be kept close onboard. There is a notice put up on the point on its N.E. side warning masters to "Round close-up to the point."

With strong W. or S.W. winds the danger is that a vessel is taken all aback as she opens Stepper Point, when, before she can gather steerage-way, she is set on the Doom Bar, where she does not take long to break up, and nothing can save the crew if there is much swell or sea on.

To avoid this danger as much as possible, sailing masters are urged to carry on all the sail they can, and shoot round the point as close as possible, keeping as near to the cliffs as they can, with an anchor ready to let go and a warp to run ashore. No sailing vessel, unless unusually handy and quick, should attempt to enter on the ebb, and after the **Doom Sands** are uncovered the stream is so strong that none but a steamer could enter. The **flood-tide** will always **help** a vessel up at least as far as **Hawker's Cove, half a mile within the point.**

There are **capstans** and bollards along the cliff to warp a vessel out of danger, and assistance is always on hand if necessary.

From "**The Ketch,**" the dangerous extremity of the Doom Bar, a bar of sand and shingle crosses the channel to Stepper Point, with 16ft. of water on it at low-water springs, and 36ft. high-water springs, after which the channel becomes deeper, with four fathoms at **Hawker's Cove,** where the **anchorage** is secure in a blue-clay bottom, as close to the W. shore as possible, with the **Newland** shut in by **Stepper Point.**

Above **Hawker's Cove** the channel divides, and has only 4ft. least water between the banks for half a cable. It deepens after this slightly, and has 12ft. least water off **Horseshoe** Bank for nearly half a mile; thence it gradually shoals to 6ft. a little N. of the entrance of Padstow tidal basin, two miles from Stepper Point. The **banks shift,** and there are no **buoys, perches,** or **beacons** anywhere to guide a stranger, so that it is risky to attempt to go above **Hawker's Cove** without local assistance. The tides, too, are strong.

The **best time** to **enter** is from **half flood** to **high-water,** and to **leave** as near **high-water** as possible.

Tides.—It is high-water, full and change, at 5hr. 13min. local time, or 5hr. 33min. Greenwich time. **Springs rise 26ft. ; neaps, 17ft.**

The wrecks that take place here nearly always happen through vessels trying to enter on an ebb-tide, when, if they do succeed in shooting in round the point, the tide seizes them, and they go inevitably on the Doom Bar, as they lose steerage-way. With on-shore winds the sea is very heavy on the ebb, and a vessel runs a great chance of broaching-to.

The **channel** up to **Padstow** turns a good deal, and the banks alter. They are all hard sand, and can be seen usually to the depth of 8ft. or 9ft. as the vessel passes over them at high-water; but a pilot is, if not an actual necessity, yet a great safeguard, and although I got in without any aid, and sailed right up to the bight off St. Michael's on the E. side, and then stood over to Padstow on the W. shore, I did not feel at all comfortable, and the banks seemed very close under me.

Padstow Harbour dries 6ft. at low-water springs, with 16ft. high-water springs, and 10ft. high-water neaps.

During winter a **red light** is shown on the S. pier, and a green one on the N. pier, but they are usually extinguished after midnight.

On the E. shore, nearly opposite **Hawker's Cove**, is the ancient and solitary church of St. Enodoch. The **channel** lies along the **W. shore** opposite this church, and then bends across **slightly** to the **E. side**, when it again turns S. and keeps along the **W. side**.

The total absence of any buoys or marks of any kind is singular, considering that this is really the only approach to a refuge between Penzance and Penarth Roads.

There was a talk of making it a harbour of refuge, and it might easily be done, seeing the excellent position of the rocks for supporting the breakwaters.

From **Pentire Head** to **Tintagel Head** is nine miles, with the bays of **Porth Quin** and **Porth Isaac** in between.

Both these bays are occasionally used by coasters for shelter against W. winds, or to wait a tide. The shores are steep-to, the cliffs high and bold, and the holding ground good close to the shore; but the N. wind sends in a heavy sea.

The **Cow Rocks** are the only danger in **Porth Quin, drying** at **half ebb**. They lie **N.N.E.** one cable from **Dordon Point. Porth Quin** is at the **E. side** of the bay, under Kellan Head; it stands on a narrow inlet, dry at low-water, with **Dordon Point**, marked by a summer-house, on its W. side and Kellan Head on its E. side.

Endellyon Church, with a square tower 462ft. above high-water, with a clearly-defined road leads up to it behind Porth Quin.

Porth Isaac is one mile and a half E., and affords shelter at high-water, with **Porth Gavorne** just beyond in another little cove, with an inn close to the head of the creek.

This is a safe place to run ashore if caught in weather too heavy to work against or run in. Steer boldly for the centre of Porth Isaac, and run on the sandy beach at its head. Life at all events would be saved, and perhaps the vessel, too, if the tide were on the ebb.

The inlet lies on the S.W. side of the bay, about a mile from **Kellan Head** and five miles from **Tintagel Head**.

There are no outlying dangers between **Porth Gavorne** and **Tintagel**. The Otterham Rock is a bold islet, 130ft. high, lying half a mile from the shore, and one mile and a half S.W. of **Tintagel Head**. This headland is bold and steep-to, 250ft. high, and easily known by the ruins of the castle on it and Tintagel Church behind it, recognised by its short, square tower.

Castle Cove and **Bossiney Cove** lie to the E. of it. A road leads down to the former, and coasters load slate here when they can.

The **Sister Rocks** lie off the W. side of **Bossiney Cove**, and about **two miles** further E. is the **picturesque inlet of Boscastle**, or **Botreaux**, with the **Meachard Rock** lying at **its entrance**, which may be **passed on either side**. It is 120ft. high, **two cables** off shore. **Wellapack Point**, with a **low tower** and **white house**, is on the W. side, and **Pelly Point**, with the **coastguard station**, on the E. side. The cove dries right out, but in very settled weather **temporary anchorage** may be obtained **inside of Meachard Rock**.

The land is high on each side of the creek, and a pier is at its head. Only small coasters, however, can make use of the place.

Beyond **Boscastle** the cliffs are very high (705ft.) before the headland of **Cambeak** is reached, on the E. side of which is

Crackington Haven, a poor place for shelter. St. Genny's Church, 317ft. above the sea, points out the cove. **Dizard Head** is the S.W. limit of **Widemouth Bay**, or **Bude Bay**, **Upper Sharpnose** being its N.E. boundary. The whole appearance of the coast from the sea is monotonous and forbidding, with cliffs varying from 120ft. to 650ft.

In the centre of the bay is **Bude Haven**, whence a **canal** communicates with **Launceston.** The **lock of the canal forms the haven.** The entrance is protected by Chapel Rock, dry at low-water, and connected with the shore by a breakwater. There is 10ft. at high-water springs over the lock-sills, and vessels lie secure enough inside, but it is not always easy to get out.

A **red flag by day** and a **white light by night** show when the lock-gates are open (one hour before high-water, and one hour after). These signals are shown on Chapel Rock. The W. side of the haven is 120ft. high, with a flag-staff. The E. side is low for half a mile. S. of Bude is Efford Beacon, 193ft. high.

Bude is a very dangerous place to **make** for, except in very fine weather, and none but those who know it go there. There is a lifeboat and coastguard station here.

Tides.—It is high-water, full and change, at Bude at 5.43; **springs rise 23ft., and neaps 17ft.**

From **Bude** to **Hartland Point** the course is N.E. by N. ¼ N., and the distance eleven miles and a half. **Hartland Quay, two miles** S. of Hartland Point, is a little boat harbour, with a pier extending N.E. ; there is 18ft. at high-water springs, but the harbour dries 6ft. above low-water, and the bottom is hard.

Hartland Quay is foul on each side. The course to steer for if intending to enter is S.S.E. ½ E. The sea is usually very heavy, with a strong under tow.

Hartland Point is known by its **dark brown** colour, with a steep slope down to the edge of the **perpendicular cliffs.** The table-land behind is **350ft.** high. There is a **gap** close to its head which seems to separate it from the shore.

The **lighthouse** is erected **below the summit** and is a circular **white tower, 59ft.** high. **It shows** at an elevation of 120ft.

above high-water a revolving red and white light, at half-minute intervals, exhibiting **two white flashes** and **one red, visible seventeen miles.**

Fog-signal.—There is a powerful fog-horn, giving two blasts (high and low notes) in quick succession, every 2min.

Off **Hartland Point,** lying a quarter of a mile distant, are the **Tings Rocks,** which uncover at low-water springs. They lie in a northerly direction, and have from six to nine fathoms close to them. Sharpnose Point, bearing S.S.W. ½ W., leads W. of them, and as long as **Gallantry Bower** above **Clovelly** is visible, bearing S.E. ½ E., a vessel is clear to the N.

The first of the ebb-tide sets W. over the rocks.

There is a tide-rip, or race, extending two miles off Hartland Point. Between Lundy Isle and the land the tidal stream runs from two to three knots at neaps and springs, respectively, and flows E. and W., turning at high- and low-water by the shore.

Remarks on the appearance of the coast and objects of interest visible from the sea between Trevose Head and Hartland Point.—There is no doubt that the entrance to Padstow is very forbidding to a stranger. Not only is the appearance of the coast wild and desolate in the extreme, but the cautions and advice given one rather tend to excite one's nerves, especially when it is remembered that the actual **channel** is only a cable wide, and that you may meet with quite a different wind in the entrance from what you are sailing with outside at the very moment when you most want a true breeze. When I opened the Gulland Rock the tide had very nearly done running to the eastward. I had never been here before, and only had one hand with me, who was even more ignorant than I was of the place. The wind was fresh from N., and the sea was dashing up the Gulland and the Newland in towering masses of foam.

It was nearly a dead run in, with the possibility of a gibe at the critical moment of rounding Stepper Point. As I ran in and saw how very near to that iron-bound cliff we were to go—so near as to be able to read the notice-board on the cliff—I began to think we had our work cut out for us, for the old tub is high out of water, and only draws 6ft., so that she does not steer any too easily when running.

We stood on. I told the boy to sing out directly he could read the words on the board, but he was so alarmed at the appearance of the sea and the certain destruction we seemed to be inviting, that he never even saw the board. I was watching the waves and steering all I could to anticipate their rush, for once a sea should take her no helm would bring her round.

The sea was nasty. I never looked the Doom Bar way, I only heard it. What I looked at was how close I could go to that cliff without hurting it. How the sea did rush up the precipitous rocks; how it curled back and dashed against the following waves, making a grand struggle and uppish fight as to who should have the mastery; while a bigger sea would come along and overwhelm the frothy turmoil in a huge green wall, which swept on to thunder against the cliff and recoil in broken fury, white with rage and churning with foam.

Through this we hurtled; and I saw at last the board and read the words. How we flew round the point, with eased-off peak halyards, and everything ready for a gibe; but it did not come until we were well round the head. and then the sea was running in with long but placid rolls. I was glad it was over.

I had no chart of the place, and only knew there was 30ft. of water in the channel up to about half a mile from the entrance. However, I told the boy to look out over the bow, and sing out if the sand seemed much nearer; but as he was always doing this, and I wanted to get to Padstow, I told him to stop it. The thing tried my patience too much.

At last, when he called out very urgently, saying we were ashore, I told him to heave the lead. We had 18ft.

But I must say they take it easy in the matter of buoys. Surely one or two might be placed to show where the **Razor, Middle, and Horseshoe Banks** are, even if they could not keep one on the W. extreme of the Doom Bar. For it is all very well to say keep close to the point, but one would like to know also how far off it there is safety.

E

I sailed right up to the bay on the left hand or E. side, thinking to find shelter there from the swell which reached even as far as that ; but it was all shoal water, so I crossed over to Padstow and anchored on a level with the S. pier-head, in 19ft. of water. This was not enough for I took the ground, but remained water-borne, although the tide caused the boat to swing rather heavily to her cable as her stern touched.

I left Padstow as soon as I could next morning, but had the satisfaction of a quiet night, while it blew freshly outside and rained in torrents.

Padstow is a poor place. The effect of the inlet as one sails up it is most depressing. It was absolutely deserted ; the old church of St. Enodoch standing bleak and forlorn on the E. shore, the pilot-houses at Hawker's Cove, and the bare landscape without a tree to be seen.

Padstow does not come open until the headland on the starboard hand S. of Hawker's Cove is passed. The town stands in a valley. The population is 1749, but it is said to have been much more flourishing ; one does not see why it should have been. The town furnished two ships to the fleet which blockaded Calais in Edward III.'s time. How those vessels ever got round the Longships is a wonder, seeing the way they were built with their high freeboard and strange castles on bow and poop. And there were no lighthouses or yachting-guides in those days, while the tides and winds were just as strong then as now.

In Henry VIII.'s time the Doom Sand began to silt across the entrance, at least, so it is reported, although a rock-bound coast like this of North Cornwall does not change like the gravelly and clayey coasts of Hants, Sussex, and parts of Kent, so that I am inclined to think the Doom Bar has been there since the days of history anyhow.

The church is dedicated to St. Petrock, a disciple of St. Patrick, who is said to have lived here. The original name of the town was Petrockstow, but after King Athelstan conquered Cornwall and the Scilly Isles its name became Athelstow, under which name that ancient writer of Guides, Leland, knew it in Henry VIII.'s reign. Why it changed to Padstow again does not seem clear. There is a fine old Norman font, with figures of the twelve apostles. A superstition long held among the country folk that no one who was baptised in that font could ever be hung; unfortunately for the belief one, Elliot, who, on the strength of the immunity he enjoyed from having been baptised there, robbed the mail-coach under circumstances of some atrocity, was caught and condemned, and in spite of his place of baptism suffered the extremity of the law.

Place House is the only interesting bit in Padstow. It was built in the sixteenth century, and used to be called Prideaux Castle, and before that Garthandrea. The Prideaux family have resided here since the sixteenth century. The house was built on the site of a monastery, plundered by the Danes in 981. The river, which is the cause of the harbour, is the Camel. There is very little water in it at any time. At low-tide it nearly all runs away, and then there is plenty of sand. "If only it were cleared away, they said it would be grand," as the walrus and the carpenter remarked elsewhere. However, it is a very fast Camel, and runs in and out at a great rate. At Wadebridge, about ten miles up the river, is a very old bridge of seventeen arches, built in 1485, at the instigation of the Vicar of Egloshayle, who left £20 a year to keep it repaired—a large sum in his days.

After passing Pentire Point on the way to the E., the next important object which catches the eye is Tintagel Head. Porth Quin and Porth Isaac are not likely to be visited or even seen, as they lie hidden in the recesses of the cliffs.

Tintagel ought to call up all our romance, if we have any. The Passing of Arthur, the Coming of Arthur, and all the Arthurian cycle, whatever that is, should arouse our chivalrous ardour. We are sailing within sight of the very shrine of that mystic company, whose noble deeds were to serve as a mirror wherein a dark age was to see the perfection of manhood.

Arthur is said to have been born in Tintagel. Everybody can talk about King Arthur and the Knights of His Table Round; but

E 2

ask anyone a little closely to tell when he lived, or what he did, and not much information will be forthcoming ; perhaps, as a matter of fact, no one knows if he is a legendary or an historic character. That he was mysteriously born by the connivance of magic, that he married Guinevere as his second wife, that he married a third one on her death or elopement with Launcelot, and that he died in battle fighting against his nephew, Modred, are, perhaps, the chief points in his life. From an historic point of view he is said to have lived about 452, and to have defeated the Saxons at Mount Badon, or Bath. Legend, however, knows a great deal more. It knows, for one thing, that a good man makes a poor husband. Not only did the fair and frail Guinevere pursue a line of conduct which, to say the least of it, was risky, but the good king's third wife actually married his nephew in the aged king's lifetime, and incited this nephew to rebel against his lord. Truly, King Arthur was very unfortunate in his wives.

But there is Tintagel and the ruins of the castle. Opposite, in shore, is High Cliff, the abrupt termination of Resparvel Down, 850ft. high. St. Teath lies inland of Porth Isaac Bay. There is an old church with memorials of the Carminows, who were one of the most distinguished families in the West, claiming descent from King Arthur. They possessed estates all through the county and their ancient lineage was so well proved in the celebrated heraldic trial, that after tracing it back to the remotest recorded time, it was admitted that their origin was lost in antiquity. However, in spite of their magnificent genealogy, their descendant in 1620 is recorded in the Herald's Visitation to be Arthur Knight, son to Master Knight, haberdasher subsequently to "Her Majestie Queen Henrietta Maria."

Pengelley, nearer the shore, is a centre of the slate quarrying district, and the best slate in England has been quarried here since the fifteenth century. Camelford, where the fatal battle took place, and where Sir Bedivere trifled so long over Excalibur while the sore-stricken king grew faint with his wounds, is about five miles inland ; but one need not be too precise in the locality of that battle. The island of Avallon could, however, be reached from the shore of Porth Isaac Bay, as it is said to be an island in the Severn.

Strangely enough the finest monument to King Arthur is to be found far away from British shores. It is to the chivalrous imagination of the last of the knightly Kaisers that the splendid statue is due. In far away Innspruck, under the shadow of the towering Alps, stands King Arthur, clad in full armour, with vizor raised, and belted with Excalibur on thigh, the most graceful, as well as the most stately, figure of all those Paladins of old who mourn around dead Maximilian, one time Emperor of the Holy Roman Empire.

It is possible to land at Castle Cove and climb the steep paths. The castle was nobly placed. Like Dunstaffnage, or Dunaverty Castle, in Kintyre, it is placed, as that ancient British stronghold of Castle Treen was placed, on a headland, joined by a neck of land only to the main-land.

Henry III. held his court here, but in Henry VIII.'s time the castle had fallen into decay. There are the remains of an ancient chapel, with a grave on both sides of the altar, which is dedicated to St. Juliet.

However, we are slipping up with the tide ; neither Boscastle nor Bude will tempt us to turn in unless it falls calm and the tide should fail us, when an anchorage inside of the Meachard Rock might be worth exploring.

Boscastle is well worth a visit, and the legend of the Bells of Botreaux* is pretty, reminding one of those other lost bells in the far away Sussex creek, where, amid the marshy land, the sluggish tide winds up to quaint old Bosham. In each case the sound of the chimes is heard before the coming storm.

---

* In case this legend is not known I will briefly give it : Lord Botreaux sent over seas for a peal of bells, which should be better than those of Tintagel. The vessel had weathered all the storms, and was rounding Willapark Point, when the pilot, a Tintagel man, heard the sound of his village bells, and thanked Heaven for their sweet assurance of safety. The captain said the good ship was to be thanked, not Heaven, for having brought them there, and backed up his opinion with a plentiful vocabulary of oaths. Thereupon the sky grew black, and before Meachard Isle was passed the ship had sunk, and bells and all were lost except the pilot, who gave God thanks. Whenever a gale is coming the bells are heard to stir or chime under the sea—so they say.

Botreaux, or Boscastle, is most picturesque, with delightful excursions all round, and old world memories to while away the time.

Bude is a most forbidding-looking place, exposed to the full fury of the Atlantic and the wild westerly gales. The sooner one is out of Bude Bay the better. The canal is used mostly for taking sand and shells for agricultural purposes.

Giving the **Tings** a respectful berth, for the sea breaks heavily on them, and so should we, we are soon opening Hartland Point with the strong flood ; and as we hurtle through the tide ripple—for it is not well to go near the Race, unless wind and tide are both together—**Clovelly Cove** and **Bideford Bay** come more and more before us. We are entering the **Bristol Channel.**

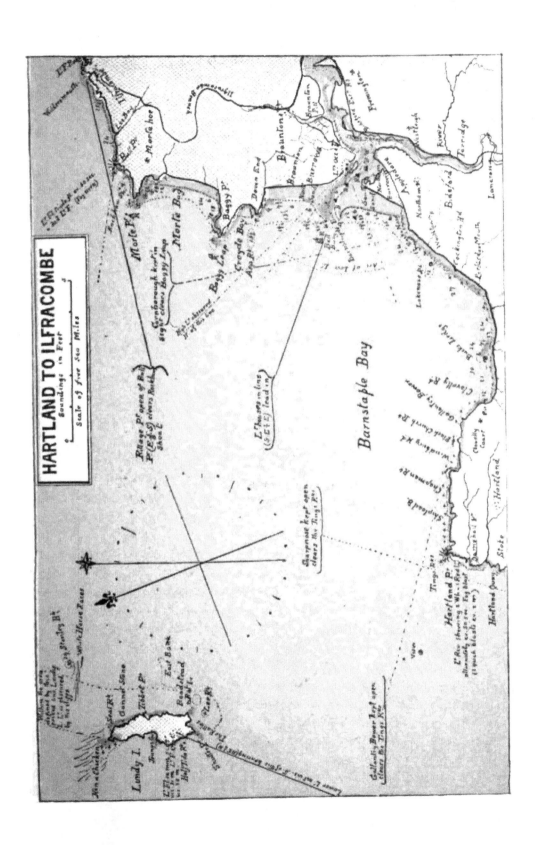

HARTLAND TO ILFRACOMBE
Soundings in Feet
Scale of Five Sea Miles

Barnstaple Bay

Lundy I.

CHAPTER V.

THE BRISTOL CHANNEL—LUNDY ISLE AND BARNSTAPLE BAY.

Sailing Directions, Bearings, Dangers, &c.—From Hartland Point, Lundy Island bears N. ¾ W., distant ten miles; St. Ann's Head, N. ¾ W., forty-eight miles; and Trevose Head, S.W. by W., thirty-four miles.

The entrance to the Bristol Channel is reckoned to lie between **Hartland Point** and **St. Ann's Head**, in Pembroke-shire, **Lundy Island** lying **exactly** in the **line of bearing**.

Lundy Island.—As this small island, two miles and a half long by three-quarters of a mile broad, is so well placed at the threshold of the **Bristol Channel**, and **Hartland Point** is the nearest land to it, I will describe it now, although **Bideford** or **Barnstaple** is our next port of call.

This island **forms a natural shelter for vessels beating down channel** against **westerly winds**. It is high, **443ft. above high-water,** and has **good anchorage** on the E. side, and shelter on the W. might be found in cases of necessity.

Bearings.—From the lighthouse, which stands half a mile from the S.W. point and 100yds. from the edge of the cliff, Hartland Point bears S. ¾ E. ten miles and a half; Barnstaple Bar, S.E. ½ E., seventeen miles; Morte Point, E. by S. ¾ S., seventeen miles; and Ilfracombe Harbour, E. by S. ½ S., twenty-one miles.

From the **N.** point of the **island**, **St. Ann's Head, Milford Haven,** bears **N. by W. ¼ W.,** thirty-four miles and a half; **Caldy Island, N. by E. ¾ E.,** twenty-six miles; **Small's Light,. N.N.W. ¾ W.,** forty-nine miles; **The Mumbles, E. by N. ¾ N.,** thirty-five miles; and **Cape Cornwall, S.W. by W.,** seventy-four miles, from the S. end of Lundy.

Lundy Lighthouse.—From a **white circular tower,** 96ft. high, **two white lights** are shown at an elevation of 540ft. and 470ft., respectively, above high-water. The **high light** shows **one flash every minute** and is **visible thirty miles.** The **low** light is fixed, and is only visible **from the W.** between the bearings of S. by E. and N.E. It is intended to warn vessels from keeping too close to the cliffs at night, when lying on and off to save the tide, or seeking shelter from the E. wind. The **low light should never** be shut out by the **edge** of the cliff as it is only **17ft.** above the edge of it. All **outlying** dangers are **cleared** with this in **sight.**

Fog-signal.—On the **W. side of the island,** four cables from the **lighthouse,** is a rocket station. A rocket is **discharged every ten minutes,** which **explodes** at a **height of** 600ft. with a loud report.

Dangers.—Lundy Isle is nearly inaccessible. At the S.E. end is the **only landing-place.** Hence, a road leads up to the top of the island. A landing can only be managed in fair weather, on a small beach E. of Marisco Castle, which stands conspicuously on the top of the S.E. point of the island.

The **dangers** are on the **N.W., N.E.,** and **S.E. ends** of the island. The **Hen and Chickens dry** from **5ft.** to **10ft.** at low-water springs, and **extend three cables N.W. from the N. point** of Lundy. The outer patch dries at 5ft. low-water. **Close** to there are **sixteen or eighteen fathoms;** care must be taken not to pass too near, therefore. A conspicuous **black rock,** off the **S.W. point,** kept open of the cliffs clears them to the W.

On the **N.E.** side there are **a few rocks** from 6ft. to 8ft. **above high-water,** but the **Knoll Pins cover** at half-tide. They are nearly a cable from **Tibbet Point.**

At the S.E. end is Rat Island, a grass-covered rock, connected with Lundy at low-water. Off it lies a **rocky ledge, dry** at low-water springs, and **bearing** in a **S.E.** direction a distance of **one cable. Beyond** this is a **rock** with **15ft.** over it at low-water springs, S.S.E., distant two cables.

Lee Rocks are dangerous. They are two heads with only 9ft. on them at low-water springs, and lie a quarter of a mile from the S.E. point of Lundy, with the castle bearing N. It is necessary, therefore, to be careful in rounding the island, not to go too close.

There are rocks, mostly showing, on the W. side. **Black Rock**, 15ft. above high-water springs, lies off the S.W. point, about a cable away, and **outside** it is a **rock** which **dries** 6ft. at low-water, distant nearly two-thirds of a cable. **Under the lighthouse** is a **half-tide** rock, drying 7ft. But none of these rocks lie more than one cable and a half from the cliffs, and the **low lights covers** them all.

There are three banks, with seven fathoms, four fathoms and a half, and five fathoms and a half, least water on them, respectively; but the sea breaks heavily on all, especially on **Stanley Bank**, in westerly gales.

N.W. bank extends E.N.E. and W.S.W. one mile W. of the N. end of the island; its length is about two miles. It is out of the strongest of the ebb-stream, and as it is sandy vessels in fine weather sometimes anchor on it in a head tide. The least depth is seven fathoms.

The **White Horses**, on which is **Stanley Bank**, with four fathoms and a half least depth, extends four miles N.E. of Lundy. The shoalest patch lies with the N.W. point of Lundy bearing W. ¾ S., distant two miles and four-fifths, and the lighthouse S.W. ¾ W. westerly. Over this shoal the tide races are very strong.

The E. bank lies one mile E. of the S. half of Lundy. It is one mile in length and three-quarters of a mile wide. The least depth is five fathoms and a quarter, with **Rat Island**, distant eight cables, bearing W.S.W.

The **Shutter** is the S.W. point of the island.

Tides.—It is high-water, full and change, at Lundy at 5hr. 15min. local, or 5hr. 33min. Greenwich time. Springs rise 27ft. and neaps 20ft. Three miles W. of the island the stream divides and passes N. and S. of the island. The ebb is not felt within this three miles' limit. On the E. side of the island the ebb runs to the S. from half-flood to low-water. The N. stream is barely felt close in, and does not run stronger than one knot.

There are two **strong races** off the island. That **off the N. end** is the **strongest**, as the tide **runs five knots**, decreasing **to three knots**, at **an offing of three or four miles.**

The **Hen and Chickens Race**, and that over the **Stanley Bank,** is **very heavy.**

The race off the **Black Rock** is heavy, but does not **extend so far.**

These **races**, when there is a **westerly** gale and **ebb-tide**, are **formidable** to encounter.

Anchorages.—Lundy Roadstead **lies** between **Rat Island** and **Tibbet Point** on the **E. side.** There is plenty of room, and it is said as many as one hundred vessels may be seen here in westerly gales. With easterly winds one has to clear out.

The anchorage for **small vessels** is **close in to the** shore, with **Gannet Island** just **open of Tibbet Point** (**Gannet Island** is an islet 8oft. high on the **N.E.** of Lundy), and **Rat Island,** bearing **S.S.W.** in **ten fathoms**; but a small weatherly craft could go much nearer in, and yet be able to work out. There is also a good berth near the signal station (Lloyds).

At night it is **safer not** to **lose sight of the light,** or only just inside of it, unless one knows the anchorage well.

On the W. side there is shelter from E. gales, and one may anchor close in in ten fathoms, but the water deepens quickly to twenty fathoms. The best place is in Jenny Cove, with six fathoms, only take care of the rocks lying one cable and a half off **Needle Rock,** which is **S.W. of Jenny Cove.** They dry 7ft. at low water.

Rattles Bay is at the S. end of Lundy. Some vessels anchor there in N. gales, but it is a very uncomfortable berth.

Remarks on the appearance of Lundy and objects of interest it presents.—Lundy is a very uninteresting island to look at. It is simply a precipitous mass, three miles long, nearly level at the top, with a broken-off piece at the S.W. end. Here a chasm, called the Devil's Limekiln, cuts off the **Shutter** from the rest of the island. It affords, however, very safe shelter in W. winds, and is not to be despised. The soil is poor in places exposed to the wind, and there are no trees except in the valley, where is the house of the proprietor, to the right of the road up to the top of the island from the landing-place.

To explain the name of the Castle Marisco. It is said that a family of that name possessed the island in the reign of Henry III., and that one of them, having to flee for his life, sailed over here and built this castle, where he lived the life of a bold buccaneer—until he was caught and hung.

A story is told of the capture of the island by the French in the time of William of Orange, which is simply a reproduction of one told by Peter Heylyn, in his "Historie of ye Raignes of King Edward and Queen Mary," of how the Dutch took possession of Sark in the Channel Islands. Curiously enough the Lundy story makes out that the island was taken by a French vessel, also flying Dutch colours. The legend says that a vessel ran into the roadstead short of supplies, flying Dutch colours. The crew reported that their master was sick. In a few days he died, and permission was asked to bury him. This was granted on the condition that they landed unarmed. As they were foreigners, the crew claimed to be allowed to inter their captain according to their own rites, and without observation. This was acceded to also. The funeral *cortege* entered the church. The door was shut. After a few minutes of solemn silence the door was opened. Then every one of the burying party emerged fully equipped, with their captain armed to the teeth at their head.

The inhabitants made no resistance, and Lundy Island became French for a few days. The coffin, of course, was full of the swords and muskets of the sailors, and the device was as successful as it deserved to be—only, did it ever take place?

The island contains about 2000 acres. Oats, barley, and potatoes are the main crops; and a good number of sheep and cattle are reared here. Rabbits and sea birds' eggs and feathers are also among the exports of the island. It is a part of Devon, and was sold for £10,000 in 1840.

The only historic remains are the ruins of the castle and St. Ann's Chapel. The population is 177.

Water, poultry, and vegetables can be obtained.

Barnstaple and Bideford Bay.—This wide and deeply-recessed bay lies between **Hartland Point** and **Morte Point.** There is **considerable in-draught** into the bay, and it would be a good craft which could work out on the flood if caught in a N.W. gale. There is not the least shelter with the wind between W.N.W. and N.E. With off-shore winds, however, there is anchorage anywhere E. of **Clovelly.**

Clovelly Village is built up the side of a steep pitch, or cliff almost. The houses peep out among woods and undergrowth. It is five miles S.E. of Hartland Point, and the cliffs between are mostly precipitous and steep-to. **Gallantry Bower** is a conspicuous clump of trees, 360ft. high above high-water, and lying W. of **Clovelly.** There is little or no flood-stream all along here, and there is a depth of eight fathoms within a quarter of a mile of the shore. On the ebb there is a perceptible current.

Clovelly Court stands clearly out on the N.W. of the village, and is a large stone building on the brow of the hill, half a mile from Clovelly.

There is a pier, but it does not afford much shelter from the ground swell. Coasting craft, however, find refuge here frequently.

There is a **fisherman's light** exhibited from September 1 to February 1. It shows **red** when there is **5ft.** least water and more in the harbour, and **white** for the rest of the tide.

The anchorage off Clovelly is safe with the wind any way W. of N.W. round southerly as far as E., and the sea is quiet. The holding ground is good, in a muddy bottom, at two or three cables off the pier, in four fathoms, taking care to avoid **Bucks Ledge,** which lies one mile and a half S.E. of Clovelly, and dries nearly half a mile off Buckish Mill at low-water. There is only 6ft. of water at two-thirds of a mile off shore. To clear the shoal, **keep Chapman Rock open of Clovelly Bluff.** This leads **N. of it.**

E. of Clovelly the land keeps high, with woods and brushwood for six miles, to Rock's Nose. This is the end of the high rocky ground. The coast then becomes lower, sweeping round in a N.E. direction to the mouth of the **Taw** and **Torridge.** It is bordered by sand hills, which extend as far as **Downend,** and wide-reaching sands stretch in front of it to the distance of half a mile at low-water.

Nearer the bar of **Barnstaple or Bideford** river, the sands dry out fully a mile from the land.

The **Lakenose Rock** lies **one mile and a quarter W.** of **Rock's Nose Point** and **half a mile** off shore ; it is **awash** at low-water springs.

Through this sandy tract lies the entrance to **Barnstaple** and **Bideford** ; but the **bar** has only **4ft.** least water on it at low-water springs.

Bideford Bar.—This is a sandy obstruction, with gravelly patches here and there. It is one mile long, with an average breadth of one cable and a half between the sands on each side, and is one mile and a half outside the points of land on the N. and S. banks of the river. After the bar is passed, the water deepens from three to six fathoms in a narrow pool, half a mile long, when it again shoals to four fathoms for one mile as far as **Appledore Pool.** Beyond **Appledore** Pool vessels lie aground. There are other dangers on the bar. Abreast its in-shore end on the S. side is a **gravel patch, drying 7ft.** at low-water springs ; while on the **N. side another patch dries 19ft. Oldwell Rocks** and the **Crow and Sprat Ridges lie abreast the light-houses on the N. shore,** so that here the **channel bears nearer to the W. or Appledore side.**

The usual anchorage outside, where vessels wait for sufficient water over the bar, is in seven or eight fathoms, distant half a mile from the Fairway Buoy, with **Cornborough Summer-house** on a summit **half a mile inside Rock's Nose,** bearing S. ¾ W.

Buoys.—The **Fairway Bell Buoy,** with staff and globe, **red,** lies in seven fathoms, half a mile outside the bar, with the high lighthouse, bearing S.E. ¼ E. A conical black buoy lies on the bar at the edge of the S. sand in 5ft. low-water. This marks the S. side of the channel. This is succeeded by two conical black buoys in 16ft. on the same side, which dry, marking respectively the Middle Ridge and the Pulley Sand. Beyond these, on the N. side, is a black and white vertically-striped can buoy in 4ft. at low-water, marking the W. end of the Sprat Ridge. In Appledore Pool there is a black mooring buoy.

Bideford Lights.—On Braunton Sands, on the N. side of the river, two lights are shown. The high light shows from an octagonal white tower, 86ft. high, with a red vertical stripe down it, at an elevation of 93ft. above high-water, a white occulting light, eclipsing for 2sec. every half minute, visible between N. 68deg. E. and S. 22deg. E. From S. 22deg. E. (over Baggy Leap and Asp Rocks) to S. 87deg. W. the light is obscured. Between S. 87deg. W. through N., and N. 68deg. E., a light of less power shows for the harbour navigation, visible seaward fourteen miles.

The Low Light.—In a white hut, with a red vertical stripe, 15ft. high, erected on a tramway lying N. and S. and at 311yds. from the high light, a fixed white light is shown at an elevation of 44ft. above high-water. The light is only visible between the bearings of E. to S. 31deg. E., and is only shown while there is 15ft. over the bar. It is moved as the bar shifts. Visible seaward eleven miles.

Tide Signals by Day.—A red ball is hoisted on a flagstaff at the low lighthouse while there is 15ft. water and over on the bar.

Tides.—It is high-water, full and change, at Appledore, at 5hr. 58min. local time ; springs rise 23ft. At **Bideford Bridge** it is high-water at 6hr. 7min. ; springs rise 16ft. At **Barnstaple Bridge** at 6hr. 28min. ; springs rise 10½ft. Local time is 17min. **behind** Greenwich time.

It is dangerous **for a stranger** to **cross** Bideford Bar at most times. With a fairly strong leading wind there is little risk, however, only as the tide makes at the rate of five or six knots an hour, and sets over **Crow** and **Sprat Ridges** into Barnstaple River, care must be taken to insure plenty of steerage way. The sea, too, is often very choppy and nasty even in comparatively fine weather, and a pilot can easily be picked up in a Clovelly fisherman.

From the **Fairway Buoy** the **lighthouses** in line lead in. When abreast of the Middle Ridge Buoy bear a little southerly for a quarter of a mile, until the easternmost of two old mills at Northam is seen over **Watertown**, bearing S. $\frac{1}{3}$ W. This leads between the **Pulley Conical Black Buoy** and the **Sprat Ridge Buoy (can, black and white stripes)**. As soon as the latter is passed steer E. and bring the low Bungalow House at **Instow** in line with Worlington Houses on the hill top above, bearing S.E. by E.; then steer up to Appledore Pool and anchor as soon as Northam Church is shut in by Appledore Customs' Watch-house, S.W. $\frac{3}{4}$ W.

The anchorage in **Appledore Pool** is limited. It is only three cables in length by two-thirds of a cable in width, with from two and a half to five fathoms water. The holding ground is not good at the lower end, and plenty of scope must be allowed at once as the tide runs very strong. To add to the difficulties of the place there are many limestone heaps scattered about the shore in the bay below the Customs' Watch-house.

Appledore possesses two dry docks and several building and repairing yards.

Opposite it is **Instow**, with a stone pier and hotels, and it possesses a bathing establishment as well.

The strong tides and shallow water make all these places bad for boating.

Coast to Morte Point.—From Braunton Burrows to **Down End**, the extremity of the sand hills which fringe the bay N. of Barnstaple Bar, the distance is two miles and a half. Off **Down End** lies the **Asp Rock**. It is **half a mile in extent**, and has only 12ft. of water over at **low-water**. Close to it **there are from five to seven fathoms of water**, Down End, bearing **S.E. by E.** distant one mile, and **Baggy Point,** N.E. ¼ E., mark its outer edge. **Morte Point, well open of Baggy Point,** clears it to the westward.

Between **Down End** and **Baggy Point** is **Croyde Bay.** There is anchorage here with off-shore winds and fine weather, and coasters frequent it in the summer if desirous of saving a tide.

Beyond Baggy Point, which is a bleak-looking headland, lies **Baggy Leap,** a rocky shoal three-quarters of a mile long, with Baggy Rock awash at low-water and with deep water close to it. There is a channel between the rocks and Baggy Point a quarter of a mile wide. The outer point of the shoal is three-quarters of a mile from the point, and a heavy breaking sea is found for fully half a mile further out during gales against the tide.

A **red conical buoy** lies in eight fathoms, distant one cable, in a N.W. direction from **Baggy Leap Shoal.**

Morte Bay lies between **Baggy** and **Morte Points.** The village of Morthoe lies in a valley E. of Morte Point, and is rapidly becoming a favourite seaside resort. With E. or S. winds the bay offers good shelter in six fathoms, with a clean sandy bottom, about half a mile off shore.

Morte Point is rocky and rugged. The cliffs at the extremity are low. **Off** it lies the **Morte Stone,** only **covered** at **high-water springs.** It **rises** from the **centre** of a **rocky ledge,** running out three cables and a half W.N.W.

A **conical red buoy,** with **staff** and **globe,** lies in nine fathoms, a quarter of a mile off the ledge, bearing from **Morte Stone** N.W.W. ½ W. There is a nasty tide race off this ledge. The ebb sets clear of it, but the flood sets **over** it from Morte Bay.

Remarks on the appearance of the coast and objects of interest between Hartland Point and Morte Point.—The coast, as Clovelly Bay is opened out, becomes much more picturesque. The desolate wildness of the western cliffs gives way to the soft beauty of wooded steeps, with crags and cottages peeping out here and there. Clovelly village is most picturesque, and it would be well worth going ashore to explore this lovely

coast, if only the wind would allow.   Anchorage in this bay is
quite safe with off-shore winds however strong, and the ground
swell is felt less here than in most other places in North Devon.
It is safe to anchor close to the pier-head, according to the
draught of the vessel.

Clovelly Court stands beautifully, commanding as it does
magnificent views over the bay.   All this country has been so
well described by Charles Kingsley, in Westward Ho! that it
would be well to revive one's memories of that delightful book.
From Lundy to Morthoe the whole district is redolent of the
Brotherhood of the Rose and the deeds of Sir Amyas Leigh.
To those who cross Barnstaple Bar and anchor in Appledore
Pool, the question may occur: How did that good ship after
all her voyages manage to navigate that difficult channel?   There
were no buoys or leading lights at that time, but they were sailors
then, and no mistake, and were accustomed to find out the
dangers for themselves.

Bideford and **Barnstaple** are both ancient towns.   The latter
has a population double that of the former (12,282 and 6499),
but Bideford is easier of access.   Both places are difficult,
naturally, and rendered all the more so by the deposits of
limestone brought over from Wales and recklessly thrown out
anywhere.   Added to these obstructions are the fishing weirs,
few of which are marked, and which cover at half-tide.

The River **Taw**, on which Barnstaple is built, rises in Dart-
moor.   It's course is fifty miles long, but can only be navigated
by boats at high-water, about three miles above Barnstaple.   Off
the town and below the bridge the river Yeo flows into it.   The
two streams then run W. for Appledore, where they meet the
Torridge flowing down from Bideford, and together the united
rivers flow into the sea, forming at high-tide a fine expanse
of water.

It is seven miles from the sea to Barnstaple and five miles
to Bideford.   There are several pools, with from two to four
fathoms of water, between Appledore and **Fremington**, two miles
and a half below Barnstaple, where there is a quay near the
Bideford and Barnstaple railway.

F

Coasters mostly lie aground on Braunton Sands sheltered from all winds. The flood-tide is slack for some short time at high-water, but the ebb runs very strong; thus, owing to the strength of the tidal streams, the difficulty of the bar in any except settled fine weather, and the shallow nature of the rivers at low-water, it is tolerably clear that for an amateur yachtsman there are reasons in plenty why he should avoid Barnstaple Bar. If he will go there as a stranger he had far better obtain local help to show him where to anchor and how to moor. Even supposing he should get over the bar and anchor in Appledore Pool, he may not be by any means at the end of his anxieties, as with such tidal streams and the wind any way up or down, the vessel will sheer about in an aggravating way, most likely fouling the anchor, and finally getting ashore or foul of some other craft.

There is a good deal of traffic up these rivers. The tonnage which enters Barnstaple annually is 101,000, carried in 2120 vessels; while Bideford boasts 5000 tons and 80 vessels.

Behind Northam Burrows the golf-links of **Westward Ho!** are laid out. There is a pier, a hotel, and a school. The place looks dreary enough from the sea, especially after passing Clovelly. It is a curious thing, but I notice it at all the new seaside places I pass. The new big hotel is always plumped down in the most exposed situation which can be found. There is no mistaking it. You see a square lump miles away; it is the first thing you see. That's the new hotel! Is it not possible to combine newness and comfort with the picturesque and a cosy situation?

The coast north of Barnstaple Bar is bleak and uninteresting as far as Morte Point, showing how the gales tear over it.

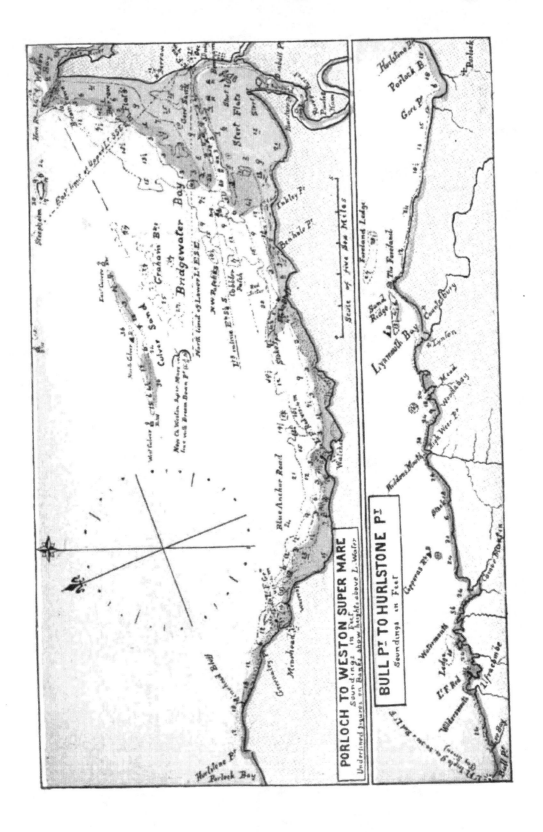

PORLOCH TO WESTON SUPER MARE

Soundings in Feet
Underlined figures on Bank show heights above L. water

BULL Pt TO HURLSTONE Pt

Soundings in Feet

CHAPTER VI.

———

BRISTOL CHANNEL—MORTE POINT
TO STEEPHOLM.

I INTEND to pass briefly over this part of the coast, as I do not think the Bristol Channel at all suited for the amateur cruiser.

The tides are far too strong, the harbours but poor ones, and the traffic too busy. The prevailing winds also blow up and down, and the seas are choppy and heavy. It is necessary, however, briefly to describe the dangers and the shelters, such as there are, so that a craft, if driven by necessity to run up the channel, may be able to know what to avoid and where to make for shelter.

I have heard men say the Bristol Channel is no worse than the English Channel, but I did not believe them, nor will any one else who considers the range of tide and the nature of the harbours in the two channels. The Bristol Channel tide is the highest in the world after the Bay of Fundy, and it is said that it nearly equals that celebrated tidal wave at certain seasons, 56ft. having been recorded at Chepstow, the average rise at the springs being 38ft. There is a tradition that it once reached 70ft.

Even a moderate westerly breeze meeting that tide on the ebb very soon knocks up a sea, which requires more skill to tackle than provides pleasure for the passengers. I was also told the Mumbles was a perfectly safe roadstead. I daresay vessels of war and merchant ships might ride out a gale there, but it would be uncomfortable work—and they might not. However, the Mumbles mud is soft. It is only necessary to look at the map to see that there is no outside anchorage protected from all winds, where vessels can lie in safety, in the whole Bristol Channel, Penarth Roads and King Roads being the nearest approach to safe roadsteads.

After passing **Morte Point, Bull Point** opens out with **Rockham Bay** and **Shoal** between the two. **Morte Stone** bears S.W. by W. ½ W. at six cables distance. There is less than 6ft. on this danger at low-water.

The clearing marks are **Rillage Point**, kept **open of Bull Point**, bearing E. ½ S. This course leads **clear** of both **Morte Stone** and **Rockham Shoal**.

The **white light** from **Bull Point Lighthouse** also **clears** it by night.

Bull Point Lighthouse.—From a circular white tower, 55ft. high, is exhibited, at an elevation of 154ft. above high-water, a flashing white light, showing three successive flashes of 2sec. duration each, divided by intervals of about 3sec. The third flash is followed by an eclipse of 18sec. A fixed red light shows 18ft. below the flashing light, between the bearings of E. by N. and S.E. by E. ½ E., to mark **Morte Stone** and **Rockham Shoal.**

Fog-signal. — The fog-siren gives three blasts in quick succession every 2min. The coast from Bull Point to Ilfracombe is three miles. The shore is steep, with a well-wooded valley about half-way. For a quarter of a mile off shore the ground is foul, and should not be approached within that distance. Coasters anchor sometimes in **Lee Bay.**

Ilfracombe is now becoming visible, but the harbour is hidden until the vessel is about half-way between **Capstone Hill** and **Helesborough,** two hills situated on the W. and E. of the town, and about a mile apart. Capstone Hill, 154ft. high, is conical, with a flag-staff on the summit, and slopes down to **Lantern Hill,** the W. point of the harbour entrance. Helesborough, 420ft.

high, is on the E. side, with **foul ground** at its base, **extending a cable from the shore.**

There is no difficulty in approaching Ilfracombe, and it is considered the **best dry harbour** on the S. side of the Bristol Channel.

There are altogether ten acres included within the piers, of which the inner harbour comprises six.

Lantern Hill, connected by a narrow neck of rock to **Capstone Hill,** forms the natural shelter. This has been improved by a transverse pier, 100yds. long, forming the inner harbour. A second pier has been carried out from the transverse pier to nearly low-water, and this has been extended to the end of the low-water rocks, off the E. side of Lantern Hill, by a pile pier.

If only a vessel could lie afloat in Ilfracombe it would be a very pleasant yachting resort. As it is, to be quite safe, a vessel should go into the inner harbour and lie aground on legs. The bottom is hard and level, covered with a muddy surface.

There is not much room in the anchorage under the lee of the inner pier, and a vessel is somewhat in the way of other craft going in and out.

Steamers lie alongside the extension quay, and in fine weather go alongside the pile pier.

The anchorage in the Range, as it is called, is exposed to the N., **and** N.W. winds send in a heavy swell. In quiet weather, and with off-shore winds, a good berth may be picked up here, the **pile** pier bearing **S.S.W.** and **Bull Point Lighthouse** just showing off **Capstone Hill.** It is better to **wait** until **half-flood** before attempting to enter the harbour, when there is 19ft. to 20ft. of water off the pile pier landing, but only 6ft. to 7ft. at the pier-head.

Lights.—On the top of the ancient chantrey, on Lantern Hill, 127ft. above **high-water, a fixed red light is shown** from **September 1 to April 30, visible ten miles.**

On the **inner pier-head a fixed red light** is shown all the **year** round, and on the pile pier a **fixed red light** is shown at the three angles of the pier all the year round. There are no tide signals.

Tides.—It is high-water, full and change, at 5hr. 42min. local time, or 5hr. 58min. Greenwich time. Springs rise 27ft. (but equinoctial tides rise 32ft.); neaps 21ft.

The tidal stream, at a quarter of a mile off shore, sets to the E. from low-water until half-flood, and then to the W. until low-water, thus making 3hrs. to the E. and 9hrs. to the W., but at about a mile out the streams run E. and W. for 6hrs. each, and turn at high- and low-water by the shore.

E. of Ilfracombe, distant one mile, is **Rillage Point,** known by an old mill above it. Off this point a ledge of rocks runs out one-third of a mile to the N.W., rising suddenly from a depth of ten fathoms to three fathoms, causing nasty overfalls in westerly winds. It is called **Buggy Overfall.**

Watermouth Bay, half a mile beyond Rillage, affords a kind of shelter in W. winds. There is a small pier.

Combe Martin Bay, lying S.E. of Watermouth Bay, also affords temporary shelter in five or six fathoms.

The coast now becomes higher, **Little Hangman** and **Great Hangman** Hills being 756ft. and 1083ft. high, with a higher hill further E. 1187ft. high. The cliffs are steep-to for the most part.

Off Great Hangman lies Copperas Rock, with 4ft. least water on it, and steep-to all round. It lies half a mile N. of **Great Hangman.** Capstone Hill, open of **Rillage Point,** bearing **W.,** leads N. of it, and the **Foreland,** in line with **High Weir Point,** leads between it and the shore, in five fathoms and a half.

There is a conical black buoy lying N.N.E. of the **Copperas Rock,** distant one cable.

High Weir Point, with a race, extending half a mile off, comes next. A bank with 16ft. least water lies off it one mile and a quarter in an E. by S. direction. By keeping Little Hangman Hill open of High Weir Point, a vessel passes it to the N.

Westward of **High Weir** is **Heddons Mouth,** a romantic valley, or cleft in the rocks, leading up to Exmoor, with a winding path through the fir woods to Trentishoe.

Eastward of **High Weir Point,** distant three miles and a half, is **Lynmouth,** the shore between being very picturesque, with woods and steep slopes. **Borthaven, Lynmouth,** and **Lynton** are all beautiful in the extreme, the latter lying 500ft. above Lynmouth. The church and hotels are plainly seen from the sea to the E.

Lynmouth Creek receives small vessels as far as the jetty, but the entrance is fronted by boulders, and it dries out two cables and a half from the shore. There is a narrow gut, marked on both sides by posts, for coasters to warp up to the jetty, where there is 15ft. at high-water springs.

Off **Lynmouth** there is good anchorage in off-shore winds, in four to six fathoms, at half a mile from shore. The ebb is hardly felt here, and the flood only runs at one knot and a half. Outside this **roadstead** lies a bank, called the **Sand Ridge,** although it is gravel. This is a **dangerous bank,** with only 4ft. least water on it. It **lies** between the **Foreland** and **Lynmouth.** It is said at very low tides to uncover. The **bank** is a mile long, and one cable and a half wide. A channel, a quarter of a mile wide, lies between it and the Foreland.

A **black conical** buoy, with **staff and globe, lies one cable N. by W.** of the **W. end** of the **ridge,** with Lynton Church bearing S.S.W. ¾ W.

To clear the ridge to the N., keep **Capstone Hill open** of Rillage Point, bearing W.

The **Foreland** lies to the E. of **Lynmouth, distant two miles.** It is a very conspicuous **headland,** being 734ft. high and very **bold.** It stands detached from the mainland, being connected merely by a neck, and is easily known by this feature.

A rocky ledge runs off with a depth of three fathoms for two cables distance, and beyond it three-quarters of a mile to sea is the W. end of the **Foreland Ledge,** running parallel to the coast for one mile and a quarter, with four fathoms and a half least depth. These ledges cause heavy overfalls.

The same marks for clearing the **Sand Ridge** clear this, or one who knows the place may pass **between** the **Sand Ridge** and the **Foreland.**

The coast E. from the **Foreland to Gore Point** is high, ranging to 1200ft., and covered here and there with wood. Beyond **Gore Point,** which is low and fronted by a shingle beach, lies Porlock Bay, six miles from the Foreland.

Porlock Weir lies on the W. side of the bay, with a quay.

In this bay coasters often anchor to escape the tide, at half a mile off shore. Behind Porlock is **Dunkerry Beacon** 1678ft. high, the highest point in Somerset.

The weir at Porlock has dock gates, and can receive vessels 30ft. wide and 12ft. draught.

The E. point of Porlock Bay is Hurlstone Point; from here to Minehead is four miles. There is shoal water off **Greenaley Point** for a quarter of a mile off shore.

Minehead Harbour affords **shelter** with **on-shore** winds for vessels which can take the ground. There is one pier curving round to the E. and S.E. The harbour is easy of access, but an awkward "scend" comes in with N.W. winds. Legs are no use in this harbour. A sharp-bottomed vessel must lie alongside the quay and look out at high-water for some knocks.

In entering, have a stern anchor ready to check the vessel's way.

Tides.—High-water, full and change, at 6hr. 24min. local time, or 6hr. 38min. Greenwich time. Springs rise from 32ft. to 37ft. ; neaps, 24ft. The ebb-stream sets W. one hour before high-water by the shore.

The shore now becomes low, and the low-water-mark is nearly half a mile from land. **Blue Anchor Road** is four miles from **Minehead.** The holding ground is very strong, stiff clay.

Two miles beyond **Blue Anchor Road** is Watchet. This is another dry harbour, with piers enclosing a space of nine acres and a half. The harbour is **easy to enter.** As at **Minehead a good deal of swell comes in** here **at high-water** when gales are blowing. Legs may be used with precaution.

Lights.—On the **W.** pier-head a fixed red light is shown at an elevation of 30ft. above high-water, visible four miles when there is 8ft. on the flood and 10ft. on the ebb. A ball is hoisted by day to show the same thing.

Tides.—The tidal stream runs from four to five knots at one mile off the pier-head, and the ebb sets to the W. one hour before high-water by the shore. In mid-channel the stream turns at high- and low-water by the shore.

The coast from Watchet eastward has no especial feature. Quantockhead Church has a conspicuous square tower with low spire. The low-water line is nearly one-third of a mile off the shore, as far as Stoke Bluff, off which a spit runs out, and dries nearly a mile from the shore, with 7ft. only at a quarter of a mile farther out.

Cobbler Patch has only 7ft. on it. It lies one mile and a half W. of **Gore Buoy** in Bridgewater Bay.

The church or pier-head at Watchet, bearing **W.S.W.**, clears this patch, as also the Klive Patch, with two fathoms and a half least water; and Burnham Lights in line, E. by S. southerly, lead N. of it, too. These lights lead clear of the Cobbler up to the Gore Buoy.

Bridgewater Bay, with the estuary of the Parret, has no attraction for a yachtsman. The bar has 3ft. on it at low-water and 38ft at high-water. The tides are strong, and there are many stakes and fishing weirs over the flats.

The coast is most uninteresting, and there is a Bore in the River Parret, which, in 1875, caused considerable damage at Bridgewater, smashing the dock gates and sinking a barge. Ordinarily, this tidal phenomenon only rises 2ft., but all the same attention must be paid to moorings.

At half-tide there is 20ft. on the bar.

Buoys.—The **Gore Bell Buoy** is the fairway buoy. It lies in 12ft. at low-water spring tides. It is conical, with a staff and globe. Up to this the Burnham Lights in line lead in the fairway. After the buoy is passed, bring the high lighthouse S. of the low light, and pass between the **red and black can buoys.** There are **three red can buoys** marking the S. side of the bar channel, and **three black can buoys** on the N. side, with **one white one**, being the last or inner one. **Three red buoys**, smaller, also mark the N. side of Stert Island, being the S. side of the **Swatch Channel**, the mark for which is **Flatholm Lighthouse** in line with the E. end of Steepholm up to the white buoy; then N. of Chisel Rocks and the **small red buoys** N. of Stert Island.

Lights.—Burnham Lights stand on the low shore N. of Burnham Village.

The **high lighthouse is a white tower, with a vertical red stripe, 99ft. high.** From it is **exhibited, at an elevation of 91ft. above high-water, a double occulting white light, visible fifteen miles.** E. of the bearing, S.S.E. $\frac{1}{4}$ E., the light is obscured. The light occults twice in quick succession every minute as follows: Light 54sec., eclipse 2sec.; light 2sec., eclipse 2sec.

The **low light is distant** from the **high light 500yds, and is a square white tower, with a vertical red stripe, 36ft. high, showing, at an elevation of 23ft.** above high-water, **a fixed white and red light, visible nine miles.**

The **white light is visible between the bearings of E. $\frac{3}{4}$ S. and E.S.E. over the bar.**

The **red light is visible seaward between the bearings of E. $\frac{3}{4}$ S. and E. $\frac{1}{4}$ S.; and also up the river between the bearings of N. by E. and E. $\frac{1}{2}$ E.**

The **lights in line lead N. of the Gore Bell Buoy.**

The tide is very strong on the ebb and the anchorage is off Burnham, the only possible place for a stranger, and here there is little room to lie afloat or swing with the tide.

A good deal of trade goes on with Bridgewater, as much as 187,715 tons entering annually.

Burnham, like Pisa, possesses a leaning tower—that of the church—and a pier extending ·nearly to low-water. Steam-boats call here, as well as at Lynmouth, in the summer from Cardiff and elsewhere.

Culver Sand is a dangerous bank, lying half-way between the English and Welsh coasts. It dries over a distance of **three miles from 3ft. to 8ft. at low-water.** The flood-tide and ebb set directly across the sand, its total length being four miles and a half.

This danger is marked by three buoys. **West Culver is spherical, red and white in horizontal stripes, with staff and diamond,** a quarter of a mile W. of the three-fathoms edge of the sand, **Nash Lighthouse,** on the Welsh Coast, bearing N.N.W. $\frac{1}{8}$ W., distant eleven miles and four-fifths. **North Culver is conical, red,** close to the N. edge of the sand. **East Culver is spherical, red and white in horizontal stripes, with staff and triangle.**

On each side there is a fairway, the northern one the deepest.

Steepholm Island lies three miles and a half E.N.E. of the Culver Sand. It is four and a half cables by two cables in breadth. The highest part of it is 239ft. It is inaccessible except at the E. end. Ledges extend off the E. and S.W. points, and from the W. point is a shoal with three fathoms and a half least water; but none of the dangers extend farther than three cables, or about one-third of a mile.

Remarks on the appearance of the coast and objects of interest visible from the sea between Morte Point and Steepholm.—The town of Ilfracombe comes in sight shortly after rounding Morte Point, the lines of terraces showing white against the dark hills. It is a pity there is no harbour along the coast where a yacht could lie safely afloat in all winds, and it would seem as if a little outlay would make a very pretty little floating harbour of such places as Porlock or Lynmouth. The cliff scenery after passing Ilfracombe becomes very striking, especially when opposite the Hangman Cliffs and Heddons Mouth.

Lynmouth is most beautiful. It is celebrated for the loveliness of the Valley of Rocks; but all this district from Combe Martin Bay to Porlock is a continual panorama of delightful scenery, and one only regrets the more the necessity of being obliged to hurry by it. The dangers, however, of the sea, if a N. or N.W. wind should get up, are too serious to allow one to dally with the beauty of the scene; and even an E. wind sends up a very nasty sea with the flood-tide.

In settled fine weather a cruise could be managed along here with much pleasure and profit ; but it would be managed more easily in a small sailing boat or canoe, which could be hauled up at night, or lie aground in the tidal harbours.

There are many excellent anchorages with off-shore winds.

Between the Foreland and Gore Point the shore is quite inaccessible, except at one spot, three miles E. of the Foreland. Here a stream runs into the sea, and forms the boundary between Devon and Somerset.

All this country is well described in " Lorna Doone." Exmoor is conspicuous all the way between the Foreland and Minehead, and nowhere is the scenery finer than here.

As Bridgewater comes open the country becomes flat and uninteresting, and so continues as far as Brean Down.

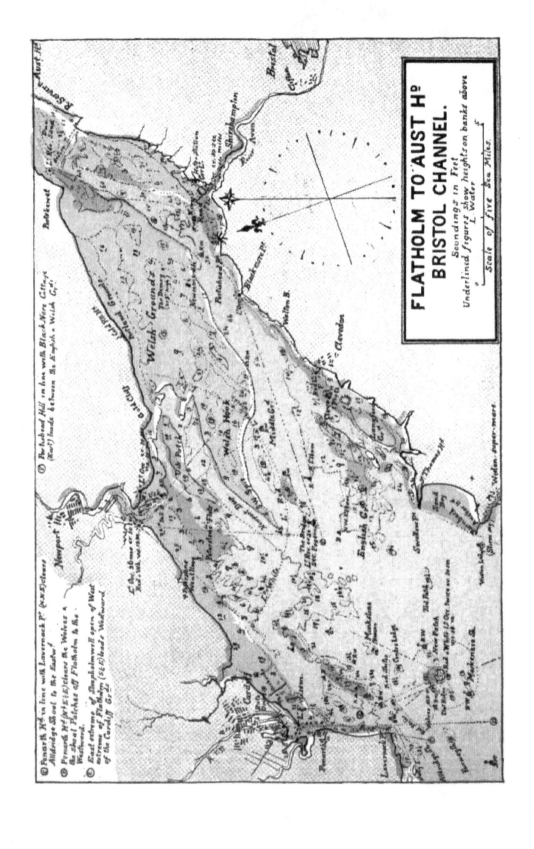

FLATHOLM TO AUST H?
BRISTOL CHANNEL.

Soundings in Feet
Underlined figures show heights on banks above
L. Water.

Scale of Five Sea Miles

CHAPTER VII.

STEEPHOLM TO SHARPNESS AND CARDIFF ROADS.

THE Bristol Channel is narrowing considerably now. Wales has been in sight for some time, and as Brean Down comes abreast a vessel is opposite Lavernock Point and Cardiff Roads.

Flatholm Island, two miles N. of **Steepholm Island,** is only **four miles** across the **water** from **Brean Down,** and **two miles and a half** S.E. of **Lavernock Point,** in Glamorgan. Unlike Steepholm, Flatholm, as its name signifies, is low, the highest part, 65ft., being at its S. end, from which it falls gently to the N. The length of the island is about a third of a mile, and on its S. or highest part is a lighthouse.

Flatholm Light.—In a circular **white tower,** 99ft. high, a **white occulting light** is shown at an elevation of 164ft. above high-water. **The light occults twice in quick succession every half-minute. It suddenly disappears for 3sec., then reappears at full power for 3sec., and disappears for 3sec., and then remains at full power for the remainder of the half-minute.** It is visible **eighteen miles.**

Red sectors are shown between the bearings S.E. ¼ E. and S. by E. ¼ E. over the **Wolves,** and S. ½ E. and S.W. ¼ S. over **Centre Ledge.** The white sector between these leads up to Cardiff Roads, between **Ranie** Spit and W. Cardiff Buoy, between the bearings of S. by E. ¾ E. and S. ½ E.

The main channel lies between the Holms.

There is **anchorage** at the N.E. side of the island in **three** fathoms, sand, opposite the landing-place.

Continuing along the S. shore, How Rock, a rocky ridge, runs off Brean Down for a quarter of a mile, causing a tide race for some distance out.

The next headland is **Anchor Head,** and between it and Brean Down lies Weston or Uphill Bay. All the bay is mud at low-water, but at its W. side the River Axe discharges into the sea, close under Brean Down. It is difficult to navigate, but there is a pool where a shallow draught vessel of 6ft. can lie afloat at neap tides.

Honeycombe Rock, a dangerous ledge, with only 2ft. on it at low-water, lies six cables W. by N. of Anchor Head. Its N.W. edge is marked by a **red conical buoy,** in five fathoms, called Weston Ledge Buoy.

Baimbach Islet, connected by a pier to Anchor Head, lies off the land, and near by is the **beacon,** which, **in line with the square church tower in Weston-super-Mare,** indicates the line of the **submarine telegraph cable.** Vessels are prohibited anchoring in this line.

Weston-super-Mare lies in the N.E. corner of Uphill Bay. Worle Hill lies to its N., with a mill at its extremity, 260ft. above high-water.

Next comes **Clevedon,** with the **Langford Grounds,** which dry at low-water, filling in **the bay** to the distance of one mile off shore, which is low.

Clevedon Pier shows a fixed **red light,** at an elevation of 27ft. The pier is 270yds. long.

From here to **Portishead** the coast is fairly straight. Off **Walton Bay,** so called, is anchorage in three to four fathoms. The low-water-mark is only about one cable off shore, between **Portishead Point and Pier,** but, as is the case all along this shore, fishing stakes are abundant and dangerous.

Behind **Clevedon,** and as far as Portishead, a hill runs parallel with the coast. It is 300ft. high in places. The ruins of **Walton Castle** mark the W. end, and above Portishead are two peaks ; the seaward one is crowned by a flag-staff, 164ft. above high-water.

Anchorage in Portishead Pool is off **Portishead Pier**, between **Firefly** and **Flatness Rocks**. On the former there is only 3ft. at low-water ; the latter is a bed of gravel and stones, and it dries. A red conical buoy, in seven fathoms, lies half a cable N. of Firefly Rock.

The anchorage is confined further by the training-ship **Formidable**, which is moored stem and stern close to the low-water edge, two cables above Portishead Pier. She has five anchors down—three to seaward and two inshore. The anchor ahead and the inshore ones have three hundred fathoms of chain out ; the N. anchors one hundred and fifty fathoms each. The anchors are buoyed.

Tides.—It is high-water, full and change, at 7hr. 13min. local, or 7hr. 24min. Greenwich time. **Springs rise from** 31ft. to 40ft. ; neaps, 22ft. In the third hour of the flood the tide rises most, about 9½ft., or nearly as much as is the whole rise and fall in the lochs of the Clyde.

The average strength of the ebb in the main channel is five or six knots ; of the flood about four knots and a half.

The coast is low between **Portishead** and **Avonmouth**. At the mouth of the River Avon is **Dumball Islet, low and marshy**, with beacons on it.

The red hut on Dumball Islet in line with the white hut behind it, bearing E. by S., leads clear of the **Firefly** and **Flatness Rocks**. At night green lights are shown in these huts.

Light-vessel.—On the **Bridge Shoal**, on which the least water was four fathoms, the Grounds Light-vessel is moored in four fathoms. From an elevation of 38ft. above the water a flashing white light, giving a flash every 30sec., is shown, visible eleven miles. The vessel carries a ball at the mast-head.

Fog-signal.—A foghorn, giving two blasts, high, low, in quick succession, every 2min. The vessel lies between the **English** and the **Welsh Grounds**, the latter of which dry from 10ft. to 12ft. at about one mile and a half S. of the Grounds Light-vessel. The **Welsh Grounds** also dry as much as 27ft. opposite Clevedon.

The **Middle Ground** lies between the **English** and the **Welsh Hook**, and dries 2ft. The **English Grounds** front the coast from Weston, a distance of ten miles.

Buoys.—The **Middle Ground** is **three miles** in extent, and parallel to the **Welsh Hook.** On S. Middle there is a **can buoy, red and white chequered**; on E. Middle, a can buoy, red and white stripes.

The **Welsh Grounds** are connected with Newport, Monmouthshire, and cover fully two-thirds of the high-water space of the upper part of the Bristol Channel. The S.W. spit is a prong lying out from the Welsh Hook.

Buoys.—On the **S.W. spit** is a **black conical buoy**, with a **staff and globe**, in 27ft.

The **Welsh Hook** is marked by a **can buoy, red and white chequered,** in 23ft.

The **Newcome Buoy** is a can buoy, red and white stripes, in 19ft.

The **Cockburn Rock**, E. of Newcome Shoal, **which shifts**, lies at the entrance to **King Road, with 4ft. over it at low-tide. It is marked by a red and white chequered can buoy,** in 18ft.

The **Denny Rock** is 21ft. high above high-water, and 410ft. in length. It is a useful guide to King Road.

Anchorages.—There are no good or comfortable anchorages for small yachts in all weathers. The docks at the great ports are the only really safe places. Off **Walton Bay** there is fairly safe shelter out of the full tidal stream in from three to four fathoms, one cable and a half off shore.

King Road lies off the mouth of the **Avon**, seventeen miles above **Flatholm.** The ordinary anchorage is half a mile on either side of **Avon Lighthouse**, in line with Penpole Tower. At night a **red sector** indicates the anchorage in some four to six fathoms. It is better to anchor to the E. of this bearing to allow a clear way for vessels to Bristol.

Light.—**Avon Lighthouse** is an octagonal white tower. It shows an **occulting white light** (eclipsing suddenly for 3sec., and then as suddenly reappearing at full power once in every

half-minute), **73ft. above high-water, visible fourteen miles.**
A red sector shows over King Road, bearing S.E.

A fixed red light, 18ft. high, is shown 230yds. N.W. of
the **Avon Light.** These lights, in line, lead up the River
Avon.

The Portishead anchorage has already been noticed.

The tides run **five knots in King Road.**

The **Port of Bristol** is not a place for a yacht to sail to with
comfort. A tug boat or steam is requisite. There is 40ft. of
water at high-water and 3ft. at low-water. This speaks for
the navigation.

There is good dock accommodation at either Avon Mouth
or Portishead.

From Avon Mouth to New Passage is five miles. The
channel is now only one mile and three quarters wide, and
this is further narrowed by the **Mixons** and the **English stones**
to the passage called the **Shoot. Charstone Rock** lies three
cables off Portskewet, and shows a revolving white light.
Above this, to **Sharpness Dock,** whence there is canal communication with nearly all England, the services of a pilot are
indispensable. The velocity of the tide, the various obstacles
and the traffic, causing difficulties an amateur yachtsman would
be foolish to encounter on his own responsibility.

**Passing now to the N. side of the Severn, Chepstow, on
the Wye,** is a **possible port** for a yacht, but here the tides
rise highest. The shore-going authorities say it has reached
70ft. The Trinity House authorities say not more than 56ft.,
which is enough to cause a pretty strong stream.

There are, however, attractions at Chepstow to induce a
hardy amateur to risk the worry. A vessel will lie afloat here
at low-water, which is a comfort, as it is actually the first
sheltered place where this has been possible since leaving
Padstow, without resorting to artificial means.

On no account should a stranger attempt to get up here
from **King Road** without a pilot. The risk is too great, as
the tide runs with great rapidity through the **short passage,**
and there are obstacles.

G

To start from King Road weigh with the first of the flood, as most of the dangers show. **Charstown Rock**, in line with **Mathern Cliff**, above **Portskewet**, on both of which are white lights—the first revolving, the latter fixed—leads through the **Shoot.** Pass **S.** of **Charstown Rock**, and when **abreast of Mathern Upper Pill**, or Creek, keep half a cable off shore, and bear round for the **Wye.** Tidenham Stone lies 7oyds. N. of **Ewen's Rock, opposite an old oak tree; leave this on the starboard hand.** There is 6ft. over it, **when another rock**, called **Fair Tide Rock**, is covering at **Redcliff.**

On the E. side of the Wye is **Old Chapel Isle with a ruin on it**, off **Bleachley Point.** The Severn is barely a mile across here. The best anchorage at Chepstow is near the **Railway Bridge**, where vessels drawing 12ft. may lie afloat at all times in perfect safety.

The **Castle of Chepstow** stands magnificently, and the scenery of the river, with the delightful boating excursions it offers, affords some compensation for the difficulty of getting to the place.

When once at Chepstow, provided a vessel is moored well, there need be no further anxiety upon the score of weather. The strength of the tides and the local traffic, which is not great, are the only worries.

Tides.—It is high-water, full and change, at Chepstow at 7hr. 30min. Springs range from 38ft. to 56ft ; neaps, 29½ft.

The Bore, or Hygre, as it is locally termed, is felt here, but mostly on the Severn above Sharpness. It is usually highest at the fifth flood, after full and change. The tidal wave rarely exceeds 4ft. to 5ft.

There are two fine bridges over the Wye at Chepstow, with 51ft. below them at high-water. One is a railway bridge, the other an iron bridge for ordinary traffic.

Tintern Abbey and the celebrated Wind Cliff are within a day's excursion up the river, and are well worth seeing.

Continuing to sail W., for which purpose the ebb-tide is a necessity—and extra caution is, therefore, required in the navigation — the course leads over the Severn Tunnel from

New Passage to Portskewet. It is safer to keep the regular channel, about four miles off the low shore, between the **Usk** and **Redstone**. It is possible, of course, to pass over the flats at high-water, but care must be taken, as the water falls so rapidly.

To enter the Usk it is better to have **local help**. There is a great deal of traffic, and the tides are, as usual, strong. Newport is a very busy place.

The **Peterstone Flats** lie off the N.W. side of the **entrance** to the river. They are a continuation of the **Cardiff Flats**. **Usk Patch** lies directly opposite the river, and E. of **Peterstone Flats**. It **dries** for a distance of three miles, with a breadth of four cables, the highest part drying 24ft., and is connected with the **Welsh Grounds** by a ridge, with **less** than **6ft**. over it. **Usk River Light**, bearing N.N.W. ½ W., distant two miles and a half, crosses the shoalest part of the **Usk Patch**. **Two buoys mark** the **entrance** to the river. They lie aground at low-water. **E. Usk** is conical, red, and **W. Usk** is a bell buoy with red and **white stripes**.

Lights.—There are two lights. **W. Usk** exhibits from a circular **white tower**, at an **elevation** of **57ft. above high-water**, an **occulting red and white light**. There are three occultations every half-minute, viz.: dark 1½sec., light 1½sec.; dark 1½sec., light 1½sec.; dark 1½sec., then light for 22½sec.

The **white light shows between** the bearings of N. **62deg**. E. to N. **22deg**. E., and between N. **21deg**. W. to N. **32deg**. W., **leading between** the buoys at the **entrance** and **between** S. **71deg. W. and S. 57deg. W.**

The **red light shows** between N. **22deg**. E. to N. **21deg**. W., and between N. **32deg**. W. to the **land**.

E. Usk light is ten **cables** and **a half** S. **68deg**. E. of the **W. light**. It shows white, red, and green. It occults **2sec**. every **10sec**., and **shows** white from N. **56deg**. W. to N. **51deg**. W.; also in **main channel** from N. **35deg**. E. to N. **51deg**. E., and from S. **46deg**. E. to S. **41deg**. E. It **shows** red from N. **51deg**. W. to N. **35deg**. E., and **green** from N. **51deg**. E. to S. **46deg**. E.

The coast from Usk to Cardiff is low, with muddy flats, drying out for three-quarters of a mile.

Anchorage off the Usk.—**Newport Deep,** or Road, lies **between Peterstone Flats** and the **Welsh Grounds.** It is three miles in length, with good holding ground in from four to six fathoms. It is one of the safest anchorages above the Holms. The tides are easy here, and there is not much sea.

Newport lies three miles up the Usk.

Cardiff is another very busy port, as many as 800 vessels entering in a month. 9,000,000 tons are annually exported, and as many as 1,000,000 imported. Under these circumstances it is not suited for yachting. The port ranks as the third largest in the kingdom.

The castle is now transformed into the residence of the Marquis of Bute.

Between **Cardiff** and **Penarth** are the Penarth Flats, on which vessels lie aground on a muddy bottom.

From **Penarth** to **Lavernock Point** the shore dries out a quarter of a mile, and is mostly rock and stone. Off **Penarth** lies the **Cefn-y-Wrach,** a bed of stones, which dry at low-water. Another patch lies half a mile S.E. of this, with 9ft. least-water, close to the W. side of Cardiff Roads.

Cardiff Grounds front the mouth of the River Taff, on which Cardiff is built. These are two miles off shore, and are liable to change. The bank dries as far as one mile and a tenth from **Lavernock Point,** bearing W., and from thence extends for one mile and three quarters N.E., with a **swashway** with 4ft. at low-water, two cables wide, half a mile from the S. end. The average width is two cables, and it dries as much as 13ft. From the N.E. extremity a ridge of sand, with only 3ft. to 6ft. water on it, extends N.E. one mile and three quarters to Cardiff Flats.

Buoys.—Four buoys mark the Cardiff Grounds on the **N.W.** side and one the E. spit.

West Cardiff Grounds is a spherical buoy, black and white stripes, with staff and globe, lying in four fathoms.

Middle Cardiff Grounds is a black conical buoy, in four fathoms, at the N.E. end of the swashway.

The **Hook Buoy** is black, conical, in two fathoms. **E. Cardiff Grounds** is black, conical, with staff and globe, in two fathoms and a quarter.

Cardiff Spit, on the E. of **Cardiff Grounds** is a red and white chequered can buoy.

Penarth Roads inside of this bank is the safest anchorage on the N. side of the Bristol Channel.   The two Holms in line bearing S. by W., and Penarth coastguard flag-staff open S. of the lifeboat house, W.N.W., is a good anchorage ; or even a little N.W. of this is a good berth.

In **approaching** this **anchorage** from the **W., Lavernock Spit** and **Ranie Spit** lie off **Lavernock Point.** The former dries one third of a mile in a S.S.E. direction.   The latter is a spit of stones, three cables in extent, in a N. and S. direction, with one dry spot on it at low-water, distant half a mile from Lavernock Point in an E. by S. ½ S. direction. The tide sets ·very strongly over these shoals.

Barry Island kept in line with **Sully Island,** bearing W. ¾ N., leads S. of **Ranie Spit.**   There is a black and white striped çan buoy, surmounted by a staff and cage, one cable and a half S.S.W. of the dry spot on **Ranie Spit,** distant five cables.

Penarth Head is the highest headland on the N. shore of the Bristol Channel.   The cliff is bold, and there is a church tower near the summit, a little inland, 216ft. above high-water. From **Penarth Head** to **Lavernock Point** it is two miles and a half. W. of **Lavernock Point** is **Sully Island,** three miles E. of Barry Island, two cables off the low coast.   It is connected by a half-tide ledge and is 53ft. high.

Lavernock Point is one mile and a quarter E. and 50ft. high, rising behind to 105ft.   Off **Sully Island** is Sully Ledge, nine cables distant, bearing S.W. by W., with two fathoms and a quarter least water over it. **Aldridge Shoal,** lying between Sully and **Lavernock,** has three fathoms and one-sixth least water.

One fathom bank is one mile and a half in length, with two fathoms and one-sixth least water over it.   It is marked by a spherical buoy, painted black and white rings, in six fathoms.

New Patch lies half a mile E. of Flatholm Island Lighthouse. There is 7ft. least water on it. It is marked by a chequered black and white can buoy, E. of a 10ft. patch, in four fathoms.

Mackenzie Shoal is one mile from S. point of Flatholm, bearing S.W. by W. ¼ W. The least water is one fathom and a half. It is marked by a spherical buoy, black and white rings with staff and diamond.

The Wolves lie N.W. ¼ W., distant eight cables from Flatholm. They consist of three rocky heads which dry 5½ft. at low-water. Two buoys mark this danger. The W. buoy is spherical, black and white rings. The E. buoy is spherical, with red and white rings, distant from Flatholm one mile.

The Monkstone used to be very dangerous. It dries 10½ft. It lies N.E. ¾ N., distant two miles and a half from Flatholm.

A stone beacon with a safety cage, 40ft. above high-water, is erected on it.

Sailing in or out, keep N. of the One Fathom Bank, with Breaksea Light-vessel bearing W. by S. ¼ S., leaving the Wolves on the S., passing between Ranie Spit and Cardiff W. buoys.

Tides.—It is high water, full and change, at Cardiff at 6hr. 56min. Springs rise from 37ft. to 40ft.; neaps, 29ft. The stream runs fair between the Holms, the flood at three knots, and the ebb at four knots, turning at high- and low-water by the shore.

Off all the points and over the banks there are overfalls and tide rips.

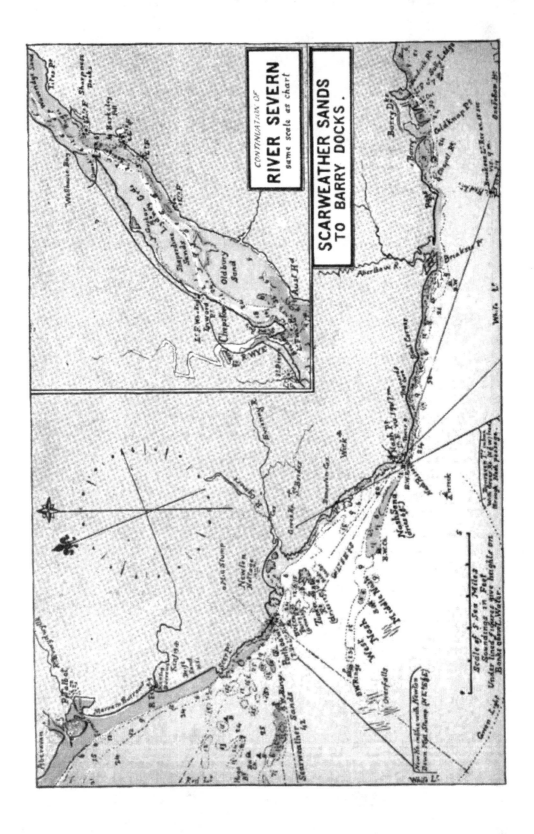

CONTINUATION OF

RIVER SEVERN
same scale as chart

SCARWEATHER SANDS
TO BARRY DOCKS.

CHAPTER VIII.

CARDIFF ROADS TO THE MUMBLES.

ALWAYS with the proviso that I consider this part of the coast unsuitable for cruising purposes, but yet unwilling to give it the go-by in case strangers might have to run up here, I continue the cruise from **Lavernock Point**, westwards.

There is fair anchorage out of the tide half a mile W. of Sully Island, but it is better not to lose sight of the S. point of the island in line.

Barry Island and Roadstead are three miles W. of Sully Island. There is anchorage in Barry Roads in quiet weather at half a mile off the docks.

Barry Port has been made by connecting the island with the mainland. There are large docks here. W. of Barry Island is an inlet where vessels can take the ground.

Coldknap Point forms its W. side, off which a spit, partly dry at low-water, extends three-quarters of a mile in a westerly direction.

Beyond this is Porthkerry, with **Chapel Rock**, dry at extreme low-tides, on its W. side, and three-quarters of a mile from Roos Point, the most southerly point in Wales.

Breaksea Point comes next, off which the low-water limit, encumbered with boulders, stretches to a quarter of a mile. **Breaksea Ledge** is marked by a black and white chequered can buoy, in four fathoms.

Aberthaw River lies E. of Breaksea Point. There is shallow anchorage at its mouth in quiet weather. Over **Breaksea Ledge** there is a considerable overfall.

Breaksea Light-vessel is moored in **eighteen fathoms in the fairway, nine miles S. 50deg. E. from the Nash Lights,** and one mile and three quarters W.N.W. from the **One Fathom Bank Buoy, Flatholm Light bearing** E. six miles and three quarters. A ball is shown at the masthead. From a height of 35ft. above the sea a **revolving** white light is shown, attaining its **greatest brilliancy** every 15sec. Visible eleven miles.

Fog-signal.—Two explosive reports are sounded every 10min., the interval between the reports being 5sec.

From **Breaksea Point to St. Donats Bluff the coast is low. Colhugh Reef** dries one-third of a mile from Colhugh Point, one mile and a half from St. Donats Bluff, and the bay between is shoal to the distance of four cables off the land.

St. Donats Bluff is five miles from Breaksea; behind it are the ruins of St. Donats Castle. The cliffs here are 100ft. high.

Nash Point is an important headland in the Bristol Channel, lying just opposite **Minehead.** The head is 77ft. high, and is crowned with two lighthouses. The high light, which bears from the low light S. 65deg. E. and is 333yds. from it, exhibits at an elevation of 182ft. above high-water a fixed white and red light. The **white light** shows between the bearings of S.E. by S. and N.W. ½ W. Visible eighteen miles. The **red light** is shown over **Breaksea Ledge** between the bearings of N.W. ½ W. and the land. A ray of red is also shown from a window below the lantern over **Tusker and Fairy Rocks.** Both the high and low lights are seen over this sector.

The low light is fixed, white. It is obscured westward of N.N.W. ¼ W. The lights in line lead S. of **Nash Sands and Scarweather Sands.**

The high lighthouse is **painted in black and white bands. Nash Sands are dangerous.** They extend seven miles in a N.W. direction from Nash Point, with a breadth of from one to six cables, steep-to on both sides, with six to eight fathoms water. There are three parts of them.

The **Nash** dries 6ft. at its E. end, and is one mile in length. A spit runs out one mile and a half W. with less than 6ft. on it. This sand is six cables wide.

The E. **extreme** is marked by a **spherical buoy, painted black and white in rings, lying in three fathoms, and distant from Nash Point 800yds.**

Nash Middle is a quarter of a mile in length, with from 3ft. to 6ft. least water on it. It is **marked at its E. end by a black and white chequered can buoy,** in three fathoms ; and at its **W. end by a black and white vertically striped can buoy.**

West Nash extends two miles and a half W. from the Middle with depths at low-water of one fathom and three quarters to three fathoms. Beyond it are rocky patches, with four fathoms and a half on them. It is marked by **W. Nash Buoy,** in five fathoms and a half, **a spherical black and white buoy painted in rings.**

To pass to the **E. of Nash Sands, keep Groes House in line with Dunraven Tower,** bearing N. ½ W. The channel is one cable and a half wide.

The **ebb- and flood-tides set across the sands in a N.N.W. and S.S.E. direction; but when the high light is open S. of the low light** the streams set along them. The velocity is five knots at springs.

Dunraven Castle stands about half-way between the Nash and the Ogmore River. It is conspicuous by its flag-staff, 232ft. high above high-water, and its tower, with a summer-house close to the cliff.

The shore should be given a good berth, as a ledge runs S. all along here. Ogmore Down is 321ft. high. On the hill, half-way between Dunraven and Ogmore River, is Groes House. This in line with **Dunraven Tower leads** through the **Nash Channel.**

There is a good landing-place at Dunraven.

From here to the Ogmore River the coast is fairly bold to look at, the low-water limit extending about two cables.

Beyond the river to **Porthcawl** it is sandy.

Off **Porthcawl** and the **Ogmore River** is the **Tusker Rock,** which dries 12ft. It is the **highest point of a mass of rock half** a mile long. There is shoal water inside of it. It lies S.S.E. one mile and two-thirds from Porthcawl Light, and one mile and a half W.S.W. from the Ogmore River.

A can buoy with staff and cage, painted in black and white stripes, lies in five fathoms W. of the S.W. point of the Tusker.

Fairy Rock, awash at low-water springs, lies S. six cables and a half from Porthcawl Lighthouse. It is marked by a black and white chequered can buoy, in four fathoms, one cable and a half W. of it.

Porthcawl is not a place for a yacht to go to unless obliged, or for special reasons. The harbour dries out. There is a wet dock, but the harbour has to be protected by booms in heavy weather, when a considerable sea comes home here. The anchorage outside is bad, and the ground swell frequently heavy.

Light.—From the pier-head a fixed light is shown, visible eleven miles. It shows red N. of E. by S. to S.E. ½ S., white between N.E. by E. and E. by S., and green from N.W. ½ N. to N.E. by E.

The coast from Porthcawl to Port Talbot is low, with sand hills here and there and higher land behind. The little stream, the Kenfig, dribbles through sand, and the gray square tower of Kenfig Church stands in a clump of wood. Margam Wood is a fir copse on a hill 302ft. high, and Newton Nottage disused mill is one mile and three quarters N.E. of Porthcawl Lighthouse.

All this E. side of Swansea Bay is unapproachable in any fresh wind from the S. or W., as a heavy surf beats all along the sands, which dry out in places as far as a mile from the shore, interspersed with rocky ledges.

Port Talbot, also called Aberavon, is a lately-constructed port for colliers and other vessels which load minerals. The floating dock is 300ft. long by 45ft. wide, with a depth of 22½ft. over the sill.

A heavy ground swell beats along here and right up to the entrance. The coast continues low and sandy. Behind is

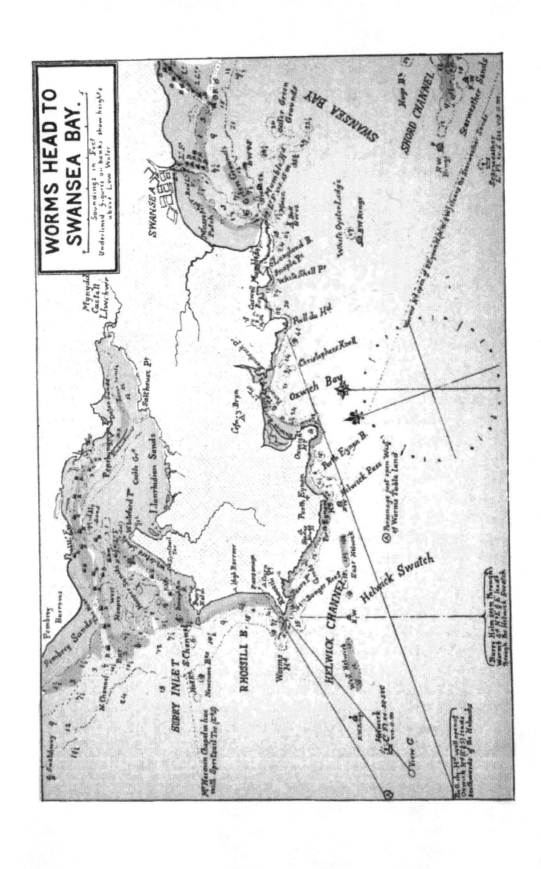

Mynydd Dinas and Cwm Bychan, 832ft. and 1178ft. high, respectively.

The **Neath** River is another wasted opportunity. It looks as if it should be a comfortable place. Owing to the tides and the sand it is practically useless for a yacht unless she goes into dock. The whole of the entrance dries out, and is filled with mud and sand to the distance of two miles off shore.

The **navigable** channel at high-water runs close along the embankment, 2ft. above high-water, which extends half a mile W. ¾ S. from the S. pier-head of **Briton Ferry Docks**. There are several **black buoys** lying along this to mark the loose slag which has been thrown down. The **Fairway Buoy** lies in two fathoms, and is painted **red and black, in vertical stripes**, with a **staff and cage**. A **red can buoy**, dry at low-water, lies seven cables within the **Fairway Buoy** to mark the E. side of the channel.

Above **Briton Ferry, on the E. side**, is the **Giant's Grave Pill**, or creek, where vessels can lie out of the tide.

The coast W. of the Neath is low and sandy as far as **Swansea**, with high ground behind.

Swansea looks a vast place from the sea, and recent improvements have made the harbour and dock accommodation ample and extensive. The entrance **channel** between the piers at the mouth of the **Taw** is dredged to a depth of 12ft. at low-water. The docks afford any amount of shelter suitable, in many quiet corners, for yachts—if quiet corners can be found in this busy place—the aggregate tonnage of which is over 2,000,000 annually, entering and leaving.

Light.—From a **white lighthouse**, 23ft. high, near the end of the W. pier, is exhibited a **fixed red light**, 35ft. above high-water, visible seven miles.

Tidal Light and Signal.—A **black ball is hoisted by day** at the W. pier-head from December 1 to April 1 when there is 16ft. at the piers, and all the rest of the year when there is 14ft. An **electric white light** is exhibited from the **E. pier** at night for the same purpose.

Time Signal.—A gun is fired every day, except Sundays and public holidays, at 0hr. 44min. 18sec., local time, *i.e.*, 1hr. 0min. 0sec., Greenwich time.

Dangers in Swansea Bay.—The bay is encumbered with the following shoals: The **Kenfig** and **N. Kenfig** Patches; the latter with least water, 10ft., over it, otherwise there is from two to three fathoms. They lie one mile and a tenth from Kenfig River, bearing E.S.E. from them. A **black conical buoy**, in four fathoms, lies E. by N. ¼ N., one mile and two-fifths from the **Hugo Bank Buoy.** The largest Kenfig patch is one mile long.

Hugo Bank is a V-shaped shoal, extending N.W. by W. and N.N.W. one mile and a quarter each way.

The shoalest part has only from 2ft. to 6ft. least water, and lies one cable inside its S. edge. It is **marked by a black and white chequered buoy,** in four fathoms and a half, lying one cable and a half S.S.W. of the W. end of the shoalest part.

The passage between **Fairy Rock, Porthcawl,** is N.W. ½ W., passing to the northward of the E. and N. Scarweather Buoys.

Scarweather Sands are four miles and three quarters in extent by a mile in width. There are three patches which dry. **W. Scarweather** is near the centre and dries 6ft., with several patches awash half a mile to the westward. **E. and Middle Scarweather,** at its E. end, dry only at low-water springs. A heavy sea breaks over these sands, and the tide sets obliquely across them.

To clear them **keep** Worms Head open of **Porth Eynon Head.** This leads S. of them. The **Mumbles,** bearing N. ½ E., leads W., and Kenfig Church, in line with Scar House, leads E. **Scar House** is a dark-looking farm, half a mile behind Scar Point, the last point, rocky and brown-looking, at the end of the long row of sand hills at the E. side of Swansea Bay, two miles and a half N. from Porthcawl.

Scarweather Light-vessel lies in fourteen fathoms, S.W., one mile and a half from **W. Scarweather Buoy.** The light is a **quick flashing white light, showing one flash every 5sec., visible ten miles.** It carries a half globe over a globe at the masthead.

Fog-signal.—The siren gives two blasts in quick succession every 2min. The **Scarweather Bank** is **marked** by **three buoys.** W. Scarweather is spherical, **black** and **white** bands or rings, with **staff** and **diamond.** It lies in five fathoms, three cables W. of the three fathoms' limit.

E. Scarweather is a spherical red and white ringed buoy, with a staff and triangle, in seven fathoms, S.E. of the E. extreme of three fathoms.

N. Scarweather is a **black conical buoy,** in five fathoms and a half.

Shord Channel lies between the Scarweather and Hugo Sands. It is four cables wide, with a least depth of four fathoms and a half.

White Oyster Ledge lies S.W. by S., two miles and three quarters from the Mumbles Light. It has four fathoms and a half least water over it, but a **heavy** sea on the **ebb-tide** breaks on it with **W.** winds. A **buoy, spherical, black and white bands,** lies in **eight fathoms, one cable S. of the least-water patch.**

The **Green Grounds** are detached rocks, from 7ft. to 10ft. over the inner **grounds** and **two fathoms and a half** over the outer. The **W. extreme is one mile E. by N. from the Mumbles Lighthouse,** and the outer grounds are S. by W. ½ W. from the E. or inner Green Grounds.

Two buoys mark this danger on the S. edge. The **S.W. is a black and white chequered can buoy,** in four fathoms. The E. is a black and white striped buoy, in three fathoms and a quarter.

The **Mixon Shoal** lies S. of the **Mumbles.** It is a bank of fine sand lying in a N.E. and S.W. direction, eight cables long by two cables broad, with least water on its S.E. side, from 1½ft. to 6ft. The shallow spot lies with the Mumbles Light N.N.E., distant 800yds. The **flood-tide sets directly over the shoal.**

A **bell buoy,** black and white stripes, in ten fathoms, marks the S. corner of the **Mixon,** with **Porth Eynon** and **Oxwich Heads** in line.

Just inside and N. of the **Mumbles Light** the shingle does not dry out farther than a cable for half a mile towards Swansea, but after that the flats extend three-quarters of a mile at low-water, with fishing weirs all about.

There are patches of stone and mussels here and there.

Approaching Swansea from the W. keep Porth Eynon open of Oxwich Bay, and pass S. of the Mixon Bell Buoy. Then steer—when **Sketty Church Spire,** lying N. of Oystermouth, is open of the Mumbles Light—N. ¾ E. southward of the **inner Green Grounds Buoy,** and anchor in the roads.

It is possible to pass W. of the Green Grounds.

The anchorage in Mumbles Road. — When Oystermouth Castle opens of Mumbles Lighthouse, steer N.N.W. until Mumbles Church bears N.W. by W.; then steer for it and anchor when the **light-keeper's house chimneys** at the Mumbles come in line. There is from 14ft. to 15ft. here at low-water.

It is possible at **tide time** to pass between the **Mixon** and the **Mumbles.**

Tides.—It is **high-water, full and change,** at the Mumbles at 6hr. 1min. local, or 6hr. 17min. Greenwich time. Springs rise from 27ft. to 31ft.; neaps, 20ft.

The flood-tide in the fairway, **between the Mumbles and Scar-weather,** sets to the E. from low-water until 1hr. before high-water by the shore, at about four knots at springs. S. of the Scar-weather it sets more south-easterly and so draws out of the bay over the bank. The ebb runs 7hrs. to the. W.

Near the shore an eddy sets round the bay on the flood from the E. The ebb runs out strongly past Mumbles Head, creating a nasty race with S.W. winds.

Mumbles Head is 60ft. high; off it are ten rocky islets, connected by a shingle bank, covered at half-flood. Ledges lie off, drying in a S.E. direction to the distance of **200yds.,** ending in the **Cherrystone,** which dries 4ft.

Oystermouth Castle is a conspicuous sea-mark, being 170ft. above high-water.

Mumbles Light.—On the **outer islet is a white octagonal tower,** 56ft. high. From it is exhibited, at an elevation of 114ft. above high-water, a fixed **white light,** visible fifteen miles.

Remarks on the appearance of the coast and objects of interest visible from the sea between Cardiff and the Mumbles. —The coast W. of Lavernock Point as far as Nash Point is mostly hilly. None of the heights are great, but the cliffs are tolerably bold.

St. Donats Castle is an ancient building, restored recently. It was the seat of an ancient family, the Stradlings, or De Esterling, the last male representative of which died in 1738. At his funeral the picture gallery was burnt down and the castle otherwise damaged. The Stradlings were allied to the chief South Wales families, such as the Herberts of Colebroke, and Cadogans of Trostry; but the lands have changed hands since the eighteenth century. In the church are some tombs of the Stradlings, which are worth a visit.

As Nash Point is rounded **Dunraven Castle** comes in view. It is a modern castellated mansion on the site of an ancient stronghold, called Din or Dinas Dryfan. The castle stands well on the rocky headland, looking out over the wide Atlantic, and is a fitting residence for one who so worthily upholds the honour of the yachting world, and so pluckily challenges for the America Cup. Let the yachting journals wrangle how they like over the " Deed of Gift." The main object of the gift was to promote racing, and they who do their utmost to act fair and square to make the best race on most equal terms are the men who deserve most credit from public opinion.

It is a costly business to keep building a new racing craft, such as the *Valkyrie*, every year, and race her over in America.

The whole district is full of castles, more or less in ruins. Coity and Ogmore Castles stand farther inland. Behind Porthcawl is Morlais Castle and Ty Mawr, where Anne Boleyn is said to have stayed. From Rochford, in placid Essex, it was a long ride to this little out-of-the-world nook overlooking the Bristol Channel.

Margam Park lies between Kenfig and Porthcawl. It is five miles in circumference and well wooded. There is a collection of orange and lemon trees here with a curious history. Sir Henry Wotton, Ambassador to Venice in the reign of

James I.—and whose too truthful remark that ambassadors were sent to lie abroad for the good of their country was taken amiss by the English Solomon—sent these trees as a present to Charles I.

The vessel was wrecked on the Nash Sands, or the Kenfig Patches, and the plants were taken up to Margam, where they remained. No question seems to have been asked until the reign of Queen Anne, who was approached upon the subject; but as the trees were thriving so well, and would have cost a good deal to take by land to Hampton Court, or Windsor, Her Majesty made a free gift of the trees to the owner of Margam, and there they are to this day.

Some say they were sent by "the King of Spain" to Queen Elizabeth. One can hardly realise the grim Philip sending these oranges and lemons as well as the Armada.

Others say a Dutch merchant sent them to Queen Mary. Anyhow, they never got to the royal conservatories, and never crossed the Taffy. Why they ever came up the Bristol Channel at all, if intended for royalty, one does not quite see.

The country is pretty behind the sea-shore, being rich and fertile.

Port Talbot has been formed by making a cut through the sand to the N. of the old outlet of the Avon. There is a conspicuous row of white cottages here, rejoicing in the name of Constantinople.

Baglan is a country house, standing back in the Avon Valley. The poets, Mason and Gray—the one known by his Elegy on the death of Lady Coventry, the other by "The Elegy"—used to visit here.

Neath, in spite of the exports of minerals of all sorts, is a place of great antiquity. The abbey ruins stand forlornly in the midst of the grime and dirt of the toil for wealth. Canals, coal-pits, chimneys, and railways surround it. The abbey was once remarkable for its artistic beauty and wealth of decoration, The Vale of Neath is celebrated for its beauty.

Swansea is well backed by high ground, and the town is most flourishing in appearance. There are drawbacks however as the black cloud hanging over the country suggests. Smelting works and collieries are splendid things, no doubt, for putting money into somebody's pocket, but they also put nasty fumes into the air. Copper, sulphur, arsenic, smoke, all combine to rob the country of its fresh look; and tall chimneys, vomiting black smoke, do not add to the attractions of the landscape.

South Wales is a busy place.

The Mumbles is a watering-place, connected by tramway with Swansea. It is a fishing village, backed by steep limestone cliffs, 200ft. high, and the situation is very pretty. Altogether 120 boats are employed in the oyster dredging, and the population is nearly 4000.

Oystermouth Castle is quite worth a visit. It is in good preservation, and the gate and towers are well proportioned. It was built by Henry Beaumont, Earl of Warwick, in 1113.

H

CHAPTER IX.

THE MUMBLES TO CALDY ISLAND.

Bearings from the Mumbles Light.—Nash Light bears from the Mumbles S.E. ½ S. southerly, distant eighteen miles and a half. Lundy Island, W.S.W. southerly, thirty-six miles. Hartland Point, S.W. ½ W. westerly, thirty-nine miles.

The coast from the Mumbles to Pwll-du Head is rocky and bold. There are three shallow bays in between and limestone quarries.

West of Pwll-du is **Oxwich Bay,** with good anchorage in N. or W. winds. On its E. side is Pennard Pill, where small vessels can lie aground in E. winds. It dries out at half-ebb.

Sir Christopher's Knoll lies seven cables off the N.E. side of the bay, with 7ft. least water over it. It bears W. by N. one mile and a half from **Pwll-du Head.**

Oxwich Head is 235ft. high. The sand dries out to one-third of a mile in the bay, and a ledge of rocks runs off Oxwich Head. A berth of half a mile should be allowed in rounding it.

Porth Eynon Bay, W. of Oxwich Head, is fringed with sand for 600yds. seawards. Anchorage can be had here in off-shore winds. A patch of rocks lies in the centre of the bay, with two fathoms and a half over it, with the church bearing N.W. ¾ W. distant one mile and a fifth.

Porth Eynon Head is 141ft. high, ending in a cliff, off which the foreshore of rocks extends 400yds. to the S.W., with from three to five fathoms close to. On the E. of the head it dries out to one-third of a mile, with two low islets on it, and shoal water extends two cables farther in a S.E. direction.

From Porth Eynon Head to **Rhos-sili Point** is four miles, trending in a N.W. direction, with rugged cliffs ; off which a rocky foreshore extends about one cable, with a depth of three fathoms at three cables off.

The **Helwick Sands** lie off **Porth Eynon Head**, and the E end is barely half a mile from the head, leaving what is known as **Helwick Pass** in between.   The sands lie in a **W. by N. ½ N. and E. by S. ½ S.** direction, and are six miles and a quarter long by a quarter of a mile broad, with a swashway in between.

The least depth on them is two fathoms near the centre of the **W. Helwick** sand.   The **E. Helwick** has a least depth of 13ft.   **Three buoys mark the sands.**

E. Helwick is a red and white spherical buoy painted in rings, lying in four fathoms, half a mile from Porth Eynon Head.

Middle Helwick, marking the centre of the S. end of the swashway, is a **red and white striped can buoy,** in six fathoms.

This is a good guide for the swashway, which is one mile and a half wide, with three fathoms and a quarter least water.   Burry Holm, seen through **Worms Sound,** bearing N. by E. ¾ E. leads through.

W. Helwick buoy is a red and white striped spherical buoy, with staff and diamond, lying in eight fathoms, with **Worms Head** distant three miles and three-tenths, bearing E.N.E.

There is a good passage through Helwick Pass, in five or six fathoms least water, and the E. Helwick buoy is the best guide for it.

Helwick Light-vessel is moored in seventeen fathoms, two miles W. of W. Helwick sand, with Worms Head bearing N.E. by E. ¾ E., distant four miles and three-fifths.   From it is exhibited, at an **elevation** of 36ft., **a flashing white light,** giving **one flash** every **30sec.**, visible eleven miles.   **A ball is carried at the masthead.**

Fog-signal.—The siren gives blasts of 5sec. every 2min.

H 2

The **flood-tide sets across the Helwick Sands** out of Caermarthen Bay, but the **ebb sets along it. A heavy sea** beats on
these sands in W. and S.W. gales, especially on the ebb. The
sands are steep-to on the S. side, and rise from twelve
or fourteen fathoms to three or four fathoms pretty quickly.
They are not so steep on the N. side.

Worms Head is at the N.W. end of a narrow islet, lying at
two cables and a half from Rhos-sili Point, from which it is
separated by Worms Sound, dry at half-tide, but with 13ft. of
water in it at high-water springs.

The head is 162ft. high, with an inner summit 139ft. high.
On its N. and W. sides it is steep-to, but the **S. side is foul
to the distance of two cables.** A reef, called **Danger Reef,
extends six cables S. of Rhos-sili Point,** with only 4ft. **least
water,** and foul ground **extends the same distance S. of Worms
Head Table-land.**

**Rhos-sili Bay is two miles and three quarters wide with a
sandy shore, drying out a quarter of a mile.** The S. part of
the bay is bordered with limestone cliffs, 100ft. high, which have
been greatly quarried. Behind it the land rises to a steep hill,
called High Barrow, 595ft. high, and Beacon Hill, 620ft. high.

At the N. end of the bay is Burry Holm, a grass-covered
islet, 105ft. high, with steep cliffs on the W. side, and sloping
towards the E. It is joined to the mainland at half-tide by a
rocky spit. A **rocky ledge** extends a little way off its W. side,
from which the sands sweep round on each side to Rhos-sili
Bay and Broughton Bay, respectively.

Whiteford Point is three miles and a half N.E. of **Burry
Holm,** which is the **S. boundary of Burry Inlet.**

Tempting as Burry Inlet looks at high-water, it is a **very**
dangerous trap for the unwary. It is the largest estuary on the
South Wales coast, being four miles wide by nine miles deep.
Unfortunately, with the exception of a few pools and shallow
channels, nearly the whole of this wide mere is a mass of sand
banks, dry at low-water.

Vessels desiring to enter must anchor in **Rhos-sili Bay,** or
keep the sea until high-water. An immense deal of trade is

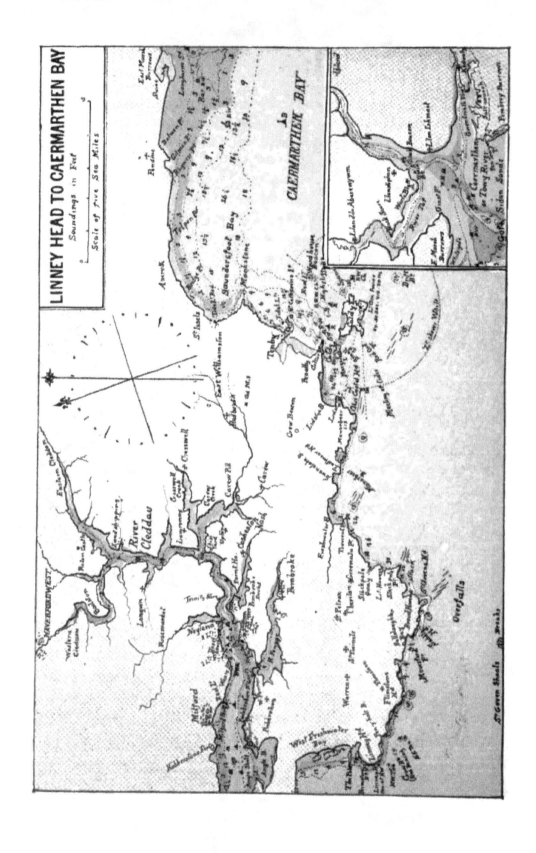

LINNEY HEAD TO CAERMARTHEN BAY

Soundings in Feet

Scale of five Sea Miles

CAERMARTHEN BAY

carried on with Burry Port, on the N. side, and Llanelly. The channels leading to them are well buoyed and lighted, but can only be navigated by those well acquainted with the shifting banks. Anchorage can be picked up here and there in the pools, but at tide time with S.W. or W. winds there is a great deal of sea, especially as the tide begins to ebb, and until the banks uncover.

From Burry Inlet to **Saundersfoot Harbour,** on the N.W. side of Caermarthen Bay, the whole coast is fronted by sands. Off the estuary off the Taff and Towy Rivers, the sands extend four or five miles to sea. There is a channel over **Caermarthen Bar,** with only 2ft. on it at low-water, 15ft. at half-tide, and 28ft. at high-water springs ; but the river dries just within the entrance and between Nos. 3 and 4 buoys. There are pools between Nos. 2 and 3 buoys, with 7ft. to 14ft. at low-water, but the tides are very strong.

I do not, therefore, intend to include Caermarthen River, any more than Burry Inlet, among the places I advise the amateur yachtsman to attempt. If he should be obliged to tackle the sands he must get local help, and then let him look out also, and be prepared for risk when moored. The buoys have constantly to be moved owing to the shifting sands.

Sand hills skirt all the bay, with higher land behind.

Saundersfoot Bay, with the little tidal harbour of Saundersfoot, provides shelter with off-shore winds. It is shallow, but anchorage in 13ft. low-water can be had with **Tenby Castle** open of the **Monkstone.** Vessels take in minerals here. A considerable sea comes home with S. or even S.W. winds. S.S.E. is the worst wind.

The same remark applies to **Tenby Roadstead,** where there is good shelter with winds from S.W. round to N.E., in two fathoms and a half to four fathoms, with **Tenby Church** seen over the **old castle,** W. ⅓ N., and **Giltar Point in line** with the outer edge of **St. Catherine Island,** S.W. by W., or even a little nearer in for light-draught craft. There is here three fathoms and a quarter at low-water. Perhaps there is better anchorage N.N.W. of this berth at a little distance off the pier-head.

Between **Saundersfoot** and **Tenby** is the **Monkstone**, 48ft. high. It is the outer of two islets off **Monkstone Point,** one mile and a half N. of Tenby.   A ledge **dries** 100yds. beyond the rock, and other rocks S. of it to the same distance.

Skear Rock lies 100yds off **St. Catherine's Island,** and is nearly awash at high-water springs ; 100yds off it the water is three fathoms and a half in the pool.

St. Catherine's Island is connected with Castle Head at half-tide. It is 92ft. high, with steep cliffs, and with a cavern at the inner end.

The cliffs between Monkstone and Tenby are about 170ft. high.

Tides.—It is high-water, full and change, at Caldy Island and Tenby at 5hr. 55min. local time, or 6hr. 13min. Green-wich time.   Spings rise from 25ft. to 28ft. ; neaps, 19ft.   The E. stream through **Caldy Sound** begins at 4hrs. ebb, *i.e.,* 1hr. before high-water at Liverpool Bar.   The W. stream begins at 4hrs. flood, or 1hr. before low-water at Liverpool Bar.   Close in shore, between Giltar and Monkstone Points, the stream sets N.E. from 1hr. before low-water to 1hr. after low-water, when it sets S.W., causing an eddy off the point for 50yds.

Woolhouse Rock would be very dangerous were it not for the **beacon** on it.   It is awash at half-tide, and on this portion a stone beacon, with staff and ball, 41ft. above high-water, has been erected.   The rocks extend 600yds. in a N. and S. direction, and lie one mile N.E. of the High Cliff Bank.

The **High Cliff Bank** has 8ft. least-water on it, and lies 800yds. N.E. of Caldy Island, being a high part of the sands lying off the island.   It forms the S.E. side of **Caldy Sound.**   A buoy on the N. end of it lies in three fathoms, with **Woolhouse Beacon** bearing E. ¾ N. 1400yds.   The buoy is painted **red and white chequers.**   The **S.E. end of the bank** is marked by another buoy, **red conical,** in two fathoms and a half.

The **Yowan Patch** has two fathoms and a half on it, bearing E. ½ S. one mile and a tenth from the Woolhouse Beacon. **Tenby Spire in line with the N. end of St. Catherine's Island, N.W. by W. ¾ W.,** clears this patch **to the N.**

Giltar and Eel Spits.—The Giltar Spit extends nearly half a mile in a S.E. direction towards Caldy, with less than 6ft. on it in places. The extremity of it is marked by a red and white striped can buoy, in three fathoms, but the spit trends in a N.E. direction some distance inside of this.

The Eel Spit lies off in a N. direction from Eel Point on Caldy Island, and has patches of about 6ft. least water. It is marked on its N. extremity by a red conical buoy, in three fathoms and a half.

A heavy race sets in here, with strong winds against the tide. Between these buoys is four fathoms least water.

Drift Rock, with four fathoms and a half least water, is only dangerous because of the sea over it. It lies distant from **Caldy Light** one mile and a third, bearing from the light S.S.W.

The same remarks apply to **Trawler's Dread,** four miles and one-eighth in a S.E. by E. $\frac{1}{3}$ E. direction.

Spaniel Shoal has 10ft. on it least water. It lies in a S.E. $\frac{1}{2}$ E. direction from Small, or Little, Ord Point, the E. end of Caldy, distant 700yds.

A red and white chequered can buoy, in six fathoms, marks the end of this shoal.

Lidstip Ledge has 10ft. least water on it. It lies in the fairway of the sound. The W. end of St. Margaret's Island, bearing S.E by E. $\frac{1}{2}$ E., distant 1300yds, leads over the shoalest part. The danger is only one cable and a half long. There are five fathoms close-to. Sound Rock, with 14ft. least water, lies 300yds. S.E. by E. of Lidstip.

W., distant 300yds., of St. Margaret's, lies a rock with only 9ft. over it. The channel lies between it and Sound Rock.

Anchorages round Caldy Island.—The roadstead is between Eel Point and **High Cliff Bank, off Priory Bay.** The tides are strong, but there is shelter from all winds except from N.E. to S.E. Anchorage on the N.W. side of Caldy is not recommended. Shelter from S.E. winds might be found there, but the tides run very strong and the ground is not good.

Tenby Harbour dries right out, with the low-water line 100yds. outside the piers. There are good quays, but the space is limited. Vessels moor in tiers and lie on legs.

The harbour and roadstead are easy of access, and the place would be a first-class yachting resort if only there were shelter in all winds. The anchorage is entirely exposed to S.S.W. round to N.E. winds.

A harbour light is shown on the pier-head. It is fixed, red, visible three miles.

Caldy Island Lighthouse.—From a circular white tower, 52ft. high, 180yds. inland of the S. point of the island, and at an elevation of 214ft. above high-water, an occulting light is shown. It disappears twice every half-minute, and is visible twenty miles. It shows white to seaward, red towards Old Castle Head between the bearings of S. 72deg. E. and S. 58deg. E., and red towards Woolhouse Rocks and High Cliff Bank between the bearings of S. 53deg. W. and S. 13deg. W.

There is a beacon half a mile N.E. of the lighthouse. Near the edge of the cliff is an obelisk. This is to clear Woolhouse Rock.

St. Margaret's Island is connected with Caldy at low-water. There is not much dry foreshore at that state of tide, and none extends beyond two-thirds of a cable, or about 130yds.

Remarks on the appearance of the coast and objects of interest visible from the sea between the Mumbles and Caldy Island.—At last the voyage is becoming a little more interesting. Smoke stacks and coal dust are being left behind. The **Mumbles** is quite a yachting resort in its way, and the *habitués* are loud in their praises of its perfection. One man declared, on the strength of having seen it in print, that "as a natural place of shelter it is not surpassed by any in the British Islands." All I can say is, that if the British Islands can offer no more protection from S. round to S.E. winds I am sorry for the shipping interests, underwriters included, although a run on the mud banks, or a retreat to the splendid docks of Swansea, may prevent a final catastrophe.

The peninsula now slipping past on our starboard hand as we go W. is called **Gower**. It is a peculiarly interesting part of South Wales, and would repay a visit if one stayed long enough at the Mumbles.

The country is pretty, the history curious, and the geology interesting. Oysters, too, and shell-fish are excellent.

Henry I. allowed the Flemings, or Esterlings, to settle here, and as England, somehow, has always benefited by these colonies of strangers, so the Flemish strain gave a solidity and practical turn to the poetic and fiery Welsh blood. Sir Walter Scott has introduced these people into his little-known novel, "The Betrothed." **Pennard Castle**, on Pennard Pill, is a crumbling old ruin, on the edge of a sandy heath. It dates from the twelfth century. **Penrice Castle**, behind Oxwich Bay, is a modern fortalice, with a lovely garden, but there is an old ruin near it.

The caves along this coast, too, are remarkable. W. of Pwll-du are two strange caves, **Bacon Hole** and **Minchen Hole**. Bones of all kinds of extinct animals were found here. To the W. of Porth Eynon Head is another remarkable cave, called the Culver Hole.

Behind the cliffs, and some distance inland, is the high land of Cefn-y-Bryn, on the N.E. side of which is a remarkable cromlech, the top stone weighing over twenty tons. It is supported by many other stones.

Rounding Worms Head, which is a decidedly picturesque headland, with its highest peak defiantly standing out to the ocean, Rhos-sili Bay cannot fail to strike a stranger by its beauty. On its sands the Atlantic rolls its waves unbroken from the W., and it is seldom there is not a fine head of water sweeping in from the ocean.

The high land immediately behind, rising steeply to 620ft., makes a noble background.

The dreary mockery of promised shelter and a commodious haven, which Burry Inlet and Caermarthen Estuary so heartlessly express, is not realised from the sea. Yellow sand hills, backed by high land some miles behind them, are all that

are visible as one sails across the bay towards Tenby. More
and more, as the miles decrease and the beautiful situation of
the town begins to dawn on the mind, come regrets that there
is really no safe shelter offered even here. A vessel in the
roads is quite at the mercy of a change of wind · and with E.
winds there is no refuge except Milford Haven.

But chimneys, and smelting works, and all the abominations
bred of man's insatiate craving after wealth, are being left
behind. Once more the cruise is taking us towards pleasant
places.

Tenby, with its Castle Hill jutting out into the bay, its lines
of houses sweeping round the strand, and the tall spire of
its ancient parish church, St. Mary's, makes a delightful
picture.

In this church are some curious monuments of merchant
adventurers, of the fifteenth century. The town walls also
remain in parts, showing how the place was defended, for the
builders of the place were the Flemish colonists of the time
of Henry I. They lived at war mostly with the Welsh, and
were useful allies of the Norman barons, who were always
carrying on a feud with the natives. The Strongbows and the
De Windsors were never happy unless sallying out in full
armour to harry the unhappy Celt, or be harried by him.

Queen Elizabeth had the place refortified; and Queen
Victoria's reign has seen a fresh example of the military
engineer's work, St. Catherine's Rock being turned into a
battery.

Caldy Island and St. Margaret's muster ninety inhabitants
between them. The sound between the island and the mainland
is not more than half a mile across. Its greatest length is one
mile and three quarters by two-thirds of a mile wide. There
are two picturesque bays on its S.W. side, and the proprietor,
Mr. Hawkesley, lives in a house near the ruins of the ancient
priory, of which a low square tower with a spire still remains.
The highest part of the island is near Red Ord Point, 170ft. high,
on the S.W. Off Little Ord is Spur Islet, and High Cliff has
another detached rock lying off it. There is good water on the

island, but the landing-place is in Priory Bay, on the N. side, some distance from the well.

A large amount of limestone quarrying is carried on here and at St. Margaret's, which is barely a quarter of a mile long by 200yds. wide. The cliffs are precipitous and pierced with caverns.

Yachts often lie off Tenby in the summer, and a very delightful place it is with its promenade and breezy walks. That across the sands, called the Burrows, to Giltar Point is an especially attractive one.

Manorbier Castle, standing on its little bay, should certainly be visited. Here that excellent old chronicler was born, Gerault de Barri, of the ancient house of De Barry, who gave its name to several places, as Barry Islet and Port. Some of the family attended Strongbow to Ireland, and, judging by the popularity of the name over there, the Barrys fulfilled the command given to Adam and Eve. Giraldus Cambrensis—to give the Monkish historian his best-known name—was born in that dark old Norman castle, which has stood many a howling gale from the Atlantic since first it was built in the days of the third king of the Norman line. Part of it has been recently fitted up as a residence by Mr. Phillips, the owner of another ancient castle in this county, and is used by him as a seaside retreat. The castle is a striking object at the head of its little bay amid the sand hills, backed by the darker slope of the Ridgeway behind.

Behind Tenby and S. of Gumfreston, where there is a mineral spring with properties allied to those at Tunbridge Wells, is Trellwyn, or Trefllwyn. This was a fortified manor-house in the days of the Great Rebellion, and was held by the Earl of Carberry. Some parts of the old house are still used as labourers' lodgings.

During westerly gales a very heavy sea sets into Caermarthen Bay, and the swell runs round into Tenby Harbour, causing a nasty "scend" at tide time. It is this which makes this place, charming as it is, so risky, for there is no escape except by riding it out or running ashore during S. or S.E. gales.

The tide races, too, off all the heads, but especially off Old Castle Head and St. Goven's, or St. Gowan's, Head, make it nasty work going round to Milford, as a vessel has to stand off to avoid the overfalls.

What Tenby wants is a good breakwater, thrown out in a N.E. direction, curving round to the N. from St. Catherine's Island, then one could lie there and be happy.

CHAPTER X.

CALDY ISLAND TO MILFORD HAVEN.

Bearings from Caldy Island.—St. Ives bears S.W. ½ S. southerly, distant ninety-one miles. Trevose Head, S.W. by S. southerly, sixty-six miles and a half. Padstow, S.S.W., sixty-five miles. Lundy Island, S. by W. ½ W. westerly, twenty-eight miles. Barnstaple Bar, S. ½ E. easterly, thirty-seven miles.

The coast from Giltar Point to St. Goven's, or St. Gowan's, Head is mostly limestone cliff, with several bays in between. Sunken rocks lie off here and there, but to no great distance, and the coast is mostly bold.

A berth of three-quarters of a mile clears all dangers, only it is not advisable to pass too close to the headlands, owing to the races off them.

Giltar Point is a narrow projection of limestone, 100ft. high.

The highest cliff W. of this point is called **Proud Giltar**; it is 170ft. high.

There are caves all along these cliffs.

Lidstip Bay affords anchorage in off-shore winds. The point is a ridge of limestone, 140ft. high.

Old Castle Head is a bold headland, 213ft. high. On the summit are the remains of ancient earthworks. Between this and Lidstip Point is a little landing-cove, called **Shrinkle Haven.**

W. of **Old Castle Head is Manorbier Bay,** with the old castle at its E. side. A ledge of sand and gravel, with six and seven fathoms on each side, fronts the shore from Manorbeer Bay to **Old Castle Head,** at a distance of one-third of a mile from the shore; the least depth on it is 9ft. at its E. end. By keeping the first valley, W. of Lidstip Point, well open of Old Castle Head, a vessel passes S.E. of it.

E. Freshwater Bay lies W. of Swanlake Bay, on each side of which are cliffs. Sands extend at low-water some distance off it, with sand hills behind, through which a stream struggles to the sea.

The coast gradually trends round in a S.W. direction, forming **Stackpole Road** with **Stackpole Quay,** a little jetty under limestone quarries at the head of the bay. The anchorage is S. of this opposite a little bay, called Little Haven. Vessels ride here safely with off-shore winds.

Stackpole Head lies S. of the bay, and is a bold feature, jutting out in a S.E. direction from the land.

Between this headland and St. Goven's Head lies **Broad Haven,** where a vessel may run ashore in cases of necessity. The tide runs in one-third of a mile at high-water; farther in are lock gates, forming the ornamental waters of Stackpole Court. This haven is one cable and a half wide. On its E. side is the Stack Rock, and seen up the valley are the woods and slopes of Stackpole Park. The haven is fronted with sand at low-water.

S. of this is **New Quay,** a sandy cove in the cliffs, lying 400yds. inside of St. Goven's Head. This is a useful landing-place when it is impossible to land anywhere else along the coast.

St. Goven's Head is a precipitous cliff, 122ft. high, with level ground behind it. Half-way up the cliff are the chapel and well of St. Goven, half a mile to the W. of the head. The chapel has a belfry.

A spit runs off for nearly 1200yds W. by S. from the head with two fathoms and a half at its extremity. A tide race sets heavily over this for fully half a mile off the head.

S.W. of the head, distant four miles, lie St. Goven's Shoals. There are three rocky patches, with three fathoms and a half least water on them ; but the overfalls are heavy on these banks, and they should be given a wide berth. Four miles is none too much when the wind is against the tide.

The coast continues bold in appearance to **Saddle Head**, with rocky ground extending 200yds. off shore. **Two miles beyond Saddle Head** are the **Elegug Stacks**. They are two precipitous rocks of considerable height, standing in a bight of the cliffs. **Flimston Head** is two miles and a half from Saddle Head ; Bullslaughter Bay and Flimston Bay lie in between.

Linney Head is another bold weather-worn promontory. Between this and Flimston Head the cliffs are dark and precipitous, except where the sea-mews have whitened them. Stacks or isolated pinnacles of rock stand out a little way, with deep chasms behind. There is a coastguard watch-house on **Linney Head,** and five cables and a half S. of it lies the **Crow Rock**, not more than 20ft. in **extent, which dries 18ft. at low-water** springs. **A red pyramidal beacon, with staff and ball,** is erected on it.

Off the Crow are the E. **Toe,** with 15ft. least water, lying E.N.E. from the Crow distant 200yds. S.E. **Toe,** nearly awash at low-water, lies S.E. ¾ S. distant 1100yds. N.W. **Toe** lies 500yds. N.W. by N. of the Crow and is nearly awash at low-water. All round them there are from five to eight fathoms.

Crow Sound lies between the Crow with its Toes, and the **shore. The channel is 400yds. wide with three fathoms and a half. Saddle** Head, just open of Flimston Head, bearing **S.E. ¾ E. leads through.**

W. Freshwater Bay is about two miles and a half wide. The sandy foreshore dries out some little distance. A spit of **shelving rock,** called the **Pole,** stretches out one-third of a mile in the S.E. angle of the bay, forming on its S. side **Bluck's Pool.** An eddy tide sets round **Sheep Island,** where the stream is always running to the S.E. The cliffs between **Freshwater Bay** and **Studdock Point** are high and steep-to.

Sheep Island lies off the point. It is only 400yds. long, and at half ebb is connected with the land.

Sheep Island forms the S.E. point of the entrance to Milford Haven.

Dangers in the approach to Milford Haven.—Turbot Bank lies three miles and three quarters S. from St. Ann's Head. The least depth on it is five fathoms and a quarter, and it is only noticed because a heavy sea breaks over it in bad weather.

Sheep Rock has three fathoms and a half least water on it, and lies in the fairway of the E. channel, five cables from Sheep Island, which bears E. ¼ N. from it.

The Rows, Middle Rocks, and Chapel Rocks, with 12ft. least-water on them, lie nearly in the middle of the entrance, dividing it into two channels, of which the W. is the better.

These rocks are marked by three buoys. A red conical buoy, with staff and diamond, lies in seven fathoms, one cable W. of the nineteenth rock on Middle Rocks. A red conical buoy, in seven fathoms and a half, lies on the N.W. side of Chapel Rocks, and a red and white striped can buoy marks the S.E. side of Chapel Rocks.

Off St. Ann's Head is a shoal lying S.W. for nearly a mile, with three fathoms least water on it. In Mill Bay a shoal, with two fathoms least water, lies S.W. of W. Blockhouse Point.

On the E. side lies Thorn Island, with Thorn Rock a third of a mile S.W. by W. ¾ W. from the island. The least water on it is 9ft. A ledge of rock extends 250yds. W. of the island, and dries at low-water. There is a channel between the island and the shore, with 10ft. at low-water.

Thorn Rock is marked by a red conical buoy, in five fathoms.

There are no further dangers in the approach. The cliffs are fairly bold, and may be approached to a reasonable distance.

The rocky ground at the entrance causes a heavy sea on the ebb-tide with S.W. or W. winds, or, in fact, with any winds from the S., and the tides run fairly strong all through the haven.

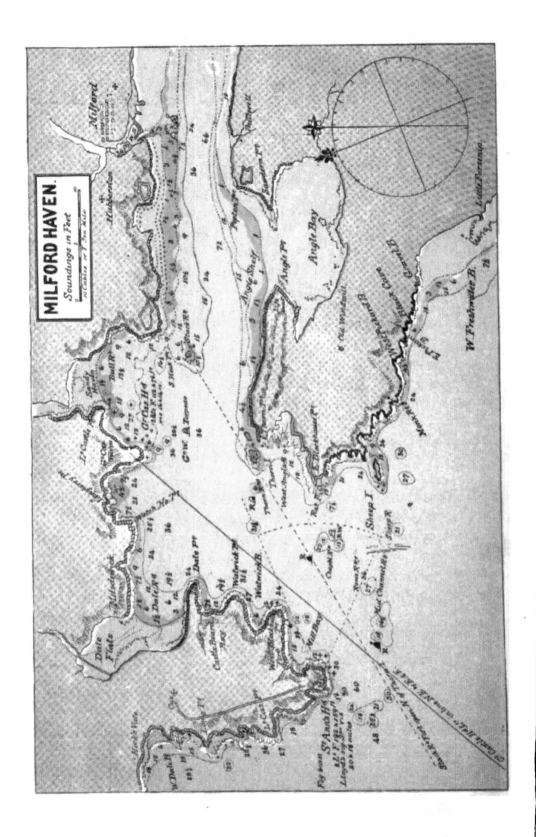

Tides.—It is high-water, full and change, at St. Ann's Head at 5hr. 56min. local time, or 6hr. 16min. Greenwich time. Springs rise, 24ft.; neaps, 18ft.

The stream turns to the N.W. off St. Ann's Head at 3hrs. flood by the shore, and runs till 3hrs. ebb; that is, it turns 2hrs. before high- and low-water at Liverpool. At 2hrs. before high-water at Liverpool it runs S.E. for 6hrs.; and at 2hrs. before low-water at Liverpool it runs N.W. for 6hrs. at the rate of three knots. The stream inside the haven turns at high- and low-water by the shore.

Lights.—St. Ann's Head. From a circular white tower, 75ft. high and 192ft. above high-water, a fixed red and white light is shown. It shows white seaward, and red between the bearings of N. 45deg. W., and W. covering Chapel and Thorn or Harbour Rocks; visible twenty miles.

At 205yds. S.S.E. of the high light is an octagonal white tower, 42ft. high and 159ft. above the sea. It exhibits a fixed white light, visible eighteen miles. The lights in line lead between the Turbot Bank and Crow Beacon.

Fog-signal.—A fog-siren gives one blast every 3min. There is a telegraph and signal station close to the lighthouses.

At Great Castle Head two lights are also shown. In a white square tower with black stripe, at an elevation of 112ft. above high-water, a fixed white light is shown, visible sixteen miles. In a white turret on the keeper's house, 174yds. in front of the high light and 76ft. above high-water, a fixed white light is shown. Both buildings have a black stripe down them. When in line they lead clear in the W. channel.

Milford.—A fixed red light is shown from the W. pier at the entrance to Milford Docks, and one at the W. side of Castle Pill and the pier at Newton Noyes.

Pembroke.—In the dockyard two fixed red lights are shown. The high light, 46ft. above high-water, is visible between the bearings of E. by S. ¾ S. and S.E. ¼ S. The low light, 23ft. above high-water and 1130ft. from the high light, is visible between the bearings of E. by S. ½ S. and S.S.W. A green sector marks Carr Spit from S. ¼ E. to S. by E. ¼ E.

I

The Great Western Railway Co.'s Pier has four small fixed white lights, not shown on Sundays.

After opening up the haven when Thorn Point is rounded, **Great Castle Head must not** be approached **too** nearly. The ground is foul for the distance of two cables, with a rock off it, with only 9ft. least water.

Stack Rock has a ledge, dry at low-water, extending 200yds. E. of the fort. S.E. of South Hook Fort shoals lie out, and it is better to keep between the buoys marking the channel. There are three fathoms at two cables and a half off shore all the way up to Milford.

On the S. side **Angle Shelf is nearly straight.** All **Angle Bay dries** out.

Pwllcrochan Flats, between Popton and W. Pennar Points, dry out and are steep-to, leaving the channel between them and Newton Noyes Pier on the N. side little more than two cables width, although at high-water there looks double that distance of deep water.

Off Weare Point on the N. shore is a tongue of shingle and mud. It dries out in a S.E. by E. direction for a quarter of a mile. **A black and white chequered can buoy** marks the extremity in three fathoms.

There are **two black and white chequered can buoys,** lying on **the S. edge of Milford Shelf,** between South Hook and Milford, and **three black conical buoys** marking **Angle** and **Pwllcrochan Flats.**

Pennar Flats are mud, and dry two cables and a half between Pennar Creek and **Carr Rocks.** A very narrow channel leads into Pennar Creek, with a pool of 9ft. low-water just inside the points. The tides set in and out **strongly** here, although a berth might be found. The mud is all soft. Jacob's Pill lies on the N. shore in Pennar Creek, where are shipbuilding yards.

The **Carr Rocks** lie two cables and a half N.W. by N. from the N.W. end of the dockyard. The highest rock dries 10ft. Carr Spit extends two cables beyond the rock. The N.W. end of Carr Spit is marked by a **conical black buoy,** with staff and globe, in four fathoms. Another black conical buoy marks the N.E. end of the spit, in four fathoms.

Dockyard Bank lies E. of Carr Spit, with a swashway in between. It lies in the middle of Pembroke Reach with 6ft. to 9ft. least water on it. Two buoys mark the danger. A conical black buoy lies at the W. end of it, and a similar buoy marks its E. end. There is 19ft. in the swashway at low-water. The dockyard chimney, bearing S. by E., or in line with the third top window from the N. end of the building shed E. of it, leads through.

Mud flats lie all along the S. shore, filling in all the bights. Lanion Pill dries right out.

The mud, with stones here and there, lies out two cables from the N. shore. Off Neyland Point is a chequered black and white can buoy, in two fathoms. A beacon lies on the mud, within the buoy.

The end of Neyland Pier is marked by a boat showing a fixed white light at night. A black can buoy marks a shoal, extending from Neyland Point one cable and two-thirds; it lies in 12ft. at low-water.

Anchorage.—The tides run strong in the haven, so that vessels must moor securely. A nasty sea can very soon get up with the tide against the wind. In Dale Road there is good shelter with W. winds, but the ground is covered with seaweed, and if once the anchors drag it is no use paying out more scope; they must come up and the vessel seek another berth. This is not a place to remain any time.

Sandy Haven Bay, if not used for torpedo experiments, is a good place in winds from N.W. to N.E. A buoy, painted in green and white bands, is moored here, in four fathoms and three quarters, when torpedo practise is going on. Small vessels may pass on the W. side into Sandy Haven.

Angle Bay dries out entirely. It is a mud flat, with 19ft. on it at high-water. A patch of flat rocks lies a quarter of a mile E. ½ S. of Angle Point. This bay affords perfect safety for vessels which can take the ground.

I 2

Pennar Mouth has a pool, called **Crow Pool,** just inside the points ; there is 10ft. least water here, but there is only 3ft. over the bar at the entrance.

Above Neyland there is anchorage anywhere. Off Neyland Pill is a good berth, or in the bight beyond off Cosheston or **Lanion Pill.** Here a vessel is out of the way of the traffic.

There is no difficulty whatever in entering Milford Haven, as all dangers are provided for. The only obstacle is the tide. With scant winds it is impossible to get in against the ebb.

Above the Trinity Wharf, opposite Pembroke Ferry, as far as **Laurenny,** there is good anchorage anywhere in five fathoms, except at a place a little below Benton Castle. Here a bar of stones crosses the river, with only 9ft. over it at low-water.

Two creeks open out on the E. side of the river here ; one goes to Carew Castle. These are navigable at high-water, but dry out at low-water.

Above **Laurenny** there is deep water to **Garron Pill.** The **Tuns Rocks** dry out nearly half-way across the high-water channel, opposite Benton Woods, to the distance of one-third of a mile. The best water is on the W. shore as far as Langreen Pool, where there is good anchorage in three fathoms. The river now runs nearly N.N.E. as far as Landshipping Pier, where is anchorage in two fathoms, but there is little water farther on.

The river divides here into the E. Cleddau and W. Cleddau, both rising in the Precelly Mountains behind Fishguard. On the W. Cleddau is Haverfordwest, but there is barely 9ft. of water at high-water springs as far as the town. A considerable amount of traffic, however, is carried on. It is better, therefore, in anchoring, to pick up a berth in the bight, as much as possible out of the set of the ebb-tide and the traffic.

The E. Cleddau is nearly all dry at low-water.

Remarks on the appearance of the coast and objects of interest visible from the sea between Caldy Island and Milford Haven.—The coast scenery grows finer as we sail W. The indented nature of the shore forms beautiful bays, of which Lidstip, Freshwater E., and Stackpole Bays are the finest.

Manorbier Castle, behind the Old Castle Point, is a striking feature, and the woods round Stackpole Court look peaceful behind the dark cliffs on the shore. The Cawdors inherited this beautiful property from an ancestress, a Miss Lort, the heiress of Stackpole. Stackpole Quay is a curious little nook in the cliffs, and the gap at Little Haven shows at once where a safe anchorage could be found in winds from W.S.W. round to N.E. It is a pity there are these tide ripples off the heads, for the coast deserves a closer inspection.

St. Goven's Head is very bold. The little chapel is not seen until the head is rounded to the W. There is a weary flight of steps leading to it, which, it is said, no one has ever counted twice the same number. Near the chapel is a cleft in the cliff. Here St. Gowan stepped in, and was hidden from the pursuing pagans, who wished to show their appreciation for their beloved missionary in the good old-fashioned way. After they had gone on the chasm opened, and St. Gowan came out. The well below has been credited with wonder-working properties.

The cliff scenery becomes finer and grander towards Linney Head. All the way there are caverns and chasms, with isolated rocks and precipitous cliffs. The Elegugs are only two out of many other stacks which gird the cliffs.

Without doubt the sight of St. Ann's Head looming up round Linney Head is one to cause considerable satisfaction. At last a harbour is at hand where the skipper may rest and take his ease ; where the craft may lie afloat in perfect safety without the aid of artificial protection.

Since leaving Falmouth this is the first time, with the poor exceptions of Padstow, Appledore Pool, and Chepstow, this has been possible.

It is a fine entrance between E. and W. Blockhouse Points, with Great Castle Head right in front. To a certain extent it reminded me of the Goulet de Brest. The shores are alike. There are the mid-channel dangers. The entrance is to the W., and the roadstead turns abruptly E., round the sharp point of Thorn, corresponding to the Pointe des Espagnols.

But there the similarity ends. There is no comfortable and convenient Port du Commerce. Nowhere, except up the Cleddau River, is there a quiet spot where a yacht will lie out of the way of traffic and uneasy tides.

But let us be thankful; we are entering one of the three grand harbours of the United Kingdom—Falmouth, Milford, and Cork—of which to my mind Falmouth is out and out the best, because of its very mild tides, allowing a vessel always to ride head to wind if it is of any strength.

As we pass Dale Road it is easy to see with what a force the W. wind must rush through Dale Gap, rendering an anchorage off the wide stretching sands difficult at times, especially considering the weedy nature of the bottom. After passing South Hook Fort, a berth may be taken up anywhere along Milford Shelf, but the farther up the better.

CHAPTER XI.

——

MILFORD HAVEN AND ROUND ABOUT.

THIS is not going to be a sailing chapter. It is about time one took a stretch ashore. The neighbourhood is attractive, and there are many excursions to be made. For my part I should not anchor at all until I had passed Neyland, and then I should be guided by circumstances, anchoring either off Laurenny, or just round Hobbs Point, to the E. of Neyland.

All the excursions can be done in the dingey, or on foot.

Milford is comparatively a new place. It owes its origin to Charles Greville, who owned the land. It was in 1790 when the first change was made. Packets were to sail regularly to Waterford, where Dunmore Harbour was made for their reception. South Sea whale fisheries were to have their headquarters in Wales, and make it a Welsh Dundee, and, finally, a dockyard was to be built and ships of war constructed.

Of all these schemes none now remains. In 1814 the dockyard was removed to Pater, as the peninsula between Pennar and Cosheston Pill is called. The packets are now steamers, and they run to Neyland and Waterford. The Whale Fishery Company has gone to the dogs.

Sir William Hamilton, whose wife is better known to fame, died here. The life of Lady Hamilton is a remarkable one. Many men loved her; but as she confessed the only one of her three Charlies she ever cared for, was Charley Greville, and

he very soon ceased to care for her. Her maiden name was
Duggan, if I remember right, which she or her mother altered
to Cadogan, but it made no difference. Her *début* in life was
as a nursemaid, and she ended Lady Hamilton, sometime
Ambassadress to Naples. Perhaps none of Romney's portraits
are better known than those of this successful adventuress.

There is a memorable piece of wood here. Most of us have
learnt or read "Casabianca." Part of the main-mast which
"stood on the burning deck" of the *l'Orient* is preserved at
Milford, as well as an antique porphyry vase, with an inscription
to Lord Nelson. In fact, memories of the great war and the
scandals connected with it hover round Milford.

The French always had an eye on this remote, but safe,
haven. A force of 1200 men landed here to help Owain
Glyndwr, and they would fain have accomplished the same
thing in 1797—only the report of the new dockyard and the
strength of the place frightened them. The expedition landed
at Fishguard instead, and there surrendered to the Lord
Lieutenant of the county, Lord Cawdor, and a muster of the
good women of Pembrokeshire, dressed in their red cloaks,
which the Frenchmen took for His Majesty's uniform.

Henry of Richmond and Richard II. both landed here, the
one to win a crown, the other to lose one; Henry VII. to
win crown and life from Richard III.; and Richard II. to lose
crown and life to Henry IV. In Pembroke Castle the first of
our Tudor kings was born.

Pembroke old town stands on a rocky shore on the edge of
Pennar Creek. At high-water there is about 14ft. alongside
the quay, but the creek presents but a forlorn spectacle of
mud at low-water. The Royal Dockyard is two miles by road
from Pembroke, and three miles beyond Milford. It occupies
eighty acres, surrounded by a high wall, and is protected, in
addition to the forts at the entrance and at South Hook, by
Pater Fort at the N.W. end of the dockyard.

Neyland, or New Milford, has grown up by reason of the
Great Western Railway. Here the mail steamers come alongside, and a hydraulic lift takes goods and passengers up to

the level of the railway, according to the tide. The steamers leave at 2.30 a.m., and get back about midnight. Somewhat of an improvement on the old sailing packets of Lady Hamilton's days.

There is ample means of communication between the two sides of the harbour by means of ferries. Newton Noyes Pier, 200yds. long, where vessels are coaled, is one mile E. of Milford. From **Weare Point,** a mile beyond it, is a ferry to the dockyard, and from Pembroke Point to the Trinity Wharf there is another, as well as the railway ferry between Hobbs Point and Neyland.

The Trinity Wharf is three-quarters of a mile E. of Neyland. The jetty is 250ft. long, but dries 3ft. at low-water. Here are all the appliances for buoys and lighthouses, laid out and stowed away in the orderly manner in which all the Trinity House work is done.

The glory of Pembroke, apart from its dockyard, is the ancient castle. The grim old ruin stands well on its rock beside the muddy creek. The whole town was once defended by walls, but very little remains of them now. Under the castle is a cavern, rejoicing in the name of "The Wogan." It formed a means of communication with the river from the castle. Of course, the indefatigable Strongbow turned up here. As he was Earl of Pembroke he naturally is in his place, but Arnulph de Montgomery built the castle in 1094. Plenty of fighting has been done round these old towers. The last siege it stood was from the Parliamentarians, by whom it was taken in 1648, after a six weeks' siege.

Talk about the Rhine for old castles—why, it is not in it with this neighbourhood. Gower was as thick as could be with them, but round here they simply crowd.

A very pleasant picnic could be enjoyed if the tide were consulted by rowing up to Carew Castle or Carew Pill. Upton Castle will be passed on the way, and Benton Castle is a little beyond, while Picton Castle and Rose Castle are up the next turning.

Carew Castle, however, will be enough for one day's antiquarian picnic if it is to be an aquatic one as well. This old place was originally one of the houses of the Tewdwrs, or Tudors, and was given to Gerald de Windsor as a marriage portion for his bride Nesta ap Tudor. Unfortunately the lady was carried off by Blethyn ap Cadwgan, from whom, by the way, Nurse Duggan claimed to be descended after she became Lady Hamilton. The land, however, remained, and Gerald de Windsor's son, apparently disgusted at the goings on of his parents, took the name of Carew, which the learned say is Welsh for "fortification" (Caerau). However that may be the Carews held it for some centuries, when one of them being in difficulties mortgaged it to Sir Rhys ap Thomas, who, in the fifteenth century, was as big a man almost as Strongbow in the twelfth. "Old Sir Rhys," as Leland calls him, did things in grand style here. He was wise enough to take the side of the Lancastrians at the end of the wars of the Roses, and supported Henry VII. heartily. After Bosworth Field the old knight held high feast and holiday in this castle, including a joust, or tournament, for five days, during which time the "Nobility and Gentry" of South Wales were entertained to the number of six hundred "free of charge."

Sir Rhys ap Thomas and his wife are buried under an altar tomb, with their recumbent effigies above, in Caermarthen Church.

Carew Castle seems to have been an improvement on the grim feudal castles, such as Manorbier and Oystermouth. There are evidences of art and culture in the banqueting hall— once a noble chamber—and in the large Tudor windows, as well as in some of the chimneypieces. The building reminds one more of Raglan, which was built by Sir Rhys' grandfather, Sir William ap Thomas, or Herbert, about 1420.

By the way, nothing is more perplexing in Welsh county history than the way in which families change their names every generation. The well-known families of Vaughan and Herbert are good illustrations of this. The possessor of the familiar name of Jones is, or may be, a descendant of the Vaughans, as any Thomas may, for want of proof to the contrary, be a descendant of Charlemagne through Heribert de

Vermandois, ancestor of the Herberts of Coalbroke, otherwise ap Thomas, the progenitors of the noble families of Pembroke and Carnarvon, of whom the fighting and philosophical Lord Herbert of Cherbury is a typical example, uniting in his person the fiery and dreamy element of the true Celt—quick to take up a quarrel and unpractical in its issue.

Carew Castle is a rare instance of ancestral property once alienated reverting to its original owners after a lapse of years. In the seventeenth century Sir John Carew recovered possession, and the good knight lies at rest beside his dame under his tomb in Carew Church hard by.

In the churchyard, too, is a fine old cross, worth stepping over to see. If rowing up the creek, keep to the starboard or right side after entering; the other "pill" goes to Cresswell. Take the right-hand pill; then keep to the left after passing Upton Castle, and so continue until Carew Bridge and Castle come in sight. By road it is four miles from Pembroke and six from Tenby. The ruins and surroundings make a lovely sketch.

Another excursion should certainly be taken up to Langwin, if, indeed, the yacht does not go up and moor off here in one of the snuggest anchorages in the Cleddau. This is the head-quarters of the oyster dredgers, of whom a great number, both men and women, find plenty of occupation in the fisheries.

From Langwin Picton Castle can be visited. This castle is most interesting, and, if permission can be obtained, it is well worth going over. As a castle it stands almost unique in its continuous history. Like Windsor, Arundel, Alnwick, Warwick, and Leeds (Kent), it can boast that it has never been uninhabited since it was built in the eleventh century. Walter de Picton was one of the knights who accompanied William the Conqueror in his Welsh expedition when the Norman duke paid his visit to the shrine of St. David. He obtained a grant of the land— as much as he could get from the rightful owners—and in the days of Rufus built his castle. From that day to this the old walls have been inhabited. In the history of all castles the critical time was the period of the Parliamentary wars. Almost every one of the ancient strongholds was occupied by the local gentry for the king, and, as a consequence, local fighting was abundant. One reads of the great actions of that struggle, such as Marston Moor and Naseby, but they were only the great bubbles on the seething turmoil of domestic strife. Wales and Cornwall were especially the scenes of these picturesque but bloody contests between aggressive Puritanism and defiant culture. As usual, and as will always be the case when men are in earnest, refinement and chivalrous ideas, allied to free living and rollicking bravery, succumbed to the stern purpose of a grim faith, backed by self-seeking and hypocrisy.

The cannon of Cromwell battered down the walls of the feudal strongholds, and the Ironsides did the rest of the Lord's work. Sergeant Smite-Them-Hip-and-Thigh and Corporal Praise-God-Barebones, backed by Private Sword-of-the-Lord-and-of-Gideon, were hard facts to strive with.

Picton Castle, however, survived this crisis. Sir Richard Philipps held it for the king, and yet managed to keep his head and his property. Since then the Philipps family have held it uninterruptedly, and hold it still. Among other manorial possessions of theirs is Manorbier Castle. Picton Castle boasts that it was never forfeited, never deserted, never vacant, and long may its owners continue to utter the same vaunt. The plan of the castle is an oblong, with three towers or bastions on each side, with the gateway at the end.

Time has mellowed the stern aspect of the fortress, and domestic needs and the altered conditions of life have introduced modifications in the internal arrangements; but Picton Castle is still the castle of the twelfth century, adapted to a dwelling-house of the nineteenth.

Speaking of Picton reminds me of that stout warrior of our own day, General Sir Thomas Picton, who was born here at Pembroke. The fiery old chieftain of the celebrated "Fighting Division," who fell while leading the final charge at Waterloo, came of a soldierly stock, and no knight of feudal times ever showed himself a better captain or man-at-arms. Another Welshman, too, who came from this neighbourhood, and who distinguished himself as a skilful captain and brave man, was Sir William Nott, of Ghuznee.

Who knows how far the tales told in childhood in this land of castles and legends may have fired the imagination of these combative and ardent spirits, prompting them in turn to achieve great deeds? It is good for children to see ancient ruins and hear tales of the brave deeds of old. Health, enterprise, and imagination are alike fostered by a scramble over a hoary ruin.

If there is time Haverfordwest might be visited. It is nine miles from Milford. There is a fine church, standing well ; also a castle, in ruins, built by Strongbow. The French tried to take it in Henry IV.'s time, but failed, and the Parliamentarians made a more successful attempt 200 years afterwards. Now the donjon has become a dungeon—it is the county gaol.

There is a parade and a priory, or rather the ruins of one, founded by one "Hwlffrdd." This spelling, by the way, is nothing to what we are coming to presently. We are in Wales now, and shall be more so by-and-bye.

Slebech Hall and **Lamphey** could be visited. The latter is a modern house, the residence of Baron de Rutzen. It is built on the site of an old Commandery of the Knights of St. John, but nothing remains of it except, perhaps, a sword—which is a large one—a veritable excalibur. **Lamphey,** on the Tenby road, possesses the ruins of a palace, once the "palatial residence" of the Bishops of St. David. There are the remains of the chapel and several other parts of the building. For an example of domestic architecture in feudal times it is useful. It passed into the hands of the Earls of Essex, of the Devereux line. There is a curious connection between the eastern counties of England and these western ones of Wales. All round the neighbourhood of Maldon and Witham there are legends of the FitzHamons who conquered South Wales ; and in the times of Henry I. and II. South Wales was much the fashion with the Norman followers of the last Norman and first Angevin kings.

They seem to have regarded Wales much as we regard South East Africa now, and treated the natives accordingly.

It seems to me a great pity, from the romantic point of view, that these modern settlers should not call themselves knights. When the descendants of these new ancestors came to look back on their past, they will like to be able to say they were descended from Sir Thomas Smith or Sir William Jones, "a right hardie knyghte and full worschipefulle," as the old chroniclers used to say—and spell, which, after all, is no worse than the Americans are doing now, when they call a traveller "a traveler" and splendour "splendor."

The full enjoyment of a title is not to the acquirer or first possessor, it is to his posterity: hence comes the dislike of hereditary titles. Jealous minds feel their bearers have had nothing to do with it.

Well, we are in the country of romance. Poetry and dreamy speculation are a part of the national character. When at Rome, do as Rome does. However, as there are many more miles to be sailed, let us get aboard before we become lotus-eaters and, thereby, loiterers.

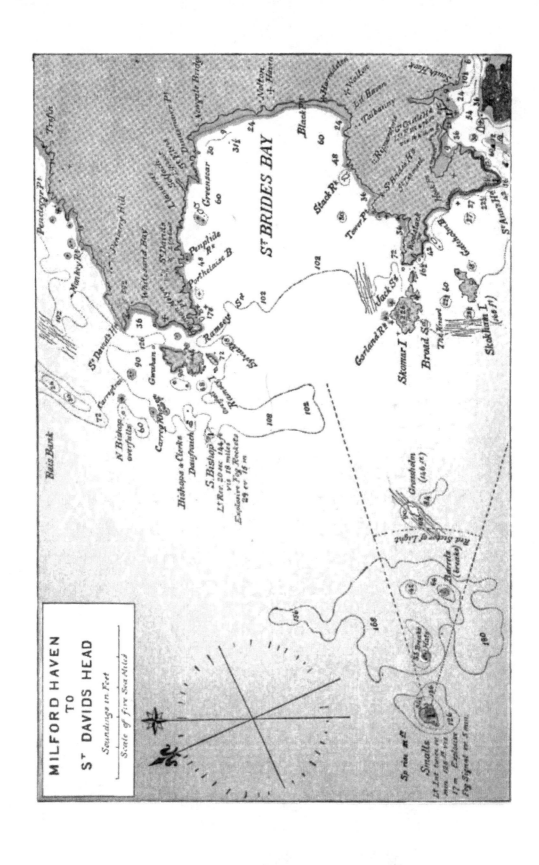

MILFORD HAVEN
TO
ST DAVIDS HEAD

Soundings in Feet

Scale of five Sea Miles

CHAPTER XII.

ST. ANN'S HEAD TO THE BISHOPS AND CLERKS.

Bearings from St. Ann's Light.—To Saltee's Light-ship, N.W. ¼ W. westerly, distant fifty-nine miles. To the Smalls Light, N.W. by W. ½ W., eighteen miles and a half. Scilly Islands (St. Martins), S.W. ¼ S., one hundred and eleven miles. Cape Cornwall, S.W. by S. southerly, ninety-five miles. Trevose Head, S. by W. ¼ W., sixty-eight miles. Lundy Island Light, S. by E., thirty-six miles and a half. Barnstaple Bar, S.S.E. ¼ E., fifty miles and a half.

Tides.—The tides are most important and should be attended to carefully, as between Skomar and Skokham Islands the streams diverge. The flood stream flowing past the former towards the Irish Sea, and S.W. of Skokham towards the Bristol Channel. In other words, between the Smalls and St. Ann's Head, the ebb from Liverpool becomes the flood in the Bristol Channel.

Whilst the water is falling at Liverpool, the stream sets S. by W. ½ W. off the **Smalls Rock**, and then, a little S.E. of the rock, sweeps round into the Bristol Channel at the rate of from two to three knots, causing high-water in the outer parts of the channel. It is high-water at St. Ann's Head, at full and change, about 6, and it is low-water at Liverpool at the same period, at about 5.

At the **Smalls** it is slack water about 20min. before the times of high- and low-water at Liverpool. **Off St. Ann's Head** the N.W. stream begins to run at 2hrs. before low-water at the Liverpool bar, and the S.W. stream at 2hrs. before low-water, or 3hrs. before high- and low-water on the shore.

In **Jack Sound** the stream sets to the N. from 2½hrs. before low-water until 3½hrs. before high-water at Liverpool bar and to the S. from the rest of the time. The N. stream sets directly towards **Ramsey Sound** with much vigour for a short distance, causing heavy overfalls. The S. stream sets equally vigorously through the sound, but **S. of Mid Island**, and creates a powerful eddy which might be dangerous.

Wildgoose Race is a dangerous race to the W. of **Skokham** and **Skomar**, between which islands lies the **Knoll**, with three fathoms and three quarters least water on it. Over this bank the streams run in uncertain ways, and the tide is much slacker, **Wildgoose Race** being to the W. of it. Coasters anchor on this bank in adverse tides, but there are several rocks on it, although a good part is sandy. In Wildgoose Race craft have been known to founder, and it is not un-common for a vessel to be dismasted in the heavy, breaking sea.

At two miles off St. Ann's Head, and about one-third of a mile W. of Skokham, the N. stream begins 1½hrs. before low-water at Liverpool, and the S. stream at 1½hrs. before high-water at Liverpool.

There is no doubt the amateur sailor who sails this cruise will have to expect a good deal of rough and tumble. The best wind for continuing the cruise is a S.E. one, as this means smooth water. Most likely, however, such luck will not happen. The wind is more likely to be from the W. A vessel bound up the Irish Sea requires to be at St. Ann's Head at 3hrs. flood by the shore if she wishes to profit by all the tide, and as this means going out against the flood stream through Milford Narrows, it is difficult to be managed without a leading wind and plenty of it. If possible, it would be better to take the last of the ebb out, and creep up towards **Jack Sound** for the first of the N. going stream, or else go out with the first of the ebb and carry the remaining 3hrs. of the N. going stream into St. Bride's Bay.

Coast between St. Ann's Head and Wooltack Point.—The coast is mostly steep-to, with bold cliffs as far as Dale Gap, where there is a remarkable break in the cliffs.

Gateholm Bay is round **Hook Point**, and is a fine sandy bay, backed by dark red cliffs, facing S.W. In off-shore winds a quiet weather anchorage could be had here if necessary to wait the tide. **Gateholm Island** lies off its W. end, but is only an island at high-water. From here to Wooltack Point the coast is rocky and high (150ft.) Behind it is a peak 175ft. high.

Skokham Island is two miles from the mainland. It is one mile long by half a mile wide, and is highest towards the W. (165ft.) The cliffs are precipitous, and it is mostly steep-to. The island slopes slightly to the E., and at that end there is a stack rock connected by a neck of rock and sand. There is a white farmhouse near the landing-place on the E. side; this is seen from Jack Sound.

Skokham Spit, on the N.E. of the stack, has three fathoms least water on it.

On the N. side, one cable from the shore, is a rock awash at low-water. The only anchorage is in seven fathoms close in to the cove on the S.E. side. The bottom is foul.

Wooltack Point, four miles and a half from St. Ann's Head, is dark and precipitous. It forms the S. point of St. Bride's Bay.

Jack Sound lies between it and **Mid Isle**, which is 154ft. high, and separated from **Skomar** by a narrow channel 80yds. wide, with 9ft. least water, but with sunken rocks in mid-channel on its N. side.

Skomar Island is one mile and three quarters long by one mile broad. Steep cliffs, seamed with chasms, surround it to the height of 200ft. The top is a level, with rocky knolls here and there. A flag-staff stands on the highest of these. There is only one house on the island on the N. side. The E. part

K

of the island is a peninsula, connected by a narrow neck, forming on each side, respectively, N. and S. havens, where there is safe anchorage with off-shore winds. In entering, keep close to the W. side in both havens, as rocks lie off the E. side. These anchorages look snug, but they might be traps if the wind shifted, as there is not much room to work out if a vessel goes too far in.

The island is mostly steep-to, except off the S. point of the peninsula, at the E. end. Here rocks lie out some little distance.

The **Mew Stone** is an islet as high as the island off the S. side, and the **Garland Rock** is another remarkable islet on the N.

Wildgoose Race carries on its villainy from the W. ends of Skokham and Skomar, and forms a considerable obstruction to the navigation of **Broad Sound** between the islands.

Jack Sound is only one cable wide between the **Horse** on the **Wooltack** side, and the **Bitches** off Mid Island. The **Benches** lie a quarter of a mile off the mainland, and the **outer rock never covers.** A sunken rock, with two fathoms and a half least water, lies one cable and a half S.W. of this rock. The **Inner Benches,** off Anvil Point, dry and extend three-quarters of a cable from it.

It is **possible to go** between the **Benches,** but it is **better not,** unless very well acquainted with the locality.

The Blackstones lie a quarter of a mile S. of **Mid Isle,** and never cover. The **W. Blackstone** dries 7ft. at low-water, lying N.W. by W. ½ W. from the Blackstones.

The **Horse Rock,** which is **very dangerous,** dries 8ft. only, and lies one cable off the mainland, N. of Anvil Point. Midway between it and inner Bench Rocks are two other rocks, which dry 12ft.

The **Bitches** dry 16ft. to 18ft. at low-water. They lie E. of Mid Isle, and leave a channel of only 260yds. wide between them and the **Horse.**

Off **Wooltack Point** is Tucker Rock, which always shows 5ft. above high-water. There is an eddy with a nasty overfall setting round this.

Jack Sound is a very ugly place in strong winds and weather tides. At all times the overfalls and eddies are bad. At spring-tides they are very bad, and in gales of wind from the N. or N.W., or S. and S.W., they are abominably bad. If the passage perilous must be taken, try to get there at slack water (2½hrs. before low-water and 3½hrs. before high-water at Liverpool).

Coming from **the S. pass close E.** of the **Blackstones** and steer towards **Tucker Rock, which always shows,** keeping the W. end of Skokham just open E. of the E. angle of the Blackstones, bearing S.W. ¼ W., a vessel then will pass between the Horse and the Bitches. When the Garland Islet N. of Skomar opens, steer more N. In coming from the N. keep nearer to the W. side until the **Garland** is shutting in, when keep **Skokham** open E. of the Blackstones as above, so as to avoid the eddy and overfall off the Tucker.

An amateur skipper had better not go through here for the first time without local knowledge and help.

Six miles away W. of **Skomar is Grassholm.** It is three-quarters of a mile round. The island is 146ft. high, and is steep-to mostly, except on its E. end, where a rock dries 2ft. at low-water; and off the W. end, at the distance of about half a cable, are a few rocks which dry 13ft. at low-water. A tide race sets off both ends of the island, with a back eddy between.

W. again of **Grassholm** and at **three miles** distance are the **Barrels, extending half a mile under water,** except a rock at the N. end which dries 10ft., the Smalls bearing N.W. by W. ½ W., distant four miles and a quarter.

Tide rips and overfalls generally indicate the rocky bank.

N.W. again of the **Barrels** are the **Hats,** extending a mile under water, with many shallow heads, on which the least depth is 8ft., and is distant from the **Smalls** two miles, bearing W. by N. ½ N.

Still going W. at last the end of this long and dangerous submerged promontory is reached, the **Smalls** being a cluster of rocks, all of which are beneath the sea at high-water except the lighthouse rock and two others E. of it.

K 2

The reef extends half a mile N.E. and S.E., and is about three cables broad.

The lighthouse is eighteen miles and a half westward of St. Ann's Head. From a tower, circular, and painted in red and white horizontal bands, at an elevation of 125ft. above high-water, an intermittent light, giving two occultations every minute is exhibited. It is light for 54sec., eclipsed for 2sec.; light 2sec., eclipsed 2sec. Visible seventeen miles. The light shows white except between the bearings of W. $\frac{1}{3}$ N. and N.W. $\frac{3}{4}$ W., where a red sector covers the Hats and Barrels.

W. of the lighthouse there are no dangers. N.E. rock lies two cables N.E. $\frac{1}{4}$ N. from the lighthouse, and dries only at low-water springs. It is steep-to on its N. side. E. rock is awash at low-water springs; it is a quarter of a mile S.E. by E. $\frac{1}{3}$ E. from the lighthouse. S.W rock dries 5ft., and lies S.W. by W. $\frac{1}{3}$ W., three cables from the lighthouse.

In entering the Irish Sea, or St. George's Channel, as this part of it is called, it is better to go outside the Smalls, if only to avoid the overfalls off the islands and over the reefs; but there is a very good passage on either side of Grassholm, only care should be taken to keep well clear of the races off the islands by giving Grassholm a berth of a mile on either side, and Skomar a berth of about the same on its W. side.

When Wooltack Point is passed St. Bride's Bay suddenly opens out, the coast forming an acute angle at the point.

Close round the point is Martin Haven, a small cove where a landing could be effected out of the tide. Musselwick Bay is edged with steep cliffs, and skirted by a few outlying rocks to no great distance, and with two fathoms close ashore at low-water. There is anchorage here to wait the turn of the tides, sheltered from all winds except from W. to N.E.

Tower Point is the N. extreme of the bay. A little inlet, with shelter for boats, runs up to St. Bride's, on the W. of which is St. Bride's Hill. From this cove to Mill Haven, opposite the Stack Rocks, the cliffs are bordered with rocky heads and ledges. The Stacks are a group of conspicuous high rocks, lying **two miles** W. of **Goultrop Road** and nearly three-quarters of a mile off the shore.

There is a good channel between them and the cliffs. The coast now turns S.E. round **Goultrop Head** and forms **Goultrop Road** with **Little Haven** at the head of a sandy shore. There is anchorage in the road with winds S. of W.S.W., but anything W. or N. of that sends in a heavy sea, when a vessel, if caught, would have difficulty in working out. There is a life-boat here.

Broad Haven is beyond, with a wide sandy strand, on which a vessel might run at a little after high-water, and save life if not property.

In anchoring in Goultrop Road bring up as near to the E. of the head as convenient, in a bight under Talbenny. There are three fathoms close in.

St. Bride's Bay is six miles and a half wide and seven miles deep. Nearly all the shore facing the W. is bordered by sands, and the bay is sandy, with good holding ground throughout. Unfortunately, it lies exposed to the full drift of the W., W.N.W., and S.W. winds, sending in a heavy sea.

The only anchorages are **Goultrop Road,** and off the little land-locked tidal inlets of **Solva, Porthclaise,** and **Porthllisky.**

Tides.—The W. stream runs on the S. side of the bay for 9hrs., turning 2hrs. before high-water by the shore, the flood-tide, or N. stream, setting across to Ramsey Island for 6hrs., beginning at 2½hrs. before low-water by the shore.

From **Cwm Mawr,** a sandy bight at the N. end of the long sandy shore, the coast turns nearly at right angles to **Penmaen Melyn,** the S.E. point of the entrance to **Ramsey Sound.** Precipitous cliffs front the sea. They are mostly steep-to, with outlying islets and rocks at intervals. **Dinas Mawr** is a rocky point, jutting out E. of **Solva,** and **Greenscar Islet,** with the **Mare Rock** lying 200yds. E. of it, lies half a mile S.W. of Solva. **Greenscar** is 108ft. high. A rocky ledge, and a rock always above water, lies half a mile W. of it.

Between these islands and the shore there is plenty of water and good anchorage with off-shore winds. **Solva,** or **Solfach, Creek**

has capabilities if only utilised. It is very narrow, with a rocky
islet on its E. side, nearly blocking the entrance. Off this islet
there are two fathoms at low-water. The channel is only 50yds.
wide, and shoals quickly within the islet, drying out to within
a cable of the islet. At high-water there is a pretty little
harbour, where vessels can run in and be in perfect safety.
There is no getting out, however, with S. winds. This is a
snug place for vessels that can lie aground.

Porthclaise Inlet lies two miles and a half W. of Solva.
The coast is all clear in between. Off Porthclaise there is
rock dry for 5ft. at low-water. It is half a mile S.S.W. ½ W.
from the W. point of Porthclaise, with the S. point of Crow
Rock in line with the Bishop's Rock off Porthllisky. The highest
hill on Ramsey, open of the Bishop, clears it to the S.W.

Porthclaise Inlet is 50yds. wide, and dries out to the pier
half a cable within the entrance. This is a handy place for
seeing St. David's, as it is only one mile away. The cathedral
cannot be seen from the sea as it lies in a hollow, but the
hotel is very visible.

Crow Rock, 58ft. high, lies to the W. of Porthclaise, and on
its W. side is Porthllisky Bay. The Bishop's Rock lies S. of
the bay, and another rock, awash at low-water springs, lies one
cable and a half S.E. of Crow Rock. Anchorage could be
had here with off-shore winds, in six fathoms, in the bay while
waiting the tide.

Tides.—The tides are mild in St. Bride's Bay. The stream
runs round for 3hrs. from the S. side of the bay to the N., and
for 9hrs. the other way on the S. side. There is a strong eddy
on the N. side on the ebb. When coming through the sound
on the ebb a vessel must keep well to the W. side so as to
avoid this eddy. In entering with the flood a vessel must
keep to the E., or Porthllisky side, to ensure being carried
into the sound. There is no in-draught into the sound until
within half a mile of it. Then it begins with a will. Half
way across the entrance of the bay the flood stream begins at
5hrs. before low-water at Liverpool, or 4hrs. after low-water
by the shore.

Ramsey Sound lies between Ramsey Island and the mainland. It is a quarter of a mile wide at its narrowest part at the **Bitches,** and two miles long. Like **Jack Sound** the tides rush through at an alarming rate, causing heavy overfalls at each end and eddies at the sides.

Ramsey Island is one mile and a half long by half a mile wide. There is one farmhouse on it, and the only convenient landing-place is on the E. side abreast the Bitches. At **Aber Mawr Bay,** on the W. side, a landing could be effected in fine weather. High cliffs surround the island, which is barren mostly, allowing scanty pasture for a few sheep. The highest part of the island is 444ft. high on the W. side, and Ramsey Saddle on the N.W. side is 326ft. high.

There are several outlying stacks and rocks, but all are above water and close to the island. **Ynys Berry,** or **Margery Island,** is the largest, lying S.W. of Ramsey, with two rocklets on its E. side. **Carreg Eilun** is 80ft. high; **Pontyr Eilun** is just above high-water springs; **Sylvia Rock,** with three fathoms least water, lies S. ¼ W. half a mile from Carreg Eilun.

Shoe Reef lies one cable S. by W. ¾ W. from Penmaen Melyn, on the E. side; it dries 9ft. at low-water, with a few small heads N. of it. **St. David's Head,** kept open of Pencarnen Point, clears them to the W.

The **Bitches** lie off the middle of Ramsey Island, to the distance of nearly two cables in the sound. Two rocks, dry at low-water to the extent of 4ft., lie 50yds. E. of the outer Bitch. The Bitches are high rocks and never cover.

The **Horse** dries 3ft. at low-water springs, and lies near the middle of Ramsey Sound; overfalls and rips generally mark it sufficiently. **Carreg Trai,** nearly always above water and lying N. of the Bishop and Clerks group, just open of the N.E. point of Ramsey, leads over it, and **Gafœliog,** a rock 10ft. high, off Pencarnen, in line with Pencarnen Point, leads over it, too. To clear it, **Gwalian Rock,** 5ft. above high-water, lying four cables N. of the N.E. corner of Ramsey, touching the N.E. point of the island, leads W. of the Horse and E. of the Bitches.

St. David's Head, shut in with Pencarnen Point, leads E. of the Horse. The E. side of the sound is practically clear of sunken dangers except the **Horse** and the **Shoe.**

There is safe anchorage in all weathers, except a gale from the N., in the bay on the E. side of Ramsey Island in the sound, one cable and a half N. of the **Bitches** and as near the island as the draught of the vessel will allow. Take care to anchor out of the tide. A long vessel cannot lie here easily, as she would be in danger of swinging into the tide unless great care were taken.

There is an eddy on the flood-tide, extending beyond the Bitches and from the N. of the island. To anchor, therefore, one must go past the Bitches and shoot into the eddy, allowing for its taking the vessel back towards the anchorage. It is easier picking up a berth on the ebb.

Tides.—It is high-water full and change in Ramsey Sound at 6hr. 0min. local, or 6hr. 21min. Greenwich time. Springs rise 17ft. The stream runs 3hrs. after the turn of the tide by the shore, the N. stream ending 2½hrs. before high-water at Liverpool. There is 20min. of slack water at each tide.

When within half a mile S. of Penmaen Melyn a vessel will feel the in-draught. Outside of that the tide runs across the sound and outside Ramsey.

The great point is to keep well in the centre of the stream and avoid the eddies. The rate of tide is six knots, more or less, according to wind. Off Gafœliog it slackens to three knots, and sweeps round St. David's Head half a mile off shore. The flood outside Ramsey causes a back eddy round the N.E. end, reaching as far up the sound as a few yards past the **Bitches.** On the E. side is another eddy reaching as far as the Horse, where it creates whirlpools, to be avoided.

The ebb sets close round St. David's, and rushes towards the **Gwalian Rock, where it divides, one stream going outside the island, the other** through the sound. There are two eddies on the ebb, one working back along the W. side of the island from Ynys Berry, the other beginning at the Horse and running back to St. David's Head. They are not felt during the first quarter of the ebb.

It is needless to say that slack water is the best time for Jack Sound and Ramsey Sound. In any case, it is advisable to avoid them at spring tides and with head winds. A vessel in these tide races sheers about a great deal, and a good hand at the helm is necessary. The great thing is to keep in the tide. Even with a leading wind, it is not always easy to steer going through the sound.

Outside of Ramsey Island lie the **Bishops and Clerks**; they cover a space of three miles. The sunken dangers lie between the four Bishops, who are above water, while the Clerks are kept below.

South Bishop Lighthouse.—On the S.W. rock, 100ft. high and 250yds. long, distant two miles W. of Ramsey, with the Smalls lying W. by S. ¾ S., distant twelve miles and a half, is a circular white tower, 36ft. high. From it is exhibited, at an elevation of 144ft. above high-water, a **revolving** white light every 20sec., visible eighteen miles.

Fog-signal.—At intervals of 15min. two explosive reports, sounding like the report of a gun, are given by means of rockets. The interval between the reports is 5sec.

The S. Bishop has sunken rocks off its N.E. end for half a cable, and a tide race off its W. end. Between it and **Daufraich** is a clear channel with true tides. Daufraich is a flat rock, 300yds. long, with ledges off its N. and E. sides. It is two-thirds of a mile from the S. Bishop. **Carreg Rhoson** is 250yds. long, with rocks above water at its E. and W. ends, thus making it nearly two-thirds of a mile in length. The rock is steep-to, with eddies and rips off its ends.

North Bishop lies two miles and a half W. of **St. David's Head.** It is 120ft. high, with outlying rocks, E. and W., in all half a mile long.

Bell Rock, with 8ft. water over it, lies E. by S. ½ S., distant two cables and a half from the E. rock. There are **heavy over-falls** over the rock and for one mile W. of the N. Bishop.

The **Clerks** are five rocks, lying **between the Bishops and Ramsey Island. None of them lie N.** of the N. Bishop nor **S.** of Daufraich.

Carreg Trai has been already noticed. It hardly ever dries, and is the northernmost of the group; it is steep-to. **Maen Rhoson** is a rock 3oft. high, and also steep-to, two cables N. of **Carreg Rhoson, Moelyn, Cribog, and Maen Daufraich,** the latter being one cable N. of Daufraich, Cribog one cable and three quarters E., and Moelyn one-third of a mile E. This latter rock dries 14ft. at low-water, covering at the last quarter of the flood, but the other two are just uncovered at low-water. There are no safe passages between them. **Llech Uchaf** and **Llech Isaf** are half-way between Daufraich and Ramsey; they are four cables apart. The first is 5ft. above high-water; the other is covered 3ft. at high-water. There are heavy overfalls on and near these rocks. At one cable S.W. of Ramsey is a rock dry 12ft. at low-water.

The passage W. of Ramsey, close to its W. side, is preferable to the **sound,** as the tides are true and less rapid. Take care to give the **Llechs** a good berth. **Bais Bank,** with depth of **four fathoms least water,** begins one mile and a half from the N. Bishop, and trends N.E. by E. ½ E. for four miles and three quarters, being above half a mile wide. There are **heavy overfalls** on this in bad weather.

Carreg Eilun, seen through **Ramsey Sound,** bearing S.S.W. ¼ W. leads E. of the Bais Bank. Ramsey Hill, in line with the N. Bishop leads S. of the bank. The tides run nearly six knots near the N. Bishop. The flood stream at two miles W. of the Bishops sets N. by E. ½ E., about five knots at springs, and draws round St. David's Head as it goes N. The force eases off at 2hrs. before high-water at Liverpool, near Ramsey Island, but W. of the Bishops it runs half an hour longer. S.E. of **Carreg Trai,** the ebb sets inside the Bishops with varying tendency as it passes the obstructions. It sets fairly through between Ramsey and the Llechs.

For a stranger it is better to pass outside, or W., of all these dangers. He will find a true tide and have a lighter heart if he keeps W. of the S. Bishop Light.

———————————•}••••{•———————————

CHAPTER XIII.

THE BISHOPS AND CLERKS TO ABERDOVEY.

Bearings and distances from the Smalls Light.—Longships Light bears S.S.W. southerly, ninety-nine miles. Lundy Island, S.S.E. ½ E., fifty-one miles. St. Ann's Head, S.E. by E. ½ E., eighteen miles and a half. St. David's Head, E. by N. ¾ N. northerly, seventeen miles. The same for the S. Bishop, twelve miles and a half. Cardigan Bay Light-vessel, N.E. ½ N., forty-seven miles and a half. Bardsey Island Light, N.E. ¼ E., seventy miles. Chicken's Rock, Isle of Man, N.E. by N. northerly, one hundred and forty-two miles. Mull of Galloway, N.N.E. ½ E. easterly, one hundred and seventy-eight miles. Tuskar Light, N. by W. ¼ W., thirty-five miles.

Bearings and distances from the S. Bishop.—Kish Light-ship (Dublin Bay) N. ¾ E., ninety miles. Wicklow Head, N. ¼ E., seventy one miles. Tuskar Light, N.W. ¾ N. northerly, thirty-six miles. S. Stack, Holyhead, N.E. ¼ N., ninety-one miles and a half.

St. David's Head, although not more than 100ft. high, makes a good land-mark by reason of the high peaks just within it. **Llaiethy Peak** is 592ft. high, and looks like the cone of an extinct volcano. It is steeply sloping all round. **Penberry** is one mile and two-thirds E. ½ N. of it, and is only 19ft. lower. Both the headland and the peak are of trap rock connected by a bed of slate.

Whitesand Bay lies between Pencarnen Point and St. David's Head; there is good anchorage here out of the tide in off-shore winds.

The coast now turns sharply to the E. for nine miles and a half, with few outlying dangers far from shore. It is a rugged coast with several indentations.

Abereiddy Bay is an occasional anchorage, but dangerous sunken rocks lie in the approach to it. All dangers are cleared, however, in a course from St. David's Head to Strumble Head. A wide bay, with a few deeper inlets, lies between **Penclegyr Point** and **Penbrush Point**, the W. end of **Pen Caer**, as the promontory is called, to the W. of **Fishguard Bay**. The highest point of this rocky headland is **Carnfawr**, 700ft. high, which slopes steeply to the sea at **Strumble Head** and **Penbrush Point**. Sandy beaches lie at the end of these coves, and **Abercastel** and **Aber Mawr** afford beaching places, if nothing else. In the latter place anchorage could be found in winds from S.S.W. to E.N.E., but it would be an awkward place if caught in a W. or N.W. wind.

The Trai-Maen Rocks, drying at half-tide, lie in the bay between Pen Bwlch-du and Penbrush, and two islets—**Ynys Owen** and **Ynys Michael**—lie close to the W. side of Strumble Head. It is as well to be careful when standing in to cheat the tide, for one or two other heads lie close in. On the ebb there is an eddy round Penbrush, but it is very close to the point.

Strumble Rocks.—One is E., distant one cable, and the other W.N.W., one cable, off the N.E. angle of the head, but only half a cable from the shore. They dry at low-water springs only.

Strumble Head is a noble feature. It is one of the finest headlands on the W. coast. It consists of a barren, rugged mass of trap rock, and is seamed and scarred by the weather in a remarkable way.

From this head to **Pen Anglas** is two miles and three quarters, with the little cove of **Aberfelyn** one mile and a half E. of Strumble Head, memorable for the last invasion of the United Kingdom by the French.

Fishguard Bay is three miles wide by one mile and a half deep; rocky cliffs, rising steeply behind to lofty hills, surround the bay. **Dinas Head**, on the E. side, is a remarkable headland, nearly separated from the mainland by a narrow ditch. Llanllawer Mountain is 1107ft. high, and runs parallel to the coast for three miles, ending in another rugged head 1152ft. above the sea. Separated from this range by a valley is Precelly Mountain, 1754ft. high.

There are slate quarries in the cliffs which surround Fishguard Bay. The only out-lying rocks in the bay are the **Cow** and the **Calf**, extending one cable off **Pen Cow**, the point S. of Pen Anglas. The Cow is 17ft. above high-water, and the Calf is then just below the water. A few rocks dry out a little beyond.

Goodwick lies in the S.W. corner of the bay, and Fishguard is in the S. corner of the bay on the estuary of the Gwaen River. There is a pier, dry at low-water springs, extending 300ft. beyond the quay, but the harbour dries out some time before low-water. The bottom is mud and clay, with gravel over it. At high-water there is about 8ft. at neaps and 12ft. at springs in the harbour. Many limestone heaps lie about on the W. side. The best place to run ashore is alongside Goodwick Pier. Sands lie out from Goodwick to the extent of two cables for half a mile, but at half a mile off shore there are three fathoms.

The town of Fishguard is on the higher ground at the S. side of the Gwaen. The village on the other side, and nearer the harbour, is called Abergwaen.

Fishguard Roadstead is safe from all winds except those between N. and E. It is a pity this very easy little anchorage is not improved. A first-class harbour of refuge could be made here, and Cardigan Bay sadly needs one. As it is, Fishguard is the only approach to a shelter between St. Ann's Head and St. Tudwall's Roads. The best anchorage is off Goodwick Village, as near in as the draught of the vessel will allow, and with a view to getting away with on-shore winds.

Dinas Head, 452ft. high, separates **Fishguard** from Newport Bay. Owing to the low land behind the head it looks like an island.

The coast is clear of dangers up to the entrance of the **Nevern River.**

Newport Bay lies between **Dinas Head** and **Pen-y-Bal,** two miles further E. Both heads are steep-to and high. **Carreg Drowy,** always above water, lies close to Pen-y-Bal, and is connected by a ledge, which covers at half tide.

The bay is clean sand, gradually decreasing from nine fathoms to the ands, which dry out a long way off the Nevern outlet. In the channel of the river there are some boulders. It is better, therefore, to cross the sands on its N. side at high-water if desiring to enter the river. It is impossible to get in with on-shore gales, owing to the heavy sea on the sands.

Tides.—It is high-water, full and change, at 7hr. 0min. local, and 7hr. 20min. Greenwich time. Springs rise 13ft.; neaps, 9ft. If a vessel can take the ground there is fair shelter when once inside.

Newport lies on the S. side of the bay. It is a pretty watering-place, at the foot of the fine hill Carnengyle.

From Newport Bay to Kemmaes Head, at the W. side of Cardigan Inlet, the coast is mostly slate, steep-to, and without outlying dangers.

Kemmaes Head is 500ft. high, and on the E. side of the inlet is Cardigan Island, one mile and a half distant, 178ft. high and 800yds. long. It is mostly steep-to except off its W. end, where rocks lie out to the distance of half a cable. The bay runs in for one mile to the edge of the sands, where the River Teifi dribbles to the sea. Cardigan is three miles up from the low-water margin. The entrance is shallow and sand-blocked.

Anchorage in Cardigan Port.—This is an exposed anchorage, except with S. or S.E. winds. An inn on the E. side of the bay, in line with a point at the E. side, called Craig-y-Cwbert, marks the direction for anchorage.

Tides.—There is 14ft. on the bar at springs and 9ft. at neaps. There is 2ft. in the channel at low-water. It is high-water, full and change, 7hr. 1min. local time. At low-tide there is not enough water for a boat at two miles below Cardigan.

A **beacon** is placed on the W. side of the channel at two cables N. by W. of the sandy point ; there is also a pier on the W. side, but rocks dry out at low-water beyond the pier.

Tidal Streams from St. David's to Cardigan Port.—The flood stream sets E.N.E. and the ebb W.S.W., about two knots an hour, about three miles off shore. The streams follow the line of the coast, but **close** into **Penbrush Point** on its S. side there is an eddy on the ebb, and from Pen Anglas to Strumble Head there is an eddy for the last 3hrs. of the flood. Here the stream sets within a distance of half a mile off shore to the W. for 9hrs. ; this is useful for going to the W. and S. There is very little tide in Fishguard ; what there is runs from Dinas Head, round the bay, and out W. by Pen Anglas for 9hrs. The last 3hrs. of the flood there is no perceptible current.

The coast continues to run E., gradually sweeping round to the northward beyond **Aberystwith**. There are a few **coves** between **Cardigan Island** and **New Quay. Traeth Mount** and **Aberporth** are the best of them, but they offer no shelter, except as a temporary anchorage in quiet weather at about a quarter of a mile off them. **Ynys Fach** is another of those remarkable narrow headlands, like Castle Tryryn, or Tintagel. It is the termination of Pen Dinas Llochtyn. Behind the headland is **Moel Badell.** Under this promontory on the E. side there is a pretty little bay, and good anchorage for fair weather close in shore.

There are no dangers between **Ynys Fach** and **New Quay,** but the ground is foul in many places. **New Quay Head** is conspicuous by the two stack rocks lying off it, and the wind-mill on the hill three-quarters of a mile behind it. There are no outlying dangers. **Carreg Drenog** is joined to the **head** by a low neck, but Carreg Waltog is an islet. Between this rock and **Carreg Ina** on the E. side there are no dangers. **Carreg Ina** and the rocks between it and the E. side of the bay cover at the first quarter of the flood, and might be dangerous. It lies three cables out, and is **marked** by a can buoy, in one fathom and a half N.W. of the rock.

The anchorage is safe with winds from W. to N.E., but anything N. of those bearings sends in a heavy sea. The rock, **Carreg Weltog,** may be rounded pretty close, and when it is shut in by the headland then anchor on sandy bottom, in three fathoms.

Tides.—It is high-water, full and change, at 7hr. 30min. local time. Springs rise 13ft.; neaps, 15ft. There is very little stream of tide off here.

The harbour is formed by a pier curving round E. off **Pen-y-Wig Point,** with a small lighthouse at the end from which a white light is shown from September 15 to March 12. Over **Ina Rocks** it shows red. The harbour dries right out.

Cardigan Light-vessel is moored in thirty-five fathoms as a fairway mark, in a straight line between the **Smalls** and **Bardsey**; the former bearing from it **S.W. ½ W.** forty-seven miles and a half, the latter **N.E. ½ E.** twenty-one miles and three quarters. It exhibits a red revolving light every half-minute, visible ten miles. A black watch-buoy lies half a mile E. This is to warn vessels not to get embayed in Cardigan Bay, into which there is a good deal of in-draught.

Between **New Quay** and **Aberaeron** the only outlying danger is **Carreg Gloyn.** It is only two cables from the shore, off **Pen-y-Gloyn,** but there is only 1ft. of water on it at low-water. It is half a mile W. of **Aberaeron Pier.**

There is no inducement for any yacht to go to Aberaeron. When the wind blows hard, the natives even cannot secure their craft, if they have any. Repairs to boats can be effected here.

About one-third of the distance between **Aberaeron** and **Aberystwith** is a ridge lying out to sea, with only 8ft. on it, at half a mile from shore. It is called **Cadwgan Reef.** There is a heavy sea on it at times. The tower of Llansantffraid Church lies close by, S. of it. **Moel Badell,** bearing S.W. by W. ¾ W., open of the cliffs off New Quay Head, clears it to the W.

Patches of stone lie off between here and **Aberystwith** to the **distance** of three-quarters of a mile. A white farmhouse,

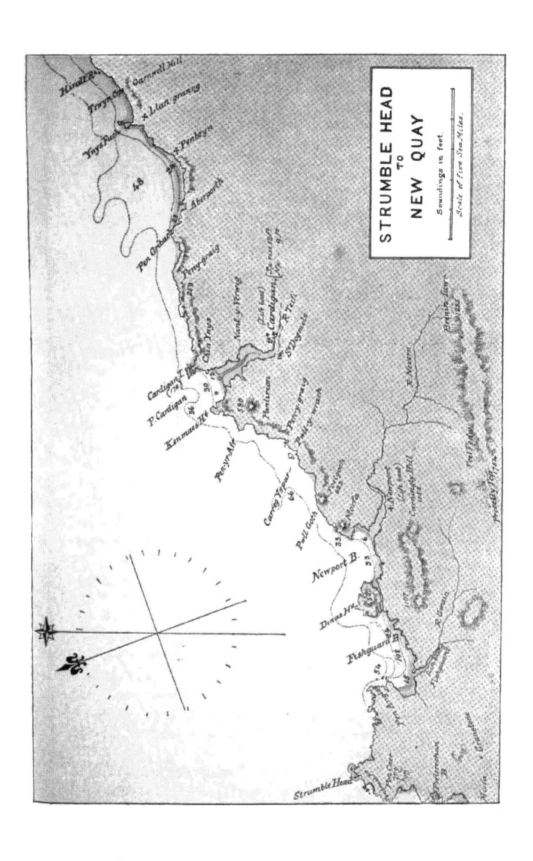

STRUMBLE HEAD
TO
NEW QUAY

Soundings in feet.

Scale of Five Sea-Miles.

Garrell Hill

Hirall Bay

Trevn Opn

Llan grang

Yny Pwll

Penbryn

Aberporth

Pen Gronant

Penygraig

Cilie Teifi

Nant y Wryg

Lit Cardigan

R. Teifi

Cardigan I.

S. Dogmaels

P. Cardigan

Planwen

Penygrang

Kenmau He

Poll y wrach

Penyyhir

Goroy Tyger

Pwll Goch

Newport B.

Dinas He

Fishguard B.

Strumble Head

R. Nevern

Prescelly Top

Carningli Hill

R. Gwaun

Penglais, on **high ground** above Craig Lais, or, as it is called, Constitution Hill, N. of **Aberystwith**, with one chimney on its gable, **open W. of Aberystwith Castle, clears these.** The **tendency** of both **tidal streams** is to **set in shore** here.

Pen-y-Dinas, with a monument on its top, is a conspicuous hill, 406ft. high, S. of Aberystwith. It stands between the two streams of Rheidol and Ystwith.

Aberystwith is a **conspicuous** place, with its terraces, piers, ruined castle, hotels, and college, all fronting the sea. It is a poor place for a yacht though. The promenade pier is 200yds. long, with 3ft. of water at its outer end at low-water. The **anchorage** is one-third of a mile off the pier-head, in five fathoms sand and clay, or nearer in, depending on draught.

Rocky ledges lie out one cable and a half S.W. of the Castle Point. Pen-y-Dinas Monument, in line with the South Pier-head Lighthouse, leads S. of this ledge.

The harbour entrance lies S. of the castle. A pier runs out in a N.N.W. direction from the S. side for 230yds., and at its head is shown a fixed light—red to S. of **E.S.E.** ; **white** to N. of E.S.E.

Tidal Lights.—In a field behind the inner end of the **S.** pier two **movable white marks are shown.** These **marks** in **line** lead in. **Fixed white lights** are exhibited here **when required,** and when there is sufficient water. From September 1 to November 30 they are red.

When there is 9ft. on the bar a **black ball** is hoisted by day on the yard-arm of the flag-staff, and when **there is water** enough in the **harbour a red flag** with **white letters is hoisted** at the **mast-head.**

Tides.—The same as at **New Quay.**

The harbour dries at **low-water springs** ; at high-water there is from 13ft. to 16ft. **inside.** Between **Aberystwith** and Borth (four miles) lie the **first** of the **strange shoals** which make Cardigan Bay so dangerous.

Clarach Patch, however, comes first. It stretches out half a mile from the cliffs at the N. side of **Clarach Valley,** and

L

has only 2ft. on it at low-water. **Castle Point on the middle of the S. pier clears it to the W.**

The **Gynfelin Patches** stretch out from a deep gully abreast of **Wallog Farm** for a distance of six miles and a half off shore, and the bank is barely more than a cable wide, if that. The first part is a narrow spit of shingle and large stones, extending in a W.N.W. direction, and **dries** for one-third of a mile at low-water, but is covered when the tide has risen 6ft. or 8ft. At its end is a shoal, with 3ft. on it, which extends to the distance of one mile from shore, when the water deepens to two and two fathoms and a half. The **leading mark for the inner swashway** is **Pen-y-Dinas Monument** on with the centre part of **Aberystwith Castle ruins.** The **swashway is half a mile wide.**

Then the shoal **rises again with depths** of from **one fathom and a quarter to one fathom and three quarters for two miles and a quarter** from shore. This part is called the **Sarn Gynfelin.** After this it deepens again, forming a channel one mile wide.

Pen-y-Dinas, open N. of the S. pier light S.S.E., leads through, in three fathoms.

Beyond this channel lie the **Gynfelin Patches**, with not more than 3ft. water on them at low-water. Beyond them the water deepens to one fathom and three quarters for one mile, where there is a narrow swashway, with from two fathoms and a half to two fathoms and three quarters least water.

The outer patch begins with three large stones, one measuring 15ft. by 20ft., with only 2ft. of water over it. This patch is **one mile and a half long**, and at the W. end is another pile of stones with only 1½ft. of water on them. The E. and W. stones used to uncover. They never, or rarely do now except in the dip of a sea.

Pen-y-Dinas Monument, bearing S.E. ½ E., distant six miles and a quarter, leads over the W. stones.

A red conical buoy, with staff and globe, marked "Patches," lies in seven fathoms off the W. edge of the outer patch.

Cader Idris, in line with Foel Wyllt, a dark peak over Dysynni Valley, bearing N.E. by E. ¾ E., leads two miles W. Dysynni is the deep valley N. of Aberdovey and Towyn.

Tides.—A distinct tide rip is visible over the patches, even in fine weather, when the wind is against the tide. Off the patches the N. stream begins 1½hrs. before low-water at Liverpool, and runs 1½hrs. before high-water. In shore and N. of Gynfelin Patches it turns half an hour earlier.

Borth stands on the S. side of the Dovey Estuary, and is conspicuous by its large square hotel. Sand heaps lie all along N. of it to the Dovey Bar. All behind this shingle and sandy tract is marsh, called Cors Fochno. The high land now recedes, leaving a wide estuary, blocked by sands, and discharging at the N. side under the high land of Aberdovey.

It is advisable to keep well out to sea until the Fairway Buoy is seen when approaching Aberdovey, as the sands lie out a long way on each side. When Aberdovey bears E. by S. then one may steer for the Fairway Buoy (black conical, in four fathoms); then steer to pass S. of the black and white chequered can buoy, in 7ft., on the S. edge of the N. spit; and then steer to pass N. of the red conical buoy, in 11ft., on the N. edge of the S. spit. The bar is between these two buoys. The bar shifts, and the buoys are altered accordingly, but by keeping close to the buoys, if in doubt, there will always be water at near high-tide, before which time a stranger should not enter. There is about 3ft. of water at low-tide in the channel.

Tides.—It is high-water, full and change, at 8hr. 0min. local, or 8hr. 16min. Greenwich time. Springs rise 16ft.; neaps, 13ft. The flood stream sets across the entrance at the outer buoy, and care must be taken in entering not to be set on the N. sands while the sands cover. In the channel the flood only runs for 4¾hrs., and is weaker than the ebb, which runs for 7¼hrs., and is very strong.

There is temporary anchorage outside, with Pen-y-Dinas Monument just showing clear of Aberystwith N. cliffs. The anchorage in Aberdovey is limited, and the strong tides make mooring a necessity, and even then the kedge, unless heavy and bent to a chain, will come home when it blows hard against the tide. The deepest pool near the village is in the channel just off the jetty. The middle of the jetty, in line with the Refuge on the S. sands and a Pink House up the harbour standing on with a little headland in line with a conical hill E. of it, is a good place, in two to five fathoms. A vessel is rather exposed here, however. There is anchorage farther on, a little past the town, but it is very limited, and the best places are taken up by other boats' moorings. The depths vary greatly, and the channels, too, rendering navigation for a stranger exceedingly difficult. Coasting craft lie ashore off the town.

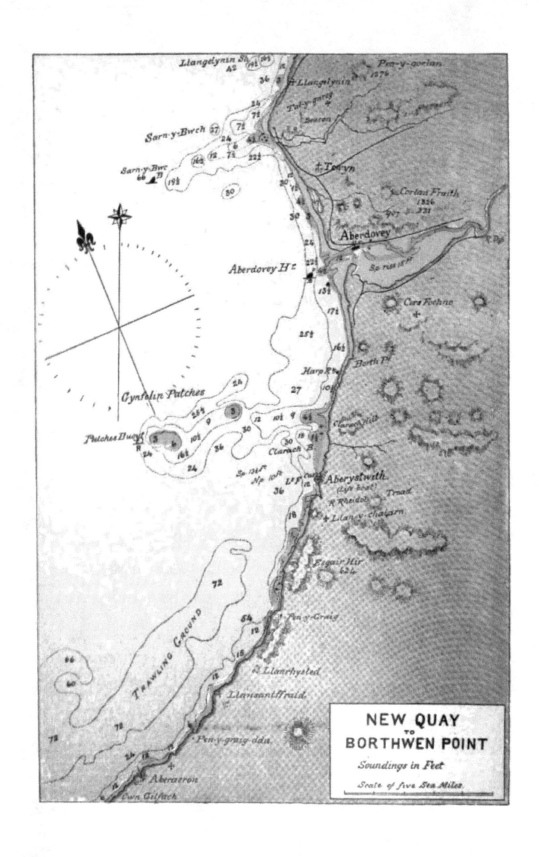

NEW QUAY
TO
BORTHWEN POINT

Soundings in Feet

Scale of five Sea Miles.

CHAPTER XIV.

THE COAST BETWEEN ST. ANN'S HEAD AND ABERDOVEY.

Remarks on the coast and objects of interest visible from the sea between St. Ann's Head and Aberdovey.—There is no doubt that the temptation to run the gauntlet of Jack Sound and Ramsey Sound is very great. If there is no strong head wind, and the tide is not too rampant, it might certainly be done, only it would be better to get as near slack water as possible. By good management and luck this could be arranged, if a vessel left at the top of high-water at Milford. She would go out on the first of the ebb, and would have an hour in which to get through Jack Sound, allowing two hours from Milford to St. Ann's Head. Then, by keeping in to St. Bride's Bay she would escape the strength of the tide, and would most likely have to anchor off **Porthllisky** or **Porthclaise** for the flood stream at Ramsey.

The coast is very interesting, and could well be dawdled over if the weather were fine. An anchorage off **Solva**, or **Solfach, Inlet** or **Porthclaise** would do no harm, and **St. David's** is well worth a visit. It is only a mile from the latter creek. In these days of Welsh Disestablishment it is as well to remember that Christianity as an organised system existed in Wales long before it re-emerged in England. St. David's See was originally at Caerleon, but, owing to the disturbed state of the Marches, it was, in the eleventh century, moved to St. David's for the sake of tranquility. There were seven suffragan bishops owing fealty to the See—Hereford, Worcester, Bangor, St. Asaph, Llanbadarn, and Margam. The buildings which exist show that the Episcopal establishment was very extensive. The cathedral, the palace, St. Mary's College, and other buildings were all enclosed in an embattled wall, 1200yds. round, with four gateways. The palace is in ruins. The cathedral has recently been almost rebuilt, at great cost. The tower was found to be so insecure that it had actually to be hung on wooden supports while the foundations and other parts were rebuilt under it. The roof of the nave, the shrine of St. David, and the stalls, should all be noticed. St. Caradoc was buried here and Giraldus Cambrensis. Edmond Tudor reposes in the cathedral under a fine tomb, and the carving of the Bishop's throne is a thing to be admired.

The number of ruined and roofless buildings standing round show how extensive was the ecclesiastical establishment, and how utterly the Reformation took all the life out of it, if, indeed, spiritual life had not sunk long before into lazy contentment and formal ritual.

A vessel that can take the ground, or that has legs, would find a snug nook wherein to rest at Solva Inlet, and the country all round is well worth exploring. **Broad Haven,** on the S. side of **St. Bride's Bay,** in **Goultrop Road,** is a rising watering-place, and Whitesand Bay, or Porth Mawr, at the N. end of Ramsey Sound, is a delightful bathing-place.

Well, the tide is slackening now, we can begin to tackle this formidable sound. Keep her head close to Pen Maen Melyn and stick to the middle of the channel, edging away from the **Bitches** on the port and the **Horse** on the starboard. All dangers are showing, and the stream is just beginning to run. It is a delightful sail at such a time, and this narrow land-locked sluice is a pleasant change from the long roll of the open sea. Ramsey Island and Skomar provide sea-birds' eggs for the wine importers of Bristol—they are used to clarify the wines. Twelve persons comprise the population of Ramsey,

so they say.   Much traffic passes through this strange alley—
a kind of Wych Street to the busy Irish Channel.

The whole collection of rocks—from the **Smalls**, eighteen miles
away, right out on the threshold of the Bristol and Irish
Channels, to the North Bishop on the N., and Skokham
at the S. point of the triangle—is a curious relic of a sunken
land.

Cardigan Bay is another example of the legend of the submerged country.

Right up from Brittany to Wales it is the same tale of an
invading flood.

The lost kingdom of Is, the drowned realm of Lyonnesse,
the flooded lands of Cantref-y-Gwaelod, all attest some great
catastrophe, unrecorded in authentic history—a page in the
unwritten annals of human misery, and the powers of nature
asserting themselves in terrific violence.   From the Sein
Island, off Douarnenez Bay, right up to Bardsey Island, the
western sea is streaked with crumbling ribs at regular intervals,
stretching their narrow and rocky remains from E. to W.   Of
these strange remnants of a prehistoric age none are more
curious than the three Sarns, or causeways, in Cardigan Bay—
the Sarn Gynfelin, the Sarn Bwlch, and the Sarn Badrig.   It is
a sure proof that this subsiding process is still going on, that
the stones of the Gynfelin Patches, which used to be visible
above high-water, are now 2ft. below it.

The sands which block the estuary of the Dovey and form
the marsh of Cors Fochno are piled on the roots of an ancient
forest, as St. Michael's Mount survived the primeval growth
which has sunk beneath the sea.

As Pencarnen Point is opened, the rugged point of St.
David's Head comes in sight, with its volcanic-like cone
behind it.

I never shall forget the first time I saw this headland.   It
was my watch from 4 a.m. till 8.   The grey mists of a warm,
quiet night still hovered over the sea.   The **Smalls Light** was
blinking lazily on the starboard beam, the **South Bishop** bore
E. ¾ N.   I took the helm sleepily and steered.

Gradually over the cold gray scene came a mellow tinge. Above the mists floating over the waves spread a rosy flush, and as I looked far away against a crimson patch loomed a purple shape, a sharp cone rising from a low base. Behind it rose the sun, flooding the gray sea with a path of glory from that volcanic peak to where the little ship was slipping lazily over the flood, sweeping her round into Cardigan Bay.

Llaiethy Hill is quite unlike any hill I know in the South of England. It is formed of trap rock and therefore of igneous origin.

The Bishops and Clerks are a dangerous chapter. The Clerks far worse than their superiors. This coast looks better from the shore than from the sea, and it is a good thing when it is past.

Strumble Head and Pencaer are noble objects, looming up across the bay. This headland came upon me quite as a surprise when I first saw it, for I had no idea the scenery was so grand. As **Penbrush Point is rounded** headland after headland comes in sight. The scenery is splendid. Carn Fawr and Carnengyle tower over the rugged cliffs below, and at last one realises that Wales is a mountainous country and that this is the country of Snowdon.

Fishguard Bay is one of the prettiest nooks I know ; the pity is it is not made a perfectly safe harbour. As it is Welsh landsmen rave about its absolute safety, one book saying that the largest ships afloat may anchor anywhere in the bay in absolute security. I recommend that writer to be on board one of them when she is caught in such N. and N.E. gales as we have had this winter and see what he says then. There is a lifeboat here fortunately for him.

But the bay is pretty, and generally safe. The country round, too, is glorious. I know of no place which makes so delightful a seaside resort ; the wonder is it is not better known. There is no place in Wales, or anywhere along this W. coast, that can touch it, unless it may be Newport ; but the bay there is not nearly so beautiful nor the shelter so safe.

There is a romantic story told of the little cove of Aberfelyn, just one mile and a half W. of Strumble Head. In 1797 the French Government sent out a fleet to invade England or Ireland—or anywhere, in fact, where they could effect a landing. The ships had on board some 1400 men, of whom 800 were the refuse of the prisons. It was a cheap way of getting rid of their dangerous criminals.

The fleet escaped the vigilance of our cruisers, and giving Milford Haven the go-by, for reasons best known to the French admiral, dropped anchor, or hove-to, between Strumble Head and Pen Anglas. Why they did not put into Fishguard Bay is not clear. The troops and criminals were landed. General Tate, the French commander, made a strategic move on the farmhouse of Trehowell, which was occupied without resistance, the garrison, consisting of the farmer and his household, performing a masterly move to the rear. There was much slaughter, nevertheless. The pigs, sheep, and poultry, who had not shared in the skilful tactics of their owners, were ruthlessly slain, and that night the French enjoyed all the triumphs of conquest. Perfidious Albion was occupied; the victories of the armies of Italy and the Rhine were eclipsed; the name of Tate would go down to history accompanied by those of Moreau, Jourdan, and Buonaparte.

Next day operations began. Hardly, however, had the criminals and others pulled themselves together preparatory for a renewal of the conflict, when news came that the insolent, but cowardly, English were to be seen massed in overwhelming numbers on the slopes of Pencaer. This was serious. The general reconnoitred the position. It was too true. Skilled soldier as he was and brave man, he recognised at a glance the futility of resisting a force so superior, and placed so admirably, on the heights.

There was no possibility of remaining where they were. All the eatables of Trehowell had been consumed, all the drinkables had been drunk.

It was a case of dying or surrendering. The Frenchman never surrenders; at least the "Garde" never does. So the French prepared to die; but as the cowardly Englishmen did not come on, and they were getting hungry, there was no help for it—they had to be taken. In this way Lord Cawdor, at the head of a few Pembroke militia and farmers, backed up by the brave lassies of Fishguard, dressed in their red whittles, or shawls, and with their high beaver hats on their heads, captured the whole force, except those who were able to get on board the fleet again.

This is the veracious account of the very last invasion of the United Kingdom, and long may it prove so.

The French, of course, with their accustomed gallantry, said they saw at a glance who the enemy was. They could not think of resisting the fair sex, and yielded, as true chivalrous sons of Gaul should yield, to the charms of beauty ; besides, English prisons were better than French jails.

From Fishguard many rambles among the Precelly Mountains can be made. The view from the summit is said to be magnificent.

Certainly **Pen Dinas**, or **Dinas Head**, is a most picturesque object, facing the ocean with abrupt front as it does, and sloping steeply to the marshy isthmus behind. It looks from the sea just like an island.

As **Newport Bay** comes open the ancient castle of the Lords of Kemmaes dominates the town. Built in 1215—not by Strongbow—it was beseiged by Llewellyn Mawr and dismantled. It is now the property of Sir I. D. Lloyd, who has restored some of it, and uses the castle as a seaside retreat. The ancient Manorial Courts are still held here.

This, too, is a rising watering-place, and like Fishguard deserves to be more known. When I see such howling tracts of dreary shingle or bleak sand, with monotony stretching for miles on each side, developing into seaside resorts, I marvel where is the taste of the age that can choose a blistered desert instead of a richly beautiful scene ; where mountain and sea and dimpled meadows, with "winding streams round ruins hoar," meet the explorer on every side.

At Newport excellent water can be obtained easily from the brooks which brawl into the bay on the S. side. Cwm-dwi is as pretty as its name, and the water comes clear and sparkling from the heights of Carnengyle.

Nevern is beautifully situated in the valley, surrounded by orchards and green meadows.

Leaving Newport Bay with regret, the young flood soon takes us round Pen-y-Bal, with its stack rock acting sentinel below.

In a short time Cardigan opens, and the deceptive estuary of the Teifi spreads before us. It is a pity there is no shelter here. The country is well worth exploring.

There is **St. Dogmael's Priory,** one of the earliest and most important of the Norman foundations. Martin de Tours—his very name is redolent of sanctity—was the knight who carved out a property for himself and his descendants on this beautiful western shore, and it is interesting to see how early these military adventurers saw the need of employing the help of the monks in introducing culture and a reverence for things holy among the half-subdued Welsh. All round Wales, from Chepstow on the S. to Denbigh on the N., the Norman barons lived in their isolated castles among a foreign people, always at feud, always ready to attack or be attacked, with little mercy shown on either side. Such was the life of the knights and their descendants from the eleventh to the thirteenth century.

Very little of St. Dogmael's is left, but the village is pretty, standing one mile and a half within the estuary on the S. side. Fishermen chiefly live here, and their cottages are scattered about on the wooded upland as taste or convenience prompted. Cardigan itself has little to attract. There are, of course, the ruins of an ancient castle—this time built by the Welsh—and the history of its early days gives us a curious side glance at the history of the time, and one can understand how it was the English invaders managed so well. Rhys-ap-Gryffydd built the castle, and his son Gryffydd-ap-Rhys inherited it, but his brother Maelgwyn-ap-Rhys attacked the stronghold, took it with the help of his English allies, and sold it to his friends ; but in the next generation, another Maelgwyn-ap-Gryffydd attacked it, and having taken it put the garrison to the sword and destroyed the castle, after which, as usual with the Welsh chieftains, he retreated to the mountains, whereupon the English built the castle up again, and so it stood until Cromwell's troops battered it down.

There is another castle really worth visiting. Cilgerran (pronounce both "c" and "g" hard) Castle stands on the Teifi. The situation is lovely. The choice of the position shows the genius of the Norman baron who selected it, as well as his taste, if that had anything to do with it. William Marischal, Earl of Pembroke, was the builder of this stronghold, to overawe Gryffydd and his turbulent family. The fragments that remain are a ruined gateway, two towers, and a few crumbling walls, all festooned with ivy, and commanding the rapid torrent below and the valley around, where woods and undergrowth clothe the steep rocks from base to top of its rugged sides.

This is a place where people inspired with poetic ardour might make verses. Mr. Warton did, with not altogether unsatisfactory result, judging by his poem of "King Arthur's Grave."

Continuing our cruise, after passing **Cardigan Island**, and noticing the curious peninsula of Pen Dinas Lochtyn, with its attendant islet, some four miles E., we are near a cave with a remarkable name. It is just before a little cove, about one mile and half S.W. of New Quay Head, called **Cwm Tydi.** The cave is in the cliffs overlooking the shore and gives name to the parish, Llandysilio Gogo, which means Tysilio's church by the cave. This saint is answerable for a good deal of type being used up. It is he who helps to perpetrate that awful word which the natives have shortened into Llanfair P.G., and which is a parish in Anglesea, between the bridges on the Menai Straits. I will give the word when I get there, as no account of Wales is complete without it. I bought it for a penny, and it hardly went into my coat pocket.

New Quay is quite a superior place in its way, but its harbour is not good enough to explore. Nor is that of Aberayron, or Aberaeron, a kind of toorylooral word, suggesting "Aaron" on the Rhine, or anywhere else.

There is a circular encampment N. of this place, which is called the camp of Cadwgan ap Bleddyn, who has given his name to the reef lying off here. This Welsh chieftain was a conspicuous character. It was he who ran away with Nesta, daughter of Rhys ap Tewdwr, who also, by the way, carried on a considerable flirtation with Henry I., when she was married to Gerald de Windsor. He appears to have been a generally marauding, Ishmaelitish kind of person, who lived the life of a robber chief and pirate of the melodramatic order, posing as a patriot and a bitter enemy of the Normans and English. Some of his descendants developed into respectable people, and became allied to other old historic families of Wales, such as the Herberts and Glynns; but others continued the traditions of their ancestor, and kept together a band of marauders composed of all the lawless youth of the mountains, which, under the name of the Gwylliaid Cochion Mawddwy, became the scourge of all the country between Welshpool on the E. and Dolgelly on the W., and from Snowdon to Plinlymmon, until they were exterminated in a death struggle in the days of Queen Mary. From 1148 to 1552 is a long time for a robber band to exist.

Aberystwith is in sight now, and a pretty place it looks from the sea with its rows of buildings extending from the dark mass of the castle ruins, and filling up the valley of the Ystwith behind. The cliffs are growing higher again. One can even see the western slope of Plinlymmon far back over the nearer hills, Pen-y-Dinas Hill with its bare slopes and the monument on its summit.

This column, by the way, was erected to commemorate the Battle of Waterloo. Aberystwith is undoubtedly a delightful seaside resort. There is boating when the tide is up in the two streams on which the town is built. The walks are many and lovely. Among the most celebrated of them being that to the Devil's Bridge, of which a legend is told much the same as that of the more renowned structure of the same name in the St. Gothard Pass. I must say my sympathies are all with the devil in these stories. He does his work honestly, and then is shamefully cheated by a shabby trick.

The castle is kept tidy by the Corporation, who have made the old ruins quite respectable. Walks are laid out, and it is a favourite resort of nursemaids and children, or otherwise. Of course, it was built by Strongbow; but we have now sailed into the district where another name is pre-eminent. Owain Glyndwr is the hero now. In fact, we are on the threshold of the very shrine and sanctuary of Welsh independence. The country behind here, and stretching from the Forest of Ergob on the S. to Snowdon on the N., was the refuge of all the patriotic Welsh chieftains from Cadwallader to Owain Glyndwr.

In the days of Charles I. the castle was turned into a mint by a Mr. Bushell, who appears to have made bushels of money. So rich was he that he raised and equipped a regiment for the King entirely at his own expense, and fed and clothed the royal forces for some time, lending the King besides £40,000. It is needless to say, no more is heard of Mr. Bushell after that. I think the Stuarts taught the world one good lesson, and that was not to put any trust in princes. If the Comtesse d'Uzés had read the story of civil wars aright, she would not have invested so largely in General Boulanger for the future benefit of the Orleans family.

The University College of Central Wales stands on the terrace overlooking the sea. It was built for the private residence of Sir Uvedale Price, but sold for an hotel, which ultimately cost £80,000. Then it was sold for £10,000 to the Governors of the College, which is intended to promote higher education.

The harbour cannot be recommended, however, as a yachting resort.

As we slip by Aberystwith it is becoming more and more apparent that we are approaching a totally different scene to any we have met with yet in our cruise from Harwich. The scenery is becoming really beautiful.

Far away N. are peaks and headlands, looking like islands. They are the summits of the mountains in the Lleyn Peninsula, in Carnarvonshire, and the still better-known peaks of the

Snowdon Range. The sea to the N. seems hemmed in with mountains and with peaks of all shapes and sizes.

A dark-nosed promontory lies right ahead; from it the mountains rise tier on tier, ridge on ridge, until they culminate in a peak, the highest of all around. That is Cader Idris, 2929ft. above the sea. It looks quite close. One does not at first realise that each ridge, which rises in increasing heights from the yellow sands, which are blocking up the foreground, are separated by valleys at least a mile or even two miles wide, the depths of which vary from 1000ft. to 2000ft. below.

We are looking on the County of Merionethshire, a district which long ago astonished that worthy prototype of Mr. Murray and all modern Guide Book writers, excellent Master Camden, sometime Clarenceaux and Garter King-at-Arms. To look at a map of the county as delineated by Nicolas Shaxton, or others, *circa* 1610, is most surprising, and certainly filled me with a desire to go and see it. However, Merionethshire is not all pimples and pyramids as therein depicted, but it is very attractive, nevertheless.

But look out! We are nearly on the patches! Don't you see the tide ripples yonder? Mind the marks! What strange freak of nature is this? Or is it really the remains of an ancient embankment, as legend says, which stretches out to sea here for nearly seven miles?

Whichever it is, the Gynfelin Patches are a serious danger, and had better either have sunk altogether or kept above water. Aberdovey then would be indeed a splendid harbour of refuge, with the two Sarns as breakwaters.

But there they are, and we must give good heed to pick out the swashway. Fortunately the tide shows where it is, as I knew, to my good luck, when first I came up here, without either chart or book of sailing directions, and only had a " Bradshaw's Railway Map " to know the general lie of the coast. Even then I was better off than the Vikings who roamed round here, and burned St. Dogmael's and St. David's by way of a spree. They had nothing but their eyes and sounding

pole to guide them, and I had at least a railway map. But
a man must be a fool who does not see the tide rips over the
Sarn Gynfelin, if there is the least wind. It was early morning
when I first caught sight of Aberystwith, and, to confess the
truth, I was not at all sure if it was that town or Aberdovey, for
the night had been thick and quiet, and I had seen no lights
since passing New Quay, about ten the night before. I consulted "Bradshaw," but he did not tell me much. I looked to
see if there was a picture of the hotel, to give me an idea of
the place; unfortunately that part was missing. So I took a
cast of the lead and found I had nine fathoms. All looked
safe around. I stood, therefore, in as close as I could to find
out where I was. It did not take long to see that there was
no estuary there; and as the dawn had now clearly broken I
saw that beyond that line of dark cliffs there was a wide
opening, and I guessed Aberdovey was there. At first I took
Borth for the place, and was standing in for what looked like
an inlet S. of the hotel; but I soon saw my mistake, and what
was more surprising, that right ahead of me and as far as I
could see to the W., there was a very clearly defined tide ripple.
It was most remarkable in the smooth sea to see this long
narrow line of broken water. I at once divined there were
rocks; so, as the wind was northerly, I let the vessel go free
on the starboard tack and ran down the line, keeping her away
to stem the tide when I saw she was being carried too near the
race. The moon was at the full and the tides were running
strong. After sailing about half a mile I found the tide ripple
seemed to break, leaving smooth water between for a space.
Cautiously I let the tide edge me nearer and sounded. I had
nearly three fathoms, so I sailed boldly through and then
looked back. Aberystwith was some distance behind, and the
old castle loomed dark under the Monument Hill. I had picked
up the first swashway, according to what I know now is the
correct leading mark.

Then came the difficulty of finding my way into Aberdovey.
I still thought Borth was where I ought to enter, and
approached so close that I had only two fathoms under me.

Then I stood out and thought a bit. There were sands all along, blocking up the wide valley. I saw a train running along behind the sands. I wondered if there were a bridge, but "Bradshaw" showed none. Then I saw a schooner; she was coming from the N., and as she rounded the sandy point, where the mountains rise to Cader Idris behind, I saw she was bound for Aberdovey. So I stood on and worked up to her. Fortunately there was not water enough yet for her to cross the bar; she was obliged to anchor, or else she touched. Anyhow, I was able to open the channel and see the buoys before she ran in.

There was a delicious fresh breeze from the N.N.W., and as the tide was nearly high I rippled on past the buoys in fine style, and brought up as near the line of fishing-boats, moored off the little terrace of old-fashioned lodging-houses, E. of the church, as I could get, in 19ft. of water.

Then began my trouble. I found the tide ran in very hard, so I carried out the kedge. When all was stowed and snug a passing waterman told me I should take the ground at low-water, he advised going up towards some moorings a little further E. As the wind was fair I hoisted the foresail and went there. Then I found I had no more water than I had before, and another man said I ought to go further W. I did not take his advice, I was too disgusted; that was where I had just come from. So I let the vessel lie, and at dead low-water she only just took the ground with her keel. After that I went a little farther up next day, and remained there for three weeks; but at the next springs I had a lively time of it, for the wind blew strong from the S.W. and W., and the old boat sheered about so that she carried her kedge and anchor right away several times, and it was only by steering her up to the tide that I could do anything with her until I borrowed a heavier kedge, after which she lay all right.

But it is a pretty place, and a pity there is not a better shelter and deeper water.

M

CHAPTER XV.

ABERDOVEY TO ST. TUDWALL'S ROADS.

THE coast from **Aberdovey** to Barmouth has to be given a wide berth. After clearing the Fairway Buoy, a course well to the W. of N. must be steered to pass the **Sarn-y-Bwlch.** Between Aberdovey and the point of sand at **Tan Fanau,** on the N. side of the estuary of the **Dysynni River,** sand heaps and sands stretch all along the coast. **Towyn** lies S. of the **Dysynni,** and the new villas standing on the shore are conspicuous objects. Behind Towyn two valleys run inland towards **Cader Idris.** The one on the S.E. leads to **Abergwynolwyn** and Tal-y-Llyn, whence Cader Idris can easily be ascended; the other, which is the **Dysynni Valley,** leads past **Pennarth** and the **Craig Aderyn,** or Bird Rock, and continues by a path across the saddle of **Cader Idris** to **Dolgelly.** Between these valleys stands **Foel Wyllt, a clearing mark** for the **Gynfelin Patches,** as well as the **Sarn-y-Bwlch.**

Behind the sand heaps the ground rises steeply, and finally after many successive ridges culminates in Y Briddell, 2190ft., on the S. of Tal-y-Llyn, and Cader Idris, 2929ft., N. of it.

The Bwlch, or **Pen Bwlch,** is a rugged hill close to the point at the N. of the Dysynni mouth; it is 635ft. high and has a **white beacon** on it. From it the **Sarn-y-Bwlch** stretches W. for five miles, rising from a depth of five fathoms. It is a ridge of stones, and **dries** for nearly two miles off shore, with only 6ft. at two miles off shore. It is steep-to on both sides.

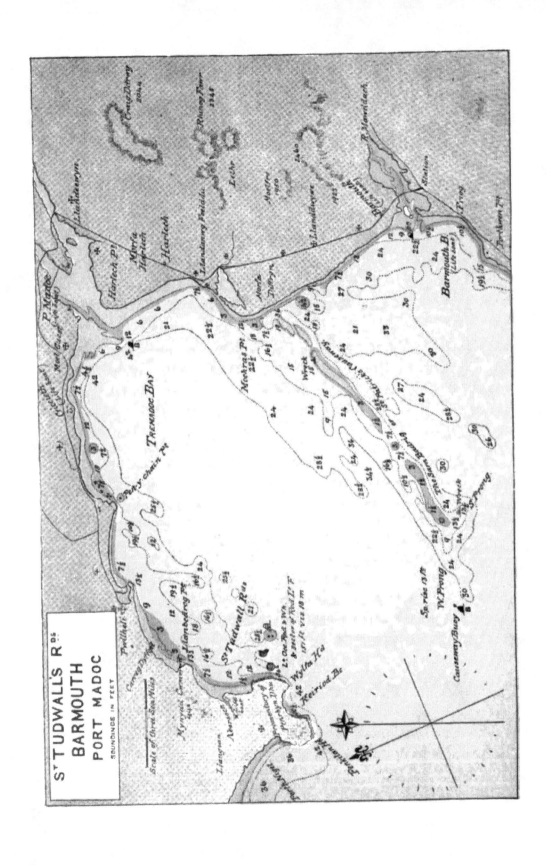

A black conical buoy, in four fathoms, lies W. of the most dangerous part, the beacon on the Bwlch Hill bearing E. ¼ N., distant four miles and a half.

A large bank of sand lies off the Dysynni mouth and dries some distance, so that the coast off Towyn should not be approached without great caution within one mile.

The S.W. point of the Bwlch Hill well open S. of **Foel Wyllt,** bearing E., leads S. of the **Sarn-y-Bwlch.** **Borthwen Point,** a low promontory, behind which the hills rise steeply, open N. of **Figle Fawr,** a hill standing by itself on the **S. edge** of the **Mawddach** or **Barmouth** Estuary, bearing **E.N.E.,** leads **N.W. of the Sarn-y-Bwlch.**

From Pen Bwlch the coast recedes in a N.E. direction to **Borthwen,** and the coast is fringed with boulders. The land rises steeply behind the low cliff, on the edge of which the Cambrian Railway runs. From this point the mountains soar abruptly to Cader Idris, with no intervening valley, the summit itself being not more than four miles as the crow flies from the S. end of the spit of sand lying off the cliffs, where they edge away to form the S. side of the **Mawddach River.**

Barmouth Harbour is another such place as **Aberdovey,** with stronger tides if anything, as the railway embankment and bridge cause the ebb to sluice through with more concentrated energy. However, there is less drift in the little pool near the railway bridge; but when I saw it last the limited room was occupied by two pairs of moorings. There is 10ft. to 15ft. here at low-water. It is on the S. side after passing Penrhyn Point, and must be steered for warily, as the flood sets strongly up to the railway bridge.

This is one of those places where a pilot would be useful, as there is very little room in this small space available for anchorage.

To enter.—Keep well out after passing **Borthwen Point** until **Figle Fawr,** the conspicuous low hill just behind the S. end of the railway embankment, is in line with a house on Penrhyn Sand Spit, the first house N. of the flagstaff about a mile W. of **Figle Fawe.** This leads up to the **Fairway Buoy.** Then

M 2

steer to pass S. of the **red buoy** on the **W.** end of the **spit which stretches W.** from the little **island** of **Ynys-y-Brawd**, on which is a **beacon marking** the S.W. end of a bank of stones stretching S. of the island; then having passed the beacon steer for the snugger anchorage described above. In passing between **Penrhyn Point** and **Ynys-y-Brawd**, keep well in mid-channel, as sand lies off the S. point. **At low-water there is only** 2ft. on the **bar**, and the channel is **barely** 200yds. wide at the entrance of **Ynys-y-Brawd**. The usual anchorage is W. of the beacon, **between** it and the **red buoy** to the S., but it is a nasty uneasy berth. The sands shift, and even in the little inner pool the anchors are liable to come home or be covered by the sand, owing to the eddies and force of the tide.

It is possible to pass through the railway bridge, as it is a drawbridge, but this would have to be by arrangement.

Tides.—It is high-water, full and change, at 7hr. 41min. local, or 7hr. 57min. Greenwich time. Springs rise 14ft.; neaps 10½ft.

Outside in the bay the flood sets N.E. by E., and the ebb S.S.W., at about half a knot an hour.

There is a quay, where coasters lie, as well as on the sandy shallow flat inside **Penrhyn Point.** Barges go some way up the river—to **Penmaen Pool.**

From Barmouth the coast is nearly straight, in a northerly direction, to **Mochras** Island. Almost directly after passing **Llanaber**, one mile and a half N. of Barmouth, the mountains recede, and sand hills skirt the coast to Dyffryn Morfa. There are no outlying dangers, only the sands uncover some little distance at low-water. Bemar Bank has only 4ft. on it. It is three-quarters of a mile off shore at high-water. **Mochras Spit** stretches out one mile and a half off Mochras Point. It is formed of loose stones, with a least depth of 4ft., half a mile off shore.

Off **Mochras** lies the Sarn Badrig, or St. Patrick's Causeway, the most extensive of these three remarkable stone ridges running out into Cardigan Bay.

The **Sarn is separated from Bemar Bank** by a passage, **half
a mile** off shore, with a least depth of two fathoms and three
quarters.

The causeway is altogether ten miles in length. A great
part of it **dries,** and of the rest a great deal has only from
1ft. to 3ft. on it at low-water. It rises from **Badrig** E. Pass,
at about a mile off shore, to a bank which extends for two
miles, and is dry 2ft. above low-water. For the next two miles
and a half there is only from 1ft. to 3ft. on it, when it sinks,
leaving a swashway one mile and a quarter wide, with depths
of from 7ft. to 9ft., except for a patch of only 3ft. in the middle.
Then the **Sarn** continues under water for one mile and a half,
with from 1ft. to 3ft. least water on it, and ends in a rock which
dries. W. of that, four cables, is another rock, which dries
1½ft. at low-water, with other rocks under water, with from 2ft.
to 3ft. on them round it. One ridge goes W. for one mile, with
from 6ft. to 9ft. on it, and another S. for the same distance from
the dry rock, with about the same water on it as the other
ridge. They are steep-to, as is the causeway on its S. side;
but on its N. there are patches with only two fathoms and a
half to three fathoms on them, two miles from it.

A **conical buoy, black, with staff and diamond,** lies two
miles **W. by N.** of the **W. ridge, or prong,** of the **Sarn
Badrig, St. Tudwall's Light** bearing **N. by W.,** distant
**seven miles and one-sixth, and Bardsey Light N.W. by
W. ⅛ W.**

To go through **Sarn Badrig** E. Pass keep the W. shoulder
of Moel-y-Gest, a hill 861ft. high close to the shore, half a
mile N.W. of Port Madoc, over the low point of **Mochras Island,
bearing N. by E. ⅜ E.** This **leads between the E. end of the
Sarn and Bemar Bank.** Then when **Moelfre Mountain,** the one
nearest to Dyffryn Marsh and round topped, bears E. by S.,
steer W. by N. until Moel-y-Gest is in line with **Moel Hebog**
(2566ft. high), just to the S.W. of **Beddgelert,** and distant as
the crow flies some seven miles from the N. shore of Port
Madoc Inlet, bearing N.N.E. ¾ E. This leads clear of the
Mochras Spit.

To clear the **W.** end of the **Sarn Badrig**, Snowdon in line
with **Moel Hebog** leads over the buoy, and the **Rhiew Mountain**
at the W. end of **Lleyn Peninsula** well open of Penkilan Head,
S.W. of St. Tudwall's, bearing N.N.W., leads between the
buoy and the W. prong in five fathoms. Carn Madyrn, the
next sugar-loaf mountain (1221ft. high), N.E. of Rhiew Mountain, open W. of **Wylfa Head** between St. **Tudwall's Island** and
Penkilan Head, leads **W.** of the buoy.

At night St. Tudwall's Light, showing white, bearing E. of
N. ¼ E., leads W. of Sarn Badrig. The ten-fathom line is two
miles W. of the causeway.

It is needless to say that this is a most dangerous obstacle,
lying as it does so far out in the bay. The general direction
is nearly parallel with the **Lleyn Peninsula**, and a vessel caught
in a gale in Barmouth Bay would have great difficulty in
working out.

Tides.—The ebb and flood set N. and S. on the S. side of
the Sarn Badrig, and in Barmouth Bay ; but on the N. side
they set in and out of **Tremadoc Bay.** The rate is about one
knot, and the streams turn at the W. end of the Sarn at 1hr.
before high- and low-water at Liverpool. Nearer to Tremadoc
Bay the flood turns 1hr. earlier and runs 7½hrs.

From **Mochras Island** to **Harlech Point** the coast is low and
marshy. A little tidal creek runs in behind Mochras Island,
broad and shallow, meandering ditch-like through Morfa Dyffryn.

Opposite Harlech Castle the foreshore becomes narrower, and
the old castle stands finely on its craig, overlooking the marshes
around.

Large boulders lie all along the shallow shore nearly to
Harlech, where a fine stretch of sand runs off N., skirting
Morfa Harlech and forming the wide sands of **Traeth Bach**
and **Traeth Mawr.**

The estuary of **Port Madoc** looks a noble piece of water at
high-tide. It is a dreary waste of sand at low-tide, the channel,
as at Aberdovey and Barmouth, being nearer the N. shore, only
in this case there is no dry dover (pronounced duvver) or
sand spit at high-water, as there is at both those places.

Harlech Point marks the S. side of the estuary, and **Ynys Cyngar**, one mile and a half N. of it, forms the N. point.

The estuary is divided into two inlets by a promontory 250ft. high. The S. one is called **Traeth Bach**, or Little Sand, and the N. one **Traeth Mawr**, or Great Sand. Both dry out at one-third ebb. The **Glasslyn River** flows into the sea through the latter outlet.

Port Madoc has only recently come into existence. The channel nearly dries out at low-water, there being no more than 2ft. then; but one mile below the quay there is a pool with from two to three fathoms. There is a rock here, which dries at low-water, called the Gomer; it is 70yds. off shore, 200yds. N.E. of Fechan Point. Ring-bolts are placed along the shore near this point for the convenience of vessels mooring. As the tides run strong this is necessary.

There is 2ft. least water on the bar, and 17ft. at high-water springs. The channel alters now and then, and the buoys are moved accordingly. Usually they are placed as follows: The **Fairway Buoy, black conical,** lies one-third of a mile S.W. of the bar, in four fathoms. On **Morfa Bychan Spit**, which is **one mile and two-fifths** S.W. of **Ynys Cyngar**, and bends round **Harlech Spit**, there is a **black cask buoy, a black and white striped buoy,** on the E. side of this spit, and three more black buoys, all to be left on the port hand. One mile N.E. of the Fairway Buoy is a small red buoy, with staff and cage, lying in 6ft., and a **red buoy** marks the end of Harlech Spit.

A pilot is an advantage, if not an absolute necessity, in going in here.

There is a good deal of traffic to Port Madoc, and a regular packet every week to Liverpool.

Tides.—It is high-water, full and change, at the bar at 7hr. 56min. local time. Springs rise 15ft.; neaps, 10¾ft. It is 17min. later at Port Madoc, which is two miles and a half above the bar. A heavy sea sets over the bar in S.W. gales.

The channel is liable to change, owing to this heavy sea, and the strong freshes which come down from the mountains after heavy rains. The Glasslyn, rising in the Snowdon range, is peculiarly liable to these influences.

Opposite Harlech is **Criccieth Castle, three miles W. of Ynys Cyngar.** The shore is low and sandy, with one promontory 156ft. high. Criccieth Castle, like Harlech, stands well on a headland, washed by the sea. Three miles W. is the promontory of **Pen-y-Chain,** low but steep, and looking higher than it is because of the marshes behind.

A rock, with only 4ft. on it at low-water, lies one cable and a half off **Pen-y-Chain,** and all the way between it and **Afon Dwyfawr** it is foul to half a mile off shore. Two ledges also dry N.E. by E., distant from the point 650yds. and 1400yds., respectively.

Gimlet Rock, off Pwllheli, well open of **Pen-y-Chain,** clears the ledges, but not the rock off the point.

Pwllheli Roadstead is a safe anchorage in winds from W.S.W. to E.N.E. through N., but directly the wind begins to blow S. of that it is time to clear out. The harbour is dry at low-water, and is a dreary enough place at best. The entrance is narrow and shallow, with not more than some 2ft. in the channel at low-water. The bottom inside the harbour is mostly hard shingle. A fairly strong tide sets in and out.

The Gimlet Rock, which is in danger of speedily becoming a thing of the past, stands like the ruin of a castle at the S. point of the harbour entrance. Behind it is a marsh, and then comes, near the shore, a terrace of new lodging-houses, and the inevitable new hotel. Pwllheli proper is nearly a mile away, across the marsh.

The best anchorage for small craft is just inside Gimlet Point, with **Llanbedrog Point** almost shut in, in about two fathoms and a half, only this is too near in if there is much swell on ; but in any case, anchorage here should only be regarded as temporary. Safety could be obtained by running into the harbour and lying alongside the quay, but not comfort.

Sands dry out for some distance in **Penrhos** and **Llanbedrog Bays.** N. of Carreg Dyffed stones dry out for half a mile, and stones lie about on the W. side.

Llanbedrog Point is also called **Mynydd Cwmmwd.** It is a hill, 440ft. high, with small piers on each end for shipping stone. The point is fairly steep-to.

Abersoch Bay is also blocked with sand as far as **Penrhyn Du Point,** under which is **Porth Bach.** Beyond is **Wylfa Head,** with high cliffs, but the bays of **Abersoch** and **Porth Bach** are blocked by sand, which dries out to a level with Penrhyn Du Point, after which the cliffs to Wylfa Head are steep-to, **with no outlying dangers in the sound.**

St. Tudwall's Islands lie off Penrhyn Du. The West Island, on which is the lighthouse, is 700yds. long by 200yds. wide, and 120ft. high. **A rocky ledge** extends one cable and a half N.E., with a rock on which is 16ft. at low-water, one-third of a mile farther.

The East Island is a quarter of a mile long by 200yds. wide, and the sound between the islands is a quarter of a mile wide; but the navigable channel is on the East Island side. There is shoal water one cable N. of East Island.

Carreg-y-Trai dries 9ft. at low-water. It is one cable long and three cables S.E. of East Island. A reef lies off its N. and E. ends for about 200yds.

Wylfa Head, open S. of West Island, leads S. of the rock.

A bell buoy, in black and white stripes, lies two cables E.S.E. of the rock, in ten fathoms. **New Patch has three** fathoms and a half on it. It lies E. of Carreg-y-Trai.

St. Tudwall's Light.—From a circular white tower on West Island, at an elevation of 151ft. above high-water, an occulting red and white light is shown. It shows bright for 8sec., followed by an eclipse of 2sec. **The white light shows between** the bearings of S. $\frac{3}{4}$ W. through S., and E. and N. $\frac{3}{4}$ E.; also from N.W. $\frac{1}{4}$ W. to S.W. by W. $\frac{1}{4}$ W. The red light shows between the bearings of N. $\frac{3}{4}$ E. to N.W. $\frac{1}{4}$ W., and from S.W. by W. $\frac{1}{4}$ W. to S. $\frac{3}{4}$ W. The **East Island** hides the light between the bearings of S.W. $\frac{1}{4}$ W. and W. by S. $\frac{3}{4}$ S. The light is visible eighteen miles.

A fixed red light is shown from a window, 16ft. below the occulting light, on the same tower; it covers **Carreg-y-Trai** between the bearings of W. $\frac{3}{4}$ N. and W. $\frac{3}{4}$ S.

St. Tudwall's Roads are sheltered from all winds, but those from S.W. through S. to E.N.E., when a heavy sea comes in, and a vessel would be in danger if caught here in a gale with anything S. in it. With N. winds strong gusts come off the land. The **inner road** has good holding ground. N. of **Porth Bach**, with the lighthouse bearing S. ½ W., or three-quarters of a mile E. of Abersoch, is a good berth, depending on the wind.

A bank lies between the **inner and outer roads**, but there is 12ft. to 13ft. on it least water. A conical red buoy lies in three fathoms on the edge of the shoal, which lies in a line from Llanbedrog Point to East Island.

The **sound between St. Tudwall's West Island** and **Wylfa Point** is free from dangers, but the tide sets through fairly strong.

The roadstead is easy of access, and affords ample shelter in off-shore winds.

Tides.—It is high-water, **full and change**, at 7hr. 45min. local, or 8hr. 3min. Greenwich time. Springs rise 14ft; neaps, 9¾ft.

Remarks on the coast and objects of interest visible from the sea between Aberdovey and St. Tudwall's Roads.—Aberdovey is a delightful little place. There are good golf links, excellent bathing, plenty of sand, and a society which devotes itself to the enjoyment of nature. The country abounds in beautiful walks, and the rowing excursions up the estuary of the Dovey to Glandovey Junction are endless in the variety of experiences one may encounter. The channel is uncertain, and the sand banks the reverse.

The wooded slopes beyond Porth Helig, and the whole panorama of hills reflected in the water at high-tide on a still evening, form a beautiful picture. The shapes of the hills are most graceful, and the colouring rich.

At **Aberdovey** anyone may become the tenant of a lighthouse. There is one on the hill behind the station, but it is not lighted unless anyone hires it. I did not know this when I first arrived here with my "Bradshaw's Guide," but learnt the fact soon afterwards. Two other leading lights are lighted if a vessel is expected. If she arrives without notice she has to find her way in herself or wait outside. I was much rebuked by local opinion because I came in without a pilot. It was not correct, and I was regarded accordingly.

I explained that there was 19ft. of water when I came in. If I had signalled for a pilot and waited outside I should most probably have missed the tide, and why on earth should I not come in when all the conditions were in my favour? No matter, it was not usual. It had never been done by a stranger, and public opinion was against me. I find it always is where-ever I go, because I don't do things as others do them.

The scenery along the coast between Aberdovey and Barmouth is very attractive. The mountains are so very near. To be only six miles from the top of **Cader Idris**, and yet to be in one's own boat, seems unnatural.

As the valley of the **Mawddach** comes open, the scene is even more beautiful; but the vale on the S. side, which leads up the Dysynni stream, is nearly as charming. In the wooded slopes of Pennarth stands the home of the Wynnes, and there is preserved the most valuable of all the Welsh MSS., the famous Hengwrt Chronicle. Beyond is the Bird Rock, a very pretty bit of scenery, rising abruptly as it does from the winding valley against the background of rugged mountains; while farther still, and on an outlying spur of Cader Idris, stands **Castell-y-Beere**, almost rivalling **Caerphilly** in the extent of its ruins, and of whose history scarcely anything is known. That, to me, is one of the strangest things about all these castles, the total absence of records telling us what happened in them. Take such large places as these two castles I have mentioned. Caerphilly, near Cardiff, encloses thirty acres. For over 500 years these splendid buildings were the home of a large society; at least for 300 years they were so continuously. A household of over two or three hundred souls would be none too large for such places. One would think that the annals of such a garrison, the domestic life of such a collection of people, would leave some incident recorded, but we know nothing, absolutely nothing, of the actual existence. All we can do is to conjecture, to piece together a page of Froisart, a little of the Morte d'Arthur, as related by Sir Thomas Malory, a side view such as Chaucer gives in his Canterbury Pilgrims, illustrated by the illuminations of such a chronicle as that of Froisart, or Monstrelet, or the book of the Tournois of gentle King Réné. That is all. What shadowy phantoms are these to occupy such solid and extensive ruins as Castell-y-Beere, of which nothing is known, scarcely, save that Edward I. is said to have stayed there?

What a record for such a place!

As we put up the helm to run down towards the Fairway Buoy, off Barmouth, the dark slopes of the N. side of **Cader Idris** bring the sunny sides of the Barmouth Hills into brilliant contrast. The town looks pretty at their base, with the new church, above the station, standing out conspicuously against the dark, almost blue rocks and cliffs behind.

Barmouth is a very much more crowded place than Aberdovey, and was quite busy with tourists and visitors when I was there in August. It is a pity the anchorage is not better, as it is a beautiful place to visit, with a glorious country to explore. It is in places like these that the craft I recommend for cruising purposes has such a pull, for it can take the ground and be quite comfortable, lying on the sand behind Penrhyn Point out of all harm, and starting away when the crew have done the place. As one sails farther in to the deep bay ahead, thoughts of the Sarn Badrig begin to interfere with one's comfort. The long, low coast offers nothing attractive as **Mochras Point** and **Dyffryn Ardudwy** is neared. The tide ripples are very strong over the Sarn, and the wind will not allow the vessel to clear the W. end. The E. pass is all before us, and with the leading marks in sight, and the lead going, it is not a difficult job to pass between **Bemar Bank** and the E. end of the **Sarn**.

But what a prodigious ridge it is, stretching away ten miles to the W. The stones which dry are said to be **hewn** stones. If so, the whole dyke is artificial, and is the remains of a stupendous embankment, the fellow to the Sarn Bwlch and Gynfelin Patches.

But who made them, or when were they made? It is all a mystery, and no satisfactory answer is possible.

But now Harlech Castle is full in sight, and nobly the gray old ruin stands. This is one of Edward I.'s castles, a foretaste of the noble edifices that ablest ruler of the Plantagenet line erected at intervals from here to Conway. The sea at one time evidently washed the base of the cliff on which the castle stands, as it still does at Criccieth, across the bay. There is a magnificent view from Harlech Castle over the marshes of Traeth Bach and Mawr to the range of Snowdon, rising abruptly from the level of the sea. The celebrated "March of the Men of Harlech" is said to have been composed in memory of the relief of the castle, when it was defended by the Herberts *alias* Ap Thomas, in 1468, against the Yorkists. Colonel William Owain, brother of Sir John Owain, of Cleneny, near Criccieth, held the castle for King Charles, and it was the last garrison in North Wales to surrender to that redoubtable taker of castles, General Mytton, ancestor of Jack Mytton, of sporting memory.

The names of Owain and Mytton will turn up again all round the coast of North Wales, for wherever there was a castle to be defended or taken there these two names are pretty sure to appear in the annals of the Parliamentary Wars.

It was Sir John Owain who, when taken by the Roundheads and condemned to be beheaded, was so very grateful for the honour, for he thought he would only have been hung. But to be beheaded together with the other Royalist nobles, in fact, "like any lord," was quite nice. However, he was disappointed. He was let off and died in his bed instead. We pass this excellent gentleman's house of Cleneny standing back some distance inland between Criccieth and Tremadoc.

Port Madoc, in spite of its old-world name, really only came into existence in the early days of this century, when a Mr. Madocks bought the place, and began to enclose part of the Morfa, or Traeth. Tremadoc was the first settlement on the reclaimed land, but when the slate quarries of Festiniog became so important, a port had to be made, and so arose Port Madoc, a very busy place indeed, by reason of its toy railway to Festiniog, with the wonderful little Fairlie "double bogie engines," the largest driving-wheel being but 2ft. 4in. in diameter. These trains run up hill, the greatest incline being 1 in 68, and think nothing of it. The line is 1ft. 11½in. gauge, and the embankments are merely stone walls, 8ft. wide at the top. Some of these walls are 68ft. high. It seems a great pity to rattle over this country without giving it the attention it deserves. To my mind it is out and away more interesting than the much-be-praised Highlands of Scotland. Every valley has a legend, every mountain a romance. Robber chieftains were quite as common in Wales as in Scotland, and their deeds were quite as disreputable.

Away there behind Harlech where that sharp-peaked mountain top soars aloft to the height of 2362ft., with the table-topped summit between it and **Llethr**, 2475ft., are the "Roman steps." Why "Roman," nobody knows, for they only lead up the side of **Rhinog Fawr** and through a stoney pass, called **Drws Ardudwy**. But they are curious relics of the past, and if anyone likes a good walk—why, there it is, eight miles up from Llanbedr Railway Station at Pensarn.

But here we are cruising off Criccieth. As one looks at the ruins of the castle it seems as if the builders were a pretty steady-headed lot. The towers rise right up from the very edge of the cliff, with the sea below. It must have been ticklish work laying the foundations.

We are now sailing at right angles, or even less so, to our former course, for Tremadoc Bay is a really splendid specimen of its kind. I know of no finer sweep than this curve of truly land-locked water, with the amphitheatre of stately mountains all round, and the dim valley of the two Traeths winding among the towering heights beyond.

This flat marsh at the head of the bay, with the mountains rising abruptly from the level, reminds one of the delta of the Rhone at the upper end of the Lake of Geneva.

Pwllheli has little to attract. I lay off here in a hard gale from W. to N.N.W., and did nothing but roll and pay out chain, until I was sick of the place and had no more chain left. Then I went down and tried St. Tudwall's Roads, with a like result.

The country behind looks pretty, and certainly the mountains make the most of themselves. The Lleyn Peninsula, being only a narrow strip of land, the hills stand up exceeding well, and look a great deal higher than they are in reality. **Carn Madryn,** just forming the three points in an equilateral triangle, of which Pwllheli and Wylfa Head are the other points, is only 1221ft. high. **Yr Eifl,** of which one hears everlastingly in accounts of views in North Wales, is only 1887ft. Then comes the valley of the Dwyfach, with the railway to Carnarvon, after which a higher mountain rises up, **Carnedd Goch,** 2315ft. high, with **Moel Hebog,** 2578ft. high, across another valley, and **Snowdon** behind, the summit being not more than twelve miles, as the crow flies, from the shore at Ynys Cyngar. One seems on quite intimate terms with all these famous hills.

Port Madoc would be a good place to make one's head-quarters for visiting this part of Wales, only there are better places for a yacht.

CHAPTER XVI.

ST. TUDWALL'S ROADS TO HOLYHEAD.

THE coast from **Wylfa Head** to **Penkilan** Point forms a bay, with a sandy beach on its N.E. side. On the side of **Penkilan** it is steep-to.

A wide bay now opens up W. of **Penkilan Head**, called **Porth Nigel,** or **Hell's Mouth.** It is clear of dangers, and could be used as **temporary anchorage** at **three-quarters of a mile off shore.** There is a strong **in-draught** of the tide, and a **S.W. wind** very soon sends in a **heavy sea.**

Talfarach Point forms its W. limit, with **Cadlan Bay** beyond. Trwyn Point, W. of this, has two islands lying off, **Ynys Gwylan** and **Ynys Bach.** There is a passage within them, with three fathoms and a quarter least water.

Next comes **Aberdaron Bay,** one mile deep and one mile wide. It affords good shelter, with the wind from N.W. to E. through N. The holding ground is bad, however, and there is usually a swell from the channel.

Pen-y-Kil is the S.W. point of **Aberdaron Bay,** off which there is a considerable tide race whenever there is the least excuse for it, with the breeze against the tide.

Carreg-du is a rock which is always above water, lying one-third of a mile **W. of Pen-y-Kil.** There is a passage, one cable between it and the cliffs, which enables a vessel to escape the full force of the tide, but it looks very narrow as you go through.

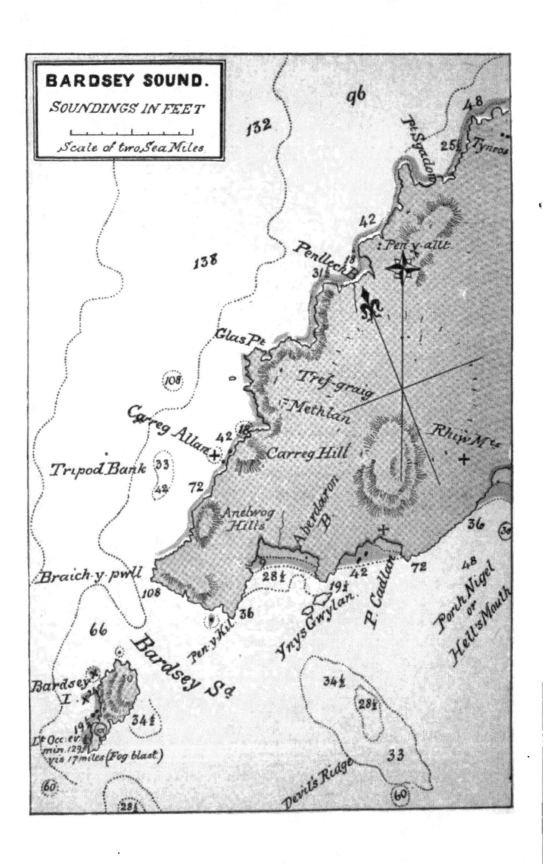

Bardsey Sound begins at Pen-y-Kil. It is one mile and a half wide and free of dangers, with the exception of **Carreg-du**, which **always shows**, and **Maen Bugail** on the island side, and which **covers at high-water springs only**. This rock is one-third of a mile from the N. end of Bardsey, with deep water between. It is very rarely that the rock, which is of small size, is not above water, but if it is covered there is always a heavy race extending half a mile N. of it.

Tides.—It is high-water, full and change, at Bardsey at 7hr. 40min. local, or 8hr. 0min. Greenwich time. Springs rise 15ft. Both flood and ebb incline to set toward **Ynys Gwylan** and into **Porth Nigel Bay**. The **flood stream** sets to the **N.N.W. at six knots**, and begins 3¾hrs. before high-water at Bardsey or 1hr. before low-water at Liverpool. The ebb runs to the S.S.E.; both streams run for 6hrs. Near Pen-y-Kil the flood turns at high- and low-water by the shore. It sets towards **Ynys Gwylan**, round **Aberdaron Bay**, and runs out round **Pen-y-Kil** and between the **Carreg-du** and the cliffs of **Braich-y-Pwll**. By keeping to the **Carnarvonshire side**, therefore, a vessel will have the N.N.W. tide 2hrs. earlier than if she kept in mid-stream. The ebb, too, turns to the S.E. 2hrs. before the mid-channel stream on the N.E. side of the sound.

Bardsey Island divides the **flood stream**, causing an **eddy** at the **N. end on the flood**, and a **similar eddy** at the **S. end on the ebb**. Both **eddies set back to the island** from the distance of about one mile and a half off it.

Two miles N.W. of Bardsey Sound the **flood stream** sets to the **N.E.**, and the ebb to the S.W., turning with high- and low-water at Liverpool.

There is a strong tide race off **Braich-y-Pwll** and over **Tripod Bank**, although the least water is five fathoms and a half, one mile and three quarters distant in a N. by E. direction, from **Braich-y-Pwll**. At **Carreg-du** the tide rips are bad also.

Bardsey Island is one mile and a half long by two-thirds of a mile wide. The S.W. point is low, but Mount Bardsey on the E. end is high (541ft.), with a bold front to the sound and steep-to.

N

The island is cultivated, and the population amounts to about 80. The usual landing is on the S.E. side, or with S.W. winds on the beach of **Porth Solach** at the N. of the island. It is difficult to land in bad weather anywhere. **Porth Mewdwy,** on the W. side of Aberdaron Bay, is the usual place of departure from the mainland.

Bardsey Island Lighthouse.—From a square tower, 99ft. high, painted in white and red bands, standing on the low land at the S.W. end of the island, **a white occulting light** is shown at an elevation of 129ft. above high-water; visible seventeen miles. It is bright for 27sec. and eclipsed for 3sec. The **light** is **hidden** by the **high land** on the **N.E.** side, and also in **Carnarvon Bay** when bearing **W. of S.W.**

Fog-signal.—A siren gives three blasts in quick succession every 5min. The first note high, the second low, the third high.

Bearings and distances from Bardsey Island Light.—Tuskar Rock bears from Bardsey W. by S. southerly, distant sixty-one miles. The **Blackwater Light-ship,** W. $\frac{1}{4}$ N., forty-eight miles and a half. **S. Arklow Light-ship,** W. by N. $\frac{1}{4}$ N. northerly, forty-two miles. **The Codling Light-ship,** N.W. $\frac{1}{4}$ N. northerly, thirty-nine miles. **Bailey Light, Howth Head,** N.N.W. $\frac{3}{4}$ W., fifty-eight miles and a half. **St. John's Point, Dundrum Bay,** N. easterly, ninety-three miles and a half. **The Mull of Galloway,** N. by E. $\frac{1}{2}$ E. easterly, one hundred and thirteen miles. **The S. Stack, Holyhead,** N.N.E. $\frac{1}{2}$ E., thirty-three miles and a half. **Cardigan Light-ship,** S.W. $\frac{1}{2}$ S., twenty-one miles and three quarters. **Smalls Light,** S.W. $\frac{1}{2}$ **W., seventy miles.**

Bardsey is pretty free from outlying dangers. There are none outside for one-third of a mile. **Maen Bugail has been described. Maen Ian** lies a quarter of a mile off the W. side. It uncovers at half-tide. **Carreg Rona** is generally above water. It lies a quarter of a mile off the W. shore, half a mile N. **of** the lighthouse. There are heavy overfalls all round Bardsey, by reason of the rocky nature of the bottom, and various shoals, none of which have a least depth than three fathoms and a half.

Braich-y-Pwll is a bold headland, 500ft. high, steep-to, and forming the S.W. extremity of the Lleyn Peninsula and of Carnarvonshire. The coast turns sharply to the N.E. for twelve miles as far as Porth Dynlleyn, bold and steep-to nearly all the way. Tripod Bank has been mentioned; the least depth is five fathoms and a half. **Carreg Allan** has 10ft. least water on it, and lies two cables and a half off shore N. of Braich-y-Pwll two miles and a half, with two stack rocks inside against the cliff.

Maen Mellt, 20ft. above high-water, has a passage between it and the shore.

Carreg-y-Chad is 1400yds. W. of **Porth Dynlleyn Point** and a quarter of a mile off shore. It has only 4ft. on it at low-water. Between it and the shore is Carreg-y-Trai, a half-tide rock. **Yr Eifl Head** open of **Porth Dynlleyn Point** clears these dangers to seaward.

Porth Dynlleyn is an open bay, sheltered on its W. side by the point of the same name, which is 100ft. high, and projects seaward half a mile. Off the point E. is **Carreg-y-Chwislen**, which **dries** at the last quarter ebb. On it is a **beacon, surmounted by a mask and globe, painted red.** It is 400yds. off the point, with a passage between, but small rocks, dry at low-water, lie off the point. The bay dries out at low-water for some distance.

Tides.—It is high-water, full and change, at 8hr. 30min. local, or 8hr. 48min. Greenwich time. Springs rise 16ft. The set of the stream is westward for 9hrs. There are some heaps of stones thrown down, with an idea of affording shelter from N.E. winds; but they do not realise the notion.

East of Porth Dynlleyn is **Nevin Bay** and Pier. The coast now becomes lofty. **Yr Eifl**, called by the English The Rival Mountain, is 1880ft., and rises almost directly from the sea, **Yr Eifl Head** being a fine cliff of very bold outline. The mountain itself is conspicuous from more parts of Wales almost than any other, owing to its isolated position, standing, as it were, in the midst of the sea, for Tremadoc Bay is not more than six miles from it as the crow flies. From Carnarvon Bay

N 2

the mountain looks like three peaks, sharp and well defined, the middle one being the highest. S.W. of Yr Eifl Head is Carreg Llan, a perpendicular cliff, 488ft. high.

To **Trwyntal** Point the coast is free from outlying dangers, but E. of that headland there are boulders lying about over the low-water sands. Yr Eifl Head, kept open of Trwyntal Point, clears all dangers. Six miles beyond this latter point the bay sweeps round to the Carnarvon Bar Sands, with a low sandy shore, while the mountains recede towards the Snowdon range.

Just E. of Trwyntal Point is **Porth Trevor, or Gwydir,** a little tidal harbour with a pier, dry at low-water.

Rising in the sandy marsh land, two miles and a half S. of the entrance to the Menai Straits, is a hill 110ft. high. It is called Dinas Dinlle, an ancient stronghold, and W. by N. of it, at three-quarters of a mile from the sandy shore, is a patch of rocks and shingle, called **Arianrod.** It uncovers at low-water. It is half a mile N. of the mouth of the Afon Llifon stream. This is supposed to be the site of **Caer Arianrod.**

Carnarvon Bar is a very awkward place, and should be approached with the greatest caution. It lies three miles or more from the entrance to the **Menai Straits,** and the sands shift with almost every heavy gale from the W. The **buoys are** constantly **being altered,** and what **may be right to-day may be all wrong in a week's time.** For my own experiences I refer the reader to the remarks on the coast, &c., in the next chapter ; that will give him some idea of the place, and what may happen to others if they try to navigate this place as a total stranger without any local help. Local help is very necessary here.

The Fairway Buoy lies in about **seven fathoms and a half.** It is a **large black pillar buoy, with staff and globe.** When this is made out, steer for the next black buoy E. of it. Leave this on the port, keeping close to it. There are two more black buoys on the port, and two red buoys to be left to starboard. Then there is a **black and white chequered buoy,** which is left to port. The channel turns S.E. here, and then at the **black buoy** off the Mussel Bank turns E. again. Leave this buoy on the port, as also the beacon ; keeping near all the buoys is the safest plan, and so steer between **Belan Point** on the S. and **Aber Menai** on the N. As the points are neared the flood-tide sweeps with great velocity along the S.E. shore, and from the offing into the narrow entrance. On the ebb, the inclination of the tide is to set round Belan Point and on to the banks which lie a long way out from the S. side. In a calm, when going out with the tide only, at the first of the ebb, every effort must be made to keep nearer the Mussel Beacon than the S. side. It is better to go out under such circumstances when the banks are uncovering, so as to have a truer ebb stream. The streams of ebb and flood are very strong within the points, and for some distance outside.

Carnarvon Bar lies three miles outside the entrance points. The depths vary, but usually there are from 5ft. to 6ft. at low-water, and from 19ft. to 20ft. at high-water. Off the Mussel Bank there is four fathoms at low-water. Off Carnarvon there is the same depth.

Tides.—It is high-water, full and change, at Carnarvon Bar at 9hr. 0min. local, and 9hr. 17min. Greenwich time. Springs rise 15ft.; neaps, 11ft. The stream turns with high- and low-water by the shore. The ebb runs S.W., the flood N.E., the ebb running half an hour longer than the flood. At Carnarvon the tide is 27min. later.

Belan Point is low, with sand hills skirting the shore. Behind it is a large marsh, with an extensive flat, covered at high-water. On the point are some buildings—a castellated kind of villa, some sheds, and a flag-staff.

Aber Menai Point is also low. It is the end of a strip, or dover, of sand, nearly two miles long, enclosing a sandy flat covered at high-water. There is a white building and the ruins of the ferry-house on the point, which is the S.W. extreme of the Isle of Anglesea.

Llandwyn Island is connected with Anglesea at low-water. It is three-quarters of a mile long by 300yds. wide, and from 60ft. to 80ft. high, and is the best guide for the entrance of the Straits. There is a little cove on the S.E. side where temporary anchorage may be obtained for small craft, but the approach is somewhat hampered by rocks. The most dangerous lie S.S.W. ½ W., distant three cables, and S. ¼ E., five cables, from the light. There is only 2ft. to 3ft. on these. **A green nun buoy** is placed S.W. of them. A rock awash lies one cable and a half E.S.E. of the low tower. This is also marked by a **green nun buoy**. Another rock, dry 9ft. at low-water, lies close to the N.E. of the island. It is marked by a perch. To clear these dangers, Aberffraw Point, on the N. side of **Maldraeth** and Aberffraw Bays, of which **Llandwyn** forms the S. point, kept open E. of Holyhead Mount will lead W. of these rocks.

Lighthouse.—On the island are two towers, painted white. From the highest or **N.W.** tower, distinguished by a **flag-staff**, is **exhibited**, at a height of 50ft., a fixed **red light**, visible five miles between the bearings of S.E. ½ S. and N.E. ½ E.

Carnarvon Bay Light-vessel.—A **light-ship**, carrying a **small ball above the globe** at the masthead, is moored in thirty fathoms in a line with **Bardsey Island** and the **S. Stack,** distant thirty miles and a half and thirteen miles, respectively. **A red watch buoy** lies half a mile E. of the vessel. **She exhibits** at an elevation of 36ft. a **revolving light** every minute, showing **twice white and once red,** alternately, each phase continuing bright for 20sec.; visible ten miles. This light-vessel is to guard against the in-draught on the flood-tide.

Fog-signal.—A fog siren gives two blasts, low, high, in quick succession, every 2min.

The navigation of the Menai Straits will be described later. (See page 205.)

Maldraeth Bay is a sandy inlet, with a valley running nearly through the island to Red Wharf Bay. There is anchorage here with off-shore winds according to draught.

Ledges lie off **Aberffraw Point,** some of the ledges lying out to the distance of one mile and a half. Some rocks uncover, others are just below the water. A berth of two miles from the shore will clear the dangers. By keeping **Penrhos Point,** the extreme W. point of **Holyhead Island,** open **W. of Rhoscolyn Beacon** all danger will be **cleared to the W.**

Cymmeran Bay, Crigyll Bay, and **Porth Trecastell** all lie open to the W. and afford a precarious shelter. There are rocks and ledges encumbering all of them. The shallow gut, which makes Holyhead an island at high-water, opens out of the N. corner of Cymmeran Bay. There is only a passage for boats through to Holyhead at high-water.

Rhoscolyn Rocks lie S., distant three cables from the point; on them is a beacon, circular, and painted in **red and white rings. Rhoscolyn Head** is bold and steep-to. There is a tide race off it. A black **nun buoy** is placed E. of a rock lying S. of **Rhoscolyn Cove** at the N. side of Cymmeran Bay, where a landing can be managed when it would be impossible elsewhere.

Holyhead Island is six miles and a half long, with an average width of one mile and a half. The highest part is Pen Gyby, or Holyhead Mountain, 709ft. high, and a conspicuous sea-mark. Between Rhoscolyn Point and Penrhos Point is **Maenpiscar,** a rock which dries at the last quarter ebb. It is three-quarters of a mile off shore, with **Rhoscolyn Beacon** bearing S.S.E. ½ E., distant one mile and a half. **Penrhos Bay,** often called **Abraham's Bosom,** is a safe little shelter with off-shore winds when the tide is running strong round the S. Stack. The anchorage is good.

S. of Rhoscolyn the tides are mild, but from off that point and Penrhos the tide races are very strong and extend some distance out. Off the S. Stack they reach their greatest violence.

The S. Stack is connected with Holyhead by a suspension bridge. The rock is 140ft. high, and from a circular white stone tower, 91ft. high, is exhibited, at an elevation of 197ft. above high-water, **a white revolving light** every minute. The brilliancy is of short duration; **visible twenty miles.**

An occasional revolving white light is exhibited in thick or foggy weather from a lantern 65yds. W. of the lighthouse at an elevation of 90ft. above high-water. It is visible seaward between the bearings of N. and S.W. ⅓ W.

Fog-signal.—A bell is sounded once every 15sec.

The N. Stack lies on the N. of the bay between it and the S. stack one mile distant. The cliffs are precipitous. On the point within the N. stack there is a fog-signal station. A gun is fired every 10min., alternately, with an explosive report. The intervals between the alternate reports are 5min.

Tidal Streams.—One mile W. of the S. stack the flood stream begins 1hr. before low-water at Liverpool, *i.e.*, a little before low-water at Holyhead, and sets E.N.E. for the Skerries. Inside of this line it sweeps round into Holyhead Bay. The velocity is from five to six knots. The ebb sets in the opposite direction. The race is very bad here, and off the Skerries, with gales against the tide. The worst part of the race is half a mile N. of the Stack Lighthouse. Off Holyhead Breakwater the stream runs E.S.E. from half-ebb to half-flood at a distance of half a mile N. of the pier. Close to it the stream sets W. from half-flood to low-water by the shore.

Tides at Holyhead.—It is high-water, full and change, at Holyhead Pier at 10hr. 11min. local, or 10hr. 30min. Greenwich time. Springs rise from 16ft. to 29ft. ; neaps, 12½ft.

E. of the N. Stack is the little cove of Porthnamarch, free from danger and out of the tide. Here vessels may wait a tide in fine weather. It is half-way between the N. Stack and the breakwater.

Behind the head the land falls steeply to the E. and is low. The quarries, whence the stone was taken to make the breakwater, lie on the E. side of Holyhead Mountain.

Bolivar Rock, with 9ft. least water, lies seven cables off South Porthwan Point, in **Church Bay,** on the E. side of Holyhead Bay, the breakwater being distant one mile and a half in a S.W. direction. A **black conical buoy,** lying in six fathoms, marks its S.W. side. **Langdon Ridge and Carmel Rocks,** lying N. of the Bolivar Rocks, have from seven fathoms to three fathoms and a quarter on them. There are overfalls over them in bad weather.

Holyhead Harbour.—The breakwater extends E. by N. for one mile and a third, forming a slight double curve, and rising from seven to eight fathoms of water.

The old harbour is formed by a pier projecting E.S.E. for 400yds. from the S. end of **Ynys Gyby,** with a wooden extension

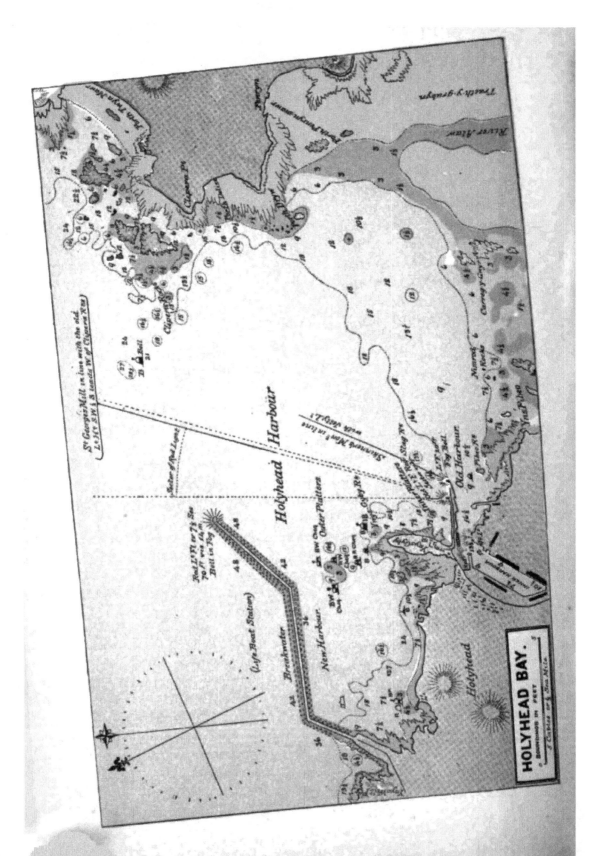

HOLYHEAD BAY.

for 170yds. in an E. ¼ S. direction. A **transverse** pier runs out for 250yds. in a N. direction from the S. shore opposite the stone pier. The space inside is kept for the Royal Mail Packets. The inner harbour is inside this, and also reserved for the London and North-Western Railway Company's steamers, where they have a yard and foundry for the repairs of their fleet.

The **Outer Platters** have only 3ft. on them at low-water, and lie three cables N. of Ynys Gyby. They are marked by a **black and white chequered buoy, with staff and ball, in five fathoms,** on their N. side, and a **black and white chequered buoy, with staff and square,** in four fathoms, on their W. side, marking the S. side of·the entrance to the refuge harbour.

A **red and white chequered buoy, in three fathoms,** marks the S.E. side of a 4ft. patch on the Outer Platters.

Skinner Rock has 9ft. **least water** on it. It lies **midway** between the **Outer Platters** and the **ledge, which dries at low-water,** extending **three-quarters of a cable** N. of Ynys Gyby, the **harbour island,** occupied by the railway station and buildings. A **black and·red chequered buoy, in two fathoms and a half,** marks its S. side.

Carreg Jordan, with 1ft. **least water,** lies N.E. by E. ⅓ E. for one cable from **Ynys Gyby,** and a **ledge, three-quarters of a cable,** dries to the N. of it.

A **black buoy** marks the N. end of this ledge, in **three fathoms,** and **another black buoy, in two fathoms and a half, lies 70yds. N.E. of Carreg Jordan.**

The **Inner Platters** lie N. of the old pier inner light, but are out of the track of shipping. They have 2ft. on them least water.

A **black bell buoy** lies, in six fathoms, three-quarters of a cable W. of a 16ft. patch off **Clipera** Rocks, and S.S.E. two cables from a 21ft. patch, the outer breakwater lighthouse bearing W. by N. ½ N., distant nearly a mile. ·The fairway to the harbour lies between. The **Pibeo Rocks** dry at low-water. They are S. of the entrance to the old harbour. A small black buoy marks their N. extreme, in 9ft.

Holyhead Lights.—On the outer end of the breakwater there is exhibited, from a white circular tower, 63ft. high, at an elevation of 70ft. above high-water, a **red flashing light,** at intervals of 7½sec., visible fourteen miles. The light appears fixed between the flashes within a distance of three or four miles.

Fog-signal.—A bell is sounded three times in quick succession every 15sec.

Old Harbour.—From a tower at the end of the wooden jetty a fixed **white** light is **shown,** and from the tower on the stone pier-head a fixed red light is shown, visible between S.W. ½ S. and S.S.W. ¼ W., to lead up the fairway between the breakwater and the bell buoy, and to clear the Outer Platters. It is difficult to find out this light unless one knows exactly where to look for it.

It is **not** advisable to enter the Old Harbour at night, because of the departure and arrival of the mail steamers.

CHAPTER XVII.

THE COAST BETWEEN ST. TUDWALL'S ROADS AND HOLYHEAD.

THE fame of St. Tudwall's Roads first reached me at Fowey, in Cornwall. Ever on the search for really practical hints for coasting I had gone on board a smart schooner lying in the tier, off Mixtowe.

I saw she hailed from Runcorn, and felt sure I should hear what shelter there was to be found in Cardigan Bay.

"Precious little," said the mate.

"If you be caught, you run for the refuge," remarked the skipper. "No vessel ever got ashore there."

Not knowing where "*the* refuge" was, I had to explain my difficulty.

"Why St. Tudwall's Roads, to be sure," growled the mate, pityingly.

When I first put in, after a long, slow drift from Barmouth, it was dark, and I thought the place looked pretty dreary, with its bare islands and the steep cliffs of Wylfa Head. There were no other vessels there.

Next morning it rained hard, and came on to blow from the W. I thought the place even more dreary, so, as I saw a steamer passing bound for Pwllheli, I weighed anchor and went up there. That was a little more lively. At least, there were shops within reach and a post-office. At Abersoch there

are these comforts, too, but it is a long row to get ashore from
the anchorage in the roads, and with a strong off-shore wind
a tidy little sea can get up for a small dingey. Pwllheli, therefore, is more convenient.

The wind blew hard for a week, fortunately off the land, but,
nevertheless, a heavy roll came in round the bay, and at last,
getting tired of the berth and the everlasting quarrying of the
Gimlet Rock, I went back to my first anchorage off Porth
Bach. There were now some thirty coasters anchored here,
and the place looked less lonely.

Next day there was a sign of the wind shifting. Then came
the usual click, click, all round ; sails were being set and
anchors were weighing. We stood out all together, half of us
through the sound, the rest outside Carreg-y-Trai, some twenty-
five sail of different rigs. It was a pretty sight, and must have
looked well from the shore. When Penkilan Head was rounded
then the wind headed us, and it was a case of short tacks to work
up to Pen-y-Kil Point. Gradually the old ship overhauled the
leading craft, until from being sixth we took the lead. A long leg
into Hell's Mouth and a short one out again ; another long leg
into Cadlan Bay and a short one to weather Ynys Gwylan ;
then another longer one, and we were up to the W. cliffs of
Aberdaron Bay and tumbling in the race which was running
round Pen-y-Kil. The coast is stern-looking and dark, but the
graceful outlines of the Rhos Hirwawn, or Rhiew Mountain, and
Carn Madryn, with Yr Eifl away to the E., give a character
to this Lleyn promontory, such as I know no other to possess.
It is far more picturesque than Cantyre or the Mull of
Galloway.

Aberdaron stands well at the head of its deep bay. Wales
must be a wonderfully healthy part of the world. Over in
those mountains behind Harlech a Welsh farmer died, in the
days of Lord Lyttleton, who was 105 years old. His youngest
descendant was eighty-one years younger than his eldest (?), and
800 people, his lineal descendants, attended his funeral. So says
Lord Lyttleton, although there does seem a little difficulty in swal-
lowing the details of the story. However Gaynor Fychan, of

Pen-y-Bont, a farm near Dinas Mawddwy, behind Cader Idris, lived to the age of 140, dying in 1686, and "Old Parr" was also a Welshman, and his age appears quite authentic. He was born in 1483, and shortened his days by too much dissipation at the age of 152, having previously been sentenced to do penance for a little love affair with Mistress Catherine Milton at the age of 105. At Aberdaron, lived Dick of Aberdaron, who had a remarkable talent for picking up foreign languages. How, living in this utterly out of the world village, in the very *ultima Thule* of Wales, he ever had a chance of hearing any other language than Cwmry is not easy to see.

The cliffs are fine at Pen-y-Kil. We all got well together as far as here, but the ebb met us and there was no getting through. I still had my "Bradshaw's map," but it did not mark the Carreg-du, and I did not know of the tide turning on the N. side before it turned in mid-stream; so as all the other craft were doing the same thing I stood across to Bardsey, but the tide swept me back and set me well to the S.S.W. At last, seeing I was doing no good, I tacked, and found, as I expected, I had lost a lot. When, therefore, I again reached Aberdaron Bay I made short tacks close to the cliffs, so close as almost to touch them before I went about, and made up my mind to see if there were not a channel between that rock and the cliffs. It was ticklish work as the rock was steep-to, and there might be heads, or even a ledge, joining it to the cliffs. I told the boy to stand in the bows and sing out if he saw any indication of rocks ahead, and tacked boldly inside the rock, going about exactly between it and the overhanging cliff. Fortunately the manœuvre was justified. There was plenty of water, and a strong tide took me along the N. shore.

I was rewarded, too, by having a beautiful view of the splendid rock and cliff scenery. There are several little coves of very romantic beauty, with grassy ledges coming down to the water's edge. In one of these, the one E. of Braich-y-Pwll, is Ffynnon Fair and Eglwys Fair, Our Lady's Well and Chapel, but little remains of the latter, and the fountain is only to be reached at low water.

Bardsey Island is attractive chiefly by reason of the difficulty of getting there. Why Dubricius, Archbishop of Caerleon, should have resigned his See in favour of St. David is not clear, but it is still more difficult to understand why he chose this very inaccessible island for his retreat, unless the inaccessibility was the attraction. He died here in A.D. 522. At one time, if we are to believe Lord Newborough's monument on the island, the little place was pretty crowded. "*In hoc loco requiescant in pace*" is the inscription on one side. On the other the legend says, "Respect the remains of 20,000 saints buried near this spot." Then the noble lord breaks into poetry, and exclaims ecstatically, "Safe in this island where each saint would be, How wilt thou smile upon life's stormy sea?" And so we leave the saints who are there—20,000 of them—all smiling. Surely there would be room for no more. There would be an unseemly riot if any others crowded in.

There is very little left of the ancient abbey of Bardsey or Ynys Enlli.

By my enterprising experiment of seeing if there were a passage between Carreg-du and the cliffs, I got through Bardsey Sound and around Braich-y-Pwll hours before the fleet of coasters, and had daylight with me nearly as far as the Carnarvon Light-ship.

The coast is strikingly beautiful as Nevin is approached. The Rock of the Leap and Vortigerns Valley are fine bits of scenery, with Yr Eifl towering above. A very large skeleton was dug out of a barrow near here, called Bedd Gwrtheyrn, so the brother of the fair Rowena seems to be called by his countrymen, although at first sight one does not recognise the name ; but it is no worse than some of Mr. Freeman's spelling.

High up in the peaks of Yr Eifl lie the remains of fortifications of a very early period in history. The place is called Tre'r Ceiri, and it is the most important prehistoric ruin in Wales. The town was encircled by a wall, some of which still stands to the height of 15ft., the base being 16ft. thick. The dwellings are said to have been circular, with a diameter of 16ft. The local name for the place is Giant City.

Beyond Gwydir, or Porth Trevor, is Clynnog, with an old church, wherein are preserved St. Beuno's chest and an instrument for dragging dogs out of church. They call them " lazy tongs "—why, is not clear.

There is a fine cromlech on the shore.

What with the drowned city of Arianrod, Dinas Dinlle, and Tre'r Ceiri, not to speak of Segontium, near Carnarvon, there is plenty about here to interest an antiquarian apart from the beauty of the scenery.

Passing the shifty bar of Carnarvon, with the two low points of sand through which the Menai Straits are entered, and where from the distance of three miles it looks as if there were no possible opening, Llandwyn Island catches the eye, with its two white towers against the low gray and yellow shore. This is the first example met in this cruise of the taste the early Christian Briton showed for building his parish church in the most inaccessible place he could find. Whether this arose from a desire to have an excuse always handy for being remiss in his weekly attendance is not quite clear—one can only conjecture. Whatever the reason may be the fact remains. There was a church on Llandwyn. Near Aberffraw there is one still at Llangwyffan, on an islet in the bay, connected by a causeway which is covered sometimes by the tide, so that there is no service at that time. There is another celebrated little church in the Menai Straits, at Llanfairpwllgyngyllgogerch—but there ! this is not the place for this atrocity in Welsh names. I will reserve it in its entirety for the time when it must be tackled.

Inland about two miles is Bodorgan Station, a name reminding one of Cornwall and Bodrigan's Leap, near the Dodman Head, as Pentreath, at the E. end of Maldreath Morfa, does of Paul Church, near Penzance. Near here is Llangadwaladr Church, where there is an inscribed stone, of the seventh century. All this part of Anglesea is historically interesting. Here lived the Princes of Aberffraw and Lords of Snowdon. It was certainly much less fatiguing to dwell in this flat country, flatter than Essex even, than to live up in those gloomy peaks, which, when they do happen to have no clouds on them, are very fine to look at.

As one sails along this rocky coast the view of the Snowdon range is very fine, if somewhat distant.

Near Rhoscolyn Head is a natural arch in the rocks. It rejoices in the name of the Arch of Caligula.

Before rounding Penrhos Point, I think a description of my own difficulties in Carnarvon Bar may be of use. Not having any chart or sailing directions of the coast when first I came up from the S., I thought the place looked too risky from the distance ; besides it was growing dark and the wind was strong on shore. I prudently left it alone and went on to Holyhead.

Afterwards, when I had obtained the latest corrected large-scale chart (up to January 1894), I felt bold enough to tackle the shoals without any help, especially as I had just come through the Swellies with no other assistance than a gale of wind and my own judgment. I left Carnarvon at 6 a.m. ; the tide was just turning. There was scarcely a breath of wind, and the old tub drifted slowly down past the low shore, and kept with difficulty between the buoys. Off **Forrhyd Bay,** where the flat all uncovers at half-tide, the in-draught set us well inside the bight, and I feared there was an eddy which would take us up the shallow mere. As we approached Belon Point the tide seized us, and we went swirling out like a straw in a mill race. There was not a breath of air, the dingey was stowed on deck, and I had no sweeps or crutch for an oar at the taffrail wherewith to keep her head on her course.

However, as the chart showed all clear between the points, and with no bank outside until well round Belon Point, I did not trouble ; only it seemed we should be some time before we saw Kingstown Harbour, if it went on like this all day.

There was another boat going out. They were natives on board, and were close to us, so I thought I had plenty of water.

The tide was sluicing out, and I saw we were being swept round to the S.W. of the point. However, I sat still. There was nothing to be done except anchor, and there seemed no reason for that. Our neighbours had begun to row, and kept away for the Mussel Bank. I tried to do the same, but there was not a breath of wind, and she would not answer her helm a bit.

Still there seemed plenty of water, and the chart showed no bank at that distance off the shore, so I sat still and let her drift. Suddenly I saw ahead an ominous tide ripple. I jumped up and bid the boy let go the anchor, but before he could obey there was a shiver, a scraping sound. The waters "stood in a heap" on each side of me and sluiced round the stern, and there we were, fixed. How the tide did run past us. Almost before I had got the sail down and made things snug for listing the best way, the water seemed to have left us high and dry. We were on a little knoll of sand, with deep water between us and the shore, and the channel just outside of us, with the Mussel Beacon bearing about N. by E., distant, perhaps, six cables. If only those men had told me of the danger I could have anchored easily, and given the boat a sheer, or even have remained at anchor until a breeze sprang up ; but they only chuckled at the plight of a fool who would go out over Carnarvon Bar without a pilot, and with no wind.

I deserved my fate no doubt.

The tide had fallen about 2ft. when we touched. By the time all was ship-shape and ready for a bad list I found we should lie very well. The force of the tide had scooped away the sand on the starboard and piled it up under the port bilge. The vessel's stem and stern were quite clear, with a pool at each end quite 3ft. deep. She lay like Noah's Ark on Mount Ararat.

Then, as if to add to my mortification, no sooner were we well planted than up sprang the most delicious little breeze possible, and boat after boat came spinning out from Carnarvon, and went foaming through the narrows to catch the sportive mackerel in the bay outside.

So there we lay, all that day, on the sand in the Bay of Carnarvon, oh !

One thing, however, came of this mishap. I was able to give the old ship such a scrubbing and scouring with the beautiful clean sand that her copper shone as it had never done before, and I was able to see all the iniquity of Carnarvon

O

Bar uncovered before me.   I saw that the channel was quite
otherwise than where it was marked on the chart.   Indeed, the
chart said so, and had quite plaintively requested me to pay
no attention to it.   I didn't ; but still I got on a sand bank.
The fact is, I don't see how any chart can be of any use for
such a place.   There were many more buoys, too, than were
marked in the chart.   However, I don't blame the chart at all,
and I hope no one will blame me if they get ashore here.
One thing I saw very clearly that I had acted with much
discretion in not attempting to come in from the W., and I was
very thankful that I got ashore where I did.   Had it been
farther out serious consequences might have ensued ; as it was
the banks prevented any sea, and luckily the day was fine.   At
6.30 p.m. I got off as easily as I went on, and made tracks for
Kingstown, where I arrived next morning, none the worse ;
indeed, all the better for the scouring on the sand.   One little
incident happened while I was on the bank, which caused me
to take a kindlier view of human nature than the conduct of
the two men in the boat had inclined me to adopt.

When I was well planted for the day, a small boat with two
watermen passed by, and the men shouted to know if I wanted
any help.   Naturally I did not, for what help could anyone give
until tide time !   It was like offering to launch Noah and his
ark after they were stranded on that Armenian mountain.   In
the afternoon, when I was walking on the shore among the
sand hills at Belan Point, I saw another boat come down and
have a look at us ; but I paid no attention, thinking it was
some more " pilots."   However, as the two people in her
began to gesticulate violently, and I had nothing to do, I
rowed off to see what it was they wanted.   When I got
alongside I found the worthy skipper and his wife had come
all that way out of their course to bring me a lot of mackerel
they had caught.   There was no refusing.   They insisted on
my taking a dozen fine fish, and their kindness was all the
more touching from the way it was done.   They would hardly
listen to a word of thanks, and, having satisfied their natural
craving to do unto others as they would be done by, this

excellent couple let the main-sheet run, and bore up for the Straits before the fresh breeze and rushing tide.

I don't know who they were. I never saw them before, nor have I seen them since; but I know that their unostentatious kindness did me a great deal of good, and I sincerely trust made them all the happier, too.

So much for the dangers of Carnarvon Bar. The S. Stack is a grim-looking rock. The white buildings look astonishingly vivid against the dark precipices and rugged slopes of Holy-head Mountain. The sea is bad off here. I know I found steering before a strong W. wind was a very serious business indeed in the dark, when first I came round this point. The worst of making places like this for the first time in the dark is that you cannot tell how far to keep off from the lighthouse. It is so difficult in a heavy, breaking sea, and with a lee shore, to judge one's distance so as to profit by choosing the best of the water. It was a gybe, too, round the N. Stack, and I was very thankful when smooth water opened before us as we ran round the breakwater. Even then our difficulties were not over, for I steered for the old harbour, not knowing the rule that sailing vessels were not admitted at the times of the departures and arrivals of the mail steamers. All was quite strange to me, and the night very dark. It is bad enough when you know a place beating up in a dark night, but it is really very anxious work when you have never seen the place before, and cannot directly tell what the various lights are in a crowded harbour, with shore lights behind to confuse everything.

Having, with much care, at last worked in between the piers of the old harbour I was hailed by a man from the shore, who said I should have to go out again as the mail steamer was expected. This was annoying; all the more so that I very much doubted if there was room to turn right round and go out before the wind. However, the old boat did it, and then I had to grope my way between the ledges and the Platters, and so work up to an anchorage in the outer harbour. I marvel now at my luck, and how I managed to pass between Ynys Gyby Reef and the Outer Platters S. buoy; but somehow

I escaped damage, and picked up a very comfortable berth off the Trinity wharf.

It was lucky I got there when I did for it blew very hard afterwards, and although I had all fifty fathoms of chain out it was as much as it would do to hold the old tub, and for two days we could not row ashore for the wind and sea. The dingey, however, was small.

I cannot say I like Holyhead. The town is a poor one. The church of St. Cybi, or Gyby, has nothing much to interest even an antiquarian. The breakwater is a fine work, and there is the guardship. That is all. The snuggest berth to lie is as far in as one can get past the Trinity establishment. A little cove, with rocks at its entrance, marked by beacons, lies round the corner in the S.W. end of the refuge harbour. There is not much water here, but it is a very well-sheltered little nook when you get there ; it is not easy, however, always to get in or out of it.

CHAPTER XVIII.

THE ISLE OF ANGLESEA—HOLYHEAD TO CARNARVON AND THE MENAI STRAITS.

Bearings and distances from the S. Stack Lighthouse, Holy-head Isle.—From the S. Stack Light the Kish Light-vessel bears W.N.W. westerly, distant forty-four miles. The Tuskar Light, S.W. by W. ¼ W., eighty-six miles. The Smalls, S.W. ½ S., one hundred and two miles. S. Bishop Light, S.W. ¾ S., ninety-one miles and a half. Bardsey Island Light, S.S.W. ¼ W., thirty-four miles and a half. Skerries Light, N.E., seven miles and a half. Chicken Rock, Isle of Man, N. by E. easterly, forty-four miles. S. Rock Light-ship, N., seventy miles and a half. St. John's Point, Dundrum Bay, N. by W., sixty-four miles and a half.

The **Skerries** are a group of seven rocky islets, with outlying rocks one mile and three quarters N. by W. of **Carmel Head.** They lie in an E.N.E. and W.S.W. direction, and are only separated from each other at high-water.

The Skerries Light.—On the highest island, from a circular white tower with a horizontal red band, 75ft. high, an inter-mittent white light is shown at an elevation of 117ft. above high-water. The light shows bright for 50sec., eclipsed 2sec.; light 2sec., eclipsed 2sec.; light 2sec., eclipsed 2sec. It is obscured between N. 24deg. W. and N. 45deg. W. covering the E. Platters, but the reflection of the light is still seen. Visible sixteen miles.

In a dwelling-house, 67ft. above high-water, a fixed red light is shown, visible between the bearings of N. 87deg. W. and S. 70deg. W., over the **Ethel and Coal Rocks.** Visible thirteen miles.

Fog-signal.—A fog siren gives three blasts, high, low, high, in quick succession, every 3min.

There are **many dangers** round **this part of Anglesea.** The **African Rock** has 15ft. least water on it, lying one cable and three quarters N. of the **Skerries.** There is usually an overfall over it.

The **West Platters** lie half a cable S. of the westernmost islet, and one rock dries at low-water. The other has 3ft. on it.

The E. Platters dry at low-water, and lie between the Skerries and Carmel Head, the Skerries Lighthouse bearing N.W. by N. half a mile away. Between these and Carmel Head there are many rocky patches, with **three fathoms and a half least water** on them, but the tidal streams cause heavy overfalls here even in quiet weather.

The **W. Mouse** is always above water, and is 20ft. high. On it is a **white** pyramidal beacon surmounted by a globe.

St. Vincent Rocks lie on the **N.W. end of the ridge, extending W. of the W. Mouse**; there is 11ft. least water on this. **Coal Rock** is a very dangerous rock, being awash at low-water. It is 20yds. across, and lies in line with the W. Mouse Beacon and two **Coal Beacons** on the land bearing S.W. $\frac{3}{4}$ S., distant from the Mouse one mile and a fifth. A **black conical buoy, with staff and globe,** lies in twelve fathoms, one cable and a half **N. by W.** of the rock.

Ethel Rock has a **least depth** of three fathoms. It lies N.W. of **Coal Rock,** 1200yds. from it, the Skerries Light bearing W. by S. $\frac{1}{3}$ S.; distant two miles.

A black conical buoy, in eleven fathoms, lies N.N.W. of the rock 200yds. from it. The two Stacks in line, off Holyhead, lead N. of these dangers, and **Lynus Point** open of the land leads N. also.

Victoria Bank has only one fathom and a half on it. It lies between Coal Rock and the shore, A **black** conical buoy, in nine fathoms, lies close to its N.E. end. The passage within the Skerries is risky, owing to the strong tides setting on the rocks. By skirting the land closely the outer dangers are avoided. A fair tide is a necessity for sailing craft.

Tides.—Outside the Skerries the tide turns with high- and low-water at Liverpool, and runs at a speed of four knots and a half at springs. Within the Skerries the tide turns 1½hrs. earlier, running often at five to six knots at springs, and possibly more, causing heavy tide rips and overfalls.

Carmel Head is a rugged cliff, with Pengarn Hill, 550ft. high, two miles beyond it. On the E. point of Carmel Head are two white conical beacons, 30ft. high, in line with each other, and the Mouse Beacon marking the position of the Coal Rock. Henborth Bay lies E. of Carmel Head, with a rock in the middle of the bay, dry at low-water. Stag Rock, lying off the W. side of Camlyn Point, is steep-to and nearly always above water.

Camlyn Point is skirted with rocky ledges all along its N. side, and off its extremity is a ledge, dry at low-water, called Harry Furlong Reef. On it is a beacon, pyramidal, and painted in black and white rings, surmounted by a staff with a triangle.

Camlyn Point is low, and merely a narrow spit, with a flag-staff at the end. Camlyn Bay affords good anchorage with winds between W. and S.E. through S. Mill Bay on its E. side is foul for anchoring.

Next comes Wylfa Head, with Kemmaes Bay and Llanbadrig Point on its E. side; here also is good anchorage with off-shore winds. The shores are high and rocky. There is a village here and a pier, dry at low water. This bay is liable to sudden shifts of wind to the N., when a heavy sea comes in. 50yds. only from the edge of the cliff stands Llanbadrig Church. Off it lies the Middle Mouse Island. It is 23ft. high and bold all round. There is plenty of water in the sound between it and the land.

Half a mile E. of the Mouse is Llanliana Head, the most northerly point of Anglesea. It is steep-to, with a cove on its W. side between high rocks. The coast now bends S.E. to

Porth Gynfor, with Porth Wen a little farther on. From here to Bull Bay the coast is bold and rocky. There is good anchorage in Bull Bay, with off-shore winds.

Off the E. point of the bay is the E. Mouse, 12ft. high, 30yds. long. It is steep-to, with a navigable sound between it and the land. It is better in going through to keep to the islet side.

S.E. of Bull Bay is Almwch Bay and Harbour. The harbour is tidal, with its tidal basin protected by booms during N.E. gales. It is used by coasters for shipping the copper from the mines in Parys Mountain. A light is shown when the harbour is open; it is fixed, white. A red light is shown when the harbour is not available.

Tides.—It is high-water, full and change, at 10hr. 30min. local, or 10hr. 47min. Greenwich time. Springs rise 18ft.; neaps, 13ft.

Off the W. side of the bay is a rock with 9ft. least water on it. Two beacons near Mona Mill, on the W. side of the bay, and two other beacons on the S. side, indicate its position.

Almwch Bay affords shelter with off-shore winds, even without entering the tidal harbour.

Lynus Bank lies half a mile off the shore, with a least depth of six fathoms, but there are overfalls over it at times.

Lynus Point is an important headland, as it juts out so far, and is easily seen from E. and W. On it is a lighthouse, and on the hill behind a disused telegraph station.

Lynus Lighthouse is a white castellated building, 36ft. high. From it is exhibited, at an elevation of 128ft. above high-water, an occulting white light, bright for 8sec., obscured 2sec.; visible sixteen miles. The light is hidden inshore of the bearing of S.E. ¼ E. so as to lead N. of all dangers between it and the Skerries, and also inshore of N.N.W. so as to lead E. of Dulas Rock.

Tides.—The tide turns at high- and low-water by the shore, i.e., half an hour before it turns at Liverpool. In the offing it runs at five knots, and there is a considerable race off the point.

In Lynus Cove there is anchorage on the W. side of the head.

The coast now bends round more to the S. to Dulas Bay. Dulas Rocks are only uncovered in their centre at high-water. A beacon, with staff and vane, is erected on it, 31ft. high. The rocks extend one cable seaward of this, and are four cables long, in a N. and S. direction. There are two fathoms least water between them and the shore. Lynus Lighthouse, kept well clear of the land, leads outside, and the lighthouse over Porth Heligon Point leads inside, of them.

Traeth Dulas is a deep sandy inlet, dry long before low-water.

Moelfre Island lies to the N. of Moelfre Roads. The *Royal Charter* was wrecked here, with the loss of 450 lives.

The roadstead is well sheltered with winds from **N.N.W. to S.S.W.**

Red Wharf Bay looks on the map like a splendid shelter. It is bordered by sands, which dry out a long way, and very heavy gusts come through the low land from Maldraeth Bay, on the W. side of the island. **Table Road,** to the E., is better for anchoring as the land is higher, but the tidal streams run at three knots an hour.

Dinmor Bank, with 11ft. least water, lies off from Menai Lighthouse nearly half a mile in a N.W. by. N. direction. A red can buoy marks the S. side of a narrow swashway, with three fathoms and a half.

Ten Feet Bank is E. of Table Road, N. of Puffin Island. There is 9ft. least water on it. A spherical buoy, with black and white bands, lies, in three fathoms and a half, a quarter of a mile W.N.W. of the 9ft. patch.

Bearings and distances from Lynus Lighthouse. — Great Orme's Head bears from Lynus Light S.E. ⅓ E., distant fifteen miles and a half. Chester Bar, E.S.E., twenty-nine miles and a half. N.W. Light-ship, Liverpool, E. ¾ S., twenty-three miles. Walney Light, E.N.E. northerly, fifty-four miles and a half. St. Bee's Head, N.E. ½ N. northerly, seventy miles. Bahama Light-ship, N.N.E., fifty-five miles. Douglas Head, N. by E., forty-four miles. Chicken Rock, N.W. by N. ¼ N., forty-two miles. Carlingford Light N.W. ¼ N. northerly, seventy-three miles.

The sound between Puffin Island and Anglesea is well marked, and there is 15ft. in the channel at low-water.

At the E. point of Anglesea, called **Trwyn Du**, is a **light-house** joined to the island by an **iron bridge**, covered at **high-water**. The tower is circular, and painted in black and white horizontal bands. It is **61ft.** high, and from it, at an **elevation of 96ft.** above high-water, a **fixed red light** is shown, visible twelve miles, except where it is hidden by Puffin Island.

There is a rock on the **seaward side, 30yds.** distant, **with less than 6ft. on it.**

A **fog-bell** is **sounded three times in quick succession every 15sec.,** in thick weather.

Puffin Island, or **Priestholm,** is 800yds. from Trwyn Du. It is about half a mile long by 300yds. wide. On the central part of the island is an ancient tower, and at its N.E. end is a white building, formerly a telegraph station, but is used occasionally by a Natural History Society, of Bangor. The buildings look dilapidated and unused. The island is mostly steep-to, except off its S.W. extremity. Here a ledge of rocks runs out in a curving direction towards the S.S.W. for a quarter of a mile. The landing-place is on a shingle beach within this ledge, on the S. side.

On the **angle** of this ledge, **where it turns more to the S.S.E.,** is a large stone **beacon,** painted in **black and white bands, with a staff and globe on the top.**

Beyond this beacon the ledge continues S.S.E. for a quarter of a mile farther, drying in parts 2ft. above low-water, with 6ft. close to it. At its S. extremity is a **red conical buoy,** with staff and globe. Beyond this buoy there is a spit extending to the S. for one cable, with only 4ft. on it. The channel on the S.E. side of Puffin is less used than the sound. The depth at low-water is said to be only 9ft., and the proximity of the **Dutch-man** and **Irishman Spits,** which dry at low-water, on the S. side, and the **Puffin Island Causeway** on the N. side, together with the strong tides, render the passage difficult, except for small craft. However, I always used it freely myself, although I was a perfect stranger, and never had the least difficulty in all weathers.

The Menai Straits are a deceptive resort. At high-water there seems a fine stretch of water between Anglesea and the mountains on the mainland; but all this tract dries out with channels here and there, leaving only a passage, more like a river than an arm of the sea, near the Anglesea shore. The channel is buoyed : black on the port side entering; red on the starboard as far as Carnarvon, from both ends, i.e., from the W. the buoys are black on the N. side as far as Carnarvon; from the E. they are red.

The Dutchman Sand and Irishman Spit, the most dangerous N.E. extreme of the Lavan Sands, leave a channel only two cables wide between them and Puffin Island. A black buoy marks the N.E. end of these dangers, beyond which there is from eight to ten fathoms.

Penmon Bay lies W. of Trwyn Du Point; the bay dries out. There is a pier here and a limestone quarry. Carreg Duon is full of boulders, some as much as 5ft. above the sand. A red buoy marks the extreme of these dangers. The channel here between the Lavan Sands is about one-third of a mile.

Trecastell Point is the S.W. side of Carreg Duon, and beyond it is Friars Bay. The foreshore dries out a long way, but there is good anchorage here, and if able to anchor close in the tide is not felt so strongly. The channel now turns more southerly to round Beaumaris Point, off which a ledge juts out some distance. A red buoy marks its southern limit.

The Lavan Sands are here very close, and the channel turns suddenly round this buoy to Beaumaris Green, leaving a deep pool on the S. side in the Lavan Sands opposite Beaumaris Point, where is a favourite anchorage for coasters, as the ebb-tide is not felt much, although there is a good stream on the flood.

The anchorage off Beaumaris is very restricted, and I would always prefer to anchor in Friars Roads, unless a good berth

can be picked up. All the berths on the **E. side** are occupied
with moorings. The best places are W. of the pier, as near
in with the pier-head as the draught of the vessel will allow,
which will probably be very little, as there is only 6ft. or 7ft. at
low-water in the bay between the **pier-head** and **Gallows Point.**

The channel is very narrow off **Beaumaris,** but it is well
buoyed. On no account should the line of the buoys be crossed
except at high-water, and then with **much caution.**

Beaumaris Light is a **fixed red light** on the pier-head.

At **Gallows Point** the **tides meet,** and here is the narrowest
part of the Menai Straits, being barely 180yds. across at low-
water. A **red buoy** marks the **S. extreme** of this danger.
Beyond this, as far as the ferry at **Garth,** the Anglesea shore
is fairly steep-to, but the sand lies a long way out from the
Carnarvonshire shore. It is marked by black buoys, but they are
rather few and far between, and there is a danger of a stranger
not noticing the two that are there, owing to their being hidden
by coasting craft at anchor.

Just E. of the **Glyn-y-Garth** Ferry, opposite Bangor, is said to
be the best anchorage in the Menai Straits. I cannot say I agree
at all with this opinion. No doubt the holding ground is good ;
but the tides are so violent that a vessel, even when moored, sheers
about in all directions, to the almost certainty of tripping her
anchor or fouling some other craft, for they do not all sheer
the same way at the same time, and when a vessel has taken up
a berth, allowing quite enough room for swinging in all ordinary
anchorages, the skipper discovers to his disgust that he is going
on a rapid voyage of destruction to meet a vessel which is coming
at five miles an hour, stern first, to ram him, while a third
craft is probably charging him furiously broadside on.

No, the only comfortable anchorages in the **Menai Straits**
are between **Carnarvon** and **Pwllfanog.** Dinorwic I consider the
safest, or as near **Plas Newydd,** on the Anglesea shore, as can
be obtained ; but in the bay W. of **Dinorwic Quay** is the best.

The worst of it is that nowhere can one escape the tidal
stream or the traffic. They are both felt least at **Dinorwic,** if
anchored as close in to the Carnarvonshore shore as possible.

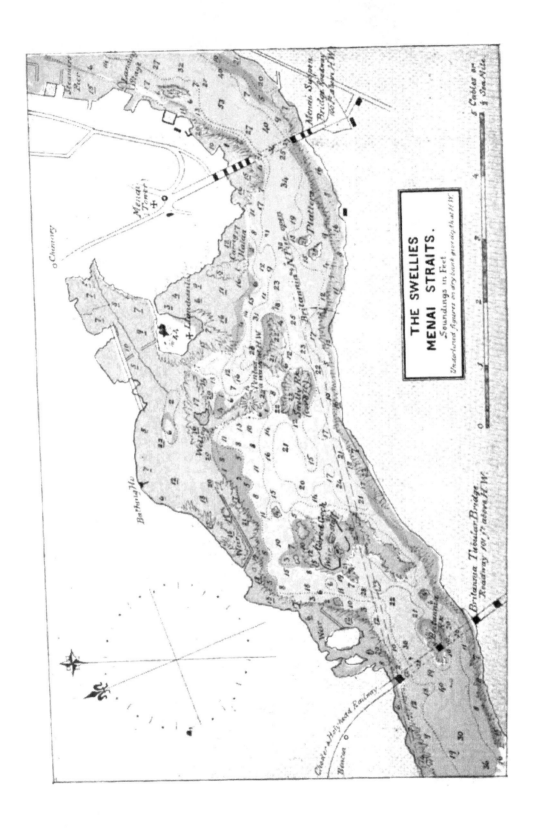

THE SWELLIES
MENAI STRAITS.

Soundings in Feet.

Underlined figures in dry bank give depth at L.W.

From **Glyn-y-Garth** to the Victoria Bridge the Anglesea shore is foul with rocks, and islands lie all along from a mile W. of the Ferry and Menai. On the Bangor side all is mud. The whole shore dries out from opposite Gallows Point right down to about a mile N.E. of the Victoria Bridge ; then it becomes fairly steep-to.

The navigation between the Victoria Bridge and the Tubular Bridge is very dangerous ; in fact, I don't know of any worse. Three pilots are required for the Menai Straits—one for the W. end, one for the E., and one for this particular part. It is called the **Swellies.** I went through the whole Straits without any pilot, and without ever having been there before ; but I confess it was a very risky thing to do. The distance between the bridges is about four-fifths of a mile. The whole space is encumbered with rocks, through which the tide swirls and sluices in a most alarming way, creating whirlpools and eddies which seem different at every quarter of an hour, and going in all manner of directions. At spring tides I was solemnly assured that the stream was **fifteen knots !** The standard authority says from seven to eight knots.

The two most dangerous rocks in the passage are the **Platters** and **Swelly Rocks,** the former lying off the S. shore and uncovering 2ft. at low-water, and the latter nearly in mid-channel and one-sixth of a mile E. of **Gored Goch Island,** on which are houses and a flag-staff. The Swelly Rock uncovers 14ft. The main channel is S. of this.

There are no beacons, or booms, or anything to show where these dangers lie. However, when the **Swelly Rock is covered there is 12ft. over the Platters,** and when the latter are visible all dangers are seen.

Gored Goch Island, at the **W.** end of the dangers, **divides the channel,** that on the N. side being used with head winds. **Cribbin Goch** is a rock off the N. side of Gored Goch. There is a narrow channel between, with only 2ft. of water at low-tide. The sea sluices through here at a violent rate. S. of **Cribbin Goch** is the main channel, 35yds. wide, with 9ft. of water. Then comes the **Swelly Rock,** with **about 8ft. of water** over it at high-water springs, and full in the strength of the tide. To clear it, **Nelson's Statue on the N. shore W. of the Tubular Bridge,** shut in with the N. pier of the bridge, will lead S. of the **Swelly.**

The **Platters** lie off the S. shore, nearly half-way between the Victoria Bridge and the **Swelly Rock.** They dry 2ft. at low-water. **To clear them** keep the Carnarvonshire shore just open of the N. pier of the **Tubular Bridge.** This leads N., and then shut in the Nelson Monument with this N. pier and steer to pass **S.** of the **Britannia Rock,** on which **stands the centre pier of the** bridge.

On the N. side of the channel is **Penlas Islet,** with a channel 40yds. wide between it and the Swelly Rock, and N. of that is **Weltog Islet,** joined to Anglesea at low-water. E. of Weltog Islet is Llandisilio Island, on which stands the little church. **Carreg Hanlan** lies S. of this, and is covered 2ft. at high-water springs, therefore it is dangerous at that time of tide. It dries 21ft. at low-water. Between it and the **Platters** is the channel, 200yds. wide.

In going through the Victoria Bridge it is better to keep the Carnarvonshire side of the channel, paying attention to the **Platters** when abreast of **Carreg Hanlan.** If that should be covered there will then be 19ft. over the Platters and 7ft. over the **Swelly Rock,** and the tide will be nearly high.

If going through, obviously the best time to run the Swellies is at slack water, provided there is a breeze. There are plenty of pilots on the look-out, and the charge is from five shillings upwards. It is usual to take one at **Garth Ferry** or **Pwllfanog.**

From the Tubular Bridge to **Dinorwic** all is plain sailing. The shore is fairly steep-to, except between Pwllfanog and Nelson's Monument, on the Anglesea side. On the S. side, **Carreg Guinog** lies one mile S.W. of the Tubular Bridge and 200yds. off the **Carnarvonshire** shore. Nelson's Monument, in line with a beacon on the railway embankment above, a quarter of a mile W. of the bridge, leads to the N. of it. After passing **Plas Newydd** a sandy spit runs out W. of the ferry at Moel-y-Don, and the sand bank dries for some distance W. of it, opposite Dinorwic.

At Port Dinorwic there is a tidal harbour, and a great deal of traffic is carried on in shipping slates from the quarries of Llanberis.

From here to Carnarvon is three miles and a half. Sands lie out a long way off the Anglesea shore from half-way between Moel-y-Don Ferry and Tal-y-Foel Ferry opposite Carnarvon. The channel is buoyed, however, and should not be deviated from except at high-water. A sand bank lies off the S. shore, too, at Llanfair-is-Gaer, but the navigation is easy by paying attention to the buoys.

Carnarvon has a tidal harbour, the River Seiont serving the purpose. It dries quite out. The usual anchorage is off the town in the channel, or a little W. of the entrance to the Seiont River. The tides run strong.

Tides in the Menai Straits.—The flood stream enters between Belon and Aber Menai Points at about 3hr. 15min. local time, full and change. It is high-water at Carnarvon at 9hr. 27min. Springs rise, 15¾ft.; neaps, 12ft. At Dinorwic the rise is 18ft. at springs, the time being 1min. later, the velocity being three miles and a half at springs.

At Pwllfanog the tide is 5min. later and rises 19ft. For 6½hrs. the stream runs to the S.W. from ½hr. before low-water, and to the N.E. for 5½hrs. until ½hr. before high-water, at the rate of five to six knots at springs.

Between the bridges the stream runs for 6½hrs. to the S.W. from 1hr. before high-water at Menai, and to the N.E. for 5½hrs. from 1¾hrs. before low-water at Menai, the velocity being from seven to eight knots.

Between Glyn-y-Garth and Beaumaris the tides meet. At Beaumaris it is high-water, full and change, at 10hr. 28min. local time, or 10hr. 44min. Greenwich time. Springs rise 23ft.; neaps, 15½ft. The stream runs S.W. for 5¾hrs. from 2hrs. flood to 2hrs. ebb.

At Menai Lighthouse it is high-water, full and change, at 10hr. 13min. Springs rise 23ft.; neaps, 16ft. The stream sets into the Straits for 4¾hrs. from ½hr. after low-water to 1hr. before high-water, and out for 7¼hrs. N. of the lighthouse the flood sets E. at first through the N.E. entrance.

It is slack water between Carnarvon Bar and Menai Bridge
at the times of high- and low-water at Llandwyn.   The flood
stream enters the E. end about 3hrs. after it begins to enter
the Straits at the W. end.   For the last three-quarters of an
hour of the flood at Menai the tide is rising there while it is
falling at Pwllfanog, and the stream is then running S.W. at
its greatest strength; and *vice versâ* for the last three-quarters
of an hour of the ebb the water is rising at Pwllfanog whilst
it is falling at Menai.   Throughout all the distance from
Menai Bridge to Menai Lighthouse the stream of the last
quarter of the ebb runs N.E., and the last quarter of the flood
to the S.W.   During the rest of the tide they run *towards*
Gallows Point for the first three-quarters of the flood, and *from*
it for the first three-quarters of the ebb.

CHAPTER XIX.

OBJECTS OF INTEREST IN THE ISLE OF ANGLESEA AND THE MENAI STRAITS.

ANGLESEA, from the sea, does not look so inviting as Essex, from the Thames. It is nearly as flat and lacks the sun. Wales is a rainy part of the world, and certainly Anglesea has its share. Holyhead Island possesses the only bit of fine rock scenery which has any approach to a mountain, and, after all, the hill of St. Cyby is very little higher than than of St. Boniface, behind Ventnor, while Mount Parys, the other elevation, is a little higher than the Laindon Hills, behind Tilbury.

It is a very nasty bit of sailing between the Skerries and the W. Mouse. After passing the black conical buoy, marking the Bolivar Shoal, it is mostly a rough and tumble for the next few miles, with plenty of work for the rudder, and a careful eye on the sweep of the tide if intending to pass W. of the Coal and Ethel Rocks. With a fair tide and breeze, however, it is easy work slipping round **Carmel Head** and **Harry Furlong Beacon**. Llanbadrig Church is another instance of the taste the ancient Celt showed for choosing his place of worship in as isolated a position as he could find. It looks as if they would hardly ever want to blow the bellows of their organ here. The organist must surely always have enough wind without. Parys Mountain, only some 484ft. high, is a mass of minerals—copper chiefly, and has been worked for

P

many years. It takes its name from Sir Robert Parys, Chamber-
lain of North Wales in the days of Henry IV. There is a
romance told about a miner of the Parys Mine which reminds
one of Sir Roger. The Jacobite Lord Lovat was beheaded for
taking part in the rising of 1745, and the story goes that his
heir fled here in disguise and worked as a miner. He married
and had one son, from whom all the claimants to the Lovat
estates are descended. Hitherto fortune has not smiled upon
their claims.

Between Amlwch and the entrance to the Menai Straits there
is very little to interest anyone. Sandy bays alternate with low
cliffs.

Moelfre Island is a melancholy spot; even now a vessel
is engaged getting up remains of the wreck of the *Royal
Charter*. The country between Red Wharfe Bay and Trwyn Du
Point is the cradle of the Tudors, at least of the latter line,
from whom Henry VII. was descended, and therefore our
present Queen. At Plas Penmynydd, about four miles inland
from Red Wharf Bay, is where Owen Tudor was born, and at
Henllys, one mile from Beaumaris, they still show his bed-
stead. The Tudor family owed their good fortune entirely to
their good looks and fortunate marriages. It was a wonderful
rise in the world for this simple Welsh squire when he married
the widow of the greatest of Lancastrian kings, as well as the
most consummate general and statesman of his age. Catherine
of France must have caused no little scandal when she
accepted the good-looking captain of the guard, although,
doubtless, Margaret of Anjou and her minion Suffolk were
not sorry to see the Dowager Queen so thoroughly efface
herself.

Right gallantly the Welsh gentleman fought for his kingly
step-son, the sainted Harry of Windsor, and Tudor blood was
freely shed in the Wars of the Roses.

The fortunes of the family, so well laid by this Anglesea
squire, were cemented by the marriage of his grandson with
the White Rose of York; and Queen Victoria, by way of doing
honour to her ancestors, sent £50 to help restore the Tudor

chapel adjoining Penmynydd Church, wherein reposes, under a well-wrought tomb, an unknown member of that house.

From Lynus Point Puffin Island has been staring at us in quite a fatiguing way. It is a bleak little spot, with its ancient peaked tower on the top, and its forlorn buildings with large bow windows looking N.E.

Whether Penmon Priory is the parent or offspring of the priestly establishment on Puffin Island is not known. The tower anyhow is very very old. I don't remember ever seeing a more grim relic of antiquity than this lonely old building on this desert island—for deserted it is nearly all the year. The second time I landed there I was surprised to find the house at the E. end occupied. Two scientific gentlemen from Bangor were just packing up after a week's stay. They kindly showed me their quarters. Luxury did not abound. Not even St. Seiriol the Bright could have housed more ascetically. Of the living I had no means of judging, it was all consumed. The cliffs are very abrupt all round, and the only inhabitants I saw were some black sheep, each with four large horns. Rabbits seemed to increase and multiply, and sea birds were not wanting.

The view from the top is very extensive. All the range of Snowdonia is spread before one—from Great Orme's Head to Garnedd Goch, nearly as far as Yr Eifl. The sands, too, of Beaumaris or Penmaenmawr Bay are well mapped out. The Dutchman is just below. Looking at it one recalls the story of the wreck of the *Rothesay Castle*, a packet which ran between the Straits and Liverpool. She missed the entrance, and went on the sands, with the loss of over 100 lives. Two men held on to the same plank, but as it would only support one there arose a contention, not as to who should hold on, but as to who should let go. The older man said his life was nearer ending, therefore he would let go. The younger man claimed to yield the *pas* because he was the younger. Then they both let go that each might let the other live. Strangely enough, both were saved. Miss Martineau tells the story, but she makes it longer than this.

P 2

Penmon Priory is only represented now by the refectory ruins and the church, which has been well restored. There is an old cross also, and a pigeon house. This ancient foundation is said to date as far back as the sixth century and to have been founded by Dubricius.

For a perfect stranger I do not know a much worse place to find one's way into on a dark night, and with a strong E. wind, than the Menai Straits. This is how I had to do it the first time I ever went there. I had come across from the Isle of Man and did not make Great Orme's Head before dark. After I had passed through the sound, and once Menai Light was hidden by Trwyn Du, there was nothing more to guide me. I could only just see the dark line of the Anglesea coast, but not a trace of the other side. The tide, too, was falling, and the wind nearly dead aft, with a considerable weight in it. It was ticklish work. Every now and then I could hear the sea breaking on the Lavan Sands, and then I drew nearer the dim darkness, which was Anglesea. The channel is very narrow, and I never saw a buoy at all until I nearly ran into the red one that lies in Friars Roads. Of course, I could not see it was red, nor did I in the least know how far I had gone in, but as the sea was getting quieter I judged I must have come some distance up. It was by that time about half-ebb, so I decided to anchor. When day broke I found I was in a good place, just E. of the red buoy off Beaumaris Point.

As I looked back by daylight and saw the place I had come through, I wondered. It was a piece of luck, certainly.

But surely they might put some leading lights up the Straits, at least, to guide one to Friars Roads. There is no light even on Beaumaris Point. In fact, nothing anywhere from one end of the Straits to the other, except pier or harbour lights.

Beaumaris is a quaint old place. The anchorage off it, too, is not bad, if only one can find a vacant berth near enough to the town to be out of the full force of the tide. It is very necessary to moor here, and have a good solid kedge down, too. It can blow very hard from both S.E., E., and W., and although there is no sea to hurt much, the tides against the wind make a nasty trouble. However, for the Menai Straits it is fair.

Beaumaris Castle is well worth visiting. For giving one an idea of the internal arrangements of a mediæval fortress, I know of none better. Without the stately grandeur of Carnarvon, or the lordly position of Conway, from an archæological point of view it is far more interesting. Those castles are mostly fair outsides and nothing more, but Beaumaris contains furlongs of passages, grim cells, dark dungeons, a beautiful vaulted chapel, and delightful walks round the battlements overlooking the sea and mountains.

There is a very hospitable little yacht club at Beaumaris— the Royal Anglesea—and the committee is most courteous in its kindly desire to welcome yachting visitors.

Altogether Beaumaris is quite a nice little place wherein to stay.

There is a good market where dairy produce can be obtained, cheaper than at Bangor, and everything needful is handy to the beach. Barons Hill, Sir Richard Bulkeley's beautiful place, is just behind the town, and visitors are allowed to go through the park on Sundays. The Anglesea shore becomes prettier as Gallows Point is passed, but the Lavan Sands lie out for miles from Penrhyn Castle and Aber in Penmaenmawr Bay.

Of course, there is a legend about these sands. All the se here, away from Great Orme's Head to Puffin Island, was once fine grazing country, and belonged to a chieftain, by name Helig Foel. He had a daughter, and she, of course, loved the wrong young man. Like most foolish people they wished to know the future, and went to consult the most eminent bard of those parts.

"My dears," said the bard, "when eels swim about in the cellars of Helig Foel's house, then know that you will soon be married."

This was cold comfort; however, they could get no better. Time went, cattle browsed and grew fat under the shelter of Puffin Island, and Helig Foel rejoiced in his flocks and herds and the richness of his land, which, protected by its dykes, kept the sea at bay.

At last, Miss Foel, getting impatient and believing in the prophetic declaration of the bard, persuaded her lover to open the sluice gates at the next spring tide so that the cellars might be flooded just a wee bit. Unfortunately, on the night that this was done there blew the most awful gale from the N.N.W. ever seen, and the sea came tumbling through the open sluice never to return again.

That night Helig Foel was a ruined man, and Miss Foel won a husband, but lost a home and all her dower. So badly was the family off that her brother had to turn saint, and live in a cave by the side of a stream 700ft. above Llanrwst. Here he died, and a church was built which is called Llanrhwchwyn, and exists to the present day, known otherwise as Llewellyn's Old Church. St. Rhwchwyn was son of Helig Foel, and, naturally, after such a flood got up as high as he reasonably could to live.

Llewellyn's wife, however, the Princess Joan, objected to walk up 600ft. every Sunday, so her husband built her a church down in the valley, but she did not profit much by it, for she carried on sadly with one William de Breos, whom her husband had taken prisoner at Montgomery; and when a wily bard came to her one day and asked her what she would give to see sweet "Gwilym," she boldly up and answered that she would give Wales and England, and her husband to boot! So the bard unfolded a cloth and showed her sweet "Gwilym's" head, neatly laid there. Such was the merry jest of those simple days, the good old days one always hears about.

The anchorage off Glyn-y-Garth, which had been recommended me in the Isle of Man, I found a fraud. The wind was E. when I first went there, and the stream was running hard against me. I brought up in a good berth, but before I could get the kedge away I found she had taken at least two turns round her anchor. Whichever I put the helm, she rode up against the tide, and then took a wild sheer straight at another yawl which was setting to us, while two more vessels were tilting at each other as hard as they could go. So I weighed anchor, and ran up above the ferry to moor between the *Clio* T.S. and the ferry; here at least I was out of the way of craft. I dropped anchor, therefore, in a clear spot, paid out twenty fathoms of chain, and went below to lunch. When I looked up ten minutes afterwards I discovered to my disgust that we were cruising down the Straits. Fortunately, we had gone clear of all the craft, so I got in the anchor and hoisted the foresail intending to try again. This time I dropped the kedge close inshore, and then luffed out into the stream with sixty fathoms of warp running out, and then let go the anchor.

This third attempt was rewarded; we held on, but sheered all over the place. Before dark, as the E. wind began to pipe up strong, I took out the third anchor and laid it on the mud ashore to the N.W., so that with three anchors down I thought I ought to do. For two days I remained there, but it is a nasty place. There is no safety for small craft, unless they have heavy moorings, anywhere about here.

Glyn-y-Garth is a pretty little place. The ferry is always lively, and the way the men manage their boats, full of people, in all weathers is wonderful. They come alongside as gently as if they would hardly break an egg. However, these boats will soon be things of the past, as there is to be a steam ferry and piers at each end. At present the landing at the Bangor side is wretched. If it is low-water one has to walk nearly half a mile over a slippery wooden gridiron, with the sea splashing up underneath, and over one's boots and everything.

This is what H.R.H. had to do when I was there, and the Prince of Wales did not like it.

Bangor is quite an ordinary country town. The cathedral is only a fairly large parish church. There is nothing whatever to induce anyone to stay here I imagine. Lord Penrhyn's castle is a modern affair, but the slate quarries at the entrance to the Vale of Nant Francon are worth a visit, and the vale itself much more.

For the amateur cruiser, trusting only to his own unaided lights, the anchorage at Glyn-y-Garth should be his limit. He may, indeed, sail down towards the Menai Bridge, but he had better be careful. To go through the Swellies without local knowledge is unjustifiable, but I do not mind confessing I did it, and this was how it came about.

I had come away from Conway at five in the morning. There was hardly a breath of air as the old craft surged over the swell. By the time Puffin Island was reached, however, it was blowing hard from the E. As I flew past Beaumaris all the yachts were jumping about in all directions, and most people seemed fighting their dingeys. They looked a sad sight; half dressed and wretched, miserably engaged in the vain effort to ward off a charge from the too-touching attentions of the faithful companion.

When I reached Glyn-y-Garth I saw that the anchorage was full and all the craft were bobbing at each other, so I ran on and brought up in a good berth, as near into the mud W. of the bathing-place on the Bangor shore as I dare go. How she did take her chain, forty fathoms went in no time before she held. It was a nasty place, however. Seeing that the wind was still freshening, and that there was every prospect of dragging during the night, I resolved to run through the Swellies and seek shelter in the bight off Dinorwic. It was a difficult job getting the anchor up, and it came home before we had got in twenty fathoms. There was still some twenty fathoms to be got on board, and all the time we were going down towards the Menai Bridge. At last the anchor was up, and then we tried hoisting the trysail, but as she was dead before the wind and the sail was pressed against the rigging it was a difficult job. The mizzen, however, was doing good work, and the foresail was fetching us along finely.

As I ran past the George Hotel, opposite Menai, I was hailed by at least three boats, offering their services as pilots. But I could not stop then, and secretly I longed to find my way through alone. The wind howled behind me. The ill-set trysail at least held the wind, and almost before I knew where we were I found the Swellies were before me. Keeping the marks I had learnt steadily ahead, the old boat flew along. It was nearly high-water, consequently the stream was running its hardest to the S.W.; but the gale was so strong aft that

I took no notice of the tide, and steered easily for wherever I thought the best of the water lay. I confess, however, I had not realised how narrow the channel was, and how many obstructions were lying about. Hugging the Carnarvonshire shore when once I felt sure the Platters were passed (although I had plenty of water over them at that time of tide), I flew past Gored Goch, with its little white houses almost level with the tide, and before I had recovered my breath the Swellies were navigated—all danger was over. As I looked back it seemed so easy, so simple, that I began to put down the dangers as the usual kind of exaggeration to which I have long become accustomed. There seemed nothing difficult in what I had just done, so I went on with lessening wind and in quiet water past the beautiful shores of Llanfairpwllgwyngyllgogerchwyrndo-bwllTysiliogogoch, with its old church in the boulder-strewn ground, sloping to the placid stream ; past Plas Newydd, ugliest of imitation castellated houses, painted white with many crimson blinds ; past Vaynol Woods until Dinorwic came in sight, and there I anchored. Here there was hardly a breath of wind, and yet only three miles back it had been whistling under the bridges at the rate of forty miles an hour.

Next day I went back to Pwllfanog, and rowed through the Swellies in the dingey. The tide was running hard to the E. I took the narrow gut between Gored Goch and the Cribbin Rock. There was no need to row, the little 9ft. boat danced through, and I sat still to take all the bearings of the place. It looked pretty bad. There was a waterman rowing a party up the Straits. He took the S. channel, and as he came up to me he called out that I ought to be drowned by this time. Naturally I enquired why?

"Why?" said the man, "because 'tis all whirlpools where you've come through. I've seen a 16ft. boat go clean down in the hole of one, and never touch water on either side, she was that sucked under by the in-draught alone."

And there the tourists sat, placidly listening, believing all the man told them, for he was a native and, of course, knew, while they regarded me as a foolhardy and reckless idiot.

I liked this imaginative Welshman, his reminiscences were entertaining. So I hooked on and listened, while the tide took us up to the George Hotel. How he did bosh those tourists, and how I envied him his fertile and reckless gift of imagination.

If only I had it how much more interesting I could make this book. There are marvellous stories told of the making of the Tubular Bridge. How they ever raised those ponderous tubes into position does seem astounding; but, somehow, the combined efforts of the most consummate skill of the engineer's art does not seem so entertaining as the story of how William Williams sat on the chains of the Menai Bridge, just after they were stretched across, and there, sitting on the top chain while his feet rested on the lower, suspended in mid-air fully 130ft. above the water he made a pair of shoes in two hours, which he sold for a sovereign.

From Dinorwic all kinds of excursions can be made. Snowdon, by the Pass of Llanberis, is easily reached. Carnarvon is only three miles and a half away. Plas Newydd Park contains the finest cromlech in Wales. The whole of this part of Anglesea is crowded with ancient remains. It was just below the ferry of Moel-y-Don that Suetonius crossed to the attack of Mona and the slaughter of the Druids. Carnarvon Castle is, of course, an object of pilgrimage, which no one who goes to the Menai Straits should fail to see. The ruins are very graceful, certainly, and, like all Edward's castles, are remarkable for the air of elegance and refinement they exhibit. Carnarvon is said to be, after Alnwick, the finest castle in Great Britain.

Somehow, to me, the castle was disappointing. I now know why. The grouping and proportions of its three towers have been copied in all the modern stucco castles which are to be found in the suburbs of almost every large town. I even seemed to recollect Jack Straw's Castle. Instead of living up to the age of the great Edward, I meandered down to the level of the successful shopkeeper, who is determined to live in baronial 'alls, and have two lodges 100yds. from his feudal fortress, defended by towers *à la Carnarvon*.

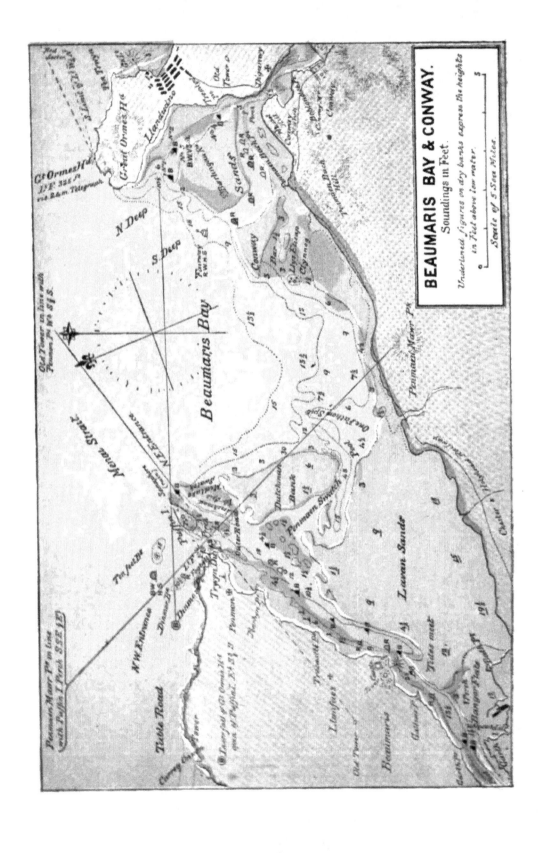

BEAUMARIS BAY & CONWAY.
Soundings in Feet.
Underlined figures on dry banks express the heights
in Feet above low water.

Scale of 5 Sea Miles

CHAPTER XX.

———

BEAUMARIS TO THE DEE.

As the tide only runs during the last quarter of the ebb to the E., it is necessary to get away from Glyn-y-Garth at the beginning of the E. going stream, which will be felt about 3½hrs. to 4hrs. after high-water by the shore. Of course, with a leading wind the tides will make less difference.

Beaumaris Bay, lying within Great Orme's Head and Puffin Island, is a dangerous place to be caught in with a N.W. wind, as the in-draught is strongly felt here, and there is not much room to work out, all the landward side of it being encumbered with sands.

Off the shore between **Penmaenmawr**—which is a conspicuous mountain, over 100ft. high, and whose sides are covered with the *débris* of blasting operations—and **Penmaenbach**, the lower mountain E. of it, is a patch of rocks, called Llys Elis or Helig ap Clynnog. It is dry at low-water, and is three-quarters of a mile off shore opposite Dwygyfylchi (pronounced Dooeguvulki).

There is temporary anchorage off Penmaenmawr, but the low-water line extends some distance out.

The entrance to the **Conway River** is marked by a **Fairway Buoy** painted in red and white stripes, with a staff and diamond, lying in two fathoms and a half. It is placed a great deal too much to the N.E., and a vessel steering from the buoy to the first **red buoy** on the Conway Bar would cross an ugly patch of rocks, which dry at low-water.

There are two approaches to the Conway River. The N. Deep and the S. Deep. The former, however, for a stranger is practically useless. At high-water neaps there is barely 8ft. in one place, and that is a patch of bumpy rocks. The channel is buoyed, but it is a matter of opinion on which side the buoys should be left. At high-water springs it might be attempted with leading winds; but I have seen several coasters left on the sand, and the position is very nasty if a N.W. wind should spring up before a vessel floats.

The S. Deep is entered by keeping Penmaenbach—the hill at the foot of which there is a tunnel close to the sea—right ahead, steering to pass to the W. of the Fairway Buoy, distant some three-quarters of a mile. The **red buoy** of the S. Deep will then be seen; leave this on the starboard, and run down all the buoys in succession. There is plenty of water, except between the third and second buoy from the Mussel Beacon. Here there is barely 3ft. at low-water. As the buoys are only placed on one side, and should all be left on the starboard, including the beacon or perch at the entrance of the river, there is nothing to tell a stranger how far he should reach over if beating in. If the wind is ahead his best course is to wait for nearly high-water, or as soon before as the draught of his vessel will permit, there being fully 19ft. or more over the shoalest part at high-water springs, and make short tacks, **never passing between the line of the buoys** on the starboard hand.

When the perch or beacon is reached, it must be passed, not too closely, on the starboard, and then round up at once to steer with the turret at the end of the railway bridge next the castle, just clear of the wooded point on the right hand or Conway side, until abreast of Deganwy Point, when bear more to the E. or left-hand shore, and pass up close to the wharf of the London and North-Western Railway. The sand lies off from the other side a long way, so that the channel is close against the wharf. Then when the end of the wharf is reached,

bear across to the wooded point and keep close up the Conway
shore. There is a black buoy on the sand at low-water, opposite
the wharf, to be left on the starboard, entering, and another
well in on the sand to the S.E. of the end of the wharf, which
is to be left some way to port.

When past the wooded point, called **Bodlondeb**, anchor a little
S. of it, and make a warp fast to the rings, which are all along
the shore. There is here a pool with from 7ft. to 8ft. at low-
water. The wooded side is steep-to, and the channel is very
narrow. There is another pool farther up, off the town, above
the quay, and in the centre of the stream below the railway
bridge, but this is an awkward berth as the streams run so
strong. There is anchorage off Deganwy, either just above
the little pontoon where the Trefriw steamers call—the landing-
stage is aground at low-water—where there are generally a few
yachts moored; or else on the other side, just above a boat-
house with a-tower. Here there is water enough to allow a
vessel to lie afloat at all states of the tide, but with N. and W.
winds neither of these berths are so good as up at Conway.

Anchored under Bodlondeb one is perfectly safe. It is as
well to take out a stern-fast when the yacht has swung down
with the ebb, so as to prevent the boat swinging. No wind
can hurt one here, and the shore is so steep it is like being
moored to a quay. At low-water one can almost step ashore
while the vessel is still afloat.

Conway is not suitable for yachts drawing over 7ft. of water;
but for small yachts up to about twenty tons, and if of light
draught, I know of no place on the W. coast, from Milford Haven
to Loch Ryan, that I like so much. I found my way in at
half-tide with a wind dead ahead, and only touched twice;
since then I have been in and out scores of times and never
had the least difficulty, and many times it was blowing hard,
too. Once I came in with the wind aft at one-third flood, and
managed to get right up to the snug berth under Bodlondeb
Point.

I was surprised to see how few people, even local yachtsmen,
frequented Conway. I received many warnings against going

there, and was told I should never get up; but the experiment proved the contrary.

The channel from outside leads S. to Penmaenbach, then it turns E. and S.E. to the perch or beacon, when it turns abruptly to the S. A bank lies off on the E. side, opposite the beacon, which must be guarded against.

Above Deganwy is the Castle Hill, a conspicuous rocky eminence. Between it and Llandudno the ground is flat with sand heaps and marshes. The N. Deep keeps along this shore, all dry at low-water, and then turns W. after the third buoy. It is obstructed with low rocky ledges, and could only be used at high-water springs and with a fair wind.

Between the N. and S. Deep is a large tract of sand, which dries some 6ft. above low-water.

The channels are said to change, so that great caution is necessary in first approaching the bar. Opposite the perch the bar is mostly gravel and stones. Between the perch and the first buoy there is over four fathoms at low-water in the channel. The flood stream runs for 4½hrs.; the ebb for 7½hrs.

Great Orme's Head is a magnificent headland, 676ft. high, and quite steep-to on its W. side. On the N. shoulder of the head is the lighthouse.

Great Orme's Head Light.—From a square, castellated building a fixed white light is shown, visible twenty-four miles. It shows red from S. 84deg. W. to N. 88deg. W. The S. limit of the white light leads to the Bar Light-ship at the entrance to the Queen's Channel, Liverpool, and the S. limit of the red light leads close to the **Constable Buoy** and **Bell Beacon** in the Horse Channel.

Bearings and distances from the Great Orme's Head Light.— Point Lynus bears from the Great Orme's Head, N.W. ¾ W., distant fifteen miles and a half. The N.W. Light-ship, Liverpool, E. by N. ¼ N., sixteen miles and a quarter. Walney Light, N.E. ¼ E. easterly, forty-nine miles. Morecambe Bay Light-ship, N.E. ½ N., thirty-six miles. St. Bee's Head, N.N.E. ¼ E., seventy-two miles and a half. Bahama Bank Light-ship, N. ¼ E.

easterly, sixty miles. Chicken Rock Light, Isle of Man, N. by W. ¼ W., fifty-four miles and a half.

Orme's Head Bay, on which Llandudno is built, affords bad holding ground. The best anchorage is between the pier-head and the Hydropathic Establishment near Little Orme's Head, opposite the big hotel, with a flag-staff on the top, at the corner of the third opening in the terraces from the pier. There is good shelter here in winds from S.S.W. to W., but the wind sweeps over the low ground from Beaumaris Bay with great violence, and it is an awkward place to be caught in by a wind with anything northerly in it.

The sands dry out a long way at the head of the bay, and the landing is awkward at low-water.

Little Orme's Head is not unlike the great one. From here to Rhos Point, the W. side of Colwyn Bay, the coast becomes lower, and off this point there are loose stones scattered about over the low-water shore. The coast should not be approached nearer than two-thirds of a mile.

Colwyn Bay is skirted by wide low-water sands, with boulders strewn about. There is good anchorage with off-shore winds, but a vessel rolls a great deal.

Constable Bank, lying almost in a straight line from Great Orme's Head to Air Point, on the W. side of the Dee, has two fathoms and a half least water over it. A spherical buoy painted in black and white rings, with staff and diamond, lies in three fathoms S. of the shoalest part.

E. of Colwyn Bay the coast extends in a nearly straight line to Llandulas, with hills, one of which rises to 666ft., behind. E. of Llandulast he shore sinks to the level of Rhuddlan Marsh, and is a dead level, with Abergele standing back half a mile from the sea.

Abergele Road has a depth of from one fathom and a half to two fathoms, and is a poor place for anchoring. The foreshore dries out some distance all along here. The coast continues flat all the way round to the Dee, with hills some distance inland.

At a little W. of Rhyl the Clwyd discharges its waters into the sea through an extensive foreshore. The estuary forms Rhyl

Harbour.   There is water enough to lie afloat for vessels drawing
6ft. just inside the entrance, off the quay, but the bar dries out
at low-water springs.   To enter, keep well off shore, and when
opposite the pier-head steer for it, passing it close on the port
hand ; then steer more W., and follow the channel between the
perches until the quays are reached, when bring up nearer the
W. side.   This is a nasty place to take, and many people get
ashore going in here.   The channel is narrow, and shifts with
the banks.

Tides.—It is high-water, full and change, at Rhyl at 10hr.
57min. local, or 10hr. 51min. Greenwich time.   Springs rise from
13ft. to 15ft.; neaps, 7ft.

The coast E. of Rhyl continues flat with high land behind,
Gwaenysgor Village having a hill 765ft. high just behind it.
Off Rhyl are patches, with from 3ft. to 6ft. least water on
them.   They lie two miles from the shore, and beyond them
are the Chester Flats, which dry at their E. end 2ft. above
low-water.   The S.E. end of these flats is the N. side of
the inner passage to the Dee.

The Chester Flats are five miles in length, and divide the
entrance of the Dee from the W. into two channels, the
Welsh Channel and the Inner Channel.

The N.W. patch buoy is black conical, with staff and cross,
and lies in 10ft. of water, two miles and four-fifths N. from
Rhyl Pier.   It marks the N. side of the entrance to the inner
passage of the Dee.

The Earwig Bell Buoy painted in black and white rings,
with a staff and diamond on it, lies in 9ft. of water.   It marks
the fairway between the Chester Flats and the shoals, extending
half a mile off shore from Talacre life-boat house, one mile
and one-third W. of Air Point.

The E. side of Chester Flats is marked with conical black
buoys, of which there are three.

The Entrance of the Dee.—The entrances of the Dee are
blocked by large and dangerous shoals.   The channels are
liable to alter after heavy gales, and the buoys have often to
be re-laid.

Should a vessel, unfortunately, get ashore, there is great danger of her falling over on her beam ends, as the sand is all shifting and the rapidity of the tides soon scours away the sand.

The system of buoyage is under divided authority. It is a great pity our Trinity House has not decided on painting all starboard-hand buoys red, as is the case almost everywhere else.

The Mersey Board paint their buoys on the starboard red, and so they are here in the **Hilbre Swash**, but the **Welsh Channel**, and the **N. channel of the Dee** above Hilbre Islet, are buoyed by the Trinity House, and all **starboard buoys** are **black conical**, while **port-hand buoys** are **black and white can buoys.**

The sand banks dry in many cases four miles and a half off shore, and show above low-water from 2ft. or 3ft. to 22ft.

The **Chester Flats** have been already described. The Inner **Channel** joins the **Welsh Channel** at or about the **Earwig Bell Buoy,** and both sweep round **Air Point,** off which **begin the Mostyn Banks,** extending nearly as far as Quay Station, on the W. side of the Dee.

The edge of the bank is marked by **black conical buoys.** The first is the **Air Buoy,** then the S.E. Air, the S.W. Salusbury, M 1 and M 2. There is water in this channel at low-tide only as far as Greenfield Gut.

Chester Bar lies at the entrance of the **Welsh Channel,** and joins **Chester Flats** and **West Hoyle Bank.** There is from **13ft. to 15ft. least water** on it at low-water, **with the exception** of an 11ft. patch in the centre. A **black and white chequered can buoy, with staff and globe,** marks this patch.

The **Welsh Channel** is three miles and a half long, with half a mile least breadth.

At the E. end of the channel is moored the **Dee** Light-vessel, in eight fathoms. It **lies one mile** from the **disused lighthouse** on Air Point, which is **65ft. high, and painted in red and white bands.** This vessel exhibits a **flashing white light** every 10sec., visible ten miles.

Q

Air Point is low, with flats extending some distance off it, and is easily known by the old tower on the point.

Hilbre Island, which **marks the E. side** of the entrance to the Dee, is 40ft. high, but narrow ; **Middle Hilbre** is the same height, but not so long ; while the **third Hilbre** is small and low, with a large black wooden beacon on it, called the **Eye.** On the land is the beach mark, a quarter of a mile E. of **North Hilbre Island ;** this is a **black wooden beacon,** also with a distinguishing mark on the top.

West Hoyle Bank lies between **Chester Bar** and Hilbre Swash. It is nearly eight miles long, lying mostly E. and W., and three miles broad. The E. part towards Hilbre Islet dries 22ft., and at the W. end it dries 13ft. The dangerous nature of this bank is shown by the wrecks on it. It is fairly steep-to on its N. side, but it shoals gradually towards the **Welsh Channel.**

Besides the **Chester Bar Buoy** this bank is marked on its N.W. end by a **red and white striped buoy,** with staff and cage, the **Horse Bell Buoy Beacon** bearing E. and the Constable Buoy bearing W. ⅛ N., with Great Orme's Head in line. This buoy should be passed to the N. All the W. side of the W. Hoyle Bank is marked by **parti-coloured can buoys, and they are to be left to port.** There are four of them, **besides the S.E. spherical buoy, painted red and white in bands, marking** the **Welshman Gut.**

The E. side of W. Hoyle Bank is marked by five conical red buoys, to be left to starboard when entering Hilbre Swash. E. Hoyle Bank extends four miles N. of Hilbre Island. The bank dries 10ft. above low-water, at three miles distance from the shore.

The bar is marked by a **pillar black buoy,** with the letters H.E. Fy. on it. This buoy lies in five fathoms, with the **Eye** Beacon open W. of the beach mark.

The **Horse Buoy, No. 1,** is one mile E. of it, **and the Horse Fairway Buoy** is N., distant one mile.

The **N.E.** and **E.** sides of the **E. Hoyle Bank** are marked by **red conical buoys,** which also show the W. side of the

Horse Channel. The W. side of the E. Hoyle Bank is shown by black can buoys, of which there are five, the last one being off Hilbre Island.

The Salusbury Banks lie within the entrance points of the Dee, and divide the river into the N. and S. channels. A swashway, going E. and W., divides the bank into two, and the N. bank is divided by another swashway, running N. and S. The W. bank is called Salusbury Middle, and the E. part Great Salusbury; this part dries 19ft.

Welshman Gut leads between the N. edge of the Salusbury Banks and the W. Hoyle Bank. There is 7ft. least water on it at low-tide.

This gut is marked on the N. side by the red and white spherical buoy at the S.E. end of W. Hoyle Bank, and on the S. side by Salusbury Middle Buoy, spherical, black and white in bands, with staff and diamond, lying in three fathoms. The S.W. Salusbury, off the W. side of Salusbury Middle, is black conical.

Salusbury Swash is a black and white chequered can buoy, marking the S.W. side of Salusbury Middle, as also the N. end of Mostyn Deep.

Hilbre Swash is well shown by the buoys. The bar is one mile long, with 9ft. least water. The channel is altogether about six miles long by half a mile wide.

Above Welshman Gut, or Hilbre Island, the banks and channels are liable to constant change, and local help should be taken by all strangers, especially considering the precarious position of a vessel if she should ground from the nature of the sand and the strength of the tides.

There is an uncomfortable anchorage in Wild Deep if the weather is rough, with S.E. Air Buoy a little N. In Mostyn Deep there is a better berth, between buoys M 1 and M 2, off the quay. In Dawpool Deep, S. of Limestone Wharf and the Hilbre Islands, there is good anchorage, in two fathoms and a half, but a cross, choppy sea is felt here on the top of the tide with N.W. winds. The tides run here and in Mostyn Deep at four knots an hour; in Wild Road at three knots.

Tides.—It is high-water, full and change, at Air Point at 10hr. 54min. local, or 11hr. 7min. Greenwich time. Springs rise from 25ft. to 28ft.; neaps, 22ft.

A dangerous wave, or bore, goes up the Dee. It begins one mile below **Connah's Quay** and runs up at eight miles an hour, with a crest 2ft high. It is most dangerous near the mud flats. In the stream it does not break, only in the shoal water. The first of the flood is generally the strongest.

The Dee can hardly be called a good place for yachting. For the local people it may be all right, but the tides, banks, and exposure to the N.W. winds make it anything but a perfect, or even tolerable, boating resort. Every winter the fishing-boats suffer greatly from the gales, and the anchorages and channels are fast filling up.

A good many small craft hail from Hoylake, and people fond of yachting, who live about the Dee, have to make the best of their surroundings; but for the amateur cruiser, who can choose his own cruising-ground, the Dee is certainly not a place to visit. I have met many yachtsmen hailing from Liverpool, Manchester, and the country thereabout; none of them but had some tale of woe to tell of broken-backed craft, strained hulls, or damage of some kind or another, which had happened in their own experience.

I have given the directions for the Dee because it is as well to know how to get there if one wants to, but for my part, I should suggest that the desire had better be unfelt or resisted.

After all, perhaps, the local people suffer most. Strangers are cautious, but those who know the place often try short cuts at a risky state of the tide, when they run on a bank and render themselves conspicuous.

CHAPTER XXI.

THE COAST AND PLACES OF INTEREST BETWEEN BEAUMARIS AND THE DEE.

WITH the exception of Tremadoc Bay and the sea between Barmouth and Aberdovey, there is no more beautiful coast scenery in Wales than is to be found between Beaumaris and Great Orme's Head.

There is this further attraction, too, in this part of the cruise, that there are the Menai Straits to take shelter in, and Conway.

I have already expressed my opinion of this snug little place, but I cannot resist the temptation to further enlarge upon its charms when I remember the scorn with which the harbour was spoken of, not only by yachtsmen but by coasters. Not a man whom I met before I went there had a good word for it. It was therefore with many qualms, and only after trying all the anchorages in the Menai Straits, that I mustered up sufficient courage to tackle the difficulties of the approach.

Had not the only anchorage recommended to me, viz., Glyn-y-Garth, proved so very uncomfortable, I should not have attempted Conway. As regards the berth in Bangor Pool, or Glyn-y-Garth, I can understand that for a big yacht with many hands, and which can veer out any amount of chain so as to moor with plenty of scope on both anchors and then haul taut, the berth is all right. Many hands make light work, and donkey-engines are handy things; but for amateurs who do not carry heavier anchors than necessary, or more chain than they can help, and who do not revel in the joys of taking out a kedge for a quarter of a mile, there is no doubt the anchorage is uncomfortable. I was there for a week at one time, for three days at another, and on and off frequently, and I heard complaints from everyone except the happy people who had regular moorings of their own, or had taken those of others. These fortunate ones enjoyed life, and rather liked cruising round and round their bridles. It gave variety to the scene.

When I had found my way up to Conway, however, and was safely berthed under Bodlondeb Woods, then I realised what contentment was. Here one could bask in the sun and watch the people walking along the favourite footpath of the town. One could even be solaced by hearing their remarks. As most of these were in Welsh, however, the pleasure, or otherwise, was a little mitigated. One conversation did cheer me:

"Is that a man-of-war?" said a voice under a parasol, one day.

"No, dear, I don't think it is a man-of-war, but I believe it is a frigate," was the masculine rejoinder.

After that I walked the quarter-deck a little.

Many small yachts came in while I was at Conway, but none picked up the only berth where a vessel lies snugly afloat. One went up to the pool off the town, just below the bridge, but as the wind happened to be right up and down he sheered about a great deal. Next to the place I always chose, a berth close off Deganwy is best, over on the Conway Marsh side, near the boat-house. The only wind that can hurt one there is a regular good blow from N. to N. by W.

Conway town is the most picturesque I have seen in Wales. Not only does it possess a splendid old castle and a most interesting sixteenth-century dwelling-house, the Plas Mawr, but it can boast of a most delightful hotel, beautifully fitted up, and most artistically furnished and adorned. The pictures which hang on the walls of the various charmingly cosy rooms and in the passages are works of art, such as are not often seen in houses intended for the entertainment of the public. The management, too, is excellent, and the charges not excessive.

The Plas Mawr is a place to be visited. It was probably built in 1580, or, perhaps, three years earlier. The rooms are now used for the exhibition of the Cambrian Academy of Art, and some of the features of the place are hidden by the efforts of modern genius, or otherwise. The fire-places, windows, and plastered ceilings are very quaint. When I went over it there was a working man going round; he told me he was a plasterer, and it was quite pleasant to hear his professional admiration for the work of a bygone age.

He told me that the ceilings must have taken a very long time to do, as each coat had to be left to dry, and work like that required several layers of plaster.

Of course, there is a Queen Elizabeth's apartment, and " E.R." is inscribed in many of the plaster mouldings; but the house was built for one of the Wynns, of Gwydir, and is now the property of Lord Mostyn.

The courtyards are very quaint. It is a pity the fine old house stands in the town; if only it was surrounded by a park, with a stately avenue leading up to it, it would look much better. The frontage up the side street is really a fine piece of domestic architecture. Considering the treatment the place has received it is in very good preservation.

Conway Castle, of all the Welsh castles, is pre-eminent for the beauty of its situation. From whichever point it is regarded, whether from the wooded hill above it to the S., or from the anchorage off Bodlondeb Point, or from the end of the cause-way where the suspension bridge begins on what used to be a rock in the middle of the river, the castle is superb. It is a veritable dream of the Middle Ages, and transports one to the time when men lived as in an enemy's country in this lovely land, and no Englishman could call his life his own outside the castle walls. In one respect Conway Castle was liable to greater risk than other Edwardian fortresses; it was difficult to

supply it with food in case of a siege—practically, it was isolated.
The passage of the river was at all times difficult; even so late
as the present century, before the suspension bridge was erected,
forty people were drowned by a ferry-boat upsetting. In time of
war it was doubly difficult, and it was often swollen by floods.
There was no provisioning the garrison from the Conway side, for
Penmaenbach was regarded then, and until quite recent times, as
a terrible pass, with the sea on one side and a precipitous
mountain on the other, the Sychnant Pass, behind Conway,
being too rough and liable to ambuscades to be of any practical use; and after that there was the foot of Penmaenmawr
to pass.

The sea was the only available means, and that was dangerous,
for the Welsh pilots were not to be trusted.

One vessel sent from Ireland, laden with wine and provisions,
was stranded on the bar, an accident which led to a fierce fight
between the Welsh and the English, and this was only typical
of many such scenes. The warfare was conducted with the
utmost barbarity on both sides, and the accounts of the mutila-
tion of the wounded read more like an Armenian atrocity than
a record of border warfare between civilised nations.

It was at Conway that Edward received the head of
Llewellyn ap Gryffydd, the last of the native princes of North
Wales. Like William Wallace, Llewellyn was betrayed by his
own countrymen.

The castle was finally dismantled in the reign of Charles II.
by its owner, Edward, Earl of Conway, after having stood two
sieges in the late Parliamentary Wars.

One of these sieges was remarkable by reason of the Archbishop of York assisting at the assault in person. It seems
difficult to realise an archbishop, the fellow Metropolitan of
Archbishop Laud, actually in arms, and serving under, or
alongside of, a Roundhead commander; yet, so it was. Archbishop Williams, being a hot-tempered and fiery Welshman,
and a native of Conway, had been aggrieved by the conduct
of Prince Rupert, who appointed Sir John Owain, the same
who was so proud of the chance of being beheaded with

noblemen, governor of the castle instead of the archbishop. He, therefore, joined General Mytton, and together they assaulted and took the castle. Every Irishman found in it was drowned. Mytton had them tied back to back and thrown from the terrace into the river. There is very little to see inside the castle, not nearly so much as at Beaumaris; but there is one little bit left in the chapel, which is worth a scramble to look at.

The view, too, from the top of the tower over the Conway River and the old town is very beautiful. I know of few places in the United Kingdom where, by means of a yacht, so much can be seen of natural beauty and archæological interest as at Conway. The excursion up the river to Trefriw is another pretty bit. One can get within two miles of Llanrwst by boat, and steamers go up every tide time. The row up is not without difficulty, for the banks in the river above Conway and opposite Llansantffraid are numerous, and the channels between hard to find. The tide, too, goes off so suddenly that great care has to be taken against being stranded for some hours.

The steamer is the better way of going. From Llanrwst, or indeed Trefriw, Snowdon is easily reached by Capel Curig, at the head of the Vale of Nant Francon, and the Nant-y-Gwryd Valley to Pen-y-Gwryd, at the head of the Pass of Llanberis. For a good walker it would be an excellent round to go up by the steamer when the tide is high early in the day, land at Trefriw, walk across to Capel Curig by Llyn Crafnant, and return through the Pass of Nant Francon by Llyn Ogwen, and so home to Conway by train from Bangor.

But after all, the excursions hereabouts are by the dozen. All beautiful, all within reach of the yacht : only moor under Bodlondeb Point, and after you have explored Conway, been over to Llandudno, heard the niggers in the Happy Valley, and done as Llandudno does for the day, you will want to see something of the mountains and the beauty of the famous Passes of Llanberis and Nant Francon.

I leave Conway with much regret, for I have found no other place like it. No other place where the past and the present,

the beauty of nature and the beauty of art, are so happily combined, with such peace and tranquillity for a harassed skipper
seeking a berth where he may have a night's rest in peace,
without fear of anchors tripping, or gales howling, or the
everlasting dingey battle, trying alike to patience, paint, and
temper.

Well, Conway is astern ; we are rounding Great Orme's
Head, and hurtling into the tide ripple off its N. end. People
make a good deal of fuss over this headland, talking of its
grandeur and solemn magnificence. I can't say it was very
solemn when I last rounded it. A char-à-banc full of festive
'Arrys was meandering along the road which goes all round the
barren rock. They greeted us below with shouts, whether of
derision or friendliness it was impossible to make out, but from
their gestures they seemed to be throwing orange peel and nut-
shells at us.

As for grandeur, it is a solid limestone mass with no form
or beauty about it.

· Now Strumble Head and Pen-y-Caer are magnificent headlands, with Pen Dinas and Pen-y-Bal beyond. There is shape,
variety, and soaring imagination in those defiant promontories,
but they are not known. There is no road round them for
the lightsome tripper to dally with the bottle or the toothsome
nut while he rides in a carriage and pair like any lord.
Excursion steamers do not run round Strumble Head or
Bardsey.

It is when I see places like Llandudno that I marvel at
the taste which selects such places for seaside resorts, and
passes by all the lovely nooks which crowd along our coasts.
Llandudno is a kind of Welsh Margate. Niggers flourish and
abound there. Promiscuous flirtations are not unknown on the
pier or elsewhere. It is even said that the *élite* of fashion
go through the labours of their toilettes three times a day.
Perhaps even oftener. The gentlemen are mostly of the pronounced dashing order, or else raw youths, who tap their teeth
with the handles of their crutch sticks and smile inanely at the
artless fair ones from under the shadow of their straw hats,

adorned with vast ribbons denoting the exclusive club to which they belong.

The bay is a fine one, no doubt, and a good refuge harbour could be made here without great cost, one would think. It is a better shelter than Holyhead and entirely free from rocks. There is plenty of stone in Great Orme's Head to make the breakwater with.

Leaving Llandudno astern we are now coming to a succession of seaside resorts, decreasing in aristocratic pretensions the farther we go E.

Colwyn Bay looks a melancholy place, but the woods behind take off a little from the straight monotony of its sea front. There was a vessel lying off there when I passed. There was not much wind, and that from the W., but the way that craft rolled was astonishing. There must be a heavy swell running along this coast at times. Colwyn Bay used to rejoice in the euphonious name of Pwllycrochan, but the hotel proprietor found his patrons did not get on very well with this word, so he wisely changed it.

There is a cursing well near Pwllycrochan. I don't mean the well curses, but if one had an enemy, the idea was to write his name down, give it to the well-keeper, who stuck a pin into it, and then, after he had received his fee, he threw the slip into the well. Whereupon the enemy was cursed. The well is called Ffynnon Elian.

There used to be a shrine over the well, but this was destroyed by the Rector in an endeavour to do away with the practice ; but cursing still goes on.

Penmaenrhos Point was once considered a most difficult pass. It was here Richard II. was taken by Henry of Lancaster and conveyed to Rhuddlan Castle.

Once more we are in the neighbourhood of many castles. A little way behind Llandulas, and near Abergele, is Gwrych Castle, once a very magnificent structure indeed, but not much to look at now.

As one passes Abergele, thoughts of that terrible railway accident occur to the mind when the Holyhead express ran into a goods train, in which was a load of paraffin oil. In a moment the whole mass of wrecked carriages and mangled people were enveloped in a cloud of black smoke, and all were burnt, the living and the dead together. The details were harrowing in the extreme.

Rhyl is now full in sight, and the navigation has to be attended to, for we are getting into the neighbourhood of the Chester Flats and Rhyl Patches.

If one has any especial reason for wanting to go to Rhyl, anchorage can be had there, and, for a trifle, any waterman would take one in. It is better when going in for the first time to have some help, as the channel is a shifty one and narrow, and also to put a stranger in the best berth for staying.

The Vale of Clwyd is pretty, and Rhyl has attractions for those who like a watering-place of the ordinary type. Near Trefnant, a little beyond St. Asaph, which is one of the excursions from Rhyl, there once lived a lady, who in her day was a celebrity. Catherine de Berain—and one wonders how a plain Denbighshire squire came to meet this young lady of foreign birth—married John Salusbury, of Llewenin, by whom she had three children. On the death of her husband she married Sir Richard Clough, who had become engaged to her on the day of the funeral of her first husband. While she was on the way back from the church, Maurice Wynn proposed to her.

"Now why didn't you say so before?" exclaimed the lady. "Unfortunately, I have already accepted Sir Richard."

Then, seeing the look of disappointment in her companion's face, she added : "But I will marry you when I have buried him."

After she had borne two daughters to Sir Richard Clough he also died, and then came Maurice Wynn's turn. When he died she married Edward Thelwall, who survived her. The Salusburys continued to flourish : her second son was known as Salusbury the Strong, and Colonel Salusbury defended Denbigh Castle stoutly against General Mytton, to whom, however, he was obliged ultimately to yield. From this branch of the family Mrs. Thrale, the friend of Dr. Johnson, was descended. This energetic Catherine de Berain is known in history as Mam Cymru. She flourished in the latter half of the sixteenth century, and there is scarcely a family of repute in this part of Wales which does not trace its descent through her. The Williams-Wynn, the Salusburys—to a member of which family the beautiful church at Trefnant owes its origin—the Thelwalls, and many others, can claim relationship through the matrimonial alliances of this indefatigable lady.

Dyserth Castle lies between Rhuddlan Marsh and the lofty hill behind Gwaensegor, called Newmarket-Cop. All round here the country bears traces of the hard fighting that once went on, possibly when the Roman legions were engaged in the conquest of the Britons, and also during the time when the Saxons and Normans were hammering at the stubborn Welshmen. It was with no wish of their own that the Celts saw themselves driven to dwell among the rugged fastnesses of Snowdon, but being forced to it they reconciled themselves to circumstances, and made it as bad for their assailants and neighbours as they could.

Rhuddlan Castle is a picturesque ruin, standing on the edge of the Morfa Rhuddlan and the banks of the Clwyd; but one is getting about tired of ruins, and after Carnarvon and Conway it is difficult to work up any fresh enthusiasm on the subject.

Besides antiquities and ancient memories there are very real reminders of the present order of things. Vitriol works, and other creations of modern society, are in full blast along here. The chimneys, and smoke, and smells, when the wind is off-shore, are much more evident than the hoary ruin or the poetry of ancient days. We are now off the Dee Light-ship, and can turn into Mostyn Deep if we like. If we get as far as Flint we can lie there, off the pier, in 30ft. at low-water, and shall be quite safe if we moor well.

Chester and Hawarden Castle, Eaton Hall, and the ancient home of the Mostyns, can be visited from here. Flint is not attractive in itself, but the excursions from it are numerous.

Mostyn Hall is a most interesting old house. It lies back about a mile from the quay, off which is good anchorage, except when it blows from the N.W. Half-way between it and Flint is Holywell, with the remarkable spring of St. Winifrid near. This well is spoken of as one of the seven wonders of Wales. It is reputed to throw up twenty-one tons of water a minute, but the amount is said to be much more than this.

Of Hawarden Castle little remains. The new mansion is of modern date.

Chester would take too much space to describe. No city on the W. coast is more worthy of a visit, however. It is even possible to go up there in the yacht if she does not draw more than 9ft. There is 12ft. of water at low-tide alongside the quays at Saltney.

However, I cannot recommend this cruise to amateurs.

For sailing purposes Flint is quite far enough, and if strangers get as far as there without getting ashore they may think themselves lucky.

Readers of George Elliot may remember the catastrophe in the Mill on the Floss. The Dee is supposed to be the scene of this closing event in the life of the misguided Maggie and her unamiable brother.

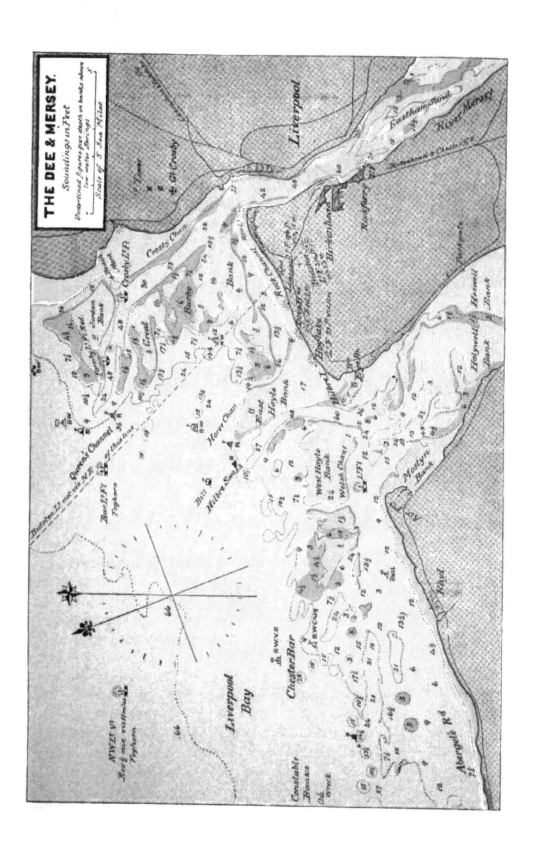

THE DEE & MERSEY.

Soundings in Feet

Underlined figures give depth on banks above low-water Springs

Scale of 5 Sea Miles

CHAPTER XXII.

LIVERPOOL BAY AND THE MERSEY.

WHILE I consider the Mersey as unsuited for amateur cruising as any estuary I know, and a place to be avoided by strangers who manage their own craft, it is necessary to give an account, as briefly as possible, of the dangers and difficulties in the approach to Liverpool, together with the aids to navigation which have been so plentifully distributed.

The buoyage of the Mersey is mercifully under the direction of the Mersey Harbour Board, who have adopted the French and the Scotch systems of colour, viz., that all **starboard-hand buoys** shall be **red**, and **port-hand buoys black**, in **main channels**, subsidiary channels being modifications of these, as far as circumstances will allow. **Conical buoys** are always **starboard buoys** and **can buoys port-hand buoys**, **spherical buoys** being middle ground buoys.

The **entrance to the Mersey** lies between **Hilbre Point** and **Formby Point**, distant **ten miles**. The whole of this space, and as far to sea as eight miles, is more or less encumbered with **banks**.

Pilots cruise off the Isle of Anglesea E. of Lynus Point, and for vessels of over **one hundred tons pilotage is compulsory**. The pilot vessels are fore-and-aft schooners, with the number painted on the mainsail, foresail, and staysail, as well as on each bow. They carry a large red and white flag—the upper half white, the lower red.

There are special port regulations in the Mersey, one of which is that two lights are to be shown at night, one at the forestay as usual, the other twice the height of the one on the forestay to show all round, in the stern.

Between the banks which block the Mersey are three channels. The **centre** and **big-ship channel** is **Queen's Channel**, leading to **Crosby Channel**. The least depth in the undredged part is 11ft. to 12ft.; 25ft. at half-tide and 38ft. at high-water springs. The bar is short, and lies between the **Bar and Formby Light-vessels**.

Horse Channel is the S. channel, and leads E. of E. Hoyle Bank and W. of the **N. spit** into **Rock Channel** off **Rock Lighthouse**. This **channel** has **only 3ft. least water** in it at low-tide in **Rock Gut**, but there is 30ft. at high-water springs and 23ft. at high-water neaps.

Formby Channel is the N. channel, and in it there is only 3ft. at low-water off **Crosby Lighthouse**.

The appearance of the coast is low and uninteresting. Low sand hills skirt both the **Hoylake shore** to **New Brighton** and also on the **Formby shore** for fully five miles.

There are **four light-vessels** altogether. The **N.W. Light-ship** lies in thirteen fathoms in the **fairway**, sixteen miles and a quarter from both **Crosby Lighthouse** and **Hoylake Lighthouse**, and from the **Bar Light-ship eight miles**.

N.W. Light-ship.—From an elevation of 30ft. above the sea a white light, revolving every $\frac{1}{2}$min., is exhibited, visible eleven miles. The vessel has two masts, and carries a black ball at the foremast head.

Fog-signal.—A steam foghorn gives three blasts, each of 2sec. duration within a period of 15sec., followed by 45sec. silence every minute.

Bearings and distances from the N.W. Light-ship.—The Bar Light-ship bears from the N.W. Light-ship E. by S. $\frac{1}{4}$ S. southerly, distance eight miles. Hilbre Fairway Buoy, S.E. $\frac{1}{4}$ S., nine miles. Chester Bar Buoy, S. $\frac{1}{2}$ W., seven miles and a quarter. Great Orme's Head, W. by S. $\frac{1}{4}$ S., sixteen miles and a quarter. Point Lynus, W. $\frac{1}{4}$ N., twenty-eight miles.

Rockabill Light, W.N.W., eighty-nine miles. Carlingford Lough, N.W. ½ W. westerly, ninety-five miles. Chicken Rock, Isle of Man, N.W. ¼ N. Douglas Head, N.N.W., fifty miles and a half. Maughold Head, N. by W., fifty-four miles and a half. Point of Ayre, N. ¾ W. westerly, sixty-one miles and a half. Ross Light, Kirkcudbright, N. ¼ E., seventy-eight miles. Walney Island, N.E. ½ N., thirty-four miles.

The **Bar Light-ship** lies in **seven fathoms and a half, two miles outside** the **Queen's Channel Bar**. From it is exhibited, at a height of 30ft., a **flashing white light, showing three flashes in quick** succession **every ½min., visible ten miles** The periods are : **flash 2sec., eclipse 2sec. ; flash 2sec., eclipse 2sec ; flash 2sec., eclipse 20sec.** The vessel has **two masts**, with a **red ball on each.**

Fog-signal.—A steam foghorn gives one blast every 20sec.

The **Formby Light-vessel** lies in **eight fathoms**, one mile and three quarters inside the bar of Queen's Channel. From it is exhibited, at an elevation of **30ft.**, a **flashing red light** every 20sec., visible eight miles. The vessel carries **two masts** and a **black ball** at the **foremast** head.

Fog-signal.—A foghorn gives every minute four blasts, each of 2sec. duration within a period of 15sec., then 45sec. of silence.

Crosby Light-vessel lies in seven fathoms abreast the N.E. elbow of the **Great Burbo Bank.** It is the Fairway Beacon to the Mersey through the **Crosby Channel.** The deeper channel lies S. of the light-ship, but there is 15ft. on the N. side at low-tide.

The ship carries **two masts,** and has a **red ball** on the **foremast.**

Gas Buoys.—Two red pillar gas buoys with horizontal white bands, marked B 1 and B 2, exhibiting a flashing white light, lie on the outer and inner edges, respectively, of the dredged bar channel, which had least water, 20ft., when last surveyed. Two **black can gas buoys,** marked Q 1 and Q 2, exhibiting a fixed white light, lie on the outer and inner edges of the N. side of the dredged channel on the bar ; and the **Bar Light-ship** is in line with the **Formby** and Crosby Light-ships, and leads through the centre of the dredged channel.

On the outer, or western, spit of Taylor Bank there is a **black can buoy, Q 4**, showing a fixed white light.

On Askew Spit there is a gas buoy, **conical red**, marked **C 4**, showing a **flashing white light**. It marks the N.E. edge of Askew Spit, Great Burbo Bank, on the W. side of Crosby Channel.

A red conical gas buoy, **showing a flashing light**, lies on the E. edge of Great Burbo Bank, about three miles S. of Askew Spit Buoy.

A gas can buoy, **black**, marked **C 8**, shows a **fixed white light**, and marks the E. side of Crosby Channel.

Lights on the Shore. — Hoylake Light exhibits from a white tower, at an elevation of 31ft. above high-water, a **fixed white light**, visible ten miles. It is obscured W. of the bearing S ⅛ E.

Upper Hoylake Lighthouse remains, but there is **no light** in it now. The **Dove Beacons** show **fixed red lights** at elevations of **30ft.** and **6oft. above high-water**, and when in line lead S.E. ¾ S. for a part of the **Horse Channel.**

Leasowe Lighthouse, which is painted white, exhibits, at an elevation of 96ft. above high-water, a **fixed white light**, visible fifteen miles. It is hidden when bearing S. of S.S.E.

Bidston Light is a **fixed white light**, and is exhibited from a dark stone tower, 68ft. high, standing some way inland, at an elevation of 214ft. above high-water, visible twenty-three miles. The light is obscured S. of S.S.E. ¼ E.

Rock Light is a **flashing white light** every 20sec., visible fourteen miles. It is exhibited from a white stone tower, **94ft.** high, at an elevation of 63ft. above high-water. **Below** the flashing light is a **fixed white light**, shown **only** in the direction of the **Rock Channel**, while there is 11ft. and more water in the Rock Gut. By day, a black ball hoisted by the side of the lantern indicates the same thing.

The lighthouse is on the low-water ledge, near the fort at New Brighton, N. of the pier.

Fog-signal.—Two bells, with different notes, are sounded alternately once every 10sec.

Crosby Light is a **fixed white light, shown from a square white tower, 74ft. high,** at an elevation of **95ft.** above high-water, visible **fifteen miles** between the bearings of **N. 87deg. E.** and **S. 31deg. E.** The first bearing leads over the S.W. end of Formby Spit, in 12ft. The latter leads **over** the **Horse Fairway Bell Beacon,** and leads N. of **Newcome Knoll.**

North Wall.—From a lighthouse on the N. wall at the E. side of the entrance to the Mersey is exhibited a fixed white light, at an elevation of 56ft. above high-water, visible between the bearings of N. by E. through E. and S. by E. $\frac{7}{8}$ E., at a distance of fifteen miles. Up the river the light shows less bright, bearing N. of E. by N.

Fog-signal.—A siren gives a blast of 3sec. duration every 30sec.

The **sand banks** are **numerous.** Beginning from the W., **Horse Channel** divides E. Hoyle Bank from **Spencer Spit,** or **North Bank** and **Brazil Bank,** and they are a S.W. continuation of **Great Burbo Bank.** They dry from 5ft. to 16ft. above low-water. Their southern edges are marked by black can buoys after the **Fairway Bell Beacon Buoy** is passed.

The S. side of this channel is formed by **Hoylake Sand** and **Mockbeggar Wharf Bank,** the edges of which are marked by red conical buoys. **On Hoylake Sand there are two red conical buoys** lying half a mile off shore on the sand, to show the channel at high-water to the **best place** for **lying aground** off Hoylake. L 1 lies off the Dove Beacon; L 2 lies W. of **this. Horse Channel Conical Buoy is marked with staff and ball.** The port-hand Horse Channel Buoy is marked with staff and **cage.** Rock Channel Buoy, No. 1, is a bell beacon buoy. No. 9 R. **black buoy** lies in the **Rock Gut, S. side of Brazil Bank.** The next buoy to it is the **Brazil Bank Buoy,** spherical, with black and white bands, surmounted with staff and triangle. Four cables S. of this is **Rip Rap Buoy,** red conical. The channel lies between the two.

H 1 black buoy is abreast H 4 red buoy, as E. Hoyle Bank runs out to the N.W. some distance beyond the dangers on the E. side.

The rocky ledge, off Rock Lighthouse, extends N. of it some little distance. **Great Burbo Bank with its continuation, N.W.,** called **Little Burbo,** dries over a space of five miles by two miles and a half. Queen's Channel lies on its N.E. side. The highest part dries 19ft., about one mile from **Brazil Bank.** From **Askew Spit,** its N.W. end, distant one mile, it dries 13ft. Between these two points there are several swashways, through which the tide, especially on the ebb, draws with considerable strength, so that it is advisable to keep to the E. side of the Queen's Channel at that time in light winds. Beyond the **Little Burbo** the water is shoal, with 16ft. to 30ft. of water for some distance, and a nasty sea gets up on this part with the ebb-tide and a S.W. wind.

Little Burbo Bank is awash only at low-water springs. The ridge connecting it with the **Zebra Flats** is the bar which is now dredged to 20ft. in the gut, and has besides from 11ft. to 12ft. on it elsewhere between the buoys. The **dredged channel is 466yds. wide.**

The **Queen's Channel** is the **main channel to Liverpool.** The bar previously referred to is now dredged to a depth of 20ft., and is ten miles distant from the entrance points of the Mersey. The channel is admirably buoyed. Q 1, red, is surmounted with a staff and ball; Q 1, **black,** with a staff and cage. There are six buoys on each side. Q 4, **black** buoy, is a gas buoy and shows a fixed white light. The **gas buoys, Q 1, Q 2, also show fixed white lights, and there are the two bar buoys, also showing flashing white lights,** as before stated.

The **Crosby Channel** is a continuation of the **Queen's Channel,** which is marked in the same way, C I to C X, red conical, on the starboard, and C I to C XI, on the port-hand, black can buoys. Inshore of C X red buoy is the **Brazil Bank** spherical buoy, painted in black and white rings, with staff and triangle; and E. of Rock Lighthouse is the red conical **Rip-Rap Buoy.**

C 4, red, and C 8, red, are gas buoys, as before stated. C 8, black, is also a gas buoy. The lights are flashing to starboard, fixed to port.

Formby Light-ship is to be passed on the S. side when entering, and the Crosby Light-ship also.

The N.E. side of the Queen's Channel is formed by Zebra Flats, Jordan and Taylor Banks, which lie between it and Formby Channel. Zebra Flats are the W. extension of Taylor Bank, and lie out two miles. From being awash they gradually sink to a depth of three fathoms at two miles off. They are marked by a black and white striped conical buoy, with a staff and disc, marked Z, lying half a mile N. of Zebra Flats, in four fathoms and three quarters, Q 1 black buoy being one mile and a quarter in a S.W. ¼ W. direction, and Crosby Lighthouse S.E. ¾ E., distant six miles and a half.

Taylor Bank is a continuation of Jordan Bank. It extends for three miles and a half and is one mile wide. These banks dry from 10ft. to 12ft. above low-water, and are steep-to mostly on the S. side.

The black can buoys of the Queen's and Crosby Channels mark the S. edge of these sands, and red conical buoys mark the N. edge of the sands, along the S. side of the Formby Channel.

Formby Channel lies between Jordan and Taylor Banks on the W. side, and Formby Spit, Mad Wharf Bank, and Formby Bank on the E. side. The channel is four miles long, with a least breadth of one cable at low-water, and with depths of from 15ft. to 3ft. on the bar off Crosby Light, where at half tide there is a depth of 17ft.

The channel is marked by red conical buoys on the starboard, and black can buoys on the port. Formby N.W. Fairway Buoy is a pillar buoy, painted in black and white rings, marked F.N.W. It lies in three fathoms and a half, Mad Wharf Beacon being three miles distant in a S.E. by E. ¾ E. direction.

There are six red buoys and three black. F 2, red, lies opposite F 1, black, distant two cables and a half. No. 3 black buoy lies off the gut, where there is only 3ft. at low-water.

F 2, **black,** lies seven cables S. of F 6, **red,** at the N. end of
Formby Deep. The **Crosby Channel buoys** are the next black
buoys.

Formby S.W. buoy is a spherical black and white buoy painted
in rings, with a staff and triangle, marked F.S.W.; it lies on the
E. side of a bank, which dries 2ft. near the centre of the bar.
This buoy is to be left on the starboard, Crosby Channel being
entered between C 5 black buoy on the port and **Crosby Light-ship.**

Anchorages in **Rock Channel** and **Formby Channel.**—Should
the tide be unfavourable for passing over the bars of these
channels, there is, in the **first-named** channel, a good place to
anchor in **Leasowe Hole,** in three fathoms, between Nos. 5
and 8 black buoys. In the latter channel, in **Formby Pool,** or
Deep, between Nos. F 4 and F 6 red buoys, and F 2 black and
F.S.W buoys, there is good anchorage for the tide, in from
three fathoms and a half to five fathoms.

All these channels are filling up rapidly.

Formby Spit, Mad Wharf Bank, and Formby Bank lie off
Formby Point and Crosby Point, and thence it forms, in a south-
easterly direction, a shelf up to Liverpool Docks. At three miles
from the coast there is only two fathoms at low-water. **Formby
Bank dries one mile and a half off Crosby Light,** and gradually
tapers off to half a mile wide off **North Wall.**

These banks are **marked** on their **S. and W. sides** by the
black can buoys of the **Formby and Crosby Channels.**

After the **entrance points are passed,** the channel is without
dangers as far as George's landing-stage. On the Liverpool side
the foreshore only dries out a little way; but on the Cheshire
side it dries out for two cables nearly, the river at New
Brighton being about seven-tenths of a mile wide at low-water,
and abreast of the landing-stages about two-fifths of a mile,
but widens afterwards.

Pluckington Bank lies off the S. end of **George's landing-
stage** as far as Coburg Dock, drying for about one cable and a
half off the shore.

Devil's Bank, the N. end of **Eastham Sands,** has 1ft. least
water on it at low-water. A spherical buoy painted in **black and**

white rings, with a staff and diamond, lies in 10ft. at the N. end of the bank, and a black and white striped conical buoy, with G.R. on it, and surmounted by a diamond, lies off the edge of the rocky ledge stretching out from Dingle Point.

Tides. It is high-water, full and change, at the N.W. light-ship at 11hr. 0min. local, or 11hr. 12min. Greenwich time. Springs rise from 25ft. to 27ft. ; neaps, 20ft. At Liverpool it is 23min. later, with a rise of 2½ft. more.

The streams are strong in the Mersey. The flood stream runs for half an hour after high-water by the shore, and the ebb likewise. Before the banks are covered the streams run strong in all the channels. After they are covered they run in from all sides towards the Rock Lighthouse.

The rate of the velocity of the tide in the narrowest part of the Mersey is seven knots. One mile N. of Formby Fairway Buoy the direction of the tide is to and from the Ribble.

At two miles N. of the Chester Flats and W. Hoyle Spit the tide sets towards Liverpool 20min. earlier than inshore, and at Newcome Knoll, with 16ft. least water on it, lying between the Horse Fairway Buoy and Great Burbo Bank, and marked by a spherical buoy painted in black and white rings, with staff and diamond, the flood stream sets S.E. for the last 4hrs. and the ebb N.W. for the first 4hrs.

The anchorages in the Mersey are not comfortable. Although the channel lies about N. and S., so that the prevailing winds do not blow so much up and down, or against the tides as elsewhere, yet the velocity of the tidal streams and the constant traffic are a source of great risk.

Between Egremont and New Brighton, which is a favourite berth, the tide runs about four knots and a half at springs, and in Sloyne Road, S. of Pluckington Bank, the tide runs from three to five knots.

Masters of vessels are cautioned to anchor as much out of the way of the track of the ferry boats as possible.

There are various ships permanently moored in the Mersey whose moorings must be given a wide berth when anchoring. Besides the *Eagle*, Royal Navy drill-ship, there is the *Conway*, training-ship, off Rock Ferry, the *Indefatigable*, for orphans of sailors, off New Ferry, and the *Akbar* and *Clarence*, reformatory ships, also off New Ferry.

For a stranger the Queen's Channel and Crosby Channel are the proper approach to Liverpool, being accessible at all states of the tide practically, and admirably marked both by light-vessels and gas buoys.

The Horse Channel and Rock Gut should not be attempted by strangers at night. The leading mark for the **red H buoy, N 4**, is **Bidston Lighthouse, open its own breadth E. of Leasowe Lighthouse,** bearing S.E. until Hoylake Light appears. From **H 5 red buoy** the **Dove Beacons**—the high light a little open W. of the low light—will lead up to the **Rock Light** and **N. Wall Light** in line; keep on this until the **Leasowe Light** disappears, when steer **E. ¾ N.** for the black can buoy R 8.

As this channel is filling up, and the Rock Gut is very narrow as well as crooked, great care must be taken in entering. The tides, too, run strong, and set over the banks before they uncover. However, as no amateur skipper is likely to choose the Mersey for yachting unless he lives in the neighbourhood, the chances are he will know the place and its dangers tolerably well, and instead of wanting or taking advice, can give it, with a good many yarns of sand-bank experiences as well.

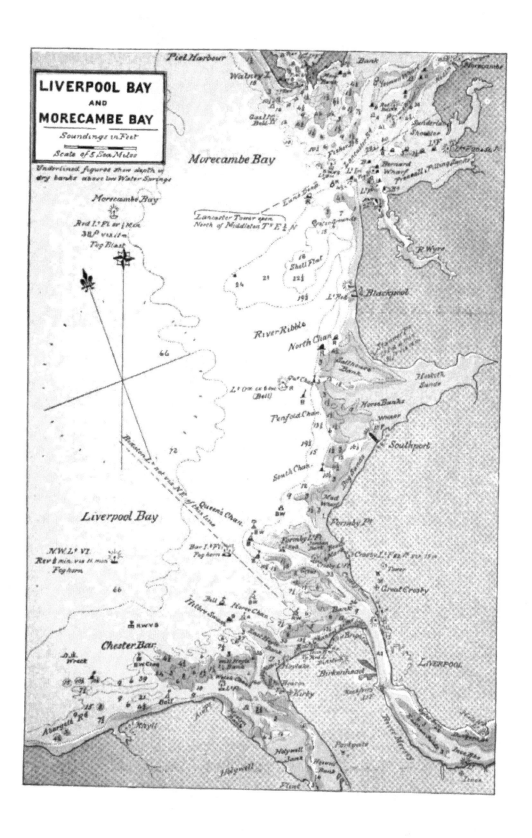

CHAPTER XXIII.

———

THE MERSEY TO PIEL HARBOUR—
MORECAMBE BAY.

BEFORE crossing to the **Isle of Man** and entering upon more congenial cruising waters, it is necessary to continue the W. coast of England as far as the Solway Firth.

I imagine few yachtsmen would care to explore this coast unless there were special reasons, but as the Lake District is readily accessible from the sea at Piel Harbour, and there are many amateur boating men in North Lancashire and Westmoreland a description of the harbours and dangers fronting them is necessary to render this work as complete as it should be. I propose, however, passing over the district as quickly as possible, and shall refrain from any comment on the shore, other than as its physical features require to be noticed in order to elucidate the navigation.

The Coast.—Formby Point separates the estuaries of the Mersey and the Ribble. The shore is low and uninteresting all the way to **Southport,** with sand hills and a low-water margin of nearly a mile. From **Southport** to **Stanner Point** on the opposite side of the **Ribble Estuary** is about five miles, the whole space being occupied with sand banks, which uncover at low-water as far as three miles and a half out to sea beyond the point.

The **Gut** is the main **entrance channel**, and leads between the **Horse** and **Salthouse Banks**. The bar, six miles below Lytham, may be a little deeper now, but its depth used to be **4ft. at low-water spring tides**, and two miles farther in it was **dry**. There were two pools with from 7ft. to 9ft. of water below Lytham; above that place the river is embanked. Works have been going on for some time to improve the depth of the river up to Preston.

Lights.—At **Stanner Point**, on the N. side of the entrance, there is a **black stone tower**, **exhibiting** from an elevation of 81ft. an **intermittent white light**, showing bright for 3½min. and eclipsed ½min., visible twelve miles.

On **Lytham Pier** a fixed red light is shown, and on **Southport Pier** a fixed white light, and two fixed red lights on St. Anne's Pier, one at each end.

Gas Buoys.—A **bell boat light buoy**, red, marked "**Nelson**," lies in seven fathoms on the N. side of the entrance to the gut, **Stanner Point**, bearing E. ½ S., distant **six miles and three quarters**. The light is **occulting**, white, 23ft. above the sea, and visible six miles. The flash lasts for 4sec., the eclipse 2sec.

Another **bell boat light buoy**, painted red and white, called "**Penfold**," lies in the Gut Channel, S.E. by E. ½ E., five miles and a quarter from **Nelson Bell Buoy**, with **Stanner Point Light** bearing N.E. ½ E., distant two miles and three-fifths. It exhibits a **fixed** white light 23ft. above the water, visible six miles.

A spherical buoy, red, called "**Ansdell**," surmounted by a **fixed red light**, 12ft. above the water, lies N.E. ¾ one mile and a half from **Penfold Bell Buoy**, in the direction of **Stanner Point Light**, visible five miles.

At two miles and a quarter distance from **Nelson Bell Buoy**, and in a S.E. ½ E. direction, is a **black conical buoy**, with staff and ball, in **four fathoms**, marked **No. 1 G**. The entrance to the gut is marked by two buoys on each side.

The outer one, on the S. side, lies nearly one mile E.N.E. of No. 1 G. The buoys are all black and have a staff and ball on them. From **Lytham** to **Preston** there are eighteen beacon lights.   **The buoys and beacons** are red on the starboard hand and black on the port.

I imagine no stranger will attempt this navigation without local help.   There is nothing to induce a disinterested amateur to explore this sand-blocked creek.

Southport, at the S. side, is a watering-place of the Llandudno order, without the natural advantages of that favourite place. To make up for their absence there are art galleries, winter gardens and an aquarium, many hotels, and some dancing saloons.   The land behind the town used to be a marsh.   It is now drained.   The promenade and sea-wall extend for two miles along the shore, and there is a pier, 1450yds. long, from which a **fixed white light** is shown.   At the pier-head there is some six fathoms at low-water.

The **South Channel** is barred by a bank, on which there is not more than 4ft. at low-water spring tides.   It lies four miles W. of Southport Pier, and from the bar up to about a mile N.E. of the pier the channel deepens to five and six fathoms at low-water.   **Mad Wharf Sands** and **Bog Sands**, which extend for nearly a mile along the shore from the S. side of the channel, are marked on the starboard hand **by conical buoys.**   The colour used to be black, contrary to the usual principle, with **red can buoys** on the port.   The outer, or Fairway Buoy, is a **black cone buoy, with staff and cross,** lying in two fathoms, just S. of the leading mark.   It lies half a mile outside the bar.

The next buoy is **black conical, with staff and globe.   The outer red can buoy, with staff and cage,** lies five-sixths of a mile within the outer **black buoy.**

The Fairway Black Buoy should be passed N., with the spire of a church (Christ Church) in line with the N.W. end of the winter gardens.

The anchorage in Bog Hole, above the pier, in five fathoms low-water, is said to be quite safe, but at high-water there is a considerable sea, and there is no protection whatever from the W. or N.W. winds.   S.W. winds, too, throw in a heavy sea for a few hours, although the banks soon uncover, and then the berth is quiet enough.

Lytham is also a watering-place, **ten miles** below **Preston.** On the **new pier-head a fixed red light is shown** from 2hrs. before to 1½hrs. after high-water; for the rest of the tide there is no approach.

N.W. of **Stanner Point** is **St. Anne's,** also a watering-place of some pretentions, with a pier, with fixed **red lights** at each end of the pier. Steamers run between these places and Southport in the summer.

There is anchorage in the pool below St. Anne's Pier, but it is not safe; there is 10ft. of water at low-water, but the bottom is loose, and the sea is pretty bad after the banks are covered.

The **N. channel** is barred by a bank, which dries 1ft. at low-water springs, and above St. Anne's Pier it also dries. The channel is marked only by **red conical buoys.** It is an uncertain channel, and filling up with sand.

Tides.—It is high water, full and change, at Stanner Point, at 10hr. 51min. local, or 11hr. 3min. Greenwich time. Springs rise 24ft.; neaps, 17ft.

From **St. Anne's to Blackpool** the coast continues low, the low-water extent of foreshore gradually decreasing in width until at **Blackpool** it is about half a mile wide. N. of Blackpool there are some cliffs, on which the hotels and houses form a conspicuous feature. There are two principal piers here, one 1650ft. long, the other 1400ft.; the longer one has a depth of 22ft. at high-water springs, and shows a fixed green light at the pier-head; the shorter pier shows a fixed red light. The town, which looks an imposing place from the sea, has a fine winter garden, over which there is a large glass dome, and many other public buildings.

Behind **Blackpool** and between it and **Rossall Point** the land is a little higher, but towards the point it declines, and the red clay cliffs merge into the low sandy banks as before.

Rossall Point forms the S. side of **Morecambe Bay, Walney Island** forming the N. point, the points being nine miles apart. The bay is fourteen miles deep and encumbered with extensive sands, which dry over the greater part of the inlet.

This is a most dreary spot, and although there are deep channels intersecting the banks the available space for navigation at low-water is much restricted.

To warn vessels of their approach to this deep bight a **light-vessel** is moored in twelve fathoms at eighteen miles distance from **Wyre Lighthouse**, which bears E. by S. from the ship.

Morecambe Bay Light-ship exhibits from an elevation of 38ft. above the sea a **revolving red light, revolving** every 30sec., visible eleven miles. She carries one **mast surmounted by a ball.**

A red can watch buoy is moored near.

Fog-signal.—A fog siren gives three blasts in quick succession every 2min. (two low notes, followed by one high).

Fleetwood lies round **Rossall Point**, on **which** there is a **wooden beacon, 57ft. high.** It is connected with **Lune Deep** and **Lancaster Sound** by the outlet of the **River Wyre**, which runs out for two miles between sand banks, all dry at low-water, in a northerly direction. At its junction with **Lune Deep** there is a bar with 9ft. least water on it. Up to **Fleetwood** there is a **depth** of from 12ft. to 16ft. at low-water springs.

The channel is **well buoyed.** The Fairway Buoy is **black conical,** lying in eight fathoms, with the **Pile Lighthouse** (Wyre) bearing S.S.E. half a mile.

After this is passed, **red conical buoys mark the starboard, and black can buoys the port hand.**

A black ball is shown at the **Wyre Pile Lighthouse** when there is 12ft. over the bar. The **same signal is shown at the lower lighthouse** in **Fleetwood.** By night the **leading** lights in **the high and low lighthouses are only shown** when there is 12ft. **on the bar.** The high lighthouse and low lighthouse are both of stone colour, and bear from each other S. $\frac{1}{8}$ E. and N. $\frac{1}{8}$ W., distant 283yds.

A **fixed** light is shown from the **red perch** on the **E. end of Blackscer.** It shows white seaward until abreast the **bell perch** when it shows **red.**

Wyre Lighthouse is a red pile iron building, standing on the N.E. corner of N. Wharf Bank at the junction of the Wyre with Lune Deep, nearly two miles from Fleetwood. It shows a fixed white light, 30ft. above high-water, visible ten miles. A red sector is shown from the balcony of the lighthouse over the Fairway Buoy when the Irish mail is expected.

Fog-signal.—A bell gives three strokes per minute, with an interval of 1min.

Fleetwood has a good deal of trade, and the Irish mail boats cause a stir in the place. If the tides did not run out with the rapidity they do the anchorage would be good, as the shelter is perfect. The place is very ugly and totally unsuited for yachting when better can be found elsewhere.

Lune Deep.—From half-way between Blackpool and Rossall Point the ground is shoal. There is only two fathoms and a half at a distance of five miles off shore. This shoal is known as Shell Flat. The inner part of these flats is known as the Rossall Oyster Grounds, and there are patches with only 3ft. on them. There is a rock, with only 6ft. on it, two miles and three quarters from Rossall Beacon.

Preesall Mill, on higher ground on the E. side of the Wyre River, behind Fleetwood, in line with the beacon bearing S.E. by E. ½ E. indicates the time of the danger.

A red bell buoy with a square cage, marked "N.W. Boulders," lies in 20ft. low-water, eight miles and a quarter W. of the boulder, Rossall Beacon bearing E. by S. ½ S., distant three miles and four-fifths.

Between it and the Wyre Light is the "Shell Wharf" Buoy, red, one mile and a half E. by N. from the Bell Buoy.

Fisher Bank forms the N. side of Lune Deep, and at its W. extreme is a rock with only 5ft. of water on it. A gas-light can buoy, painted in black and white stripes, lies in 23ft., two cables W. of this danger.

The North Wharf Flats are banks which dry at low-water, extending nearly two miles N. of Rossall and Fleetwood. The highest part, called "King Scar," dries 16ft., and within it is a black perch, 23ft. above water, with a platform on it.

Bernard Wharf Flat lies between the Wyre and the Lune, and dries out two miles and a half from the shore. Its N.W. point is marked by a conical black buoy.

The **Lune** has 3ft. on the bar at low-water springs, and at Lancaster there is only 13ft. at high-water springs, and 6ft. at high-water neaps.

Tidal Lights.—The high light is a wooden building, 54ft. high. The low light is a stone building, 20ft. high. Both show a fixed white light, visible seven miles. They are only lighted when there is 8ft. of water in the channel.

When in line they lead E. by S. ¼ S.

Tides.—It is high-water, full and change, at Wyre Light at 11hr. 11min. local, or 11hr. 23min. Greenwich time. Springs rise 27½ft.; neaps, 20½ft. The tidal streams run very strong, as much as from five to six knots at times.

The **Lune** is buoyed to **Sunderland Hole** with black buoys, placed as near the centre of the channel as possible. The sands are constantly shifting, however, and local help is indispensable for safety.

In **Abbey Hole,** just below Sunderland Point, marked by a conical black buoy, called "Barthaven," there is a depth of 11ft. at low-water, but the anchorage is very bad, and the anchor, owing to the great strength of the tide and the shifting nature of the sands, is very likely to come home.

Outside the **Sunderland Sands,** which lie a long way off Sunderland Spit, is **Heysham Lake,** the only good anchorage, in from three fathoms and a half to seven fathoms, in **Morecambe Bay,** and rather rough then at high-water with westerly winds. **Clark Wharf Scar** lies N. of it, and at the N.E. end is a shallow gut, with only 2ft. at low-water, connecting the lake with **Grange Channel.**

Clark Wharf Scar divides Heysham Lake from **Grange Channel,** five miles long and leading up to Morecambe. The Wharf dries 10ft., and the **Yeoman Wharf,** on the N. side of the **Grange Channel,** dries 9ft.

A **light-vessel** is moored in **Grange Channel** on the N. side, in 13ft. From a height of 30ft. a fixed red light is shown, visible five miles. When there is **not less** than 8ft. over the inner bar to Morecambe, a fixed white light is shown at the bow by night and a black ball by day.

Fog-signal.—A bell is sounded every 20sec.

The channel is marked by **red conical buoys** on the starboard and **black conical buoys** to port. **No. 3, red, is a bell buoy.** Between it and No. 2, red, is a red pillar buoy. Between **No. 5 red** and **No. 3 black buoys,** half a mile below Morecambe, the channel **dries.** This is the inner bar.

Morecambe Harbour is dry at low-water springs. Here are two piers and a promenade pile pier 900ft. long. A good deal of boating goes on here, as there is 27ft. of water at high-water springs over the inner bar. But it is risky work; many accidents are constantly happening owing to the strength of the tides. The flood-tide sweeps to the N. Vessels lie quite safely on the ground in Morecambe Harbour, and it is becoming a favourite seaside resort. Steamers run to Belfast daily, and to Londonderry twice a week; while in the summer excursion steamers run between Blackpool, Fleetwood, and Piel. **Lancaster is within easy reach** by train, and the Lake District lies all before the visitor from Black Coombe to Helvellyn. For small yachts, that have legs and can take the ground easily, Morecambe is a safe and convenient place.

All the bay, N.E. of a line from Morecambe across to **Foulney Island,** is a mass of sand, dry at low-water. The **Lancaster Sands, Bardsea Bank,** and **Cartmel Wharf,** dry from 3ft. to 17ft above low-water.

The **Ulverstone Channel** lies N. of these banks. It is fourteen miles up to the town from the two black buoys which mark its entrance, between the Furness and Mort Banks. At 4hrs. flood there is water enough for a vessel drawing 12ft. to get up to Ulverstone. The **shifting** channel is marked by perches and buoys. For a stranger local help is necessary here. A vessel of 12ft. draught can get to within twelve miles of Lake Windermere.

The fourth channel in this intricate bay leads to **Piel Harbour** and **Barrow-in-Furness,** and has been made a very safe and commodious channel. A **dredger** is kept constantly at work **deepening** the channel. She **exhibits two vertical lights, 6ft. apart,** on the side **vessels are to pass,** and one light on the other side.

A gas fairway bell buoy lies, in four fathoms, in the line of Nos. 1 and 2 leading lights on the S.E. side of **Foulney Island.** **Hilpsford Shoal,** with 12ft. least water, is marked by a **black buoy with staff and cage.** **A black can buoy,** with staff and cage, in 6ft., marks the W. bend of the dredged channel through the bar, and shows where the direction is altered. A small cask buoy, called "Groyne," lies off the end of the Groyne within Elbow Buoy. On the E. side, off the **Post Light,** is a **red conical buoy,** with cross, lying 50yds. S. of the **inner boulder,** or **Seldom Seen Bank,** which dries 1ft. at low-water. Above Piel the channel is marked by **red conical buoys** on the starboard, and **black can buoys** on the port.

The depths on the bar are 9ft. at low-water springs over a breadth of 200ft. Inside, there is a low-water depth of three to five fathoms.

Tides.—It is high-water, full and change, at **Roe Island, Piel,** at 11hr. 5min. local, or 11hr. 17min. Greenwich time. Springs rise 28ft.; neaps, 21ft. The strength of the stream is three knots and a half.

Light.—**Walney Island Light** exhibits a revolving white light, attaining its greatest **brilliancy every minute,** from an **elevation of 70ft.** above high-water, **visible thirteen miles.** A **fixed red light** is shown from a post on `Hawse Point, 500yds. E. of the lighthouse; it is on the S.E. part of the beach, and is visible seaward between the bearings of E. **and S.W. through N.**

Piel Pier is covered at high-water at its end. A **fixed red light** is shown from its S. end. This is to be discontinued when the alterations now being made are completed.

There are three sets of leading lights. Nos. 1 and 2 are on Foulney Island on the E. side of the entrance. Nos. 3 and 4 are near Rampside, farther in on the E. side. Nos. 5 and 6 are on the W. side, opposite **Ramsden Dock entrance.** All are fixed white lights, and burn night and day. The **front light of** each set is exhibited from a red post or pile erection. The **back lights** are shown from the top of square brick columns, faced with **white** glazed bricks.

S

On the E. side of the channel, 1200yds. below **Barrow Docks,** there is a pile lighthouse, showing a fixed white light, 26ft. above high-water, visible between the bearings of N.W. by W. through N. and E. to S. ¼ W.

The entrance to the harbour lies between **Walney Island** and Farhill Scar, dry at low-water. **In entering, the bell buoy should be passed** close on either side. Keep the Nos. 1 and 2 leading lights on Foulney in line, bearing N.E. by E. ¼ E. until off the **black can buoy;** then steer with Nos. 2 and 3 leading lights in line, bearing N.N.E. ¼ E., as far as the **black Elbow Buoy.** The turn is sharp, and if entering with much flood-tide running the helm should be starboarded before the point is reached.

When off the centre of Piel Island steer W. and bring Nos. 5 and 6 leading lights in line. There is a large mooring buoy in the channel off Piel. The best water for anchoring is above this.

The streams of flood and ebb outside the bar set across the entrance, so that allowance must be made for their force.

There are large docks at Barrow, and the glow of the blast furnaces in the district round often obscures the lights.

Although not a place at all suited for the enjoyments of cruising, a yacht could be well left here while the lakes were explored.

Windermere is only twenty miles off; Helvellyn and Skiddaw are within easy reach; and Furness Abbey, a beautiful old ruin, is just behind Barrow. There is a good hotel close by, and the country at the back is pretty.

Walney Island is a long, low, straggling island, with shallow flats lying off it on its W. side to the distance of a mile.

Bearings and distances from Walney Island Light.—The Point of Ayre, N.W. ¼ N., forty-seven miles. Maughold Head, N.W. ½ W., forty-two miles. Douglas Head, N.W. by W. ½ W., forty-six miles. N.W. Light-ship, Liverpool, S.W. ½ S., thirty-four miles.

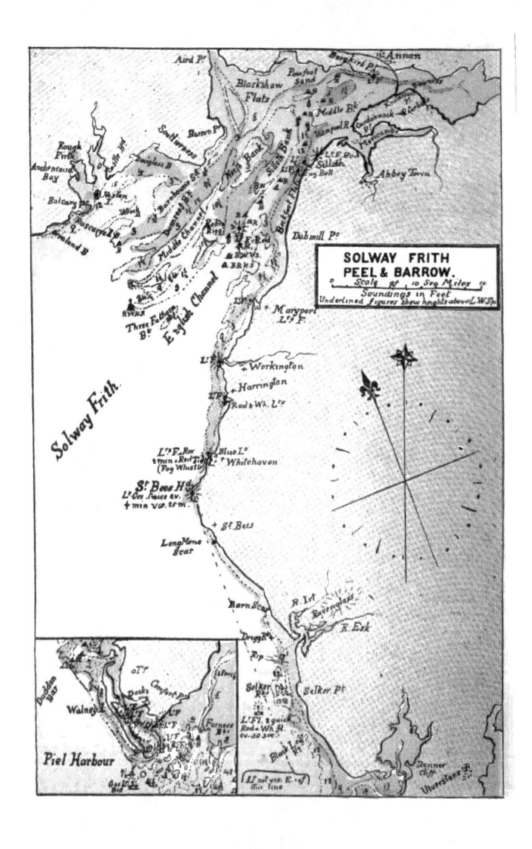

SOLWAY FRITH
PEEL & BARROW.
Scale of 10 Sea Miles
Soundings in Feet
Underlined figures show heights above L.W.S.

Solway Frith.

Piel Harbour.

CHAPTER XXIV.

PIEL HARBOUR TO THE SOLWAY FIRTH.

AFTER Piel Harbour is left behind, there is practically no safe harbour where a yacht can lie afloat at all states of the tide until **Silloth Roads** or **Catherine Hole** are reached; and here, owing to the strong stream of tide, a nasty sea gets up with S.W. winds on the ebb, even when the banks are uncovering. As a matter of fact, an amateur out for a pleasure cruise, and not bound to go up this coast unless for some especial inducement, would do well to leave unexplored all that part of the Irish Sea lying N.E. of the Isle of Man.

Coasters frequent this part in great numbers, for there is much trade in minerals all along here; but coasters don't mind taking the ground, and for them the harbours of Whitehaven, Harrington, Workington, Maryport, and Silloth do well enough.

The coast **N. of Walney Island** must be given a **wide** berth because of the sands which lie off **Duddon Bar.** A red conical **fairway buoy** lies in five fathoms half a mile outside the bar, with Walney Island Mill at the N. end of the island, bearing S.E. ¾ E., distant three miles and a quarter. **Black buoys** mark the channel within the bar, but they are not always to be depended on, and if any stranger wants to go in they had better obtain local knowledge. There was 6ft. on the bar at low-water, but it is liable to change. At low-water the channel is dry within the points.

The coast is now becoming more mountainous. **Black Coombe,** 1919ft. high, is a very conspicuous hill and only two miles from the shore. Behind it the Westmoreland Mountains rise to their greatest heights in Skiddaw and Helvellyn.

For the next four miles there are no outlying dangers **until opposite Black Coombe, where rocks** lie out nearly two miles from the shore.

Black Leg is the most **southerly, and dries 2ft. at low-water springs.** Two miles N. of this is the Scala Fold Style, **which is awash at low-water.** The **Selker Rocks** are a continuation of this.

The **Selker Rocks** Light-vessel lies in ten fathoms and a half, **N. 87deg. W., three miles distant from Selker Point, and two miles in a W. by S. ¼ S. direction from the Selker Beacon, which stands on the middle of the rocks,** which dry at low-water springs. The light-ship exhibits, from an elevation of 38ft., a double flashing light, giving one white flash and one red in quick succession every ½min., visible eleven miles. A diamond is carried on the mast.

By keeping St. Bee's Head due N. the dangers will be cleared to the W.

St. Bee's Light is masked **when bearing E. of N.**

N. of the Selker Rocks is **Ravenglass** tidal inlet. The whole of it dries out at low-water. Sand hills extend on each side of the entrance points for three miles.

Off its N. side the **Drigg Rock has a depth of only 6ft. at low-water.** It lies one mile off the shore, and bears from the **sea-mark** at the entrance N.W. ½ W. distant two miles. There is 18ft. of water into this little place on the line of the leading marks, which are the **sea-marks** on the shore, and the pillar on the S. shoulder of Newton Knot Hill bearing E. ¼ N. When abreast of the sea-mark turn up for the village of Ravenglass, where one may lie aground in safety, if not in comfort.

There is a manufactory of patent manure here.

St. Bee's Head is twelve miles from this place. The railway runs all along the low shore, which, at Seascale, rises to 111ft.

The mountains behind, however, are fine objects. **Sca Fell** is only ten miles inland, and is 3092ft. high. Some of the wildest scenery of the Lake District lies between the coast and the mountains, **Wastwater** being thirteen miles from Ravenglass and discharging its surplus waters through the sands at that place by a stream called the Irt.

At one mile and a half N. of **Drigg Rock** is **Barn Scar** and **Cochra Scar,** both dry at low-water, and three-quarters of a mile off shore. S. of St. Bee's, distant four miles, are the Longman Scar and Ben Rock. By steering a N. course from off **Duddon Bar** all these dangers are cleared. By night, if St. Bee's Light is in sight all danger is avoided. ·

Off Seascale, there are two beacons set up by the Barrow Shipbuilding Company as measured mile marks.

St. Bee's Village lies on the edge of a valley, two miles S. of **St. Bee's Head,** and the railway leaves the coast here to pass behind the high ground.

St. Bee's Lighthouse.—From a circular white tower, 55ft. high, at an elevation of 336ft. above high-water, an occulting white light is shown. It is bright for 24sec., eclipsed 2sec. ; bright 2sec., eclipsed 2sec. ; the whole occupying ½min. It is obscured **bearing E. of N., or one-third of a mile outside the Selker Rocks.**

St. Bee's Head is a **perpendicular** cliff of red sandstone, 280ft. high and flat on the top.

This is the nearest point of England to the Isle of Man, **Maughold Head** being just twenty-seven miles and a quarter from St. Bee's Head.

The **coast** now trends more to the **N.E.** for two miles and a half to **Whitehaven,** forming a shallow bay, called **Saltom Bay.** There is anchorage here in off-shore winds, in three fathoms, within half a mile of the shore. Oyster grounds lie off the shore.

Whitehaven is a tidal harbour. The entrance barely dries at low-water springs. There is from 20ft. to 26ft. at high-water. A great deal of traffic goes on here in minerals, and it is a busy place.

Lights. — On the W. pier-head, in a tower 47ft. high, a revolving white light is shown at an elevation of 52ft. above high-water, visible eleven miles. There is a fog whistle, giving blasts of 5sec. every ½min. between half-flood and half-ebb.

On the N. pier-head there is a fixed green light, shown from the same height as the other.

For a tide signal, a fixed red light is shown near the old quay inner harbour from half-flood to half-ebb while there is 9ft. in the entrance of the inner harbour. By day a red flag is shown at the head of the new quay in the outer harbour.

Tides. — It is high-water, full and change, at 11hr. 14min. local, or 11hr. 28min. Greenwich time. The tide rises from 26ft. to 28ft. at springs ; neaps, 19ft.

At low-water neaps there is a depth of 7ft. within the pier-heads. It is advisable to keep close to the W. pier-head when entering, as the flood stream sets across the mouth of the harbour.

From Whitehaven to Harrington is only four miles. Rocky ledges and stones lie off the foreshore for two cables. The railway runs along the low ground by the beach, while cliffs of from 50ft. to 100ft. rise behind.

Blast furnaces and tall chimneys vary the scenery.

The tidal harbour of Harrington dries out, there being a distance of a quarter of a mile between the pier-heads and the low-water edge.

Workington lies two miles and a half N., with the same characteristics of foreshore between it and Harrington. Off the harbour the foreshore dries out one-third of a mile. The entrance is protected by a breakwater, extending 500ft. N. of the S. pier in a N.W. direction. The River Derwent discharges through the harbour. There is a wet dock here, the Lonsdale Dock ; it is 600ft. by 300ft., with 16ft. at high-water springs, and 10ft. high-water neaps, over the sill. The width of the gates is 40ft. Small red buoys mark the starboard side of the channel, and small black buoys and perches the N. or port side, in entering.

Tidal Lights. — A fixed red light is shown at 42ft. above high-water from the end of the breakwater, while there is a depth of 8ft.   A red ball by day, at the end of St. John's or S. pier, is shown for the same cause.

Two fixed green lights are shown from white towers during the same time as the red light.   On the old wooden pier, on the S. side of the harbour, a fixed red light is shown also when the harbour is navigable.

As all this coast is illuminated at night time by the glow of the blast furnaces, the harbour lights are all difficult to see.

Maryport lies four miles and a half N.E. of Workington, the coast being low in between, and foul for some distance out for one mile and a half off shore.   There is anchorage off the port in the English Channel, but it is exposed to W. winds.

Workington Bank, off the coast opposite Workington, has 16ft. least depth on it.

Maryport is well within the entrance to the Solway Firth. The sand banks of this inlet are most extensive and liable to change, and local help is essential to penetrate farther within these dangers.

Maryport Harbour is like the previous three harbours just described.   The shore dries 50yds. beyond the pier-head. There are extensive wet docks, called the Senhouse Dock and Elizabeth Dock, and a great deal of trade is done here.   The little River Ellen discharges through the harbour, which has been lately very much enlarged.

Lights.—White and green lights light the S. side of the harbour and red lights the N.   A fixed white light is shown all night on the end of the wooden or S. pier.   It is 30ft. high and visible six miles.   A fixed red light is shown all night from the end of the N. pier.

Tide Lights.—A fixed white light is shown, from an elevation of 55ft. above high-water, from a lighthouse, 42ft. high, on the stone pier-head while there is 8ft. in the harbour.   It is visible twelve miles.   A red ball is hoisted by day to indicate the same thing.   A fixed red light is shown from the end of the N. inner pier; a fixed green light from the end of the S. jetty.

Tides.—It is high-water, full and change, at 11hr. 26min. local, and 11hr. 40min. Greenwich time.   Springs rise 25ft. ;

neaps, 19ft. There is a depth of 25ft. on the **Senhouse Sill** and 20ft. on the **Elizabeth Dock Sill** at high-water springs.

From the end of the N. pier a chain extends seaward, parallel to the S. pier, to catch the anchors of vessels which may miss the harbour. This prevents them going ashore on the N. beach.

From Maryport the coast trends N.E. to **Allonby Bay.** The coast is low, with a foreshore extending one-third of a mile out at low-water, gradually widening to two miles and a quarter off the shore opposite Dubmill, forming **Dubmill** and **Ellison Scars.** From here to Silloth the coast is **bordered by low sand hills.** In **Allonby Bay** there is **good anchorage** out of the tide after one-third ebb, as the flats then uncover off **Dubmill,** Allonby Church bearing E. by S.

Between **Robin Rigg Bank** on the W. and Ellison Scar on the E., off **Dubmill,** lies the **Solway Firth Light-vessel.** She is moored in four fathoms, is painted black, and exhibits a **fixed red light, 25ft.** above the sea, visible six miles. The **fairway** is W. of her. The channel is now buoyed, **as well** as that to **Powfort Bank,** close to **Annan,** in Scotland. **Red conical buoys** mark the **starboard** side, and **black can buoys** the port, in the Silloth Channel. They are **shifted** to meet the **alterations** of the **banks,** and have recently been changed. Pilots are necessary here. N.E. of the **Solway Light-vessel** the channel to **Silloth is barred.** There is, however, 9ft. least water on it at low-water springs and 35ft. at high-water springs.

Besides the **light-ship** there are four lights to guide the mariner up the Solway Firth, **without** counting **Hestan Island,** off the Scotch coast, which may or may not be alight. It is unwatched, so that probably it is not alight.

Lee Scar Lighthouse is a pile erection on the rocks S.W. of Silloth. It exhibits a **fixed white light,** from an elevation of 25ft. above high-water, from a building 45ft. high, visible ten miles.

A fog-bell is sounded in thick weather.

At **Cote,** or **Skinburness,** N.E. of Silloth, from a **white wooden framework,** 32ft. high, a **fixed red light** is shown at an elevation of 40ft. above high-water, visible nine miles.

At **Silloth,** on the **end** of the **wooden pier,** a **fixed white light** is shown, except when the lock-gates are open, then it is **green.**

Two fixed red lights, kept in line, lead through the centre of the dock entrance. **A red ball by day** indicates that the gates are open.

At **Barnkirk, or Annan Foot,** in Scotland, at the S.W. side of Annan River entrance, **a fixed white light is shown from half-flood to half-ebb,** visible six miles. **A fog bell is sounded in thick weather.**

Silloth lays claim to being a watering-place. There is a green or esplanade, with a pavilion and baths. There are several hotels, and communication with the Isle of Man and Dublin twice a week.

Silloth Harbour has only existed since 1856. The **Marshall Dock** is the property of the North British Railway Company. It is 633ft. long by 400ft. broad, with a depth of 24ft. on the sill at high-water springs.

Off the N.E. side of the **entrance** to the **parallel wooden jetty, a chain is laid** down for the purpose of bringing vessels up if they miss the harbour. It is marked by warping buoys.

Tides.—It is high-water, full and change, at Silloth at 11hr. 40min. local, or 11hr. 53min. Greenwich time. Spring tides rise 26ft. ; neaps, 20ft.

There is anchorage in **Silloth Roads** or **Catherine Hole,** in three to five fathoms, in sand and clay off the pier-heads. The tidal streams run about four knots, but as the main stream of the Solway Firth is now taking the N. or Annan Channel, the force of the tide is growing less strong, and there is a prospect of the Silloth Roads becoming filled up.

To enter the Annan Channel it is not necessary to cross the bar from the seaward, but to keep W. of the Silloth black can buoys, keeping on from buoy to buoy up the channel.

The sand banks in the Solway Firth occupy nearly the whole of it.

The **English Channel,** which merges into Silloth Channel and Annan Channel, is the only one which is lighted and buoyed.

Workington Bank, with 16ft. least water on it lies in the centre of the English Channel. **Heavy seas** break on it with wind against the tide.

N. of it, distant one mile, is Three Fathom Bank, with 10ft. least water on it. The ebb-tide causes a heavy overfall over this.

N.W. of this danger is Two Foot Bank, which extends **W. and S.W. from Robin Rigg**. It is marked by a **red and white spherical buoy painted in rings**, with staff and diamond, in **four fathoms**, lying at the **S.W. extreme of the bank**.

The buoys inside of this are the property of the North British Railway Company.

Robin Rigg and the N. banks lie six miles N.E. of the S.W. end of Two Foot Bank. These banks extend for ten miles, and dry over a large portion at low-water; but they are liable to alter their **position**, and have done so considerably of late years.

Silloth Bank lies between **N. bank and Silloth. The Annan Channel runs between the two**.

Ellison Scar and Far Sand Bank dry 5ft. and 2ft. They are the W. extremities of the flats, which dry off **Dubmill Point**. The **Beckfort Flats** lie between **Ellison Scar** and **Lee Scar**; **Catherine Scar** lies in between.

Above Silloth the coast is low and marshy. A wide, shallow bay, known as **Moricambe Bay**, with sand banks drying out for two miles into the Firth, opens N. of **Cote Point**. In the bay are patches of stones, known as the Tickhill Brow and W. Scars, and narrow streams or lakes meander through the sand. All these banks are known as the **Middle Banks**.

Cardunock Point and Village form the N.E. side of **Moricambe Bay**, two miles beyond which the **Solway Viaduct** crosses the Firth, here only one mile and a half wide. Half a mile farther and the Solway is fordable for carts from Port Carlisle to Dornock, a distance of one mile and a half over the sands.

Rockcliff Marsh lies between the Eden and the Esk. The little stream, the **Sark**, enters the Esk opposite **Rockcliff Marsh**, and about one mile and a half up the stream is **Gretna Green**.

The Sark formerly was the boundary between England and Scotland, but for many years this swampy bit of land was a matter of dispute, and the marshes between the Sark and the Esk went by the name of the debateable land.

The country at the head of the Solway Firth is dreary and uninteresting.

The banks are higher on the Scotch side, Barnkirk Point, at the entrance to the Annan, being 50ft. high.

The Eden flows past Carlisle and joins the Solway Firth at Sandsfield, where there is a monument to Edward I. The tide flows three miles above this place, but the river is only navigable for boats at high-water.

The tides of the Solway have now to be considered.

The usual limits of this great inlet are **Abbey Head**, in Kirkcudbrightshire, and **St. Bee's Head,** in Cumberland, distant from each other nineteen miles. From a line joining these points it is twenty-eight miles up to Annan, the practical limit of navigation.

With S.W. gales a heavy sea is driven into this estuary, but by the time Maryport is reached the full force of it is moderated by the banks and land. Thence to Silloth Roads a course could be shaped, even at night, if the leading lights are clearly made out.

In thick weather, no vessel should proceed farther in than seven fathoms until they have sighted the **Two Foot Bank Buoy or Maryport.**

The **Scotch shore should be avoided** at all times by strangers.

It is high-water at the entrance to the Firth at 11hr. 10min. local, or 11hr. 24min. Greenwich time. Springs rise 26ft.; neaps, 19ft.

At one mile S. of **St. Bee's Head** the stream runs for 9hrs. to the S.E. from the 2hrs. ebb to the last hour of the flood; then it runs for 3hrs. to the N.W. or until 2hrs. ebb.

Five miles off the head the flood sets S.E. by E. at the rate of one knot, and the ebb N.W. three-quarters of a knot for 6hrs. each way. Between **Whitehaven and Workington** the ebb begins to set out at the time of high-water, and runs for 6hrs. at a speed of about three knots at springs and one knot at neaps.

The flood sets the opposite way at the same rate.

In the **English Channel**, between **Maryport** and **Silloth**, the flood runs 5hrs. and the ebb 7hrs., the rate being about four knots.

In **Silloth Roads**, as soon as the banks are uncovered, there is little tidal stream.

Along the Scotch shore the flood sets E., and flows towards the Nith. Off Southerness the rate is as much as five knots at springs, and off Annan it attains six knots.

At Southerness the flood stream runs for 5hrs., and at **Annan** for 4hrs., so that Sir Walter Scott makes his hero technically correct when he declares that " Love swells like the Solway, but ebbs like its tide." The latter would be about half as rapid as the former, only that the freshes materially increase the **rush** of the ebb.

If any yachtsman wished to explore this part of the north, by going into either of the fine floating docks at Maryport or Silloth—the latter by preference—he would lie in perfect **safety,** and could visit the S.W. corner of Scotland easily.

Criffell Hill, 1852ft. high, just N. of Southerness and Bengairn, behind Abbey Head, are fine summits to look at.

To those who know the Solway, and the intricate **channels** between its banks, plenty of amusement can be obtained by boating among the creeks, but for a stranger the risks **are too** great for the compensating advantages.

CHAPTER XXV.

THE SOLWAY FIRTH TO BURROW HEAD.

FROM the Sark, which separates England from Scotland, to Tordoff Point is three miles and a quarter. Hence to **Seafield Point, where the Solway Viaduct** crosses the estuary, the coast runs W. for two miles, and then N.W. to the narrow entrance of the Annan River for three-quarters of a mile. There is water enough at high-water for vessels drawing 9ft. to go up to the Town Quay at Annan, the river being about 100yds. wide. **A** bridge crosses the stream one mile and three quarters above **Annan Foot** or **Barnkirk Point,** where the lighthouse stands, **exhibiting a light only** from half-flood to half-ebb.

The **tide** runs past the point, and over the scar at its foot, at a velocity of six knots at springs. It is high-water, full and change, at 0hr. 5min. local time. Springs rise 28½ft. ; neaps, 20ft.

From **Annan Foot** to **Cockpool,** at the mouth of the little **Lochar stream,** the shore trends N.W. It is low and marshy, and the **Powfort Sands** and **Blackshaw Flats** lie out a long way, as much as four miles from the high-tide mark in places.

Caerlaverock Castle, famous for its siege by Edward I., which is recorded in the celebrated Caerlaverock Roll dear to the heraldic mind, stands not far back from the shore at Lochar mouth. The ruins are very picturesque, embowered in woods facing the S. The marsh lands between here and

Cummertrees, a village on a low hill three miles W. of Annan Foot, are called the Priestwoodside Moss.

From the Lochar to the entrance of the **Nith** is some three miles and a half. Hills reaching the height of 316ft. rise a little way inland, and on the other side of the river the scenery becomes pretty, with hills rising to the height of 1852ft.

The Nith runs up to Dumfries, but its navigation is extremely restricted owing to the absence of depth in the channel and its shifty nature. Vessels of 15ft. draught can go up as far as Glencaple Quay, five miles below Dumfries, at high-water springs, and there is 12ft. as far up as New Quay, one mile and a half below the town.

A trading steamer goes up to Glencaple when the tides allow, otherwise she discharges at Carsethorn, a quay and jetty one mile N. of Burron Point.

Aird Point is the W. point of entry of the narrower part of the river from here to half a mile above **Glencaple;** there is an embankment covered before high-water, or when there is 9ft. in the channel. Perches with crosses mark this, and perches with **brooms** mark the starboard side. Two miles above Glencaple the river is 400yds. wide. After this it narrows to 100yds.

Tides.—It is **high-water, full and change, at Dumfries** at 12hr. 0min. local, or 12hr. 14min. Greenwich time. Springs rise 6ft. At **Southerness** it is 10min. earlier, and springs rise 27½ft.; neaps, 19½ft.

The town of **Dumfries** is a very ancient one. The bridge, now a foot-bridge, is one of the oldest in the kingdom, having originally thirteen arches, now there are only six. The neighbourhood is very pretty, and there are many ruins of abbeys and castles near. The population is 17,090, and there are about forty vessels belonging to the port.

The **sands,** which dry out to a line joining **Southerness and Cummertrees Village,** fill in all the estuary of the Nith, rendering the navigation most intricate and difficult, especially considering the strength of the tides.

The **Barnhowrie Sands** lie out a long way. There are patches which dry 10ft. above low-water as far out as six miles from the coast in a W.S.W. direction from Southerness. The **Scotch Deep** is on the **S.E. side** of this bank leading up to **Dumfries Channel.** S. of this lies the **Dumroof Bank.** The S.W. end of this bank is ten miles S.W. of **Southerness.**

Middle Channel lies S. of this **bank** and joins the Scotch **Channel,** N.E. of it, by narrow guts, with banks here and there leading to Dumfries Channel.

Southerness has a **square tower,** formerly a lighthouse, now disused, at the high-water extremity of the point, which is low. Behind it is the village.

This marsh, or merse, land stretches S. from the high hills behind for some little distance. Off **Southerness** are rocky ledges which extend for two cables out. These ledges continue on the E. side towards **Burron Point** for half a mile, and the sand dries out fully a mile from the shore, the Dumfries Channel being nearly dry at low-water.

Two patches dry 8ft. above low-water 1200yds. E. of the old lighthouse on the point at Southerness.

Between Southerness and Castle Head there is a wide, shallow bay, the whole of it fronted by the **Barnhowrie Sands, which dry out five miles** from Douglas Bay shore.

Castle Head forms the E. boundary of **Rough Firth,** the estuary of the **Urr Water.** **Rough Island,** 62ft. high, is connected to the shore by a causeway. It is nearly in the centre of the Firth and is a quarter of a mile long.

Coasters make frequent use of this **creek.** The mouth of the **stream** is only **two cables** wide at its **entrance** into **Rough Firth,** but there is water at high-tide for vessels drawing 9ft. to go up to the **Dub of Hass,** four miles in from **Kippford,** the village at the mouth. There is a station at Dalbeaton, half a mile farther, but only very small craft can get up there.

Below Hass are some **rocks,** which reduce the **available channel** to only 50ft. The tide **runs** up at the rate of **three knots and a half.**

Palnackie, half-way up to Hass, has a **tidal dock; with** 14ft. at high-water springs.

There is an **anchorage** on the W. side of the **Rough Firth** with from 10ft. to 12ft. at low-water. The only bad winds are gales from the S.E. at high-tide before the banks uncover. It can be entered at half-flood. The channel is close to Castle Head, and may be entered by keeping a little hill near the head of the **Firth on the E. side in line with the E. side of Rough Island. Close on Rough Island to two cables' distance,** and then steer over W. and anchor in what is known as **Gibbs Hole. Craig Roan** is a ledge, which **dries** 19ft. at low-water springs. It lies three cables E. of **Castle Head.**

The W. point of **Urr Water is Almorness,** off which lies the little island of **Hestan,** where there is supposed to be an **unreliable red and white light.**

The island is 162ft. high, connected by a causeway, which uncovers at two-thirds ebb. The **tide sets strongly** over this, from and into **Urr Water,** for the **first part** of the ebb and last part of the flood.

Off all the points the tidal streams are strong, but slack inside the bays.

Hestan Bay dries out nearly to the island. **Torr Point** separates this part of **Balcary Bay** from **Auchencairn Bay.** Bengairn Hill, 1267ft. high, is only two miles N. of this bay.

There is safe anchorage, with off-shore winds, in **Balcary Bay,** just within the point, in two fathoms and a half at low-water. There are perches marking the shoals off the head, which must be left on the port. The whole bay, nearly to the point, dries out, but the bottom is soft sand and mud.

From Balcary Point the coast trends W. **Rascarrel Bay** offers no shelter. W. of **Castle Morr Point,** off which some rocky ledges lie to the distance of 200yds., forming the W. point of **Rascarrel Bay,** are some fine caves, at a place called Barlocco. The sea flows into them, and beyond this is a little cove, called Port Mary, just a mile E. of **Abbey Head.**

Abbey Head is regarded as the N.W. limit of the Solway Firth. It is **a bold head,** steep-to, with five fathoms depth at 200yds. from the cliffs, and a hill rises behind it.

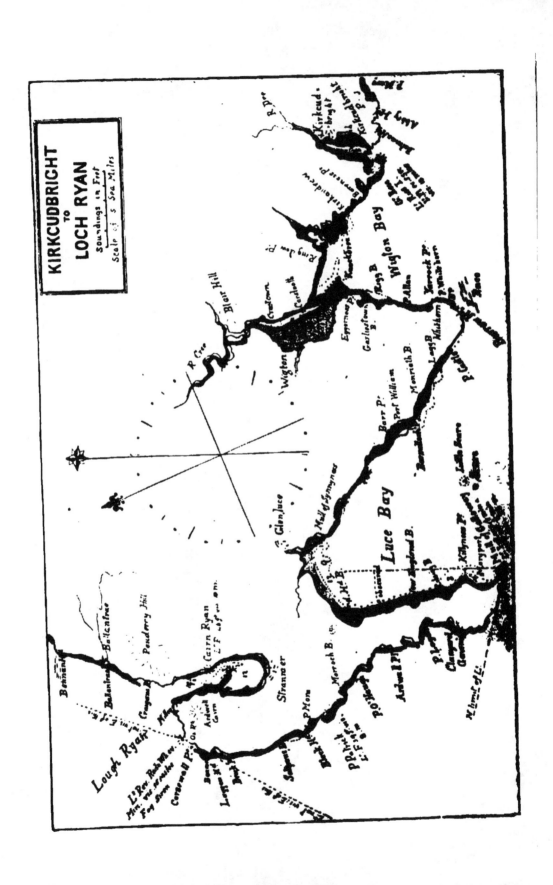

It is high-water here, at full and change, at 11hr. 10min. local, or 11hr. 26min. Greenwich time. Springs rise from 25ft. to 27ft. ; neaps, 18ft. Off the head the rate of the stream is four knots at springs.

The coast now becomes much bolder. There are no more outlying sands, and the shores may be approached with confidence. No dangers lie out farther than two cables.

Balmae Head, the E. point of **Kirkcudbright Bay**, is two miles and a half W. of Abbey Head. It is fairly steep-to for about a mile into the bay, no ledges lying farther off than 150yds. On the other side, forming the W. point to the inlet, is **Little Ross Island**, four miles W. of Abbey Head. It is of no great height, and about a quarter of a mile long. On it is a light-house and a pyramid beacon 150yds. N.E. of the lighthouse.

Little Ross Light is a flashing white light, every 5sec., visible eighteen miles. It is exhibited from a white tower, 65ft. high, at an elevation of 175ft. above high-water.

Between the island and **Great Ross**, which is 272ft. high, is a sound, two cables wide, with a rock always above water in the middle. There is 6ft. at low-water springs between this and Little Ross, off which ledges run to about 70yds., except on the seaward side, where it is steep-to.

Kirkcudbright Bay offers the only approach to a shelter where vessels may lie afloat at all states of the tide between **Silloth Roads** or **Piel Harbour** and **Loch Ryan.** The anchorage is safe in all winds except from S.S.W. to E.S.E. It is uncomfortable with winds from the S.W., although for small craft Ross Island affords shelter.

Coasters either lie ashore on the sand in **Balmangan Bay**, where there are mooring rings and where they find shelter afforded by the land as well as by Ross Island, or else they go farther in and lie on the **Manxman Sands.** Above Torr **Point three perches** mark the edge of the sand.

Abreast **St. Mary's Island**, now joined to the E. shore and well wooded, is a pool, called **Fish Pool.** In it there is two fathoms at low-water. The space is very limited, as the river itself is here only 602yds. wide at high-water. Above the

T

island it contracts still farther, until off **Kirkcudbright** it is about 150yds. wide. Here vessels lie aground, 6ft. above low-water.

The **bar**, on which there is **25ft.** at high-water springs, has only 2ft. on it at low-water, It begins three-quarters of a mile N. of Torr Point on the E. shore; a perch marks the beginning of it. **Fish Pool** is about half a mile beyond this, off **St. Mary's Island**, which forms part of Lord Selkirk's property. The **Inch** is a small island lying off the S. end of St. Mary's Island. Off it is a **low-water ledge**, extending S.W. for 400yds. and marked by a perch at its end. The channel goes close to this. The W. side of the channel is formed by the **Milton Sands**, which are **marked on their E. edge by two black buoys. The entrance to the channel over the bar is close along the E. side,** and begins a little way above Torr Point about one mile and a half N. of Little Ross Island.

Near the W. shore, and on a level with the S. end of the spit of Milton Sands, which curve round forming a shallow bay at low-water with only 2ft. in it, is **Frenchman Rock**. This danger **dries 6ft. at low-water springs.** It is well out of the **navigation, however,** as the channel is right over on the other or E. side.

Kirkcudbright is a neat **town** of some 2571 people. It stands low on the River Dee, and the country in the neighbourhood is pretty, especially towards Dumfries, where the high hills lie between the railway and the sea. The town is on the S.E. side of the river. There is a **red light** shown on the E. pier-head.

The **Manxman Sands** uncover 4ft. at low-water springs, and the Milton Sands 2ft. **Manxman Lake**, as the beaching part of the sands is called, has 21ft. on it at high-water springs. **Two perches on the W. side, abreast St. Mary's Isle,** bearing N. ¼ W. lead in the fairway.

Tides.—It is high-water, full and change, at **Kirkcudbright** at 11hr. 10min. local time. Springs rise 23ft.; neaps, 17ft. The **velocity of the tide is about three knots,** but the ebb after freshes runs stronger than that.

Boats can ascend the Dee for some distance. The ruins of Curnston Castle are on the right bank, and the scenery is prettily varied, as here the Dee receives a tributary, the Tarf. which flows into it from the W.

Meikle, or Great Ross, Point, is the E. boundary of **Wigton Bay.** The other, or W. point, being **Burrow Head,** distant from **Great Ross** twelve miles. To the edge of the Wigton or Baldoon Sands, **which dry,** the bay is eight miles deep. Beyond this, at high-water, a vessel may proceed some four miles.

The whole bay is fully exposed to the S. and S.W., and there is no shelter anywhere at low-water. At high-tide a vessel might take refuge in **Garliestown,** on the W. side, or run up to **Creetown,** at the **head** of the bay, on the **E.** side. In both cases they would **lie aground at low-water.**

A line joining **Borgue Church,** on high ground half-way between Kirkcudbright and the E. side of Wigton Bay, with **Barlocco Island** the most southerly of the **Fleet Islands,** will lead S. of the sands, in three fathoms. In off-shore winds there is anchorage anywhere all round the bay. N.W. of **Great** Ross the rocky coast is pierced by a deep inlet, dry at low-water. The edges are fringed with rocky ledges, and on the E. side there is a jetty, where, in fine weather, coasters discharge their cargoes. This creek is known as Bridgehouse Bay.

The coast continues steep and rugged to **Barlocco Island,** with a deceptive bay at Muncraig and Kirk Andrew, for the anchorage is exposed. A rock, called Meikle, or Great Pinnacle, lies off the cliffs in between. **The Islands of Fleet** are a group of four. Barlocco is 25ft. high by a quarter of a mile long, and connected with the shore at low-water. N. of it lies **Knock-brex Bay. Ardwall Island** is N. of this; and between the two islands of **Barlocco** and **Ardwall** there is good anchorage in two fathoms and a half, sand, but it is exposed to the S.W.

Ardwall Island is 100ft. high, and is one-third of a mile long. At low-water it is joined to the mainland by a ridge of sand.

Half a mile N. of this lie the **Murray Isles,** with a safe bay for anchoring in off-shore winds between. All these islands are accessible from the mainland at low-tide.

T 2

Behind the **Murray Islands**, and between **Ardwall Island** and **Ringdow Point**, is Fleet Bay. The entrance is one mile and three quarters wide, all dry at low-water, but the inlet goes some way inland.

Vessels go up as far as **Gatehouse Bridge**, five miles from the sea, and lie safely aground in a very narrow creek.

Off **Ringdow Point** the Carvellan Rocks lie some distance. They always show above water, however. **Skyre Burn Bay** lies two miles within the point, and can be reached at two-thirds flood.

The town of **Gatehouse-of-Fleet** is a borough, and vessels of sixty tons go up to it. The nearest station is five miles away and the population is 1503. The country round is beautiful, many lofty hills being in the neighbourhood, with lovely valleys in between.

Between **Ringdow Point** on the E. shore, and **Eggerness Point** on the W., **Wigton Bay** contracts to about five miles wide. The land on the E. side is high and wooded. **Kirkdale House** stands on the edge of a ravine, and behind it is the hill of Cairnharrow, 1487ft. high. The foreshore is fronted with rocky shelves, and must be given a berth of fully one cable and a half.

A narrow channel runs up level with the shore line nearly as far as Carshuth Castle **ruins**, standing among trees about a mile N.W. of Kirkdale House, with 6ft. at low-water off the little burn that here runs into the sea. Beyond this, the channel of the Cree is nearly dry.

About three-quarters of a mile N. of Carshuth Castle is **Carshuth Burn**. The shore becomes lower beyond the burn, but the land rises to a considerable elevation behind, with stone quarries here and there, granite being worked to a large extent. The refuse from these works is upset on to the shore below, causing a little promontory.

Close alongside this **shore** runs the **channel of the Cree, scarcely 100yds. wide, and bordered by the Wigton or Baldoon Sands on the W.**

The ferry, at **Creetown**, is just a mile **above** the **quarries.** The channel, almost dry, runs in front of the town, with water enough at high-tide for vessels drawing 12ft. to come up. The flood only runs up for 4hrs.

. There is navigation for craft drawing 12ft. as far as **Carty Quay** at high-water springs; at neaps there is only 7ft. of water up here.

Knockdown Ferry is one mile above **Creetown**. The shores are here only a quarter of a mile apart, and there is here a snug pool, with three fathoms at low-water, extending for half a mile above and below the Ferry House, with a width of 100yds. wherein to swing. The shore, too, is quite steep.

The disadvantages of this place are that the tides run very strong.

The river continues to **Newton Stewart**, but the railway bridge prevents vessels going up there as well as the absence of water, although the tide flows to within one mile of that place.

The country round here is very attractive, and for yachtsmen looking out for a quiet and pretty berth where there is plenty of fishing and lovely surroundings, worse might be done than dropping anchor in the three fathoms pool of Knockdown Ferry, only they had better obtain local help to get there. There is a station at Creetown, only one mile away, on the Caledonian Railway to Stranraer.

All the N.W. part of the bay is filled in with sands, which dry as far S. as **Innerwell Point** on the W. side of the bay. **Wigton** stands on rather high ground in the N.W. corner of the bay. There is a tower to the county jail, which, being white, forms a conspicuous object from the bay. About thirty vessels belong to the port, and a steamer goes once a fortnight to Liverpool, calling at the little tidal ports round the bay and Luce Bay.

There is a branch line to Wigton from Newton Stewart, and it is continued to Garliestown and Whithorn.

The **port** of Wigton is half a mile S. of Wigton on the little Bladenoch stream. Vessels of 12ft. draught can get up here at high-water springs and berth alongside the quay, of which there is 600ft. frontage.

The N. part of the bay is low and marshy, but the lofty mountain, called **Cairnsmore of Fleet**, 2320ft. high, is only three miles on the other side from Knockdown Ferry.

From the Bladenoch River the coast trends S. to Orchard-town Bay for two miles and a half, fronted all the way by the wide extending sands.

Innerwell Port lies just inside the point of the same name. There is a considerable salmon fishery carried on here. The coast is well wooded, and becomes bolder as the deeper water of the bay is approached.

From **Innerwell Point** to **Eggerness Point** there is **two fathoms** close to the cliffs, but off Eggerness there are some rocks lying out 200yds. in a S. direction.

Garliestown Bay lies between **Rigg Bay** and **Eggerness**. It is an inlet, half a mile deep, but the rocky nature of the bottom makes it a bad beaching place. A small rock dries 2ft. at low-water in the middle of the bay, just outside the edge of the shore, which dries at low-water.

By the time the tide has flowed enough for vessels to reach Garliestown Pier the rock has 10ft. over it.

A rocky patch on the W. side is marked by a perch, but several large stones lie outside it, dry at low-water.

Garliestown Pier is 760yds. long. It is dry 4ft. above low-water-mark at springs, but there is 17ft. to 20ft. alongside at high-water springs. In approaching the perch should be kept about half a cable off, not more.

There is good anchorage half a mile S.E. of the pier in all winds except those from the S. and S.E.

Rigg Bay is sandy in the centre, with rocky shelves all round. The shores are well wooded. Galloway House, in beautiful grounds sloping down to the sea, stands on its N. shore. Rocks extend off both the points of the bay.

Between **Sliddery Point**, the S. point of the bay, and **Cairn Head** the coast is nearly straight, S. by W. The ruins of Cruggilton Castle crown the cliffs N. of Pall-mullet Cove and Point, with Port Allan in a little bight S. of it.

Yerrock Port lies N. of Cairn Head, and there is shelter here, in three fathoms, from all winds except from S.E. to N.N.E.

The cliffs are high now, and the coast bends round towards the S.W. to **Whithorn Bay** and **Island**, which, by the way, is no longer an island. On it is a white tower.

Port Whithorn is dry at low-water, but at half-tide vessels may enter and lie alongside the pier, which is on the side of the island.

On the W. side there are two rocks, called the Screen Rocks, which only uncover at the last quarter of the ebb. They are **steep-to** and marked by an **iron beacon**, painted red. This little port affords safe shelter to vessels which can take the ground. They can enter here at half-tide, and there is 18ft. at the entrance of the harbour at high-water. The inlet is narrow, but there are three fathoms at low-water well inside of the beacon.

Burrow Head is steep-to, and may be approached confidently. When the ebb is running against the S.W. wind there is a nasty race off it, and small vessels should give it at such times a wide berth.

This forms the dividing point between Wigton Bay and Luce Bay.

It is a pity one cannot linger over this remote part of Scotland. It is little visited, and yet is as beautiful a part in many ways as any. In archæological interest, too, it abounds. **Whithorn** was once the seat of ecclesiastical magnificence. There are the ruins of the cathedral of Galloway, dating from the end of the twelfth century. The western doorway is fine.

St. Ninian is supposed to have lived in a cave hard by at Physgill, and Burrow Head, with its natural arch, called the Devil's Bridge, and ancient ruined fort, is well worth a visit.

The neighbourhood of Castle Kennedy is most interesting also. To enjoy this part a berth in the Cree River, above Knockdown Ferry, might well be taken, and excursions could easily be made from there.

CHAPTER XXVI.

BURROW HEAD TO THE MULL OF GALLOWAY.

LUCE BAY is a wide and deep inlet, and is a dangerous place wherein to be caught if it should come on to blow hard from the S.W. round to S.E., as a heavy sea soon gets up, and there is a natural in-draught at most times into the bay.

From Burrow Head to the Mull of Galloway it is sixteen miles, and the bay recedes fourteen miles. In fact, the Mull looks like an island, as the land connecting the Rhynns of Galloway with the rest of Wigtonshire is low.

In all this wide extent there is not one safe harbour where a vessel may take shelter at all states of the tide. Southerly winds blow for at least three-quarters of the year, and the bay is at its worst then. Beyond the **Great and Little Scare Rocks** there are no outlying dangers, the shores being mostly steep-to, with sands lying off about one mile at the head of the bay.

The **Scare Rocks** are bare masses of granite, lying five miles and a half E. ¼ S. from the Mull of Galloway and ten miles and a half from **Burrow Head**, which bears from them E. by S. ½ S. **Great Scare** is 70ft. above high-water. **Little Scare**, which is two-thirds of a mile N.E. of **Great Scare**, is a group of heads, three of which are above high-water, but several of the rocks do not show, but they are, however, all within a cable of the heads which do rise above high-water.

Between **Great Scare**, which is steep-to, and **Little Scare** there is a channel with eight and nine fathoms, the depths around being eleven and twelve fathoms. The tidal streams set between the rocks.

Tides.—The set of the tidal currents in Wigton and Luce Bays is very similar. In **Wigton Bay** the flood begins 2hrs. before low-water by the shore, and the ebb 2hrs. before high-water off **Burrow Head**; but in the offing the stream is slack for an hour at high- and low-water by the shore, which corresponds with the times of high- and low-water at Liverpool. The flood stream sets round Burrow Head and flows across towards **Muncraig Bay**, between **Kirk Andrews' Bay** and **Bridgehouse Bay**, or towards **Borgue Church.** As it draws into the bay it curves round the **W. shore** and flows up into the **Bladenoch** and **Cree Channels**, while **S. of Muncraig Bay** it follows the E. shore towards **Great Ross.** The ebb follows in the inverse direction the flood stream, and sweeps round Burrow Head with a velocity of from four to five knots at springs.

At the **Mull of Galloway** the flood stream also sets into Luce Bay 2hrs. before low-water by the shore, which corresponds with the time of low-water at Liverpool Bar. From a mile off the Mull to Burrow Head the stream runs nearly straight with a slight in-draught to the bay, but close round the Mull it sweeps to the N.E., and slackens gradually as it approaches the centre of the E. shore of the bay, between the **Mull of Sinniness** and **Milton Point,** S. of which it runs strongly down the E. side towards Burrow Head.

Off the Mull there are strong tide races at all times, but they are naturally especially dangerous with wind against the tide. The overfalls extend fully two miles off, and the stream runs at the rate of six knots at springs. At an offing of three miles the races are less perceptible.

From **Burrow Head** the coast is bold for two miles, trending N.W. as far as Port Castle Bay. Here a beach skirts the fore-shore and runs as far as Cairndoon Point, where rocks and ledges begin off the shore. Lagg Bay lies between this point and Lagg Point, off which a ledge dries as far as 400yds.

Monrieth Bay is a wider opening, and affords shelter with winds from the E. and N.E. There are three fathoms, with a gravelly bottom, within two cables of the shore. **Barsalloch Point** is the N. limit of the bay, and off rocky ledges dry out one cable and a half.

The coast from here to **Port William** is skirted with rocky shelves, extending about one cable and a half off the high-water-mark, and at **Port William** the pier dries 6ft. above low-water.

This is a little tidal harbour, affording protection by its pier to a few vessels from S.W. and S. winds. There is 13ft. alongside the pier-head at high-water springs and 9ft. at neaps. A warping buoy lies off the pier-head.

The coast continues of the same character to the **Mull of Sinniness**, which is a bold headland, 241ft. high, and steep-to.

About one mile and a half N. is **Kinfillan Bay**, where there is anchorage in 9ft., with winds from N.W. to S.E., with the **Knock of Luce**, a hill 503ft. high, seen up the burn which discharges into the centre of the bay, and at a distance of two cables from the shore.

Sands now extend from the head of the bay as far as two miles at low-water from the little island, which divides Luce Water at its junction with the sea at high-tide. Glen Luce is about a mile from the mouth of the Water, but coasters discharge their cargoes at the entrance of the burn, where a ford crosses the stream. Another rivulet meanders through the low land at the head of Luce Bay. Piltanton Burn runs out through the Luce Water Channel after a devious and sluggish course behind the sand hills at Low Torrs.

For six miles now the bay is skirted with sand hills and warrens, while the sands dry out for fully half a mile from high-water-mark.

Sandhead Bay, on the W. side of Luce Bay and at its extreme N.W. corner, offers shelter in from two to three fathoms, with winds from S.W. round by N. to N.E.

S. of this the shore begins to be rocky and steep, with ledges lying off for about one cable, and stones farther out with 8ft. over them.

Chapel Rossan Bay also affords good shelter in W. winds, but the Mull Lighthouse should be kept in sight over Drummore Point.   As far as this the tides are mild.   **The light, however, is obscured within this part of the bay.**

From **Sandhead Bay** the Peninsula of Galloway is only two miles across to **Float Bay** on the N. channel side, and about ten miles long to the Mull.

At **New England Bay** it is only one mile and a half wide to **Nessock Bay** on the W. side.   The country is bleak, devoid of trees, and intersected by valleys, with small burns running through them, and farms here and there.

From **New England Bay to Drummore Bay and Village** the coast continues to be skirted by stones and rocks lying off the cliffs.   At **Kilstay Bay** the low-water margin widens and fills up nearly all **Drummore Bay.**

There is a little dry harbour here, affording accommodation for small coasters against the quay, but it is a poor place and liable to be obstructed by shingle after S. or S.E. winds.

As the coast trends in a **S. by E.** direction to Killiness Head there is a little more shelter here with winds from the S.S.W., but the bay is shoal for some distance out, and the Mull Lighthouse should be kept just W. of Killiness Point, but not much, as there is only 12ft. here at low-water.

Killiness is a low, rocky point, with stones drying out for more than 220yds. at low-water, so that it should be given a good berth in rounding into Drummore Bay.

At one mile S.W. is the little cove of **Maryport.**   Between these places the coast is shallow for three cables off shore, but S. of Maryport the cliffs may be approached to within one cable and a half.

S. of Maryport is the only shelter in all **Luce Bay** with southerly winds.   **E. Tarbet Bay** is the first of the many Tarbets the mariner will meet if he continues to sail N. or cross to Ireland.   The word has been explained to mean a portage or land ferry, where boats can be hauled across and launched on the other side.   It is a pretty general rule that where one Tarbet, or Tarbert, is found there is sure to be another on the other side, within about a mile or a mile and a half. This E. Tarbet Bay is separated from W. Tarbet Bay by a narrow neck, barely 400yds. wide, which is low, and connects the Mull to the main part of the peninsula.

It is a snug little nook, and could be made a most excellent harbour of refuge in a place where one is very much wanted for the coasting traffic. A breakwater carried out from the N.E. corner of the Mull, in depths of eight and nine fathoms, curving round in a N. and N.W. direction, would make a perfect little harbour, and convert Mull from a dreary, out-of-the-world rock into a very flourishing little watering-place, easy of access by steamers from all ports, being about equidistant from Belfast, the Isle of Man, and Silloth, and would be for the S.W. of Scotland what North Berwick and Dunbar are for the S.E. A healthier, breezier, more quaint little spot could hardly be found, with the sea on both sides and fine rock scenery all round.

The anchorage in the bay is a quarter of a mile off the Store House and landing-place, bearing W., in three fathoms and a half, or even closer in, for there are two fathoms quite near the shore. The tide is hardly felt here, although within half a mile it is roaring in overfalls. S. and S.E. the high wall of the Mull acts as a breakwater, and the only winds which can hurt are from the S.E. round E. to N.N.E. The Mull is a bold, uncompromising headland, steep-to, and 268ft. high.

From eight to thirteen fathoms are ·found close up against the cliffs, but the normal state of turmoil in which the sea is here renders a close approach unadvisable.

Mull of Galloway Lighthouse.—From a stone tower, 86ft. high, an intermittent white light is shown at an elevation of 325ft. above high-water, visible twenty-five miles. The light is bright for 30sec., eclipsed 15sec., visible from S. 50deg. E. to S. 22deg. W., through E. and N.

Fog-signal.—A fog-siren is now erected which gives two blasts of 5sec. each, with a pause of 2½sec. between them every 3min. As the light is shown from such a height it is liable to be hidden by fogs floating at a higher level than vessels, so that it might appear clear below although the light was obscured. Accidents have happened from this cause, so that care should be taken in weather likely to be thick.

Bearings and distances from the Mull of Galloway Light.— **Burrow Head bears** from the **Mull of Galloway,** E. by S., distant sixteen miles. **St. Bee's Head Light, S.E. by E. ¼ E.** easterly, forty-three miles. **Walney Island Light, S.E. ½ S., sixty-eight miles. Point of Ayre Light,** S.E. by S. southerly, **twenty-one miles and a half.** Peel Harbour, S. ½ W. westerly, twenty-five miles. **Bardsey Island, S. by W. ½ W. westerly,** one hundred and thirteen miles. **Chicken Rock,** S. by W. ¾ W., nearly thirty-five miles and a half. **Smalls Light, S.S.W. ½ W.** westerly, one hundred and seventy-eight miles. **Tuskar Light,** S.W. ½ S. southerly, one hundred and fifty-four **miles. Wicklow Head Light,** S.W. ¼ S. southerly. The Boyne River, S.W. by W. ¼ W. westerly, seventy-four miles. S. Rock Light-ship, W. by S. ½ S. southerly, twenty-two miles and a half. **Copeland Island Light, N.W. by W. ¼ W.** **westerly, twenty-three miles.**

Tides.—It is **high-water, full and change, at the Mull at 11hr. 15min. local, or 11hr. 35min. Greenwich time. Springs rise 15ft.; neaps, 12ft.**

The Mull of Galloway is the most southerly point of Scotland. The coast now turns abruptly to the N., forming the dangerous shore of Galloway, along which the tidal streams flow at a rapid rate, and where the overfalls are nasty with the wind against the sea.

The first time I came up here I had quiet weather from Douglas to the Point of Ayre, with wind moderate from W.S.W. No sooner, however, had I headed N.W. by N. for the Mull than the wind came round to the W., and kept heading me off into Luce Bay the nearer I sailed to the Mull.

By the time I was half-way across it came on to blow very hard from the N.W., with a blinding squall of hail and wind, which caused me to take in the mizzen and lower the foresail.

Under the mainsail and second jib we thrashed through the sea. Everything was hidden, and I saw we should only just make the **Scare Rocks** as the tide was setting across the bay. After enduring an hour of this pelting, stinging misery the horizon grew more distant, the clouds lifted, and there were the rocks close to us.

It was then a beat up to the Mull. By the time we got there the tide had begun to run to the S.W. and round the Mull. This meant a very heavy sea. However, there was no help for it. By dark we were off Crummag Head and making short tacks all up the coast.

That was the darkest sail I have ever had in my life. The coast is very badly lighted between the **Mull** and **Corsewall Point,** as both are hidden at a distance of some three miles from them, and Port Patrick Light is a very poor one. It was nervous work in this head wind and short sea, for I could not tell how far we were off the shore, and I did not wish to stand off too much as I wanted to go into Loch Ryan, and had never been up here before. It was a marvel I did not get on the **Loggan Rock**; and I have often wondered since, as I sailed down by it, how I managed to escape, for I did not know then of its existence! This was in October, and I expected to have bad weather, and I was not disappointed.

The last time I went S. it was very different. Then the wind was from the N.N.W. and the sea quiet. It was June, and the air was warm. I could lay my course from headland to headland, and ran so close round Crummag Head that I could almost touch the rocks. The sea became calmer and calmer as the wind and tide swept me round the cliffs. Porth Kemin was opened and past before it was seen almost. W. Tarbet offered but a momentary glimpse, and then we were swirling round the dark precipices of the Mull.

There was no need for the caution not to go close. I went as near as if the beetling cliffs were a quay, and the startled gulls and puffins screamed at us as we flew past.

It was a lovely sail, and the dreaded race was gurgling placidly as the gentle breeze stroked it the right way, like a drowsy giant soothed by the blandishments of a dainty enchantress.

But it is not often one can be on such intimate terms with this dangerous neighbour, and I am always glad when I have passed the Mull of Galloway.

None of this coast is to be trifled with. **Luce Bay** and **Wigton Bay** can only be visited on sufferance. For little boats or canoes a good deal of pleasant sailing might be had along here in fine weather. There are plenty of places where a boat can lie aground in safety and float again with the tide. Such a craft could easily navigate the Solway, and all the coast from Liverpool to the Mull. There is shelter every twenty miles or less. It is the larger craft that are in danger here, and every winter adds to the number of the wrecks.

Kirkcudbright Bay is the only shelter readily accessible and well lighted. The entrance is wide and fully exposed to the S., but there is safety within, even if a vessel does not find out Fish Pool. No harm can come to her on the Manxman Sands, or even moored in Balmangan Bay.

I got in here at midnight, and had no difficulty in picking up a good berth, although I was a perfect stranger. There were two coasters lying in the anchorage, and they remained there the next day in spite of the wind coming up strong from the S.W.

Readers of Sir Walter Scott should be interested in this coast, as it is the scene of Guy Mannering. The caves at Barlocco might well have served for the cave of Meg Merrilees and Dirk Hatteraick, as the ruined castle of Cruggleton might have been the ancient walls of Ellangowan.

From the Mull of Galloway I propose to steer S.E. by S. and make for the Isle of Man, a place more suited for cruising than any since the Menai Straits were left, and to which most yachtsmen turn their vessels' heads on the way up or down channel.

CHAPTER XXVII.

———

THE ISLE OF MAN — ITS COAST AND HARBOURS—THE POINT OF AYRE TO DOUGLAS HEAD.

THE approach to the Isle of Man from the N. affords by far the most impressive view of the island.

The low spit, which forms the Point of Ayre, is an excellent foreground, from which the stately peak of North Barrule (pronounced N. Barōōl) rises to nearly 2000ft., being only 194ft. lower than Snaefell (2034ft.).

The summit of Snaefell is seen behind it, descending abruptly to the largest of the mountain glens, that of Glen Mooar, or Sulby Glen, on its W. side.

As the island is narrow, hardly more than nine miles across, the mountains stand up in greater stature than when looked at from the W. or E. side of the island.

The Point of Ayre is the low shingle termination of the level plain extending N.E. from the foot of the mountains, which form the greater part of the rest of the island. So low is this point that it is some time before the mariner, approaching the Isle of Man from the N., sees it at all. At night the light, which is visible sixteen miles, sufficiently indicates its position, but by day it is not distinguishable beyond eight or nine miles; while the island itself has been in sight ever since

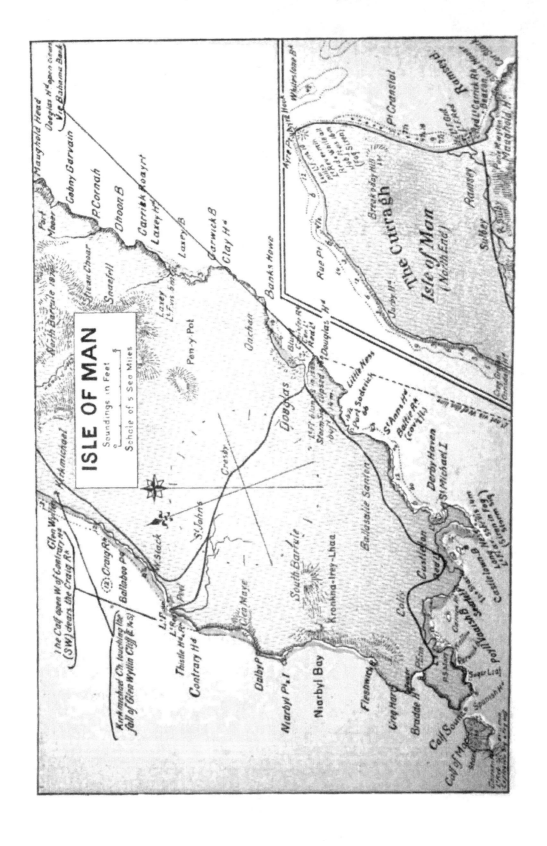

rounding Crummag Point, or, in fact, when off Port St. Patrick if the day is clear.

Point of Ayre Lights.—At a quarter of a mile within the point is a white stone tower, painted with two red bands, 99ft. high. From it is exhibited, at an elevation of 106ft. above high-water, a white and red light, alternately, every minute. It is visible sixteen miles W. of Rue Point, and S. of Maughold Head the land obscures it. In another tower, 25ft. above high-water, is a low light of less power, exhibiting a fixed white light, visible ten miles, and between the bearings of N. 8deg. E. and E.

Fog-signal.—A fog siren gives three blasts : high, high, low, of 2½secs. each, in quick succession every 3min.

Tides.—It is high-water, full and change, at Ayre Point at 11hr. 7min. local, or 11hr. 25min. Greenwich time. Springs rise 20ft ; neaps, 16ft. The flood stream begins at low-water by the shore, and runs from the W., setting S.E. over **Ballacash Bank** and King William Bank for 6hrs. E. of the point and close to it the stream sets S. into Ramsay Bay, following its curve, and on to **Maughold Head** from 2hrs. flood to 5hrs. flood ; for the rest of the 9hrs. it runs N.

At about a third of the way to Scotland the flood runs E. by S., and the ebb W. by N., for 6hrs. each way, turning at the times of high- and low-water at Liverpool, with a velocity of three knots.

Off the Point of Ayre there is a considerable race on both flood and ebb, the tide running at a speed of four to six knots.

At a distance of one mile and a quarter from the point, and in a S.E. ¾ E. direction, is **Whitestone Bank**, with a least depth of 8ft. on it. Between this bank and the point there is four fathoms least water over Ayre Hook. The sea breaks heavily on this bank in gales against the tide.

The **Bahama Bank** has a least depth of 5ft. This **dangerous** patch is near its S. extremity, and five miles and a quarter from Ayre Point Light, bearing N.W. ½ N. from the shoal. The bank is long and narrow, lying in a N.W. and S.E. direction.

U

Bahama Bank Light-vessel lies in eleven fathoms, one mile
and a quarter S.E. of the bank, with Maughold Head bearing
W. ¾ S., distant three miles and three quarters, and **Ayre Point**
N.N.W. ¼ W., seven miles and three-tenths. From an elevation of 38ft. above high-water a flashing white light is shown,
giving two flashes in quick succession every ½min., visible
eleven miles.

A fog siren gives two blasts in quick succession every 2min.

Half-way between the vessel and the tail of the bank a red
nun watch-buoy lies in eight fathoms.

Strunakill Banks, on the N.W. side of Ayre Point, have four
fathoms and a half least water, and are not important, except
that in bad weather, with wind against tide, there is a heavy
sea on them.

Ballacash Bank and **King William Bank** lie E. of Ayre
Point. The first has 7ft. least water on it, and is distant five
miles from Ayre Point. The latter has 12ft. least water on it
at eight miles and a half E. ¾ S. from Ayre Point Light. The
E. King William Bank has four fathoms and a quarter least
water on it, and lies eleven miles from the Point of Ayre. A
**spherical red and white buoy in horizontal rings, with staff and
diamond**, lies in five fathoms at the E. end of the bank, with
the Ayre Point Light bearing W. by N. ½ N., distant twelve
miles.

As a matter of fact, coming from the N. or S., a vessel
usually goes between **Whitestone Bank** and **Ayre Point**, being
the more direct route with fair winds and tide.

There is always a great deal of traffic off here, and steamers
crowd through this passage, rendering a good look out
necessary. Collisions are no uncommon occurrence, and it is
better to be careful.

Ayre Point is the **nearest** point to the **United Kingdom**,
being fifteen miles and a half only from **Burrow Head**.

Bearings and distances from the Point of Ayre Light.—The
Mull of Galloway bears from the Point of Ayre N.W. by N.
northerly, twenty-one miles and a half. Burrow Head, N. by
E. ½ E., fifteen miles and a half. Maryport Harbour, E. by N.,

thirty-five miles. St. Bee's Head, E. ½ S. southerly, twenty-six miles and a half. Wyre Light, Fleetwood, S.E. ¼ S., fifty-four miles. N.W. Light-ship, Liverpool, S. ¼ E., sixty-one miles and a half. S. Rock Light-ship, W. by N. ¼ N., thirty-five miles. Copeland Islands, N.W. westerly, forty-three miles and a half.

Ayre Point like Dungeness is growing. It is not going quite so fast to sea as that healthy promontory, but since 1818, when the first lighthouse was erected, it has grown to where it is now, or nearly a quarter of a mile in less than a century. It is possible, therefore, if it goes on increasing at the same rate to say when it will reach **Burrow Head,** but not in our time. In 6000 years it might come off. There is nothing like sailing for teaching one to look ahead.

From Ayre Point to **Ramsey** the coast is edged with sand and shingle ; the land rises about two miles S. of the Point at Kirk Bride, **Break-o'-Day Hill** being 267ft. high. Low gravelly cliffs now succeed until within a mile of Ramsey, when the shore becomes very low again, and so continues as far as the N. pier.

Ramsey Harbour is, unfortunately, tidal. It is, however, the safest harbour in the island.

The entrance lies open to the N.E., and during gales from that quarter a very heavy sea sets in and across the pier-heads. The foreshore dries nearly 100yds. beyond the piers, which are nearly 300yds. long.

There is a third pier at Ramsey, an iron landing and promenade pier, 750yds. long, and running out into 14ft. of water at low-tide. It affords no shelter, however, and it is a pity that the authorities did not utilise the money spent over this pier in extending one of the existing piers, so as to afford protection at low-water where vessels could lie afloat.

Lights.—On the N. pier, off Ramsey Harbour, a **fixed green** light is shown, visible nine miles ; and from the S. pier a **fixed red light** is shown, visible four miles. On the promenade pier two fixed red lights are shown, placed vertically.

Tides.—It is high-water, full and change, at 11hr. 12min. local, or 11hr. 30min. Greenwich time. Springs rise 21ft.; neaps, 16ft.

In the bay the stream runs 9hrs. to the N. and 3hrs. to the S., beginning to run in that direction at 2hrs. flood; but at **Maughold Head** the stream begins to run S. at 2hrs. flood, and continuing to run S. for 9hrs., only turning to the N. at 1hr. before low-water.

Anchorage.—The anchorage is good and the shelter safe with all winds except from the N. to N.E. With a N.E. wind the place is at its worst. In anchoring bring up as near the pier as is safe, there being only three fathoms at a quarter of a mile off. Just in a line with the promenade pier-head is a good berth, and a third of the distance from it to the S. pier-head.

In going in to the harbour it is necessary to have warps ready and anchor cleared, so as to let go at once. Yachts usually lie at the N. side against the innermost end of the N. pier. They are exposed to a heavy swell here if the wind blows in, and the ground is not over soft on which they lie. On the S. side the harbour takes a sharp turn at right angles to the entrance, and then the quays follow the bed of the Sulby River in a westerly direction.

The bottom of the harbour is gravel and clay. Vessels must lie alongside the quays or else on legs. There is 17ft. in the harbour at high-water springs and 12ft. at neaps.

There is a good deal of traffic in and out of the harbour. The steamers which run between Douglas and Whitehaven, and other excursion steamers, frequent the harbour, and there are many fishing-boats and coasting-vessels entering and sailing, and as the time when this is possible is limited there is a good deal of hurry when it does occur.

Ramsey is a neat, old-fashioned place in the business part of the town. Eastward there are new lodging-houses and hotels, and plenty of accommodation for visitors. The ground rises steeply to the S.E., and the slopes of N. Barrule come down to the shore between Ramsey and **Maughold Head**. Rising conspicuously to the S.S.W. of the town is a monument to Prince Albert, on a hill 390ft. high, and behind it are wooded hills, trending away W.S.W. to the entrance of Glen Mooar, or Sulby Glen.

Ramsey Bay is free from outlying dangers. The Carrick Rock is marked by a red beacon, with cage, 10ft. above water. It lies two cables off a little cove S.S.E. of the promenade pier.

Between this rock and the point, called Table-land Point, there is two fathoms. Round this little headland is a small cove, off which a vessel could lie in greater comfort than off Ramsey, with off-shore winds, and incur no further risk than in the usual roadstead. It is called **Port-e-Mwyllin.**

The advantage of this berth is that a small craft can lie within two cables of the beach, only there are no shops here. Water, however, can be obtained.

Rocky ledges skirt the little bay, in which there is 6ft. at low-water, at about 150yds. off the shore.

The **coast** from here to **Maughold Head** is steep and high, with no outlying dangers except a stack rock, called Stack Mooar, and Cor Stack nearer the head, but they are close to the cliffs and are no danger really. This piece of coast is a very fair specimen of Isle of Man scenery, as it is well varied in its features. Maughold Head is a bold cliff, 373ft. high, with a hill just within it and the old church behind. Wooded hills, more or less steep, lie inland behind **Port-e-Mwyllin**, and rising grandly over all is the peak of N. Barrule. Only from this end of the island does this mountain show so grandly. From the E. or W. it is seen to be the abrupt termination of the long ridge, or backbone, of the island, which reaches its greatest height in Snaefell—a gently sloping round-topped summit, three miles S.W. of N. Barrule. This ridge divides at Ben-y-Phott (1772ft.) and branches off into two ridges, with heights varying from 1036ft. to 1600ft., gradually decreasing as they go S.W., until both sink to the valley which divides the island at little more than 50ft. above the sea level between Peel and Douglas—the courses of the **Dhoo River**, which flows into Douglas Harbour, and the **Neb River**, which discharges at Peel, flowing in the same marshy track between Crosby and St. John's.

S.W. of the central valley the mountains rise again, attaining a height of 1585ft. in S. Barrule, which dominates Niarbyl Bay, although it is run very close in height by Cronk-na-Irey Lhaa, 1450ft., which rises abruptly from the very edge of the sea, half-way between Fleshwick Bay and Niarbyl Point, where the coast is more grand than in any other part. This district is almost uninhabited, and presents most wild features in the cliffs around Fleshwick Bay and Bradda Head.

The S. end of the island is tame, the cliffs near the Calf of Man being the only redeeming feature.

Maughold Head can be rounded very closely, and the coast is singularly free from outlying dangers all the way to Douglas Head, and even as far as Langness.

It is a pleasant sail along here, as one can keep close in, and the cliffs and shore well repay being examined. Just round **Maughold Head** is Port Mooar, which corresponds apparently to the Welsh Mawr, the Scotch More, and the Breton Meur. This is a pretty little shelter when the winds do not blow from the S. or E. Both sides are skirted with ledges, but there is three fathoms at low-water well within the points. There is a little fishing community living here, and it is an idyllic spot, with its narrow beach under the steeply-rising cliffs with N. Burrule towering above. Around **Maughold Head,** on its S. side, are several detached rocks of considerable height and picturesque appearance.

From Port Mooar to Port Cornah the coast is much the same. Steep hills slope to the edge of low cliffs, with cultivated land and copses in the valleys, while behind rise the rugged moorland to the central ridge.

Port Cornah, or Kenna, is a pretty little creek, so pretty that it is a matter of regret it is so shallow and exposed to the S. and E. At half-tide boats can get inside the little pool, where the Kenna comes brawling into the sea. The whole valley, or glen, of the Kenna deserves exploration. The stream rises in the moss at the head of Slieau Choar, 1808ft. high, and is fed by the springs on the northern slope off Slieau Lhean. After passing under the high road from Ramsey to Douglas, it descends by a succession of rapids and waterfalls through a lovely glen to the little dell by the sea shore, as pretty a

nook as any in the Isle of Man, and more sequestered than
most. The telegraph cable from St. Bee's Head is landed here.

Still cliffs and varied upland accompany the cruiser as he
sails S.W.

Laxey Head, with a snug little bay on its N.E. side, is
close ahead. Off the point here, S. of the bay, is a rock which
dries at the first quarter of the ebb. It is 200yds. from the
shore, and steep-to close around. The rock is called Carrick
Roayrt. There is four fathoms close to the cliffs in this
bight. **Laxey Head** is half a mile S.W. of this.

As **Laxey Bay** comes open the beauty of the scenery is
unmistakable. Close against the cliffs, on its N.E. side, is a
little tidal harbour. A jetty lies off the rocks on the N.
side and approaches the old pier within 200ft. Inside there is
a depth at high-water springs of 16ft., but the harbour is quite
dry at low-water.

There is a fixed white light shown on the old S. pier-head,
visible six miles. It is not seen until Laxey Head is open
S. of W. when coming from the N.E.

This bay is a safe roadstead with all winds except from the
S. and E. The holding ground is good, and there is 9ft. at
low-water within two cables of the shore. The beach is steep,
with no outlying dangers, and the cliffs rise boldly on either
side to **Laxey Head** on the N.E. and **Clay Head** on the S. In
Garwick Bay, nearer **Clay Head**, there is shelter from S.W. winds.

Laxey Valley rises steeply to the high road to Douglas
which follows the sides of the gulley. The village clusters on
the slopes, which are cultivated and bright. Laxey stream
descends from the side of Snaefell, which here rises uninterruptedly to its summit, presenting its most precipitous side to
Laxey Bay. High up above the village and towards the N.
is the celebrated Laxey mine, where there is the largest water-
wheel in the world.

A landing could easily be effected here, and Douglas is
within easy reach in case the weather changed.

From **Clay Head**, which is two miles and a half S. of **Laxey
Head**, the coast continues bold and rugged. The country

behind is less interesting. About one mile and three quarters S.W. of Clay Head there is a little bay, called Port Groudle, or Banks Howe. The bottom is foul.

Douglas Bay now opens up as Onchan cliffs are cleared, and at once the size as well as the beauty of the bay strikes one. The shore on the N.E. side is fronted by a ledge of rocks, which extend nearly to the head of the promenade pier.

The bay otherwise is clear of dangers, with the exception of the **Conister Rocks**, otherwise called St. Mary's Rocks, at the N. side of the Victoria Pier. On the highest rock there is a refuge tower of somewhat pretentious appearance.

Many wrecks have taken place on these rocks, as rocky ledges lie off in a S.E by E. ¼ E. direction, with from 14ft. to 16ft. on them.

The shore of the bay dries out to fully two cables, and shoals gradually, the deepest water being found in its N.E. corner.

Douglas Head is nearly steep-to, a low-water ledge extending off only to 100yds., and then the depths are from six to ten fathoms, with eighteen fathoms at a quarter of a mile off.

The promontory is 234ft. high, with a hideous structure on the top, and a switchback railway. The Marine Drive goes all along the head, and crosses the various chines and ravines on suspension bridges.

Douglas Harbour is formed by the Victoria Pier on the N. side, and the curved breakwater, extending from Douglas Head to Little Head, on its S.E. side.

There is an inner harbour, which is dry at low-water.

Lights.—Douglas Head Light.— From a white tower, 65ft. high, a flashing white light is shown at an elevation of 104ft. above high-water, visible fourteen miles. It shows six flashes in quick succession during 15sec., followed by an eclipse of 15sec. A vessel closing with the Isle of Man from the S., and if W. of N.E. ¼ E., will not see the light, as it is obscured by the land. It is hidden at three miles off Langness.

On the breakwater a **fixed red light** is shown in a tower, visible six miles. At the end of the Victoria Pier there is a fixed green light, visible three miles; and on the **Red**, or **Inner Harbour, Pier** a fixed white light is shown while there is 9ft. on the bar.

The iron pile promenade pier in the bay exhibits a fixed blue light, visible two miles.

There is another pier in the N.E. part of the bay, extending 120yds. in a S.W. direction from the W. side of the entrance to Port-e-Vada, but it exhibits no light, as it dries 8ft. above low-water at its extremity.

The harbour is of limited capacity, considering the number of steam-boats which ply there, and the large gathering of yachts there usually is.

In all winds, except those from the S.E. to E., there is perfect safety here; but an easterly gale sends in a nasty swell, which is felt even in the inner harbour.

Two steam ferries ply backwards and forwards, and the men who manage these boats have an especial dislike to anchor buoys.   Both of mine were deliberately cut off, and the men boasted of the achievement.   As it is necessary to moor here, and not much room in which to do it, it frequently happens that anchors get foul. The best berth is as near the S. corner of the harbour as possible, only the ferry people may object.

The inner harbour is used for the coasting traffic. Quays run up into the old part of the town for half a mile, and yachts are laid up on the shingle at the head. It is a nasty smelling place and very dirty.

If it were not for the ferry, which, after all, is a very minor trouble—although there should be more control exercised over the men, who are an insolent set if remonstrated with, in their persistent destruction of anchor buoys—Douglas Harbour would be a very quiet place.   I have never experienced an E. wind there. To judge by photographs of the tremendous seas coming over the esplanade it must be a little uneasy then.

CHAPTER XXVIII.

———

ISLE OF MAN—NAVIGATION CONCLUDED —DOUGLAS HEAD TO THE POINT OF AYRE BY THE CALF OF MAN.

THE coast from Douglas Head to Port Soderick is steep-to, with rugged cliffs of no great height, and bare, bleak ground rising behind. The shore is much indented, and trends in a S.W. direction to **Little Ness.**

Here a bay opens out, with Port Soderick in its S.W. corner. Off Little Ness there are some rocks which cover at high-water, extending for about 125yds. in an E. direction.

Port Soderick has a small jetty, and there is anchorage in off-shore winds close in to the beach in 18ft. A stream runs down the valley behind, and the little settlement looks snug and cosy.

From here to **St. Ann's Head** the coast gradually rises, maintaining the same rugged appearance. Off the S. point of St. Ann's Head is **Baltic Rock,** which uncovers at half-ebb, and outside of it is a rock with only 3ft. on it at **low-water.** They are distant from the head about 120yds.

The coast now takes a sweep round to the W.S.W. for about three miles, forming at its S.W. end the little dry harbour of Derby Haven. Rocky ledges lie all along the coast, extending off the entrance to Derby Haven.

This little shelter is fully exposed to the N.E. and E. From all other winds it affords perfect protection. A low, narrow neck of land connects the peninsula of Langness with the rest of the island, and **Castletown** is on the other side, the two bays lying back to back, the one facing N.E. the other S.W. The usual anchorage is just within St. Michael's Island. There is 9ft. at low-water, closer in to the harbour.

St. Michael's Fort is now a ruin. It was built by the seventh Earl of Derby while the Stanleys were still Kings of Man. Off the N.E. end of the island are some rocky ledges, which must be avoided in rounding into the bay.

A tidal harbour has been made by erecting a breakwater on a ledge of rocks extending S.W. from Ronaldsway Kiln on the N. side. The masonry extends N.E. and S.W. for 260yds., and the rocks on which it is built dry 13ft. at low-water. At the S.W. end of the breakwater a fixed white light is shown, visible two miles. St. Michael's Island is joined to Langness by a causeway.

From **Derby Haven** to **Dresswick Point**, at the S. extreme of Langness, is one mile and a half. This spot is noted for its shipwrecks. Off the S.W. point of Langness are the Skerranes, eight rocks which cover at half-flood, **Langness Point** being a chain of rocks 10ft. above high-water. There is a land-mark on this promontory as well as a lighthouse, the former being built some time ago as a caution to mariners not to mistake it for **Scarlet Point** on the W. side of the bay. The land-mark is a stone tower, 43ft. high, and stands on higher ground than the lighthouse, the top being altogether 105ft. above high-water.

Langness Light.—From a circular dark gray stone tower, 63ft. high, a flashing white light is shown from an elevation of 76ft., showing a flash every 5sec., visible fourteen miles.

Fog-signal.—A fog siren gives blasts of 5sec. duration with intervals of 40sec.

Tides.—The tidal stream off Langness runs at the rate of five knots at springs. The stream runs to the S. for 10hrs., from 2hrs. flood to the last hour of the ebb. In the offing, about five miles from the shore, the streams run E. and W. at

the rate of two knots, and turn at the time of slack water at
Liverpool.

Castletown Bay is a very complete horseshoe; it is mostly
occupied by rocky ledges and sunken dangers. Ledges lie off
all round, but on the **Langness** side they do not extend so far
out as they do on the W. side. The anchorage here is bad.
The tidal streams are strong. It lies fully exposed to the S.W.,
and the rocky bottom which surrounds the limited extent of
gravel and sand found in the S.E. side of the bay renders
bringing up here, unless compelled, a mistake. The usual spot
for coasters is **Spanish Head**, open of the **Stack** and **Rushen
Castle** N. by W.

The **Western Rocks** are marked by a black buoy, in three
fathoms, lying one cable S.E. of a rock called Llrecahrio, which
dries 16ft. at low-water springs.

Castletown Harbour lies on the N. side of the bay. The old
pier lies inside the new one, which is 420ft. long, and built in a
curve. Vessels of 12ft. draught can enter at high-water springs.

A **fixed red light** is shown on the end of the new pier, 22ft.
above high-water, visible eight miles.

Tides.—It is high-water, full and change, at Castletown at 11hr.
10min. local, or 11hr. 30min. Greenwich time. Springs rise
20ft.; neaps, 16ft. The current is strong to the E. across the
bay, beginning with the ebb by the shore, and forms an eddy
nearer to the N. of the bay.

The W. point is called **Scarlet Point**, and off it, on its S.E.
side, is the **Stack Rock**, a mass of basaltic rock.

W. of **Scarlet Point** lies **Poyll Vaaish Bay**, or the "Bay of
Death," as it is interpreted. Like Castletown, the whole bay is
exposed to the S.W. and S.E., and the bottom is mostly foul,
with rocky ledges all round and the Carrick Rock in the
middle, on which there is no beacon or buoy.

The **Carrick** is 500yds. long by 160yds. wide, and dries 14ft.
at low-water springs, so that at high-water spring tides there is
6ft. over it.

Langness Lighthouse open of the **Stack at Scarlet Point**
eads S. of the rock. The **red lights** on the hill, on the

W. side of St. Mary's Port, kept in line with the white light on the pier-head, leads S. of it also.

A sunken rock, 4ft. below water at low-tide, lies one cable off the E. end of the Carrick.

In the N.W. corner of the bay there is a sandy bay, with 22ft. in it, and inside the Carrick Rock there is from 18ft. to 24ft. at low-water.

Like the anchorage in Castletown Bay, this is a bad berth to lie in. It is, however, a trifle better than the former anchorage, as there is more protection in the N.W. corner, especially now the new breakwater is completed.

Port St. Mary is protected by a pier and a breakwater, 1000ft. long, called the Alfred Pier. There is shelter inside of this at all states of the tide. The harbour inside the old pier dries out, but when the Carrick Rock is covered there is 7ft. in the harbour.

Light.—From a white octagonal lighthouse on the inner pier a fixed white light is shown, 25ft. above high-water, visible nine miles.

On the Alfred Pier, at the end, in a white tower, 25ft. above high-water, a fixed green light is shown.

On a hill, W. of Port St. Mary, a fixed red light, 36ft. above high-water, is shown from a pillar. This and the white pier-head light in line lead S. of Carrick Rock. In entering at night, after giving Alfred Pier a berth of one cable and a half, open the leading lights to the N. and steer into the harbour.

Kallow Point is the S.W. limit of Poyll Vaaish Bay. Ledges lie off it for fully two cables, and the point should be given a proper berth.

The shore rises now after having been low since opening Derby Haven Bay. Porwick Bay is encumbered with a rocky foreshore, and the precipitous cliffs of Spanish Head, with the chasms on their S.W. side, loom up beyond. Spanish Head is the most southerly point of the island, and is so called, according to legend, from some ships of the Spanish Armada having been wrecked there.

The little island, **the Calf of Man**, is now all before the mariner, and he can either go through the Sound with "caution and good heed," or else pass to the S. of it. **Outside** the Chicken, however, there is a tide race.

The available channel through at low-water is not more than 100yds. wide, as a sunken rock, with only 6ft. on it at low-water, lies 70yds. W. of **Kitterland Islet, off the Isle of Man side.** **Thousla Rock**, with a perch on it and an **iron beacon,** with a **barrel-shaped cage**, painted red, 25ft. above high-water, dries at the first quarter ebb. It lies off the Calf near the N. Haven.

The Calf is about one mile long by the same in breadth. The highest point is 360ft. above high-water. There is a farmhouse on it, and part of the surface is cultivated. There are two landing-places N. of Grant Haven and S. Haven. There are also the two stone towers of the disused lighthouses near the cliff at the W. point of the island.

The shore rises from the N. to the S., being low at N. Haven and facing the W., with precipitous cliffs. The Stack Rock is a detached mass, 107ft. high, with a **boat passage between it and the Calf.** There is a sunkun rock in the way, however, and another rock, dry at low-water, a quarter of a cable N. of the Stack.

Towards the S. end of **Cargher Point** the cliffs descend to the point, which is low; but they rise slightly again as they trend S.E., and at **Burrow Cliff,** which is a bold projection, 120ft. high, they attain a rugged grandeur. Just W. of the head there is a cove where shelter may be found, in three fathoms close in, from N. winds. **Three rocks, covered at high-water,** called the **Clets of the Burrow,** lie 100yds. S.E. from the cliff.

Burrow Cliff is almost a stack rock, for it is connected with the Calf only by a low, narrow neck, covered at high-water. The cliff is pierced with a cave or tunnel, and is sometimes called the Eye in consequence; in fact, it might be called an island.

N.E. of **Burrow Head** is **Thick Head,** 250ft. high, and from there to N. Haven the cliffs decrease in height.

At **500yds.** from **Thick Head**, in a **N.E.** direction, are the **Clets of the Sound**, six rocks which **dry at the first quarter of the ebb.**

S.W. of the Calf, distant 1200yds., and separated by a Sound, with from twelve fathoms to twenty-four fathoms least water, is **Chicken Rock.** It is 5ft. above high-water springs. On it is built the lighthouse.

Chicken Rock Light.—From a tower, 143ft. high, built of light-coloured granite, and at an elevation of 122ft. above high-water, a revolving white light is shown, attaining its greatest brilliancy every ½min. ; visible sixteen miles.

Fog-signal.—An explosive fog-signal is discharged every 5min., and a bell sounded every minute.

Bearings and distances from the Chicken Rock.—The Mull of Galloway bears from the Chicken Rock N. by E. ¾ E. nearly, distant thirty-five miles and a half. Walney Light, E. by S. ¾ S., fifty-nine miles. N.W. Light-ship, Liverpool, S.E. ¾ S., fifty-six miles and a half. Chester Bar, S.E. by S. southerly, sixty-two miles. Great Orme's Head, S. by E. ¾ E., fifty-four miles and a half. Point Lynus, S.E. by S. ¼ S., forty-two miles. S. Stack, Holyhead, S. by W. westerly, forty-four miles. Tuskar Light, S.W. southerly, one hundred and twenty miles. Kish Light-ship, Dublin Bay, S.W. by W. ½ W., fifty-seven miles. The Boyne (Drogheda) River, W., fifty-three miles. Carlingford Lough, W. by N. ½ N. northerly, forty-four miles. St. John's Point, N.W. ¼ W. westerly, thirty-one miles. Strangford Lough, N.W. ¾ N. northerly, twenty-nine miles. S. Rock Light-ship, N. by W. ¾ W., twenty-nine miles. Copeland Islands Light, N. by W. nearly, forty-six miles.

Tides.—It is high-water, full and change, at the Calf at 11hr. 17min. local, or 11hr. 37min. Greenwich time. Springs rise 20¾ft.; neaps, 12¾ft. The **direction of the ebb from Spanish Head** is N.W. towards the Calf at Thick Head, and then over the **Clets of the Sound.** The flood flows through the Sound from the N., sets **over** the outer **Clet,** and thence round to Spanish Head, beginning to flow S. at 2½hrs. before low-water until 2½hrs. afterwards, the ebb flowing in a contrary sense.

At **Chicken Rock** the stream runs at four knots and a half, but nearer the Calf, from the **Stack** to **Burrow Cliff**, there is next to no stream.

The coast after passing the Sound turns sharply to the N.E., and continues rugged and steep-to, with ten fathoms close to the cliffs, except off the Mull Hill Point, three-quarters of a mile from Kitterland Island, where some half-tide rocks project about one cable and a half, and about three-quarters of a mile farther where there are two or three more; but a distance of two cables and a half from the coast clears everything.

Bradda Head is the first conspicuous object which meets the mariner as he ports his helm to turn N.E., after rounding the sunken rock off the W. end of Kitterland, a rock, however, only dangerous to vessels drawing 6ft. and at dead low-water. **Bradda Head** is a noble promontory, together with the hill behind it, rising to 766ft. To give it greater dignity the grateful inhabitants of Port Erin have erected a tower to the memory of Mr. William Milner, whose inventions are held in detestation by a branch of the community who do not disguise their envy of other men's goods. It is called in the local guide-books, "A graceful and not inharmonious edifice." As for the harmony, I don't know. No doubt when it blows from any direction there is plenty of the Æolian air about it; but the music of the winds piping loud is rather too Wagnerian for my taste.

Port Erin is now all before us. It is about two miles from the Sound, and was once a snug little shelter. The authorities have done what they could—they have thrown £80,000 into the sea. Whether the engineers did their part as well is another matter. Sir John Coode did what he could, no doubt, but it was no good, and all that remains of the breakwater is a reef extending 200yds. in a N. by E. direction E. of Castle Rocks, at the S.W. corner of the entrance to the bay. A **black buoy**, in five fathoms and a half, marks the seaward end of the breakwater, which might better be called water broken. It is a sad business to think of, £80,000 lying there, making a new feature in the outlying dangers of the Isle of Man coast. There are also the ruins of a landing-wharf along the S. shore from the landward end of the sunken treasure, but it, too, is being washed away in order to save visitors from being destroyed by what was meant for their protection. **Two fixed red lights** are placed 130ft. apart, at a height of 33ft. and 52ft. about high-water. They shine from two red wooden erections, and are visible about five miles. Kept in line they lead clear of the ruined breakwater.

The bay is otherwise free of natural dangers, except a patch of rocks, with 5ft. least water on them, opposite the breakwater on the N. side, and the **Sker Rock** beyond; but they are not so pushing as Sir'John Coode's obstruction, and only lie out 50yds. The Sker, too, is not yet sunk, and only just covers at high-water springs.

In the bay, which is very pretty, with plenty of water close in, there is good anchorage with all winds from N. round E. to S.W. The bottom is sand over clay, and the depth about three fathoms, or even less, with safety.

Westerly winds send in a heavy sea, and there is a considerable swell with S.W. winds.

From Port Erin to Niarbyl Point is about four miles and a half. On the way the finest cliff scenery of the Isle of Man is passed. Only one outlying danger lies between **Bradda Head** and **Fleshwick Bay.** The Grey Harlot Rock is close in to the high cliffs under Bradda Hill, on its N.W. side, with from six fathoms to seventeen fathoms close to.

Fleshwick Cove is a very snug little bay in S. winds round to N.E. The cliffs rise precipitously all round. The little green spot, with its steep beach in the shady recess of the towering black rocks, looks very pretty and tempting. One would like the wind to remain at E. for the pleasure of anchoring here a spell. The cliffs grow higher and higher, steeper and steeper, from 990ft. to the summit of Cronk-ny-Irey-Lhaa, 1450ft., only half a mile from the edge of the sea. This is a pretty steep gradient.

As Niarbyl Point is neared South Barrule comes in sight, but it is a poor hill beside its northern namesake. This is a

X

wild country we are passing, and the native showmen are very
proud of it. " Magnificent grandeur," " Majestic wildness,"
" Savage altitude," " Awe-inspiring solitudes "—such are a few
of the proper expressions to use when passing along here.

Niarbyl Point is three miles S.S.W. of **Contrary Head.** The
cliffs descend to this low, rocky spit, off which a ledge extends
for three cables. Then, as **Dalby Point** is rounded, the pretty
valley of Glen Maye, or Glen Moif, comes in sight. There is a
waterfall tumbling from the cliffs above, but the steep shore
recedes a little, leaving room for a green valley nestling among
the wilder hills. **Slieau Whuallian** rises behind, to a height of
1094ft., but the immediate coast line is not more than 200ft.
high, rising to the N.E. as **Contrary Head** is neared.

There are no outlying dangers from **Niarbyl to Contrary Head,**
but half-way between that point and **Peel** is **Thistle Rock,** which
is **always above water.**

Peel Castle, on the little island of St. Patrick, now opens as
Contrary Head is rounded, distant one mile and a quarter, and
one may **keep close** to it, for there are **no** outlying dangers. The
end of the N. pier comes open, and the vessel can be headed
towards the bay.

Peel Harbour is, like all the Isle of Man harbours except
Douglas, a tidal one. There is **anchorage** in the bay in two
fathoms and a half, just 300yds. E. of the N. breakwater. A
vessel is sheltered here from winds from S.W. round by
E. to E.N.E., but northerly and westerly winds send in a
heavy sea.

Peel Harbour is formed by the creek of the Neb, which runs
out in a N. by E. direction, past St. Patrick's Island. The
bottom of the harbour is hard and rocky on the W. side ; on
the town side it is sand and gravel. There is 18ft. in it at
high-water springs and 11ft. at neaps. Protection against the
inrun of the sea during N. gales has been attempted by building
the pier, off St. Patrick's Island, which extends in an E.N.E.
direction for 100yds., and there is a jetty farther in on the same
side. On the **Peel** or E. side of the **harbour entrance a pier
runs out for 120yds. in a N.N.E.** direction, leaving an entrance

5oyds. wide between it and the Island of St. Patrick. The harbour within is long and narrow.

Lights.—A fixed red light is shown in a tower, 27ft. above high-water, at the head of the old pier, visible three miles.

A fixed white light is shown on the St. Patrick's Island Breakwater, at an elevation of 37ft., visible five miles.

From **Peel to Orrisdale Head**, a distance of six miles, the coast is without interest and without dangers. **Craig Rock** has 13ft. least water on it. It lies one mile and a third off **Ballaboo Point**, two miles and a quarter distant from Peel Castle, in a N.E. direction.

From **Orrisdale Head**, which is 140ft. high, the coast continues low and straight to **Jurby Head** for three miles and three quarters. Off **Jurby Head** lies **Jurby Rock**, with only 9ft. on it at **low-water. It is 800yds. off shore and three-quarters of a mile S.W. of the Head, which is 130ft. high.**

The low ground off the N. end of the island is now well abreast of the vessel sailing N.E., and the shore trends E.N.E. for four miles to **Rue Point**, with no outlying dangers, and skirted by low cliffs.

Off Rue Point a spit of sand runs out about 800yds., with from 2ft. to 6ft. on it, in a northerly direction.

From this **point** to the **Point of Ayre**, distant one mile and a half, the coast trends about E. by N. with low land and shingle beach.

Tides along the W. Coast of the Isle of Man.—Off Contrary **Head** the tidal streams, which sweep round Ireland, meet, so that along the coast of the Isle of Man between Peel and Port Erin there is little tidal stream.

At **Jurby Head** the flood-tide sets **towards** the **Point of Ayre**, increasing in rapidity from one knot to three or four knots as it nears the points. The stream begins 1hr. before high- and low-water by the shore. Off Peel there is next to no tidal stream. Two miles N. of Peel the stream sets to and from the Point of Ayre, and five to ten miles W.N.W. of Peel they set to and from the Calf of Man, with less velocity as one sails W.

Close in to **Bradda Head** the stream begins to run N.W. 2hrs. before high-water by the shore with an eddy along Niarbyl Bay, but of no strength to speak of.

Tides at Peel.—It is high-water, full and change, at Peel at 11hr. 8min. local, or 11hr. 27min. Greenwich time. Springs rise 19ft.; neaps, 15ft.

CHAPTER XXIX.

—

THE ISLE OF MAN AND ITS
PICTURESQUE FEATURES.

FROM a dry disquisition on the possible dangers which skirt the really very tidy shores of the Isle of Man, I turn with pleasure to take a cursory view of the many attractions the island offers.

The Isle of Man is large enough, and varied enough, to be able to please all tastes. To those who prefer the glittering splendour of crystal saloons where devotees of Terpsichorean arts practise their favourite amusement to their heart's content, what place can excel Douglas in the numerous opportunities it affords? If some may object that the society is a little mixed and the gymnastic evolutions a little pronounced—that armies of the "horny-handed sons of toil" bent on enjoying themselves, and having saved up all the year for this little treat mean to do it thoroughly, are, perhaps, to put it mildly, a little too self-assertive ; that the artless innocence of the fair damsels from the purlieus of our mining and manufacturing centres is refreshing to witness, if also a little trying — to those fastidious and hypercritical souls I answer at once, go to Ramsey, or Port Erin, or Peel. If you are very exclusive indeed then try a cottage at Port Soderick, or a farmhouse at Maughold or Fleshwick if you can find one. The rocks and sands of Castle-town, Derby Haven, and Port St. Mary, are such as children

love. There connubial bliss and domestic calm might pursue
the even tenor of its way, unalloyed by the gay clamour of a
too exuberant revelry untrammelled by thoughts of others'
feelings or prejudices. Seriously, however, the Isle of Man is
quite a charming place in the variety of its pleasures.

Historically it is most interesting. Undoubtedly inhabited
from the earliest times of authentic history by Celtic tribes,
the island was conquered by Scandinavian adventurers, who
founded here a Norse kingdom in the ninth century, which
lasted for three centuries, until, after the usual manner of those
times, the dynastic feuds of the rival chieftains opened a way
for foreign interference. In 1263 Alexander III. of Scotland
defeated Haco of Norway at the Battle of Largs, and the Scandinavian possessions passed into the hands of the Scotch.
Henry IV. of England, however, managed to wrest the island
from the feeble rule of Robert Stewart, third of that name, and
conferred it on Sir John Stanley. The Stanleys, at that time
although a powerful Lancashire family not yet raised above
the richer commons, managed to obtain possession of the feudal
jurisdiction, and from the days of Sir John Stanley, in 1406
until 1736, the Isle of Man remained in the titular sovereignty
of that capable family, whose fortunes were further consolidated
by the politic conduct of Sir William Stanley, stepfather to King
Henry VII., at the Battle of Bosworth.

In 1736 the Dukes of Athole, as heirs general of the Stanleys,
whose issue in the direct male line then failed, succeeded to
the feudal kingship; but in 1765 the royalty was sold to the
Crown for £70,000, and in 1827 all the remaining rights of the
Murrays were parted with for another £417,144.

Since then the island has been governed under the English
Crown by the Governor and Council forming the Upper
House, and the House of Keys forming the Lower House.
Bills, after passing both Houses, must be signed by a quorum
of each House, consisting of the Governor and two members
for the Upper and thirteen members for the Lower House;
after which they are submitted for Royal assent, and then
promulgated in English and Manx on the Tynwald Hill.

Castletown used to be the capital, but lately an Act has been passed by which Douglas is now the seat of the Government, the technical name of which is the Tynwald.

Scandinavian habits and customs prevail in many of the legislative proceedings.   The very fact that Bills are not fully legal Acts, although passed, signed, sealed, and stamped with the Royal assent, until they have actually been promulgated in the open air of day on Tynwald Hill, reminds the archæologist of the ancient Tingvalla of Iceland, the Dingwall of Ross and Dumfriesshire, and the Thingvölly of Denmark.

The Scandinavian and Teutonic nations had a great dread of witchcraft. Assemblies held under roofs, or within human habitations, were liable to such influence, hence the choice of open-air resorts where the courts could be held without fear of malevolent or occult interference.

Tynwald Day is held on July 5 every year, unless it should fall on a Sunday, when it is held on a Monday.   It is a great day for popular rejoicing, being a public holiday, and a universal fête.   A fair is held on the low ground, near St. John's Church, to which a fenced pathway leads from the Tynwald Hill.   This mound is 256ft. in circumference, with steps leading up it from the path to the church.   It rises in four stages : The first terrace is 8ft. broad, the next 6ft., the third 4ft., and the summit 6ft.   Tradition says that the mound was composed of soil brought from the seventeen parishes of the island.

Here the authorities of the island assemble, after first attending service in St. John's Church—The Governor, the Council, the House of Keys, the Deemsters, the Bishop of Sodor and Man, the various public officials, and the officers of the garrison, if there are any.

A procession is formed from the church.   Policemen head it, then come the coroners, captains of parishes, the clergy, the four high bailiffs of the island, the members of the House of Keys, the Council, the sword-bearer (carrying the Governor's sword of state erect), the Governor (now Sir J. West Ridgeway, K.C.B.), the chaplin, the surgeon to the Governor's household, and the chief constable.

Proclamation is then made warning all unauthorised persons to refrain from molesting the proceedings, after which the laws are promulgated—that is, the titles are read ; the rest is taken as read.

The procession then reforms and adjourns to the church.

In old days, when all freemen bore arms and the chief men of the island mounted the hill clad in chain mail with sword and battle-axe on thigh, wearing those picturesque winged helmets on their heads and with their manly nether limbs encased in those thonged and cross-gartered hose, which artists would have us believe they always wore, the procession mounting Tynwald Hill must have looked dignified enough. There was no need then to cut steps up the sacred mound. Now, however, modern clothes do not suit the surroundings ; neither gowns, nor robes, nor even military uniform, nor Sunday hats, look well stumbling up the narrow steps.

Somehow, the garish day takes away from the dignity of the proceedings, and that which looks well in a deliberative chamber or cathedral nave seems mean and paltry here. Have men degenerated, or have we more sensitive tastes ?

In addition to this living relic of the Scandinavian domination, there are all over the island venerable crosses of the true Celtic type. In the most unexpected places these memorials of the devotion of long-past ages meet the rambler. They stand by the roadside, as at Maughold, or in fields and mountain sides, but more frequently in churchyards — notably at Kirk Braddan, close to Douglas.

They are usually embossed with knobs, and carved intricately with Celtic ribbon patterns, some even being inscribed with what are called Runic characters.

Monuments of a still earlier age abound. Stone circles are found in many places, mostly in the S. of the island, and nearly always in lonely places. Men feared to build their homesteads near these uncanny spots, for the Manxman was as superstitious as Celtic and Norse blood could make him, and was imbued with a profound ignorance of most earthly matters beyond fishing and mining, and eating and drinking.

Perhaps from an antiquarian point of view the Isle of St. Patrick, at Peel, is the most interesting spot in the Isle of Man. Here on this little rocky island, of seven acres and a half, are crowded together a strange collection of buildings.

There is a cathedral, a mediæval fortress, a parish church, and a very good imitation of an Irish round tower, the whole, surrounded by crumbling walls of the fifteenth and sixteenth centuries, and chafed perpetually by the girding sea.

Of these buildings the most ancient is probably the rude church of St. Patrick. It is, perhaps, when sailing in these western seas that one realises most what a very important person St. Patrick was. The mariner meets him everywhere. At St. Ives, at the Sarn Badrig or Patrick's Causeway, at the Isle of Man, in Cornwall, Wales, and Mona, the memory of the Saint is preserved by tangible survivals. Will the memory of our missionaries of to-day be preserved as lastingly in southern seas or African uplands? To be so well remembered argues that the man must have been greatly loved or greatly feared. No other name of that far-off time has so impressed itself on natural objects or artificial structures on these western shores. One grows more and more convinced that St. Patrick, worthy man, was an excellent sailor; and now I come to think of it, it was his countrymen who first started yacht clubs. No doubt, the spirit of St. Patrick inspired the Royal Cork in 1720, when the first yacht club in the United Kingdom was inaugurated, and, I believe, the first yacht club in the history of the world.

But I return to our Peel. The round tower and the ruined church are the most ancient relics on the island. The Cathedral of St. Germanus is of a far later age, probably the twelfth century, and is rapidly falling to pieces. Of the castle the most interesting portions are the gatehouse, with the guard-room in it, rendered famous by the legend of the Black Dog (Mauthé Dhoo), told in the notes to Sir Walter Scott's novel of Peveril of the Peak. What a wonderful store of legend there is in those notes to the Waverley Novels. Who would have known of the weird tale of Littlecote Hall and Wild Darrell but for Sir Walter; or troubled about Michael Scott, that knightly magician of the Hohenstaufen Kaiser, but for the greater wizard of his name and house?

Truly St. German might exclaim, "A man's enemies are those of his own house." It was a Bishop of Sodor and Man who stripped the lead off the Cathedral Church in order to cover in the Parish Church of St. Patrick. This was done by Bishop Wilson in 1710. It was the same Bishop who sent the steps for St. Paul's Cathedral, cut from the black rocks of Port St. Mary Bay. The Bishop, however, appears to have been a most worthy prelate, and his memory is said to be still held in reverence by the old families of the island.

Peel Harbour is a crowded place at times. To see the herring boats go out is a pretty sight, reminding one of the sardine boats from Douarnenez. There is a lovely view over the old town and harbour from the hill on the S.W. of the town towards Contrary Head. Here is a tower called "Corin's Folly." The story goes that one of that name lost his wife, and being deeply attached to her buried her up there; then he built the tower over her grave, and lived there until it was time to join the lost one again. I don't myself see where's the folly; in fact, I own to a liking for lonely Master Corin.

It is a pity Peel cannot prolong its piers and make itself into a decent kind of harbour. It does seem to me astounding that an island like this does not possess one first-class harbour where shelter can be found from every wind. Douglas is the nearest attempt, but to judge by the photography in the shop windows, it must be anything but a nice shelter when the sea is tumbling over the esplanade and flying over the breakwater. Surely the photographers did not invent that scene?

Castletown is the next point of interest. If it is castles one cares about, there is a neat and tidy one there. Although Rushen Castle dates from the ninth century, they say it has been so well taken care of that it looks almost new from the outside. Godred the Red, son of King Orry, who "came from the Milky Way," as he said playfully to the simple Manx folk when they inquired where he lived when he was at home, built the castle in 960, A.D., so tradition says. It is still the only fortress on the island, but about as valuable for offensive and defensive purposes as were the Welsh biddies of Lord Cawdor at Fishguard. However, they were good enough to frighten away the French, so let us hope Godred's castle will be equally effective.

The castle is quadrangular, flanked with towers, the northern one, or keep, being the highest (80ft.), and it is surrounded with an embattled wall and ditch. A modern addition is the stone glacis. This used to be the headquarters of the Government, and in the castle is the court-room and Government offices, now removed to Douglas. The country is flat and uninteresting round the town, but Rushen Abbey is a pretty place. The ancient buildings are very meagre, and an hotel occupies most of the site; but in years gone by, when I visited it on a walking tour during a stay in the island as one of an Oxford reading party, I remember the little place was comfortable and pretty enough to make up for the desecration of the monastic establishment.

The history of the place shows that it was a very important one in Manx annals. The abbot was a baron of the island. He held courts of his own, and could demand a prisoner from the Royal courts if it were proved he was tenant of the abbey. The establishment was a Cistercian colony from Furness, which Foundation elected the abbot.

King Olave, in 1134, appointed a bishop from the brotherhood, on the suggestion of Eudo de Sourdeval. It is curious to meet this name in this island of the Irish seas at this early time, for it was a Sieur de Sourdeval who made it so hot for the English and the monks in Belle-Ile-en-Mer, in the sixteenth century, that both were obliged to quit the island.

Strangely, too, this little abbey survived a long time after the Reformation had triumphed; nearly fifty years, at least, after Henry VIII. had dissolved all the other monastic foundations. It was not until quite late in Elizabeth's reign that Rushen Abbey ceased to exist as the sole survivor of the ancient religion. Like all the sites chosen by the monks, the position of Rushen Abbey is most cosy. The soil is very fertile: tomatoes, fruit-trees, and vegetables flourish as well as if they were growing in the Channel Islands, or the Vale of Gulval, near Penzance.

The little stream, the Silverburn, flows through the abbey grounds, crossed by the ancient "crossag," a little bridge so narrow that no wheeled conveyance could pass over it. There are trout in the stream, and the monks knew how to provide themselves with store of dainty fish for the Lenten, or Friday fast. The site of the fish-ponds is still plain to see.

From Rushen Abbey, which can be reached by railway from Douglas, to Port Soderick is about five miles by train. This is a favourite excursion of the tourist cars, which drive round the island. The creek is pretty, but best seen from the sea.

Douglas, of course, is the chief centre of attraction for the majority of people. The town is essentially a place of "the people." There are no duties to perform at Douglas, no antiquities, no sights, nothing by which to stir the higher emotions—the lower having probably been sufficiently stirred on the way thither from Liverpool, or Fleetwood, or Barrow.

As a contrast, however, Douglas can offer an almost unique scene in the height of the season. Excursion steamers from Dublin, Belfast, Glasgow, Silloth, Barrow, Fleetwood, Liverpool, Llandudno, and Holyhead crowd into the harbour. From Birmingham, Manchester, Leeds, and Liverpool, "the Potteries," from all the mining districts of the North and the towns of the cotton industry, crowds of people throng here. Every place is full. Even bathing machines are chartered for a night's lodging. Money is poured out on all sides recklessly in dancing saloons, refreshment rooms, drives, entertainments, in every conceivable way by which men and women bent on enjoying themselves can find an outlet for their fancy. Douglas is at once the Margate, the Donnybrook Fair, the Moulin Rouge, of the North and the Midlands of England.

That big hotel beyond the promenade pier was once the Duke of Athole's residence. It is now the Castle Mona Hotel. Everywhere one looks there are places of refreshment, hotels, lodging- and boarding-houses, and huge glass palaces for dancing. Tramcars, char-a-bancs, flys, and four-wheeled "shays" ply in all directions. Everyone is enjoying the scene, the bright sky and healthy air.

Douglas is gay, lively, amusing, and vulgar, a costermonger's holiday resort, gilt with the tinsel of a year's savings. But it is the only attempt at a comfortable harbour, and so let us enjoy ourselves.

"It is sweet to play the fool at times," so said an ancient philosopher, who probably was as good a citizen as most.

The bay is undoubtedly very fine, and the town from the sea has a decidedly handsome appearance.

The name of the town, by the way, has nothing to do with the "guid Sir James," or any other of the "proud Douglases." It is a compound word, formed from the names of the two streams which flow out through the harbour—the Dhoo and the Glas, meaning "the Black ·and the Grey" rivers. Undoubtedly this is the best centre from which to visit the rest of the island, and so it is after all fortunate that its harbour is also the best.

From Douglas to Ramsey is some twenty miles by road. The railway goes all round by Peel and at the back of the island. For those who enjoy a good walk and like hills, there is an excellent excursion before them. Take the coach to Laxey, then climb up the road from there to Snaefell, and descend either by the Sulby Glen Road or the shorter way by the N.E. of the mountain, crossing the neck between it and Slieau Choar, and so reach Ramsey by the Sulby Road. In this way the whole island almost will be seen, and if there is sufficient energy to climb the easy slope to the top of Snaefell, and the day is fine, a most splendid view will be the reward. I have seen from the top England, Wales, Scotland, and Ireland. It is not often Snowdonia can be seen, but the Mourne Mountains, Cairnsmore, and the Cumberland Hills are almost always clearly visible. The whole island lies below like a map, and one can well understand how such a view on a lovely summer's evening inspired the imagination of a mind like that of the painter, Martin, who, from the summit of Slieau Chiarn, made the study for his celebrated picture, "The Plains of Heaven."

Ramsey has, or is supposed to have, attractions of a more select order than Douglas. The place is certainly more primitive, although there are many very well-built terraces and hotels at the E. end of the town. The bay affords good shelter in off-shore winds, but a howling wind does come down off N. Barrule at times. Curiously enough the gale seems, often, purely local, and directly Maughold Head, or the Point of Ayre, is rounded, where one would expect to feel it most, all is quiet, and one wonders where the wind came from.

There is one feature of natural beauty which the Isle of Man possesses in an eminent degree. That is the multiplicity and loveliness of its glens.

To those who only go round the beaten track these are mostly unknown; but Ballaglas Glen, Sulby Glen, the Dhoon Glen, Glen Maye, and many others, are too beautiful not to be visited, and the sooner the better, for crystal dancing saloons do not improve the romantic aspect of the glens, and these erections are rapidly rising in the most beautiful and the most secluded spots. Surely the shrines devoted to Terpsichore need not invade the quiet glades and bosky dells where Il Penserosa loves to roam.

It is when these recesses are explored that one understands how really charming the island is. At first sight it looks, perhaps, bleak and rugged. There is a general absence of trees, except about Ramsey, and it is only in the depths of the numerous ravines which descend from the mountains in all directions, where the steep slopes are clothed with foliage, that one meets with a winsome beauty as delightful as it is unexpected.

One thing I have forgotten, but it is impossible to walk a yard in any of the large towns without being reminded of it in the shop windows.

It is the "Lady Isabella." This aristocratic personage is of considerable circumference, but otherwise is tall and slim. She is a giddy thing, and gyrates at a speed of twice a minute. She is never still, but whirls night and day. In other words, "Lady Isabella" is the biggest water-wheel in the world.

She is an "Overshot," and pumps up out of the Laxey Mine 250gall. of water a minute from a depth of 1200ft. A Manxman made her, and Manxmen are proud of her. Her dimensions are : 72½ft. in diameter, 6ft. in width, 217½ft. in circumference, and she weighs ten tons. She has been going since 1854, and is in good condition yet.

Of course, everyone has heard of Manx cats. Some people think they are myths. But they are a reality, and not only are the cats tailless, but the fowls, too. Why this island should be fatal to tails I don't know. There must be something in the air ; and yet writers of fiction live here. Let Mr. Hall-Caine explain.

There is another curious thing about the island—that is, its heraldry. The Arms of Man are its legs, as somebody said facetiously; but it is not content with two legs—as if to make up for its dislike to tails the Isle of Man Arms are three legs. Whether it is emblematical of the happy disposition of the Manxman that whatever befalls he will always fall on his legs, I don't know ; but wherever you go in Douglas you see the three legs—the "Trie Cassyn." Strangely enough, this same cognisance is found in the Arms of Naples, or the Kingdom of the two Sicilies, and as far back as the Punic Wars it is found on a coin of Lilybœum.

What is the connection? The cognisance is not one which would obviously be invented.

On the whole, the Isle of Man for climate, beauty, variety, and comfortable sailing, is as good a place as I know anywhere. The only thing wanting, perhaps, is a prevalence of good taste.

CHAPTER XXX.

EAST COAST OF IRELAND—FROM THE POINT OF AYRE TO BELFAST LOUGH.

From the Point of Ayre to Belfast Lough.—Copeland Islands Light is forty-three miles and a half, and the course N.W. westerly; this course leads six miles and a half S.W. of the Mull of Galloway. From Peel to the Copeland Islands the distance is forty miles and a half, and the course N.N.W. ¼ W.; while from Peel to the entrance of Strangford Lough is twenty-eight miles and three quarters, course W.N.W. ¾ N.

As the little vessel is sailing into Irish waters, it is as well to notice that the buoys and beacons under the Irish Lights Board are shaped and coloured as follows:

Buoys having a pointed top or cone, called conical buoys, are starboard-hand buoys, and are painted black.

Port-hand buoys are can buoys, and are painted red.

Spherical buoys are used to mark middle grounds, and are distinguished by horizontal stripes of colour. **Staff and globe** is only used on starboard-hand buoys. **Staff and cage** on port. **Diamonds** are used at the outer ends of middle grounds, and triangles at the inner ends.

Buoys having a tall centre structure on a broad base are called pillar buoys, and are used like bell buoys, gas buoys, and automatic sounding buoys, to mark special positions, either on the coast or in the approaches to harbours.

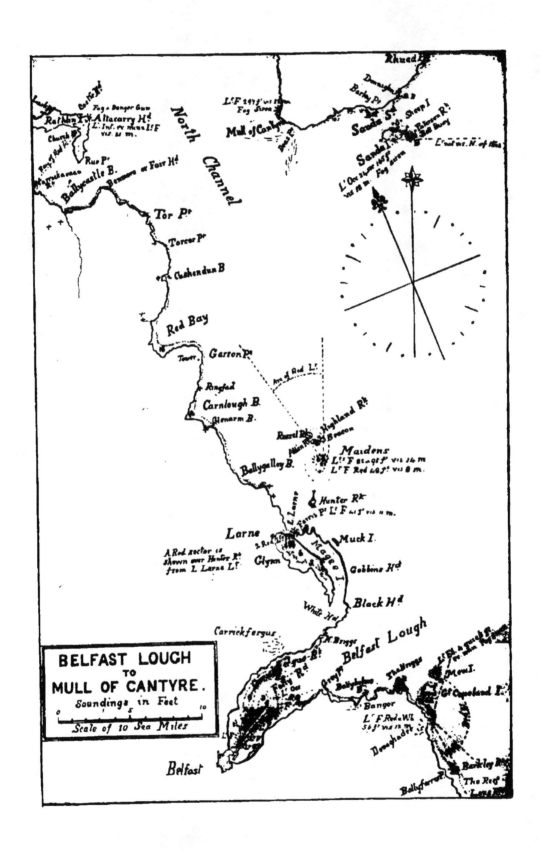

While on the subject of buoys, it is worth remarking what a pity it is the same system of colour is not of universal observance. The three authorities who arrange the buoyage and lighting of our coasts all use **different colours** for port and starboard, although middle-ground buoys, and the **shape** of the buoys, is the **same**.

Tidal Stream.—Half-way between Peel and St. John's Point, Dundrum Bay, there is no perceptible stream. At the **Point of Ayre** the ebb sets N.W. at two miles off the Point, but close to it it sweeps round towards **Rue Point** and then strikes out W.N.W. for the N. channel.

Off the **Copeland Islands the flood sweeps round out of Belfast Lough and runs down the Irish coast,** the ebb taking the **opposite** direction; but **inside the Copeland Islands** the flood sets through the **Sound of Donaghadee** for only 3hrs., after which it slacks, so that from **Ballyferris Point** to the **Foreland Point,** in the **Sound of Donaghadee, the tide runs to the N. for 9hrs. close in shore,** and only 3hrs. to the S.

The flood having turned to the N. meets the rest of the stream out of the Sound, and then the current sets round **Great Copeland,** passing over the **Ninaen Bushes,** a **shoal** with only **3ft. least water** on it on the E. side of **Great Copeland,** and runs through the channel between the islands.

At **Mew Island** there is a very rapid eddy running to the N.E., which, meeting the true flood-tide, causes a race on the S.E. of the Copelands. On the ebb there is also a race on the N.E., both of which are at times dangerous.

Through the Sound, between **Great Copeland** and **Copeland Island,** the tide sets up at half-flood by the shore, and is therefore used in preference to passing N. of the islands.

In making the land from the S.E. the coast is comparatively low and with no special feature. **Carn Hill,** on the N. side of Belfast Lough, behind **Carrickfergus,** is 1013ft. high, but it is fourteen miles N.W. of the **Copeland Islands.**

After the picturesque scenery of the Isle of Man this part of Ireland looks very tame. The Copeland Islands are low, rocky, barren-looking islets, lying off an equally bleak-looking coast.

Y

Great Copeland is one mile long by half a mile broad, and 103ft. high. Foul ground extends off it for half a mile on the S.W. side, and there are outlying rocks all round, extending to half a mile off the E. side.

In the Sound of Donaghadee, **half-way between the island and Foreland Point, is Deputy Reef, with 9ft. least water on it. It is marked by a black and white buoy painted in stripes. There is five fathoms in the channel between this and Copeland Island.**

Off the E. side of the reef of rocks at **Horse Point,** on the S. of the island, there is a red beacon, 10ft. high, with a cage on the top, showing 4ft. above high-water.

The **Platters Rocks** are patches of rocks, with less than 6ft. on them, lying three cables E. of the E. point of **Great Copeland,** and N.E. of them are the **Ninaen Bushes,** with only 3ft. on them at low-water. A **red can buoy** lies in eight fathoms one cable N.E. of them.

At the N. end of the island there is a bank, with three fathoms and a half on it.

Copeland Island lies N.E., three-quarters of a mile from Great Copeland Island. It is 67ft. high, and about a quarter of a mile long and broad. No dangers extend from it to any distance. Separated by a boat channel, and to the E. of **Copeland Island,** is **Mew Island,** which is a mere rock and almost awash in heavy gales. A spit lies S. of it, with 9ft. least water to a distance of 400yds.

Mew Island Light.—From a lighthouse, of a light gray colour, a flashing white light is shown at an elevation of 121ft. above high-water. It shows four flashes every minute. Each flash lasts 4sec., and the eclipse 1¾sec. There is an interval of 38sec. between each successive group of four flashes. A weak light appears between the periods within eight miles. Visible sixteen miles.

Fog-signal.—A **fog siren gives** a blast every 4sec. on a low note, followed by an interval of silence of 12sec; then there is a blast of 4sec. on a high note, succeeded by silence for 100sec.

As to whether it is advisable to pass through **Copeland** or Donaghadee Sound, or keep outside altogether, will depend upon the wind and state of the tide. There is really no difficulty in taking either Sound. The usual directions are that the navigation is quite safe with a pilot, but that strangers should not attempt it without a leading wind and tide. I had both wind and sea against me, but slack water, when I first went through from the S., and had no difficulty whatever, although without a pilot. By going through when the wind is N. ½ E., as it was when I tackled the **Sound of Donaghadee,** one gets into quieter water sooner and saves a little distance besides.

Dangers off Donaghadee and in the Sound.—The coast from **Skulmartin Light-vessel to Donaghadee is studded with outlying dangers which will be described later.**

S. of **Donaghadee,** however, for two miles none of these dangers lie out farther than a quarter of a mile, and they are steep-to with five fathoms close by.

Donaghadee (pronounced Don-a-dee) is a bleak-looking place, connected by a railway with Dublin and Belfast. It was originally intended as a packet station in connection with **Port Patrick,** and it was here, some say, William of Orange landed when he began his campaign, which culminated in the Battle of the Boyne, although I believe he really landed at Carrickfergus. As early as 1650 a stone quay was built, but the present harbour was not begun until 1836. The S. pier is a fine stone mole, and another pier extends in an E. direction on the N. side. The deepest water is on the S. side of the harbour, there being 5ft. to 8ft. alongside the S. pier at low-water, and elsewhere 7ft. to 11ft., but the N. side is not so deep.

The harbour is exposed to N.E. and easterly gales. At these times so heavy a sea comes in that vessels cannot remain alongside the pier, but have to moor in the harbour with a stern-fast to the S. pier.

There are about seven acres enclosed within the piers, but of this space only one-third is available for vessels that wish to lie afloat.

Lights.—From a **white lighthouse** on the S. pier-head, 53ft. high, and at an elevation of 56ft. above high-water, a fixed light is shown. It is **red to seaward**, bearing between N.N.W. and S.W., and **white** between **N.N.W.** and **N. ½ W.** This latter bearing leads **rather near the Burges Rocks** N. of Skulmartin. It also **shows white** from S.W. to **Orlock Point.** The S.W. bearing leads two cables E. of the **Platters Rocks.**

Coming from the S., as soon as vessels change the red light 'to white they will be approaching danger.

Tides.—It is high-water, full and change, at 11hr. 13min. Dublin time, which is 25min. after Greenwich time. Springs rise 11½ft.; neaps, 9½ft.

Rocks extend both N. and S. of the entrance to 200yds. from the pier-head. The church tower open of the S. pier clears the rocks S., and the N. house, on parade, open of the N. pier-head clears the N. rocks.

Foreland Point is three-quarters of a mile N. of Donaghadee, and the shore is foul. The **rocks extend 400yds.** in a **N.E. direction,** and **uncover.** They are **marked** by an **iron perch. Beyond** this are rocky heads, with from 7ft. to 12ft. over them. A **red can buoy,** called "Governor," lies in 18ft., nearly 400yds. E. ½ S. from the perch. There is another red beacon surmounted by a cage, 14ft. high, showing 4ft. above high-water at the end of the rocks, which lie out in a S.E. direction.

At night the **red light** from **Donaghadee** leads **E. of all dangers.** The **best entrance** to the **Sound** is **between** the **Deputy, Black and White, Buoy** and the **Governor, Red, Buoy.**

From the **Foreland** to **Orlock Point** the coast on the W. side is foul to the extent of two cables for half the distance. As Orlock Point is neared the shore becomes steeper. Rocks lie off the S.W. corner of Great Copeland, but the bight to the N. of it is clear. At the N.W. extremity a rock lies out about a cable.

Belfast Lough may be said to begin at **Orlock Point.**

Bearings and distances from the Mew Light, Copeland Island.— From the **Mew Light** the **Maidens' Rocks Lights** bear **N. ¼ W.,** distant sixteen miles. The **Mull of Kintyre, N. ½ E.,** thirty-eight

miles.   **Pladda Light**, N.E. ½ N. northerly, forty-five miles.
Astra Craig, N.E. northerly, thirty-six miles.   **Corsewall Light**,
N.E. ¼ E., twenty-two miles.   **Mull of Galloway**, S.E. by E. ¼ E.,
twenty-three miles.   **Point of Ayre**, S.E. easterly, forty-three
miles and a half.   **Chicken Rock**, S. by E., forty-six miles and
a half.

Belfast Lough is said to afford perfect shelter, even to vessels
disabled and with no anchor.   The banks at the head are so
soft that a ship would lie there in any weather without harm.   This
may be so, but as the Lough is fully open to the E. and N.E.,
has a very wide opening with a long drift, a good deal of sea
must necessarily come home, even at its extreme W. end.

As regards anchorages for **yachting** purposes, Belfast Lough
means **Bangor Bay** on the S. side and Carrickfergus on the N.

The approach is very easy, there being no outlying dangers
to speak of after the Copeland Islands are passed.   The **N.** and
S. Briggs are the only rocks which lie out at all, and they
extend no farther than 800yds.

The opening is six miles and three quarters wide from **Orlock
Point** to **Black Head**, and the Lough is ten miles and a half
deep in an E. and W. direction.   The N. shore is the most
conspicuous, **White Head, Black Head**, and the **Cliffs of Magee
Island** being bold and lofty, besides being steep-to.   The S.
shore is low, rising gradually to the height of 473ft. at **Helen's
Tower**, behind **Clandeboye**, Lord Dufferin's place, and **Carngaver**,
714ft. farther W.   At the head of the Lough, behind Belfast,
is Devil's Hill, 1560ft. high, and the picturesque jagged summit
of **Cave Hill**, 1182ft. high, towering over **Whitehouse Roadstead**.

Cultra Mill Stump, on a hill 455ft. high, E of Holywood, on
the S. shore, is a conspicuous mark, and a useful one, for when
it is in line with Farm Hill, near the shore, there is then only
13ft. close to the edge of the **Oyster Bank**, lying in the middle
of the head of the Lough.

After passing Orlock Point the red can buoy off the **Briggs**,
some of which dry at low-water and extend about 800yds. off
the shore, can be given a close berth, as there is four fathoms
where it lies.   Beyond this is **Groomsport Bay**, which is more

or less foul. The W. point of this bight is **Ballymacormick
Point**, with ledges drying out about one cable on its W. side.

The coast now turns sharply S. and forms the good shelter
of **Ballyholme Bay**, where there is safe anchorage in all winds
except from N.W. to N.E. The bottom is sandy, with two
fathoms at one cable and a half off shore in the centre of the
bay.

George Point separates **Ballyholme** from **Bangor Bay.** There
is a dry harbour here, with a pier and a landing-stage for
the steamboats which run to Belfast. **Bangor** is a pretty little
place, and it is a pity a breakwater is not thrown across from
its E. point. As it is the place lies fully open to the N., and
it was here Lord Cantelupe was drowned when his yacht was
wrecked. From Bangor the coast trends W.N.W. for two
miles and a half to **Grey Point**, which is 76ft. high, and steep-
to; but the bight S.E. is foul with rocks, some of which dry
at low-water. At one mile and a half W. of Grey Point
there are rocks lying out for over a quarter of a mile, but
their outer edge is marked by a **red buoy** in 12ft.

The shore now becomes low and marshy, with shallow flats
extending in a W. direction towards No. 3 Pile Lighthouse.

The **Oyster Bank**, which lies between **Holywood** and **White
Abbey** in the middle of the head of the Lough, has 7ft. least
water over it. A **red buoy**, in 12ft., lies on its W. side. **Cultra
Mill Stump**, bearing S.S.E. ¾ E. nearly, in line with No. 2 Pile
Lighthouse, leads E. of the bank in 13ft. of water.

At **Holywood Pier two fixed green lights** are exhibited at
the E. and W. sides of the W. pier. The bank dries out for
a long distance off here.

Anchorages.—**Folly Roads** is the usual berth for large vessels.
They lie in mid-channel between **Green Island** on the N. shore
and the marshes between **Holywood** and **Grey Point** on the
S. shore. There is three fathoms and a half just N. of No. 1
Pile Lighthouse.

The **safest anchorage** is in Whitehouse Roads, between
Whitehouse and Holywood Pier, about **a cable** W. of the **red
buoy** on the W. side of the Oyster Bank, in two fathoms and

a half. Half-way between, and N. of No. 2 and No. 3 Pile Lighthouses, there is 9ft. near the lake leading to Macedon Pier, but a vessel is more exposed to the E., as Oyster Bank takes off a little of the sea.

The channel to Belfast is called **Victoria Channel.** It is purely artificial, and runs nearly straight in a N.E. by E. and S.W. by W. direction. It is only about 100yds. wide, with a depth of from 12ft to 16½ft.   It leads into the River Lagan, which is connected by canal with **Lough Neagh and Lough Erne,** and so into the Atlantic at Donegal Bay.

Lights.—The channel is lighted by four pile lighthouses. No. 1 is the outermost, and shows a white occulting light 32ft. above high-water, visible five miles.   The light is bright for 6sec., then for 6sec. it is varied by one long and two short eclipses. Obscured on the S.E. side 60deg.

Nos. 2, 3, and 4 are fixed white lights, on piles, visible seaward through an arc of 180deg.   The N. side of the channel is marked by **five conical black buoys,** the lights being all on the port hand.

On Twin Island, at the N.E. end, there is a fixed white light, and at 233yds. from the S.W. end there is a **fixed green light.**

There are **nine posts,** each showing **two lights, horizontal,** marking the **N.W. side** of the channel, between **pile lighthouse No. 2 and West Twin,** but **they are unreliable.**

Red can buoys mark the E. side of the old channel, and the spot where the Holywood Light used to be.   A spherical red and white horizontally striped buoy marks the S. spit of the middle ground.

Proceeding northward from No. 3 Pile Lighthouse, **W. Bank** lies a long way out from the low shore between **Belfast** and **Whitehouse.   At Macedon Point** the foreshore dries out for a quarter of a mile.   It is mostly sand and gravel, with rocks interspersed. As Green Island is neared, the width of the fore-shore decreases, and there is 6ft. of water close in.   From **Sea Point** to Carrickfergus, however, it broadens again, and then sweeps out in a shallow flat to Carrickfergus Spit, or Bank, leaving a pool with two fathoms and a half inside.

Carrickfergus Bank begins about two miles and a half E. of Carrickfergus, and sweeps out at first gradually, and then more extensively, to nearly one mile and a half off Carrickfergus. Half a mile S. of the harbour entrance there is 12ft. at low-water, and 7ft. just off the pier-head. There is 9ft. over the greater part of the bank, and a black buoy, with staff and ball, lies, in three fathoms and a half, at the S. extremity of the bank.

Carrickfergus Harbour is formed by two piers. There is from 7ft. to 8ft. inside the harbour at the mouth at low-water springs, and vessels lie water-borne in most parts if they do not draw over 7ft.

This is the best shelter for yachts in the Lough, unless they go up to Belfast and lie in dock.

From **Carrickfergus to White Head** is four miles, with **Kilroot Point** in between, and the **N. Briggs** three-quarters of a mile W. of it.

The foreshore is one-third of a mile wide between Carrickfergus and **Kilroot**, with sand and stones uncovering at low-water.

The **N. Briggs** are marked by a beacon, and they extend a quarter of a mile off Cloghan Point. Many of the heads dry at low-water, but there is five fathoms and a quarter close to them on the south side.

At **White Head** the coast turns N.E., forming a bay which is mostly foul. Off Chichester Castle there is a rock, one cable and a half from the shore, which dries. Here the coast, which had previously been high, dips and forms a valley, through which runs a stream connecting **Lough Larne** with the sea, thus forming **Magee Island**, as the high rocky land, which lies on the E. side of Lough Larne, is called.

White Head is of limestone formation. **Magee Island** is nearly all basaltic, and the cliffs are remarkably black and steep. W. of White Head is a little dry pier harbour, used for shipping limestone.

Black Head forms the N.E. limit of **Belfast Lough**. It is a bold headland, 205ft. high, with higher land rising to 425ft.

immediately behind it.   A little boat harbour lies S.W. of it, just where the rocky ledges end and a steep beach begins, which ends, however, before **Black Head** is reached, the cliffs from here to **Muck Island** being precipitous and steep-to, with the exception of one little spot at the Gobbins, where a few boats are hauled up and laid on the steep sides of a precipitous cleft or gully.

Belfast Lough is a magnificent sheet of water, and in fine weather on a summer evening—when the sun's rays light up the western crags of the mountains which skirt the N. shore, while all the valley below is bathed in a purple and gray haze, the sea reflecting the scene above in burnished gold—it is a lovely spot.

But in a N.E. or E. gale, during the winter, it is not such a sweet spot.

Bangor is undoubtedly the place for a yachting resort, and by a judicious outlay it could easily be made one.

It is a comfort to be over on the Irish coast after the long buffet with the doubtful shelters of the English and Welsh shores.   From Belfast southward there are harbours at every thirty miles, and cruising can be carried on with greater comfort and less anxiety.

Lough Larne does not come within the limit of this volume, but it is a very handy shelter and close by.   In some ways it is the best little harbour in the whole of the Irish seas, and far safer than **Lough Ryan**, on the Scotch coast, for small yachts.

Tides.—It is high-water, full and change, at Belfast at 10hr. 43min.   Springs rise 9½ft. ; neaps, 8ft.

CHAPTER XXXI.

BELFAST TO LOUGH STRANGFORD.

FROM **Carrickfergus** to the Sound of **Donaghadee** is nine miles and a half in a S.E. ¾ E. direction. As the sweep of the tide is from **Black Head** to **Copeland Islands** during both streams and near the islands runs at five knots, and at **Grey Point** the flood runs along the shore to the **Briggs** over which it **sets**, it is as well to start from the anchorage about 2hrs. before high-water. In the Lough the streams are mild, seldom exceeding one knot an hour. It is necessary to catch the first of the flood through the Sound, as it only runs there for 3hrs. When the **Deputy Buoy** is passed, a course should be steered S.E. for two miles off the shore, or thereabouts, in order to carry the flood down the coast, as between **Ballyferris** and the **Foreland** the stream runs N. for 9hrs.

From **Donaghadee** to **Ballyferris Point** the coast is skirted by dangers, extending farther out as the latter point is approached.

At night, by keeping in the red light of Donaghadee Lighthouse all risk is avoided. The W. limit of the white light passes very near to the **Ship** and **Burges Rocks**. By day, the perch on Skulmartin in line with Halbert Point clears the reef and **Long Rock**, but **leads** rather near Ship Rock.

Between **Mill Isle** and **Donaghadee** the rocks do not lie out more than a quarter of a mile; but between **Mill Isle** and **Ballyferris Point** they are both more numerous and wider extending. None of these rocks are fine bold rocks showing conspicuously above water. They are all low heads, and are difficult to distinguish when there is any sea on.

N.E. of Ballyferris Point lies the reef, with **Ship Rock,** over which there is only 2ft. at low-water at its N. extremity. These dangers lie three-quarters of a mile from the land, and their outside edge lies in a N. ¾ E. direction, with five fathoms close to.

From the **Reef** to **Long Rock,** a distance of two miles, the whole shore is fronted with rocks. **Long Rock** is about awash at high-water springs. **Nelson Rock** is a dangerous sunken rock, a quarter of a mile S.W. of **Long Rock.** There is 7ft. least water over it, and it is half a mile N. of **Skulmartin;** between the two is the passage to **Ballywalter Quay.** There is anchorage off here, inshore of the **Nelson Rock,** in two fathoms, over a sandy bottom. The little harbour **dries** out, but some protection is afforded from N. and N.E. gales by the reefs off Ballyferris Point. E. and S.E. gales send in a heavy sea.

S.E. of Ballywalter Quay, distant nearly a mile and about the same distance off-shore, is **Skulmartin Rock,** covered at half-tide. It is marked by a red iron perch, and is steep-to on its N. and E. sides. A reef, called **Little Skulmartin Reef,** lies out in an E.N.E. direction for about three-quarters of a mile from the low point, leaving a narrow passage between the rock and the reef, with three to four fathoms in it.

Light.—Skulmartin Light-ship is moored in twenty fathoms one mile E.S.E. of Skulmartin Rock. It exhibits, at an elevation of 38ft., a **fixed** white light, visible ten miles. The vessel is rigged with main and jigger masts, and carries two half globes, the circular part uppermost.

Fog-signal.—An explosive signal is fired twice in quick succession every 10min.

From Skulmartin to **Halbert Point,** a distance of a little over three miles, the coast is free from danger. **Ballyhalbert Bay** sweeps round in a S.E. direction, with **Burial Island, off Halbert Point,** separated by a narrow channel half a cable wide, with only 9ft. on it at low-water.

In this bay a vessel may anchor a tide, in three fathoms and a half over sand. From S.S.E. to N. it is exposed. **Ballyhalbert Quay** is nearly dry at low-water springs, but affords shelter for small coasters that lie aground; there is also a small dock. From here, across the land, it is only two miles and a quarter to the shores of **Lough Strangford**. The N. end of the Lough is only five miles S.W. of Bangor on Belfast Lough. **Burial Island** is a rock 20ft. above high-water; it is the highest part of a reef lying N.N.E. and S.S.W. The N. point is just awash at high-water, and is steep-to. The E. side also is steep-to, but the S. point extends under the water for one mile, with depths of from 13ft. to 14ft. over it. A spot of gravel extends off **Halbert Point**, diminishing the apparent breadth of the Sound between to 100yds. The coast continues rocky, with outlying dangers, all the way to the entrance of **Lough Strangford**, and should not be approached so as to shut in **Skulmartin Perch** with **Burial Island**.

McCammon Rock is covered at high water; it lies one-third of a mile off shore; and from it, in a southward direction, is **Plough Rock**, covered at half-flood. **South Rock Old Light-house**, in line with **North Rock Beacon**, bearing S.S.W. ⅛ W., leads well clear of these dangers to the E.

Between **Plough Rock** and **Kirkistown Point** is **Green Island**, connected with the shore at low-water.

From **Kirkistown Point**, a narrow spit of gravel extends three-quarters of a mile towards the reef of rocks, on which is **North Rock Beacon**. This reef extends three-quarters of a mile in a S.E. by E. and N.W. by W. direction. It is composed of rocks and gravel, and is only covered at high-water springs. At its E. end is a circular stone beacon encased with iron, the upper half spiral with a ball on the top, 40ft. above high-water. There are rocks E. of this to the distance of one cable.

Inside and S.W. of these rocks is **Cloghy Bay**. **Mill Rock**, dry at low-water, lies in the middle of the entrance, with two fathoms and a half on each side of it. The bay is shallow, but there is 6ft. between **Cloghy Village** and **Mill Rock**. Vessels anchor here often as there is shelter from all winds, except those between S.S.W. and E.N.E.

Between **North Rock** and **South Rock** is a shoal, called the **Breast**, with 9ft. on it.   Along the shore between **Cloghy Bay** and **Kearney Point** rocks lie off for one-third of a mile.   The **Hems** uncover for 600yds. at half-tide, about half-way between.

From Kearney Point, which is a low, sloping promontory, in an E. by N. direction, distant one mile and three quarters, is **S. Rock,** with the tower, 60ft. high, of the old lighthouse, now disused, upon it.   This islet is the centre of a cluster of dangers, some of which uncover, but many are only just below the water.   **Privateer Rock** lies half a mile **S.W. by W. from the lighthouse**; there is only 6ft. least water on it.   Between them is **another rock,** with only 7ft.   **Crooked Pladdy,** with only 7ft. on it, lies **S.S.W. ¾ W.** from the lighthouse, distant three-quarters of a mile.   **Cammon Rocks, covered at half-tide,** are **N.E. ¾ E. 600yds.** from the lighthouse.   In an **E. ¼ N.** direction, **extending one mile** from the lighthouse, is the **Ridge,** with 9ft. on its outer edge.   To mark the dangers the **South Rock Light-vessel** is moored in thirty fathoms, **two miles in an E. ¾ S.** direction from the **old lighthouse,** and **one mile E.** of the **outer end of the Ridge.**

Light.—South Rock Light-ship exhibits, from an elevation of 38ft., a **revolving white light, visible ten miles, and attaining** its **greatest brilliancy every** 1½min.   The **vessel has three masts,** and **carries a black ball** at the **mast-head.   She is painted black with a white stripe.**

Fog-signal.—A gun is fired every 15min.

Nearly two miles S.S.W. of the South Rock disused lighthouse is **Butter Pladdy,** a cluster of rocks 400yds. in extent, on which there is only 5ft. least water.   A **black conical buoy** is moored, in five fathoms and a half, S.W. of the danger at a distance of 300yds.

S.E. of **Kearney Point, on which is a windmill,** lies **Kearney Pladdy,** with 10ft. least water on it.   It is half a mile from the point.   By keeping 200yds. W. of the **black buoy** a vessel will pass safely between the two Pladdies.

W. of **Kearney Point** is **Quinton Bay,** with shelter in off-shore winds, in two fathoms, close in; but **Mill Bay,** S. of it, is foul.

Tara Hill, 180ft. high, is S. of this bay. The coast continues foul for one-third of a mile off shore as far as **Bally Quintin Point,** the S.E. point of the entrance to **Strangford Lough.**

Tides.—It is high water, **full and change,** at the **South Rock** at 10hr. 58min. Springs rise 13ft ; neaps, 10¾ft. The direction of the stream follows the coast.

Bally Quintin Point is surrounded by a mass of dangers. **Kearney Point** kept **to the** W. of Burial Island clears them, and when **Bar Pladdy Buoy** comes open then steer for it so as to pass to the S. and W. of it.

The **Quintin Rocks** lie out 800yds. from the point in a S. ¼ E. direction, and inside the Narrows **Pladdy Lug uncovers at spring tides only.** It is marked by a **beacon surmounted by a cage.**

The **Knob,** with 7ft. on it at low-water, lies **400yds.** S. of **Pladdy Lug,** and **Bar Pladdy** is 300yds. **S. of the Knob.** There is 9ft. least water on this danger, and it is marked by a **black conical buoy,** in six fathoms. Take it as a whole the coast between Donaghadee and Bally Quintin Point is as nasty a piece of rockwork as I have ever seen. The coast is low ; the rocks are low and sneaking. There is none of the fine, bold, defiant air of other outlying rocks. None are more than a few feet above water when they do show, and that is not often at high-water ; most are under the sea, and lie a long way out. They are more like a prolonged imitation of the formidable Penmarch Rocks off the coast of Brittany ; but there, low as some are, there are many over 50ft. high. Here the highest is **Burial Island,** only 20ft.

Strangford Narrows.—This somewhat dangerous bit of navigation lies between **Killard Point** on the S.W. side and **Bally Quintin** on the N.E. The entrance is divided by the **Angus Rock** into two channels. The **W. channel is narrow,** with only 13ft. least water in it, and **not** to be taken by strangers without local help.

The **E. channel** has six fathoms in it, and is fairly easy. The leading mark is the N. end off **Portaferry,** just open of **Bankmore Head.**

Tides.—The great feature of **Strangford Narrows** is the tide. The **tidal streams** run in and out at a velocity of ten knots.

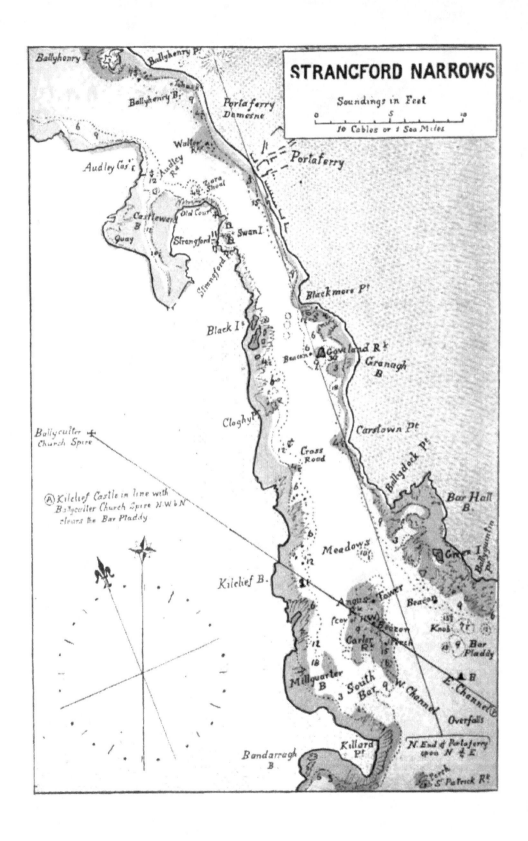

The harbour-master of Strangford Quay assured me they were the "hottest tides in the United Kingdom and Ireland"—so I was told when navigating the Swellies, and so I have since been told when passing through the Pentland Firth. That they do run strongly I know, and I should be very sorry to put to sea when an easterly or southerly gale was blowing. The race at the entrance must then be awful. This strength of tide causes many eddies and whirlpools; the largest is called the Routen Wheel, between Gowland Rock and Bankmore Head, which should be avoided if possible.

The ebb is said to be felt three miles and a half out to sea. When it is considered that Strangford Lough is twelve miles long by two miles wide, and contains many creeks and inlets, and that all the passage for the flow and ebb of the tide is through this narrow channel, five miles long, it is easy to see that the streams must be strong. By keeping in the middle of the channel, however, there is not much danger even if it should be calm; but the difficulty in that state of the weather is to manage this.

It is important to remember that both streams run from 1hr. 40min. to 2hr. 20min. after high- and low-water at Killard Point, and for half an hour after the same period at Strangford Quay. The stream runs 6hrs. each way, so that by adding half an hour to the times of high- and low-water at Strangford it is easy to know which way the stream is going.

At the N. end of Angus Rock the flood sets over the Meadows, a small patch with 10ft. least water over them, 400yds. N. of Angus Rock, and also towards Walter Rock, marked by a perch a quarter of a mile above Portaferry.

The ebb sets into the bight off Bankmore Head, and across the N. end of Angus Rock towards the E., otherwise the streams set fairly through. There is an eddy on the ebb close along the W. side of Angus Rock and under each prominent point. On reaching Strangford Lough the stream sets across towards Neill Islet, and in Chapel Road, at the N.W. end of the Narrows, there is not much felt.

At **Killard Point** it is **high-water, full and change, at 10hr. 53min.** Springs rise 14ft. ; neaps, 12ft. At **Strangford Quay** it is high-water at 12hr. 31min. Springs rise 11ft. ; neaps, 9ft.

Dangers in the Narrows, S.W. side.—Off **Killard Point**, which is of **no great height or special feature**, although the hills behind rise a little, lie the **St. Patrick Rocks**, 600yds. S.E. of the point. They are steep-to, and covered at 4hrs. flood. An iron perch, 30ft. high, marks the danger.

Killard Point is fringed with dangers. The **Craiglewey Rocks** extend 600yds. in a S.W. direction, and form a sunken reef for 600yds. farther, with only 9ft. to 15ft. over it. N. of the point a rocky ledge extends across to **Angus Rock**, with 13ft. least water on it, between a 6ft. and 9ft. patch. There is a passage between the St. Patrick Rocks and the point, but strangers had better leave it alone.

From **Killard Point** to **Kilclief Castle** the shore takes a sweep to the N.W., with rocky bottom, and so continues to the **Isle of Valla**, opposite **Bankmore Head**.

Cloghy Rocks are nearly opposite **Gowland Rock**. They uncover, mostly, at low-water. They are **marked** by a beacon on **Salt Rock**, the most northerly of the patch. They are steep-to on their E. side, and within is a pool, the entrance to which is from the N., where there is safe anchorage.

N. of this the shore is rocky and mostly steep-to; but off Valla Isle there are two detached rocks, one with only 4ft. over it, lying at the mouth of the little bay, two cables from the shore.

From these **rocks** to Strangford the **tidal streams run hardest**, slackening slightly as they pass **Strangford Quay** and **Portaferry**.

Lying in the centre of Strangford Bay is **Swan Island**; the rocks off its E. edge are marked by a perch. After **passing** Strangford the next **dangers** are **Zara Shoal**, off **Old Court Point**, on which there is **only 9ft.**, and a patch inside of it, **marked by a beacon**. The **Sleitch Rocks**, 300yds. W. of **Zara Shoal**, in Audley Roads, are marked by a beacon.

From **Audley Roads** to **Chapel Island** there are no dangers, except that shoals extend all the way between Chapel Island to the shore. **Audley Point** is steep-to. If desirous of anchoring n **Strangford Lough**, the roadstead W. of Chapel Island, in nine fathoms, is a good place ; but **Audley Roads** is the **best anchorage** in **Strangford Narrows.**

Dangers in the Middle of the Channel.—Angus Rock lies half a mile within the entrance points, and with **Garter** and **Potts Rocks** is nearly in the middle of the channel.

The reef is half a mile long and 200yds. wide, the greater part covered at high-water. **Potts Rocks,** at the S. end, **uncover** at spring tides only.

Garter Rock, 200yds. N. of **Potts Rocks, covers** at half-flood. It is **marked** by a **wooden perch** on the N. end of the reef, and on the part which **never covers** is built a stone tower, 45ft. high, **intended for a lighthouse,** but never used. On **Mid Rock,** halfway between Angus Tower and Garter Perch, there is an obelisk, surmounted by a perch. The rocks are steep-to on the N. and E. sides, but the W. and S. sides are skirted by dangerous ledges.

N. of Angus Rock, distant 400yds., are the **Meadows,** with **10ft. least water** on them. There are no further dangers in mid-channel.

Dangers on the E. side.—After passing **Bar Pladdy** and **Lug Pladdy,** both of which have been described, there are no more shoals until **Garstown Point,** opposite the **Cross Roads,** is reached. Here a berth of 150yds. should be given, as there is only 4ft. off the point. **Gowland Rock** is the next danger; it is **half-way** up the Narrows and covers at 4hrs. flood. It is marked on its **outer side by a beacon,** 16ft. **high.** N.W. of this rock are the series of whirlpools, the largest of which is called the **Routen Wheel.** For **small boats** these are **dangerous,** and for large craft they make it difficult to steer.

Bankmore Point is fairly steep-to, and there are no dangers along the E. shore until **Portaferry** is passed. At a quarter of a mile N. of this place are the Walter Rocks, marked by a **perch,** and another **rock, 150yds.** N., is marked by a pole. They lie nearly 200yds. off the shore, and the tide rushes past and over these rocks at a great pace. They lie at the S. side of **Bally Henry Road.** Off **Bally Henry Point** lies the island

z

of the same name, connected with the shore at low-water.
A beacon marks the dangers on its S.W. side, and a pole
those on the N. at the S.W. side of **Ballywhite Bay.**

Lough Strangford.—The shore of the Lough now extends in
a N.N.E. direction, with many inlets and much foul ground
to **Grey Abbey,** about eight miles and a half up. Thence it
trends N. ½ W. to **Newtown Ards,** but all the upper part
is very shoal, with numerous pladdies, rendering navigation
very difficult. Almost the whole of the Lough E. of a line
joining **Ringburn Point,** one mile and a half N. of **Ballywhite
Bay** and **Helen's Tower** on the hill behind Newtown Ards, is
a mass of pladdies, with intricate channels of varying depths
between.

The W. side of the Lough, after **Rat,** or Dan O'Neil, Island
is passed, is also much indented. Many islands lie off the
creeks, with narrow and most difficult channels in between,
most of which have from 12ft. to 90ft. of water in them, for
the depths are most abrupt in their variations, the Lough itself
having depths of from six to thirty-four fathoms in it, the deepest
part being off the shore on the E. side, near the entrance, between
Bally Henry Island and Ringburn Point. Among these islands
on the W. side many excellent anchorages could be found,
where a vessel would lie as snugly as in a dock. Above
Paddy Point, on the W. side, the Lough shoals, the greater
part drying out entirely for a mile and a half right across the
top. A little creek goes up to **Comber,** but it is tortuous and
shallow.

The S.W. corner of the **Lough** extends for some distance
towards the **Quoile River,** which is navigable to within one
mile and a half of Downpatrick, or four miles S.W. of **Killyleagh.** There are rocks and mud flats off this place, which is
on the W. shore, at the entrance to the Quoile; but a beacon
marks the E. edge of the dangers, and there is a **beacon** on
the **rocks N.E.** of **Green Island,** W. of **Chapel** and Jackdaw
Islands. The entrance to the Quoile is between the beacon
off **Killyleagh** and **Green Island.** For two miles up, as far as
Hare Island, there is plenty of water and very good anchorage,

in from four to seven fathoms; after that the river nearly dries.

For an amateur, with plenty of time and a taste for smooth-water sailing, Lough Strangford is the very place to spend a happy holiday. For canoes it is perfect, and the endless channels, islands, creeks, and rocks, which there are to be explored, make it a delightful place. It is within easy reach of Belfast, which is only seven miles and a half by train or road from Comber, or from Downpatrick one mile and a half from Quoile Quay. Newcastle and Belfast are both within reach.

Anchorage in Strangford Narrows.—On the W. side, three-quarters of a mile N. of **Kilclief Castle** and a quarter of a mile S. of Cloghy Point, there is a bight where there is good anchorage. It is marked by a pillar on the shore, in line with a pole on the hill behind, or Ballycutter Church Spire in line with the pillar. This berth is called the **Cross Roads.** The tide is not felt here if the **beacon** on Salt Rock is kept just on with the beacon on Swan Island. There is here six fathoms and a muddy bottom. S. of it is a ledge with only 3ft. on it, so that vessels should not round into the anchorage until the leading marks are in line.

The **best anchorage** is undoubtedly **Audley Roads.**

This excellent shelter is at the mouth of a creek which bends round Old Court Point, and curves behind Strangford Village. The greater part of this inlet dries out, but at the entrance, between Old Court Point and Audley Castle Ruin, there is a pool with from two to seven fathoms, with good holding ground, where vessels will lie in perfect safety out of the tide and in quiet water.

Deep-draught vessels just shut in **Rat Island, in Strangford Lough, with Castle Point or Audley Point.** The best berth is near the quay or jetty at the Audley Castle side a little W. of it, the nearer the quay the better. A charge of 2s. 6d. is made for anchoring here, and the harbour-master produces a lengthy printed document if requested to show that his claims are just, or rather the claims of Lord de Ros. It appears the beacons are kept up by this means, and they are certainly needed.

The next best anchorage is in Bally Henry Roads, just opposite. The bottom is uneven and foul in parts.

Strangford is a pretty little place, with an almost ideal harbour, curving round its little breakwater—Swan Island; but vessels are not allowed to stay there unless they are alongside the quay or waiting a tide.

Portaferry has a good beach and quay, where a vessel may lie aground to scrub; but it is more exposed to the tide and S.W. wind.

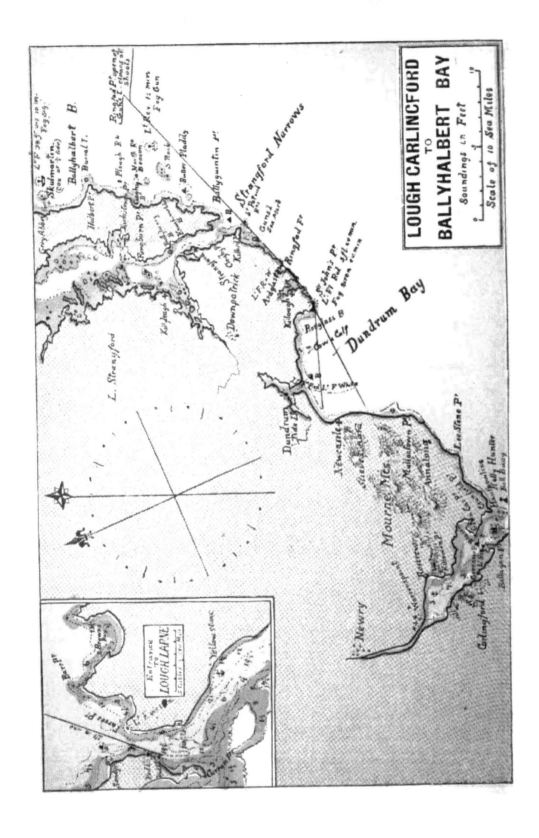

CHAPTER XXXII.

———

LOUGH STRANGFORD TO LOUGH CARLINGFORD.

FROM **Killard Point** to **Ringfad Point**, a mile S.W. of Ardglass Harbour, is about five miles and a quarter.

Bandarrach Bay lies just round **Killard Point,** with **Guns Island** S. of it. The N.E. side of this bay is fronted with the S. dangers off Killard Point, called the **Craigleway Rocks** and **Reef.**

Guns Island is connected with the shore at low-water. It is 96ft. high and about 600yds. long. A square obelisk, 25ft. high, is on the S. point of the island. The E. side is steep-to.

From here to Ardglass the coast is bold and steep-to, with cliffs of no great height; they may be skirted the whole way with safety. At Sheepland Mill there is a cove where boats can land, otherwise the cliffs are unapproachable.

Ardglass Harbour comes suddenly open in the line of cliffs, and it looks as if it ought to be a good shelter; unfortunately, it is not sufficiently protected from the S.E., which sends in a heavy sea at high-water.

The E. side of the harbour entrance is fairly bold, but the W. side is encumbered with the remains of the breakwater. A pier of concrete runs off the W. side. Vessels should keep over on the E. side until they open the pier. There is about nineteen acres of harbour at low-water. Inside there is a small dry dock, where vessels lie in perfect safety.

Inside the outer pier there is anchorage between it and the rocks N. of the harbour, which is marked by a stone beacon. There is also anchorage outside the pier with off-shore winds, in five fathoms. There are rocky ledges inside and at the head of the harbour near the dock. The E. side is steep-to, so that vessels in entering should round up at once between the stone beacon and the pier, and carry out a warp to the pier head. This position is exposed, and shelter should be sought in the dry dock in bad weather, or else clear out and run for Strangford, which is easy of access, when it is dangerous at Ardglass. There is much of interest in the little place, and it could be made a very secure anchorage.

Lights.—There is a fixed light shown at the end of the inner pier. It shows white in the channel, and the white light clears the outer pier-head. Inshore of N. 27deg. W. and N. 9deg. W. it shows red.

Tides.—It is high-water, full and change, at 11hr. 0min. Springs rise 16ft.; neaps, 12ft.

From Ardglass to Ringfad Point is one mile. The coast is bold and clear of dangers. The coast takes a sudden turn here in a N. direction, forming the tidal harbour of Killough. Killough Bay affords good shelter in off-shore winds, and at its N.W. extremity there is the entrance to the inner harbour, which dries entirely. Ringfad Point is foul to the extent of 300yds. on its S. and W. sides, and the shore continues foul all round the bay to Coney Island.

Off the W. side, and in a line with Ringfad Point and St. John's Point, are the Water Rocks, which dry 10ft. They are marked by an iron perch. Inshore of these are other rocks, all dry at low-water, and the foreshore dries for 250yds. to where the iron tripod marks its limit.

Between this and Coney Island is the entrance to the inner harbour, which is protected by a pier on its W. side.

Ardglass is a bleak-looking place, but a favourite one with fishing-boats during the herring season, and frequented by coasters. The place seemed crowded when I passed.

From Killough to St. John's Point is about two miles, and the same distance from Ringfad Point. The shores are low cliffs and steep-to.   Off **St. John's** the rocky foreshore extends for about one cable and a half.   The point is low, with moderately rising ground behind.

Lighthouse.—St. John's Point Light, Dundrum Bay, is a **revolving red light,** shown from a tower at an elevation of 120ft. above high-water, visible sixteen miles, revolving once every minute.   **An auxiliary light** is shown from a window of the lighthouse.   It shows **red** from S. 76deg. to the land, and **white** from N. 84deg. E. through E. to S. 76deg. E.

Fog-signal.—A fog siren gives a blast of 2½sec., silence for 5sec. ; a blast for 2½sec., followed by a silence of 50sec.

Bearings and distances from St. John's Point Light.—Peel Harbour bears from St. John's Point E. by S. ¼ S., distant thirty-four miles.   The Calf of Man, Chicken Light, S.E. ¼ E. easterly, thirty-one miles.   N.W. Light-ship, Liverpool Bay S.E. ¼ S., eighty-seven miles and a half.   Point Lynus, S.S.E. ¼ E., sixty-eight miles.   S. Stack, Holyhead, S. by E., sixty-four miles and a half.   Bardsey Island, S. westerly, ninety-three miles and a half.   S. Bishop Light, S. by W. ½ W., one hundred and forty-three miles. Kish Light-ship, S.S.W. ½ W., fifty-five miles.   Rockabill Light, S.W. ½ S., forty miles.

Dundrum Bay is ten miles wide from **St. John's Point** to **Mullartown,** which bears from St. John's Point **W. by S. ½ S.** The Bay is four miles and a half deep.

On its W. side it is skirted by the **Mourne Mountains,** which descend abruptly to the shore, the highest, **Slieve Donard,** rising to 2780ft. within one mile and a half of the shore, and forming a very conspicuous feature for miles along the coast.

In the N.W. angle of the bay is **Newcastle,** a favourite and pretty watering-place, with a dry harbour.   From here the coast is low, fringed by sand hills for nearly six miles, through which is the entrance to **Dundrum Harbour,** a shallow mere, dry mostly at low-water.   Sands extend all the way round the head of the bay as far as **Craigalea Rock,** off which lie the **Cow and Calf Rocks,** which are only just **awash** at **high-water** springs, and are distant one mile from the shore.   **Craigalea** is a good landmark, as it never covers but juts boldly into the bay, one mile and a half E. of Dundrum Bar. From here to St. John's Point the shore is low and rocky, with a rocky foreshore, extending in places to some distance. Between Mullartown and Newcastle, on the W. side, the coast is rocky. **Roaring Rock** lies 100yds. from the shore, at one mile and three quarters N. of Mullartown Point. It dries at low-water. The coast then becomes steep-to, with three fathoms, close in at the mouth of **Bloody Bridge River,** but shoals to 9ft. and 12ft. off Newcastle, there being not more than three fathoms at three-quarters of a mile off the pier.

The bay is dangerous at most times when there is **any** wind, as if it is on shore it sends in a nasty sea. If it blows from the W. very heavy squalls come down off the Mourne Mountains. There is, too, a decided in-draught when there is any sea running in the bay.

Dundrum Harbour has a good quay, at the foot of a low hill crowned by an old castle ; this bearing N. by W. leads into the channel. On the W. side, among the sand hills, there is a villa belonging to Lord Downshire, which also serves to show the W. side of the entrance. The bar is liable to shift. There is barely 2ft. of water on it, and half a mile in is the Scar, a mussel bank, which is now cut through, allowing a channel 100yds. wide and the same depth as the bar, over which there is 14ft. at high-water.

A **black buoy is moored outside** the bar in 24ft. It is sup-posed to be in line with the centre of the channel, but it is liable to be washed away. After picking up the buoy, the lead-ing mark in is the old castle, over the W. point of entrance, or the store on the quay, half open, bearing N. by W. When Craigalea is closing with the sand hills on the E. side the Scar is passed, and the course is then N. ¾ E. When the **first perch** is passed there is a **pool** with 8ft. at low-water in it, where vessels may lie in safety. The channel thence turns westward and northward, and is marked by perches.

Tidal Lights. — Two fixed white lights are shown from the old quay from 2½hrs. before high-water to 2hrs. afterwards.

Tides.—It is high-water, full and change, at **Dundrum Quay** at 10hr. 43min. Springs rise 12¾ft. ; neaps, 10ft.

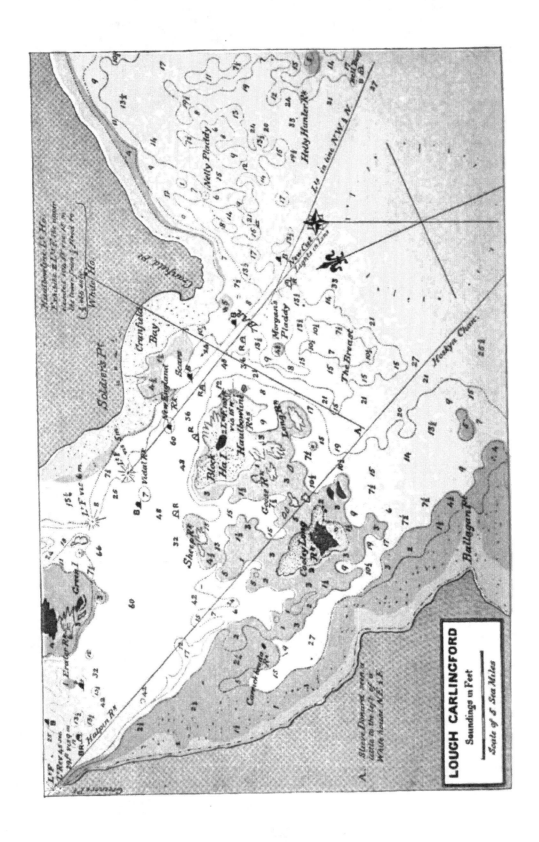

LOUGH CARLINGFORD

Soundings in Feet

Scale of 5 Sea Miles

Tidal Streams.—Off St. John's Point the streams from the N. and S. of Ireland meet, causing that curious phenomenon half-way between the Isle of Man and Ireland where the surface rises and falls, but there is no current. **Close to the shore the stream runs at one knot and a half,** but loses strength in the offing. As far as St. John's the **flood stream runs S.W.** From **Mullartown** the flood sets N.E., and the ebb *vice versâ*. The stream sweeps round the bay and out into the offing, losing strength as it goes.

Newcastle, at the N.W. corner of the bay, **has** a dry har-bour, and is unsafe with S. or S.E. winds. There are no dangers in the approach, but it is very subject to violent squalls from the Mourne Mountains.

From Mullartown to **Annalong** is three-quarters of a mile, and **Russell Point** is just beyond it. At **Annalong** there is a little dry harbour at the mouth of a stream; it is used by fishing craft and coasters for shipping granite quarried in the Mourne Mountains.

From **Annalong** to **Leestone Point** the coast is fairly clean, and may be approached to within three-quarters of a mile. At one mile E. of **Leestone Point,** and half a mile off shore, is a shoal with only 9ft. on it; that is the only outlying danger. From **Leestone** to **Cranfield Point** is four miles. The coast is mostly low, with a stretch of level land behind up to the foot of the Mourne Mountains. The foreshore is foul and rocky for some distance, gradually increasing as the entrance to Carlingford Lough is neared.

Hely Hunter Rock, with 6ft. over it at low-water, lies a good mile out from Cranfield Point. At 775yds. S.S.W. ¾ W. from it is a **black bell buoy,** in four fathoms. Between **Hely Hunter** and **Nell Pladdy,** in shore, there are two fathoms; but it is better to keep **outside** the buoy.

From here **Haulbowline Lighthouse** in line with **Greenore Light** leads up to the entrance of the dredged channel, for which the two pile lighthouses in line are the leading marks.

The entrance to **Lough Carlingford** is easily known by the white lighthouse on **Haulbowline Island** and the ruined Blockhouse on the flat rocks behind it. The dangers lie some way off the points, and the navigation is intricate; but the Lough affords abundant shelter, and the channel is admirably buoyed and lighted.

It is unnecessary to describe in detail the reefs on the E. side. The channel, or New Cut, is 400ft. wjde with 15ft. at low-water. **Black conical buoys** mark the starboard-hand, and **red can buoys** the port.

The group of rocks, of which **Haulbowline Rock** is the chief, is extensive, and divides the entrance into two channels; but the western one is **not used** much, and, as it is **unbuoyed** and **shallow**, there being only 3ft. in it at low-water, no stranger should attempt it.

The **New Cut** buoys begin at about two-thirds of the distance from Hely Hunter Bell Buoy to **Cranfield Point,** or one-third off the latter mark.

When the **Blockhouse Rock** is passed, the channel, which was previously quite straight, opens out, and a course may be steered N.W. ½ W. to pass W. of **New England** and **Vidal** black buoys, and N.E. of the red buoys off **Blockhouse Ledges** and **Sheep Rock.** Sandy flats lie off both shores. On those on the E. side the pile lighthouses are placed, which in line, bearing N.N.W. ¼ W., lead through the **New Cut.** Anchorage may be picked up anywhere here. Close to the inner pile lighthouse is a good place, S.E. of **Green Island,** but the anchorage inside the Lough is preferable.

Ballagan Point, the S.W. point of entrance, is, like Cranfield Point, surrounded by dangers, only they extend farther out and are more persistent in their attendance. Some of the rocks uncover; most do not. As all this part is unbuoyed and un-marked it need not be described, the entrance to Carlingford Lough naturally resolving itself into one channel between **Haul-bowline Lighthouse** and Cranfield Point.

Haulbowline Light.—From a **white circular tower,** 111ft. high, a **fixed white light** is shown at an elevation of **104ft. above high-water,** visible **fifteen miles.**

In the **same tower, at an elevation of 50ft.** above high-water, a **fixed white light** is shown from **half-flood to half-ebb.**

A ball is hoisted by day during the same time. Above this, at 68ft. above high-water, a fixed red light is shown between S. 39deg. W. and S. 53deg. W., to indicate the turning point in the channels.

Fog-signal.—A bell is sounded once every ½min.

Leading Lights for the Channel.—Two pile lighthouses are placed on the edge of the bank between Green Island and Soldiers' Point, distant 500yds. apart, bearing N.N.W. ¼ W. and S.S.E. ¼ E.; both show fixed white lights. The outer one is 23ft. above high-water, the inner 40ft. above; both lights are visible five miles from the outer one. They are obscured when bearing E. of N.E. by E. ½ E.

Greenore Lights.—On the S. side of the point, at an elevation of 29ft. above high-water, a revolving white light is shown, attaining its greatest brilliancy every 45sec., visible nine miles. It is obscured by a building when bearing E. of S. ¼ E.

On the pier, N. ¼ E., distant 100yds. from the above light, is a fixed red light, 33ft. above high-water, visible five miles. When these two lights are in line they lead between Watson and Stalka Rocks.

Tides.—It is high-water, full and change, at Cranfield Point at 11hr. 0min. Springs rise 16ft.; neaps, 11ft.

The rate of the tidal current between Blockhouse and the rocks on the W. side is four knots and a half, and also through the New Cut. The strongest tide is between Halpin Rock and the shore, running at five knots. Inside the Lough it slacks to one knot and a half, and off Rostrevor it is hardly felt.

The ebb, unless guarded against, might sweep a vessel through the W. channel, and the flood sets into Cranfield Bay. At Hely Hunter the streams are weak and inclined to follow the set outside, which is E. by N. and W. by S.

Dangers in the Entrance between Greenore and Green Castle Point.—From Sheep Rock—which dries 4ft. and lies almost in the middle of the apparent channel N.W. of Blockhouse Island, marked on its E. side by a red can buoy—to Greenore banks lie out on each side. They are steep-to, and uncover from

2ft. to 6ft. above low-water. The channel is clear between for nearly a third of a mile.

The first danger is **Halpin Rock**, lying S.E. of **Greenore Point**. There is 12ft. over it at **low-water**, and it is **marked** by a **red and black conical buoy**. The best water is W. of this, the channel being one cable wide. N.E. of this danger, distant 300yds., is a rock with only 7ft. least water.

Between this and **Green Island** is a **dangerous pinnacle**, with 7½ft. on it at low-water springs, and 20ft. close to. It lies 130yds. S.W. of **Frazer Rock**, and S. ¾ E. distant 500yds. from the **Earl Rock Beacon**. A black conical buoy lies close to it on the S.W. side.

Frazer Rock is N. of Green Island. Over it there is only 7ft. of water. It is not marked, but the **black conical buoy** on the **pinnacle rock** is a sufficient protection.

Green Island lies 800yds. from **Green Castle Point**, on the E. side. It is small, and surrounded by wide extending ledges. Between it and the **inner red pile light**, **close** to the latter, there is a **narrow channel** leading to a **snug anchorage**. If intending to attempt this wait until it is low-water, and go in carefully with the slack flood. There is 18ft. in this little pool, about 200yds. from the shore, but it is a difficult passage.

Earl Rock is dry at low-water. It is marked by a concrete beacon, 22ft. high, lying 700yds. E. by N. ¾ N. from Greenore Point. S. of the beacon there is a rocky head, with only 4½ft. of water on it at low-water. It is marked by a **black conical buoy**. Half-way between Earl and Frazer Rocks is another rock with only 3½ft. of water on it. All these dangers are on the E. side, as the channel passes close to **Greenore Point**.

Stalka Rock uncovers 1hr. before low-water. It is **marked** by an **iron perch**, half a mile N. by W. from **Earl Rock**, to which it is **connected** by a **ridge of sand**, which partially **uncovers** and **extends three-quarters of a mile N. of Stalka Rock**.

Between this ridge and Mill Bay Banks, on the E. side, there is a channel 200yds. wide, and with three fathoms least water. A **black conical buoy** lies 300yds. S.W. of the perch, between which there is foul ground.

On the **W. side of the channel** lies **Watson Rock**, with 5ft. over it at low-water. It is marked by a red can buoy on its E. side. This is the S. end of a bank which runs for half a mile in a N.W. by N. direction, with from 7ft. to 11ft. over its N. end. Between it and the great W. bank, off Carlingford, there is a narrow channel, with from 12ft. to 15ft. of water in it. On the outer edge of the W. bank, half a mile from shore, is **Black Rock,** marked by a perch; it is covered at half-flood. The edge of the W. bank runs from here in a N. by W. and N.N.W. ½ W. direction for one mile and a half, as far as the **red can buoy** marking the N. spit of Carlingford Bank, which is steep-to. This bank fronts the whole of Carlingford Bay. Its E. or outer edge is marked by **two red can buoys.** The bank dries and is steep-to. Between it and the shore there are 4ft. or 5ft. of water.

N. of this bank and near the Carlingford shore there is a flat, with from 8ft. to 10ft., extending 600yds. from the shore, and here is about the safest place in the Lough to anchor.

All the E. side of the **Lough as far as Killowen Point** is filled up by banks. Two conical black buoys mark the W. edge of this, and the bank dries out to the S. black buoy. From the northernmost black buoy the bank sweeps round towards Rostrevor Bay, leaving a deeper pool, with from 7ft. to 9ft. over a large part of it.

Killowen Point forms the S.E. side of this beautiful anchorage, and from here to **Warren Point** the shore sweeps round in a fine curve, with Rostrevor in the centre, forming a splendid natural shelter, and providing a scene of great loveliness.

Carlingford Lough is the first really beautiful bit of scenery to be met with after leaving Wales, and it has the incomparable advantage of providing safe anchorage and delightful sailing. I have seldom met with any place which so pleased me in every way as Rostrevor. Mountains surround the Lough. Carlingford Mountain is 1980ft. high; Rostrevor Mountain is 1596ft.; Eagle Mountain is 2061ft.; and all except the last rise abruptly from the very edge of the Lough. The colouring, shape, and abruptness of these heights is as fine as anything I have seen in the Highlands.

There is the further advantage that the prevailing winds are off shore, and that it is a far drier, as well as a warmer, climate. I always look back to Rostrevor as a really first-class yachting resort, the only drawback being that large yachts must anchor some way out, but not farther than a mile.

The head of the Lough is shallow. Off **Warren Point**, which is low and a rising watering-place, lies **Gunnaway Rock,** covered at the first quarter flood. It is marked by a **beacon,** and lies S.S.E. from Warren Point distant 600yds. There are rocks between it and the shore.

On the W. shore opposite is another **black rock, also marked by a beacon.** It is covered at 3½hrs. flood, and is on the outer edge of the stony bank which edges this side of the Lough. Between these two dangers lies the entrance to the River Newry. There is a narrow channel, marked by beacons, with a depth of 7ft. least water, dredged through the Oyster Bank at the head of the Lough; this leads to a deep hole, called Victoria Basin, where there is 72ft. of water, with moor-ing buoys for large vessels to lie and unload. One-third of a mile above it is Victoria Lock and the canal to Newry. The channel is marked by black and red beacons, and a **black and red buoy** marks the entrance to the channel.

At night two white leading lights, 48ft. and 16ft. high, bearing N.N.W. ¼ W., lead through the dredged channel.

The best anchorage in the Lough is, perhaps, that inside the last or N. red buoy of the W. bank, close to the Carlingford shore, N.N.E. of the castle. Rostrevor Bay is shallow, but there is 6ft. or 7ft. at low-water, over mud, about a quarter of a mile from the hotel, with Killowen Point just touching Greenore Point. There is a small quay at Rostrevor, but it dries out. The place is sadly wanting in a landing-stage or jetty.

As it is, at low-water the best place is under the bank near the high road, about 100yds. down the Killowen Road.

CHAPTER XXXIII.

THE COAST AND OBJECTS OF INTEREST VISIBLE FROM THE SEA BETWEEN BELFAST LOUGH AND LOUGH CARLINGFORD.

AT last the hardy Corinthian finds himself in quiet waters.

Although I have coasted all round the western shore of Wales and England, I cannot say, beyond the few places where the beauty of the scenery compensated me a little for the anxieties of the navigation and the hazards of a precarious anchorage, that the sailing was at all after the kind suited for amateurs who seek a holiday where relaxation and easy work is not entirely supplanted by downright hard toil and constant watchfulness.

Along the Irish coasts of the E. and S., cruising again becomes the easy pleasure one used to enjoy when skimming from port to port on the south-western coasts of England. Indeed, in many ways the sailing is easier, for the prevailing wind being S.W. or W. the cruising here is mainly along a weather shore. The sea is less liable to be heavy, and shelter can readily be obtained.

For natural beauty, too, the Mourne Mountains, with the splendid facilities for sailing afforded by Carlingford Lough, can compare with any part I know, and will not suffer by the comparison.

But now for details. A very few words will be sufficient to describe Belfast, as far as the purposes of this book go.

Most part of the city is barely 6ft. above the water. There are many fine buildings in it and public institutions. A great deal of money is made in the place, and it is the seat of the linen industry of Ireland.

As far back as the thirteenth century this industry was fostered by a member of that powerful and enlightened Norman family, the De Burghs, and amid all the castle-building, harrying, and blood-shedding, which those piratical Norman barons were carrying on, it is comforting to see one family, at least, introducing the arts of peace. Newtown Ards was the first seat of the industry, which another enlightened statesman also fostered, although his memory is chiefly connected with a bold scheme for rendering the crown of Charles I. secure on the basis of a military despotism, which would undoubtedly have succeeded but for the resolution of a few stubborn members of Parliament, combined with an irresolute and half-hearted monarch.

Lord Strafford invested £30,000 of his own fortune in the woollen and linen industry. Since then the business has grown rapidly, until now it has reached, perhaps, its zenith, and India and the Hindoo terror is looming ahead to undersell the western factories of Belfast, Manchester, and Roubaix.

Anchored here off Carrickfergus, with the old castle towering grandly from the very edge of the water, thoughts flit dreamily back to the time when these beautiful shores first saw the keels of the Norsemen and the galleys of their accomplished descendants, the Normans, gliding round White Head and Orlock Point, as they swept up to see what spoils could be gathered under these sunny hills.

The very name of the place causes one to wander away in a maze of thought. Tradition says Fergus McEargh started from here to settle in Scotland, and left his name on the rock behind him. But did the Irish colonize Scotland? Or did the Scotch colonize Ireland? Perhaps a little of both. Anyway, Edward Bruce, brother of the hero of the spider legend and

Bannockburn, landed here and very nearly founded a Scottish line of Irish kings.

Carrickfergus became the headquarters of an enterprising and hardy race of English gentlemen. The Chichester family, whose ancestor, Sir Arthur Chichester, was Lord Deputy of Ireland in 1612, have, by their energy and foresight, enriched themselves and the neighbourhood since that period, and exhibited those qualities of military capacity, statesmanlike diplomacy, and practical shrewdness, which have made the English the predominant partner in the United Kingdom and Ireland. In the church are many monuments to the Chichesters, among them one to Sir Arthur.

Beyond the castle, which dates from the twelfth century, there is little to see at Carrickfergus except the church.

Bangor is quite a different place. It is gay, coquette, laughing, as the French say. There is plenty of yachting life in the season, and if only there were a shelter from the N.E. a better little place could not be found.

The Royal Ulster Yacht Club has its headquarters here, and it has for its commodore that distinguished diplomatist and Corinthian sailor, the Marquis of Dufferin and Ava, among whose many distinctions that of Admiral of Ulster is not the least valued. There is something eminently mediæval about this title. Memories of Admiral Coligny and of the Duke of Norfolk, the hero of Flodden, Lord High Admiral of Spain under Charles V., suggest themselves, and that curious picture of a naval commander clad in complete armour with spurs and flowing plume irresistibly carries the mind to a contemplation of those hardy amphibii—the horse marines.

Bangor, by the way, like all the Bangors I have come across —and there is one in every country whose waters I have cruised in yet, except England—has the ruins of an abbey, and boasts the slaughter of I am afraid to say how many monks. When chroniclers kill off the poor shavelings they become very gory indeed; but, after all, few massacres come up to the awful one commemorated at Bardsey, even when committed by chroniclers and historians. Of course, there is a

castle at Bangor—an old one and a new one. This part of
Ireland really beats Wales for castles; they are so common
that one gets tired of them after a bit. Presently we shall
come to a town where there are at least five, all in the same
place; in fact, quite a street of castles, and Carlingford is surrounded by them.

About two miles from Bangor is Clandeboye, Lord Dufferin's
residence. There is a picturesque lake in the grounds, and a
museum of curios, collected by Lord Dufferin in his journeys,
voyages, and sojourns in many lands. To the brotherhood of
Corinthian sailors, Lord Dufferin may be an excellent ambassador, a bewildering diplomatist, a wily statesman, a superb
viceroy, a witty after-dinner orator, and a versatile writer. All
these in their way are useful things; but before and above all
he is a consummate sailor, a true Corinthian, who knows
how to handle his craft, as a master should. No smooth-water
sailor either; but so hardy and bold a navigator he that
he dared, under canvas only, to encounter the frozen seas of
the Arctic regions and penetrate to Spitzbergen and Jan Mayen
when tough old whalers even were turned back by the ice.

The coast from Bangor to Donaghadee is not interesting.
The Copeland Islands are a dreary monotony of barren rocks.
There is an ancient earthwork at Donaghadee, and plenty of
E. wind. A great deal of money must have been spent in
trying to make a comfortable harbour. The pity is it was not
used at Bangor, round the corner, where the efforts could have
been successful.

From here to Strangford Narrows the coast is not inviting.
It was my fate when first I came up here to have to beat all the
way against a keen and eager N.E. wind, for I was going to
Belfast. The sea was choppy and nasty, and nowhere could I
make a longer leg. In and out of all these rocks, now on the
starboard tack, now on the port, it was weary work; but at least
I had this comfort—I was able to study the outlying reefs
thoroughly. What vicious rocks they are—low, crafty, malicious,
evil-looking things, like snakes in the grass; their ugly heads
scarcely showing, and the sea tumbling over them as if in league

with their devilry to help to conceal the lurking treachery. The land behind, too, is a bleak expanse—no trees, no broken outline, no heights to relieve the monotony.

It is a comfort when Bar Pladdy Buoy comes in sight, and one sees by the fishing-boats at the entrance that the tide will be easy into the Strangford Narrows.

Of course, when I put in here I was hailed with many offers of pilotage. As usual, I declined all these attentions. So far I have explored all these coasts, and never yet, in France or England, have been helped by anything or anyone other than the Admiralty charts and my own head. This practice has drawn down upon me comments more forcible than complimentary, but I still stick to the custom, even if it shall eventually end in sticking me on a rock or elsewhere. Experience has justified me so far, and success has warranted a continuance in the habit.

I was greatly disappointed with the picturesque appearance of the Narrows. The shores are bleak-looking. Tara Hill—one of the many hills of that name, and not to be confounded with *the* Tara Hill, near Navan, celebrated by Moore—is of moderate height, and it is not until the village of Strangford is opened that one sees how pretty it is. **Audley Roads**, however, are quite pretty. Somehow I was reminded of Beaulieu Creek as I turned Old Court Point and saw the inlet winding away among the low woods and shallow shore.

As far as I can see, in ordinary weather and taking the tides at the right time, there is no great difficulty in Strangford Narrows. The tides do run at a prodigious rate it is true. It is quite absurd the way in which the ferry boats "slither" up the stream. With their heads pointing right against the tide, and a fresh wind blowing, they arrive in no time at a point which seems half a mile astern.

I rowed into Strangford Lough and towards **Killyleagh**. This is an interesting old place, shared as to proprietary rights nearly equally between Lord Dufferin and his brother-in-law, Colonel Gavin Hamilton. The Hamiltons have held the old castle since James I.'s reign, and have numbered among their titles that of Clandeboye and Clanbrassil; but, strangely enough, both titles are now lost to the family. The latter title belongs to the heir of the Roden earldom, while the former is merged in that of the heir to the Dufferin and Ava marquisate, the Roden family name being Jocelyn, and the Dufferin family name Temple-Blackwood. The castle of Killyleagh is still the property of the Hamiltons, and was nearly all re-built in 1850. The last Earl of Clanbrassil, of the Hamilton line, died in 1798, and the title passed to the heirs of his sister, who had married Lord Roden.

A tablet placed by this last Clanbrassil, of the Hamiltons, records in Greek his affection for the Marquis de Monthermer, who died in 1770. It is placed in a cave, called the Hermitage, in Tollymore Park, two miles and a half from Newcastle.

Three places of interest on or near Lough Strangford are within reach of a boat. Of these, **Downpatrick** is the most important. By rowing up the Quoile, from the anchorage under Hare Island, the quay is soon reached.

Downpatrick is the oldest town in Ulster. For a long time there were three quarters within the walls, affording the eminently Irish problem of three quarters making one whole. The Irish, the Scotch, and the English all lived apart, and no doubt the feuds were as frequent and bitter as those of the Capulets and Montagues. In the terrible Irish rebellion of 1641, the castle, which was the ancient residence of the kings of Ulster, the most memorable of whom was Celtair, son of Duach, was destroyed. Archæologists have identified the place with Dunum, mentioned by Ptolemy, but the chief claim to distinction which Downpatrick possesses is that it is the burial-place of St. Patrick. The present cathedral, which was restored, if not almost re-built, in 1790, has been subsequently considerably improved. There are, however, still standing some of the original arches of the twelfth-century building, supported by columns with quaint designs carved on them.

St. Patrick's grave is enclosed by an iron railing, and is a little to the left of the cathedral on the S. side.

The other object of interest is the ancient "Dun," or earth-work, from which the town took its name. It is a mound 60ft. high and 2100ft. in circumference.

There is a picturesque bit on the banks of the Quoile, two miles N.W. of the town, where still stand a few remnants of the Cistercian Abbey of Inch, founded by John De Courcy. Near Downpatrick are the Struell Wells. These wells used to be the object of pilgrimage at night on the Eve of St. John, but as the opportunity was too good not to be utilised as a means of suggesting scandal at any rate, these functions have been omitted in recent times.

Newtown Ards, at the head of the Lough, is another very old town. James I. incorporated it when he encouraged the settle-ment of Ulster, and by the deed a provost and twelve burgesses are appointed to govern the commonalty. The Quakers brought prosperity and quiet respectability to the place, qualities which have remained ever since the Montgomeries became lords of Newtown Ards, under the title of Viscount Ards. It seems strange that this French baronial house, whose ancestor had inadvertently slain his king, and so procured for Mary of Scotland a French crown, should become settled in this remote corner of the far West; but Ireland has always been regarded with favour by the French.

On the E. side of the Lough is an ivy-clad ruin, well worthy of a visit. Indeed, except by water, it is not easily accessible. Grey Abbey, or the Abbey of St. Mary, was founded by a princess from the Isle of Man in 1193, a daughter of the king who founded Rushen Abbey, near Castletown.

She married Sir John de Courcy, and introduced monks from Cumberland. In the rebellion of 1641 the O'Neils burnt it, but the Montgomeries restored or rebuilt the greater part of it.

As I said before in the chapter on the navigation of this Lough, a very pleasant week could be spent here, either camp-ing out on one of the islands or canoeing from inlet to inlet. Strangford Lough is a kind of Irish Morbihan.

Strangford Village and Lord Bangor's estate of Audley are pretty. Very quiet and home-like are the surroundings, reminding one more of Hampshire than any other part. By the way, it is a noble document the harbour-master hands one to justify the charge of 2s. 6d. on behalf of Lord de Ros.

As we go out Kilclief Castle stands conspicuously on our right, but the care necessary to avoid being taken out by the tide through the W. channel prevents a very attentive scrutiny.

Guns Island is not attractive—one wonders why Guns? Did Paul Jones, the pirate, threaten the peace of the good folk hereabout after he had defeated King George's ships in Belfast Lough and killed poor Lieutenant Dobbs?

But the coast is a better one to sail along now. The sunken rocks are cleared up, and the cliffs are quite tidy.

Ardglass is a delightful-looking place. I just put my nose round the corner, and seeing it was pretty full of craft went on, but the old gray town is worth more than a passing glance. Once this little place did a large trade, but what is the history of its five ruined castles no one seems to know. Not even the annals of one exist to tell us what went on, and how the châtelains, and, above all, the châtelaines got on together in such close proximity. Surely there must have been jealousies, bickerings over precedence, and rivalries of all sorts.

But now St. John's Point Lighthouse is gleaming white against the dark Mourne Mountains beyond, and the crested sea is curling under the swift squall which is flying over Dundrum Bay.

For those who wish to stay at Newcastle, the best way would be to go into Dundrum Channel and moor in the pool abreast Lord Downshire's house. The castle stands well on its wooded knoll, looking down on the Strand of the Champions, for here, when the tide was out, the young men of the country used to practise athletic sports—so they say.

This old castle has seen some hard fighting. Built by a De Courcy, it was held by Phelim Magennis against the Lord Deputy Kildare, who took it by storm in 1515, but the Magennis again got hold of it and Lord Grey had to storm it afresh.

As we sail across the bay the splendid grouping of the Mourne Mountains especially strikes one. Every mountain seems to stand up so nobly. It is not a range. It is no line of heights, but a most magnificent cluster of precipitous summits, rising abruptly from the sea on one side and the plains of Dundrum on the other. Slieve Donard towers over the whole, gaining greater majesty by reason of the perfectly level line from which he rises. This it is which gives Teneriffe its stupendous appearance, and adds height to all mountains which rise abruptly from the sea.

Newcastle is a delightful watering-place. It is a pity there is not safe shelter there. Donard Lodge, Lord Annesley's house, stands in the midst of lovely gounds. Through them runs the Glen River, with many waterfalls brawling from crags between Slieve Donard and Slieve Commedagh. The paths through the woods are endless, affording magnificent views of mountain, plain, and sea, and for those who are energetic Slieve Donard is a perpetual playground. The mountains of Mourne are a mass of granite, with veins of basalt, felstone, porphyry, and mica-trap. Their shapes indicate their volcanic origin ; and for the creation of beautiful outlines, or grand grouping, there is nothing like the fiery passions of nature. The heated moment is passed and only quiet beauty remains. There are memories along the road between the sea and the mountains which recall the fact that this is Ireland, the land of strife and bloodshed.

Bloody Bridge is so called because Sir Conn Magennis in 1641, the year of the terrible massacre of the Protestants, the St. Bartholomew of Ireland, beheaded a party of English whom he had taken. Weary of conducting the band farther, he stopped by the side of the stream and put them all to death, leaving the headless trunks on the road.

A little beyond is Armour's Hole, where a son murdered his father in 1701 ; and still farther beyond is Maggie's Leap, where a girl jumped that awful chasm by the shore to save herself from a villain whose courage was unequal to his passions, for he paused before the passage perilous, and so Maggie escaped.

It is a lovely piece of sailing on a fine day from Dundrum Bay to Carlingford, but that it can be dangerous the row of houses, called "Widow's Row," at Newcastle testifies. In the autumn of 1843, a sudden storm arose in the bay and many of

the fishermen never came home again. A subscription was made
and the Row was built as almshouses for the widows.

I look back on this sail from Carlingford to Strangford as
the pleasantest of all the cruise in the Irish Channel. The
wind was off shore, of moderate strength, allowing every sail to
be set, and the old boat went through the water in fine style.
The scenery certainly is beautiful.

As Leestone Point is passed the entrance to Lough Carlingford gradually opens. At first it is hard to make it out, for
there are many rocks about ; but when Hely Hunter Buoy
is rounded then the straight lane of buoys leads up a fine
stretch of water to the noble Lough beyond. The beauty of
the place came upon me as a surprise. I knew nothing of
Rostrevor, or Carlingford, and was totally unprepared for the
scene before me.

Green Castle, gaunt and gray, looms above the low ground
on the right. On the left Greenore looks busy and new, with
its steamboat quay and railway hotel. Behind rises Carlingford Mountain, grand and rugged, while from Killowen Point
the wooded sides of Slieve Ban soar aloft to a height of
1600ft., with "Clough More," or the great boulder, poising
on the ridge half-way.

In the dim distance fertile lands slope gently upwards to
the hills round Newry, and all is smiling repose.

Rostrevor Hotel is a large building right on the shores of the
Lough. The village is to the left, with lovely walks on all
sides, but especially up a valley behind. There is a conspicuous obelisk on the road to Warren Point. It is to
the memory of General Ross, who was killed in action at
Baltimore in 1814.

Warren Point possesses a good beach and shallow water.
There is a railway here from Newry, and it has all the appearance of a rising watering-place ; but it has none of the beauty
of Rostrevor. Both places are admirably sheltered from the
N. and E., especially Rostrevor, which faces S.S.W.

Two miles above Warren Point is Narrow Water Castle,
rebuilt by the Duke of Ormonde in 1663, after its assault by

the troops of Cromwell. The situation is romantic, standing as it does directly in the channel of the Newry River, and barring all approach to that town. It would be difficult to find a prettier picture than this old fortalice presents, crowning the rock in the middle of the water, and mirroring itself in the glossy surface amid the woods and hills which surround it.

Newry is a busy place, with regular steam communication direct with Liverpool three times a week. Vessels of 15ft. draught go right up to the town, where there is a large trade done in exporting provisions, dairy produce, linen, cattle, and other commodities.

Carlingford, at the S.E. side of the Lough, is a sleepy old place. King John's Castle as the gray old ruin is locally called, is the most conspicuous feature, and behind the town are the ruins of a Dominican monastery, founded by Richard de Burgh in 1305. The ruins stand well, nestling under the towering heights of Carlingford Mountain.

On the whole a week could easily be spent at anchor in this charming spot.

CHAPTER XXXIV.

FROM LOUGH CARLINGFORD TO WICKLOW HEAD.

BEARINGS and distances from Haulbowline Lighthouse, Lough Carlingford.—The Chicken Rock, Calf of Man, bears from Haulbowline Light E. by S. ¾ S., forty-three miles. The Bar Light-ship, Liverpool, S.E. ¾ E., one hundred and four miles. Point Lynus Light S.E. ¼ S. southerly, seventy-four miles. S. Stack Light, Holyhead, S.S.E. ½ E. easterly, sixty-five miles. Bardsey Island Light, S. by E., eighty-nine miles.

From Lough Carlingford to Kingstown there is no shelter suitable for yachts except those of very small draught at Malahide and Howth. I propose to omit minute description of the Dundalk and Drogheda Harbours as being entirely unsuited for yachting purposes, although the former does provide accommodation for vessels, in 4ft. of water, at low-tide against the quay. As for the latter, the length .of the river from the bar to the town, the strength of the tides, and the difficulties of the channel, render it an impossible place for sailing vessels, although for steamers it is practicable enough.

After clearing the New Cut, a course may be steered S. by W. ½ W. for Rockabill Light. The automatic signal buoy, moored in eleven fathoms, three miles and a half S. by E. ¾ E. from Haulbowline Light, will be left on the port, and the Imogene black conical buoy, lying in eight fathoms, one mile

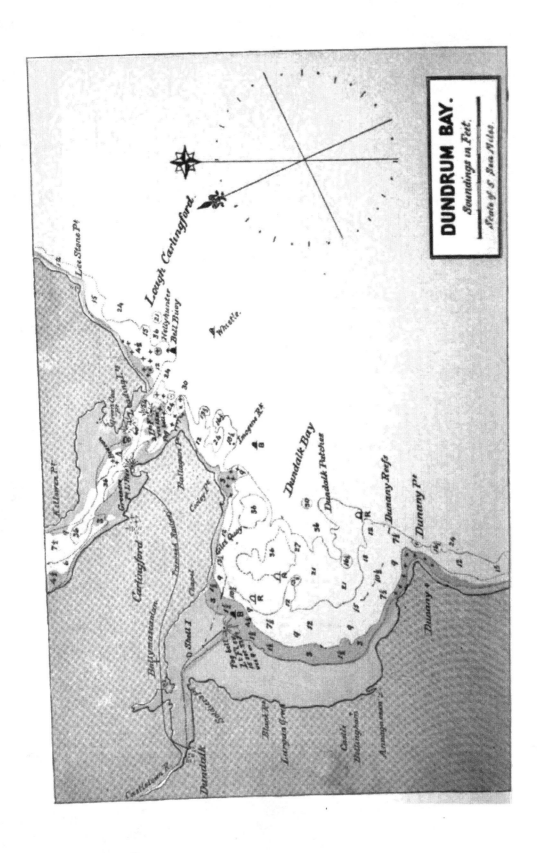

DUNDRUM BAY.

Soundings in Feet.

Scale of 3 Sea Miles.

and three-quarters from **Cooley Point,** will be on the **starboard.**
Imogene Rock lies half-way between it and the shore, with
only 3ft. over it at low-water. There is a ridge extending
two miles S.E. from **Cooley Point,** with from 7ft. to 16ft. on it.

Dundalk Bay is now well open. This extensive inlet is
nearly all foul and shallow throughout. Sand banks, which
dry at low-water for two miles from the shore, lie all round,
from Great Giles Quay on the N.E. corner to **Anagassam** on
the S.W., and continue to skirt the shore to **Dunany Point.**
In the centre of the bay is a dredged channel, with some 4ft.
on the bar at low-water, confined by submerged embankments
leading through the sands to Soldiers' Point in a northerly
direction, thence it turns N.W. to **Dundalk.** There is a pool
near Shell Island, called Rock Hole, with 20ft. of water in it.
Moorings are laid down here. The channel is beaconed and
buoyed in accordance with the rule, and at the end of the
sands on the E. side is a pile lighthouse, exhibiting, at an
elevation of 33ft. above high-water, a **flashing light at intervals**
of 15sec., visible nine miles: white seaward when bearing between **S. 87deg. W. and N. 14deg. W.;** obscured over the **Dunany
Reef** between **N. 14deg. W. and N. 22deg. E.;** red over the
S.W. banks between N. 22deg. E. and S. 33deg. E.; and white
in the direction of the channel to Dundalk when bearing between
S. 33deg. E. and S. 5deg. E. **Over the N. sand banks it is
obscured.** The channel from the **bar to the quay is lighted
with thirteen beacon lights—red on the S. side, white on the N.**
At **St. Giles Quay a red light,** in the fishing season, is shown from
September 1 to December 31.

Fog-signal.—A fog-bell is sounded every 10sec.

On the S. Bull Sand, on the W. side of the **channel,** are two
beacons, exhibiting fixed white lights. When in line they lead
up the channel on a N.N.W. ¾ W. bearing.

Off Dunany Point, which is of no great height and is conspicuous by reason of a church on a hill behind it, lies a reef,
extending in irregular patches in a N.E. direction for two miles
and a half, with depths of from 10ft. to 12ft. over it. A red
can buoy lies, in three fathoms and a half, 800yds. E. of a

patch with only 15ft. on it, or about two miles and a half N.E. of **Dunany Head.**

Clogher Head, four miles S. of Dunany Head, is a bolder feature.   It is a rocky promontory, with a fishing village on its S. side.   From here the shore is low for some miles, with the entrance to the Boyne four miles and a half S. of Clogher Head.

The Boyne very nearly saw the wrecking of my craft, for I trusted to what I was told, viz., that there were from 5ft. to 7ft. on the bar, and found to my sorrow there was barely 3ft., with a tide which I verily thought meant to roll craft, anchors, masts, everything, over and over like a ninepin and carry us away to sea.   I never saw an anchor come tearing home as mine did when the vessel's keel took the ground, and she slewed down the channel.

The Boyne River is marked by **Maiden Tower** and a small obelisk beside it, called Lady's Finger, and by stone beacons on its N.E. side and wooden perches on its S.W.   The width of the channel off Maiden Tower is barely 100yds.   Sea walls, more or less dilapidated, lie along the N.E. side as far as the third stone beacon, and on the S.W. side also.   They are covered at high-water.

Lights.—There are four lighthouses, on iron frames, from only three of which lights are exhibited.   The E. Light is a fixed **white light,** 27ft. above high-water, visible between the bearings of W. $\frac{1}{2}$ S. and N.W. by W. $\frac{1}{2}$ W. six miles, **Rockabill bearing N.N.W. $\frac{1}{2}$ W., distant eleven miles and a quarter.**   This is the low light.

W. Light is 100yds. in a W. by N. direction from the E. Light, and shows a fixed white light, 40ft. above high-water, visible six miles between the same bearings as the E. or low light.   These lights in line lead in the best of the water, and their positions are altered as the bar alters.

N. Light is a **fixed red light,** open to the channel within the bar.   It is 23ft. above high-water, and bears from the E. lighthouse N. by W. $\frac{3}{4}$ W., 780yds. distant.

The Boyne River is further lighted by six white lights on the N. side and one green and two white lights on the S. side.

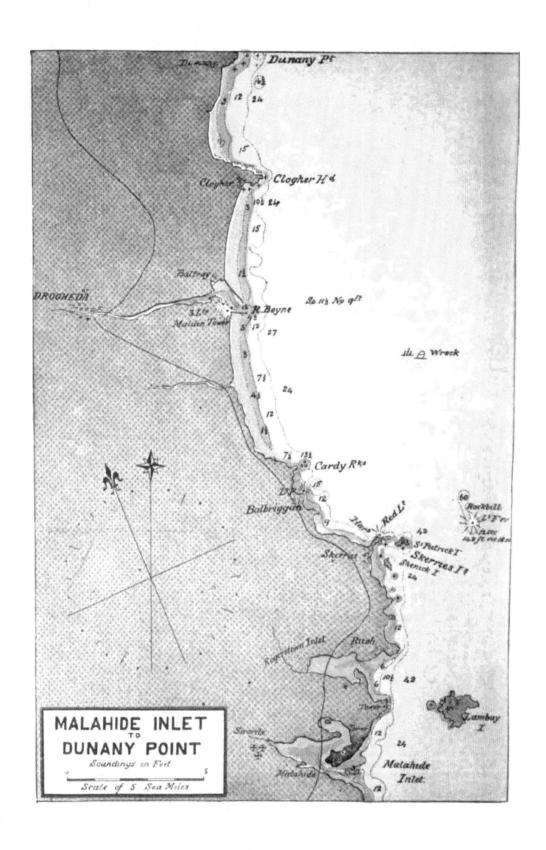

Dunany
Dunany Pt

Clogher Pt · Clogher Hd

Baltray
DROGHEDA
Maiden Tower
R. Boyne

So 11½ No q.fs.

11½ ⌂ Wreck

Cardy Rks

Balbriggan

So. 11½ No q.fs.

Hares · Red Lt
St Patrick I
Skerries
Skerries Is
Shenick I
Rockbill
Lt. Ho.

Rogerstown Inlet
Rush

Sirens
Malahida
Malahide Inlet

Lambay I

MALAHIDE INLET
TO
DUNANY POINT
Soundings in Feet
Scale of 5 Sea Miles

All are obscured seaward, and are only shown from half-flood to half-ebb.

Tides.—It is high-water, full and change, at Crook Point, entrance of the Boyne, at 11hr. 0min.   Springs rise 11¾ft. ; neaps, 9ft.   It is 45min. later at Drogheda.

From the mouth of the Boyne, which is hardly visible from our course—for the coast is low and the small gap in the sand hills very insignificant—to the Skerries, the shore sweeps round to the S., with an even margin at low-water and gradually shoaling depths.   Balbriggan lies in the S. part of it, with a jetty and dry harbour.   Half-way between it and the Boyne is Laytown, on the Nanny rivulet; and the Cardy Rocks, marked by an iron perch, lie one mile N.N.E. of Balbriggan Lighthouse, 600yds. off Braymore Point.   They uncover at half-tide, and there is a passage between them and the shore, with three fathoms in it.

Behind Balbriggan the coast is higher, but it is all of moderate elevation and uninteresting.   There is a fixed white light at Balbriggan, and a red sector covers the Skerries.   It is visible ten miles.

To Skerries Harbour the coast now trends S.E., forming Skerries Bay.   This place is a favourite fishing resort, and is considered the best dry harbour on the coast, as there is scarcely any inrun into it and the bottom is fine shingle, suitable for lying on legs.   Dublin is fifteen miles by railway.

The Skerries Islands are a group of barren rocks to the E. of the harbour.   They consist of the Islands of St. Patrick, Colts, Red, and Shenick, all of about 40ft. high, with outlying rocky foreshores.   The two last-named islands are connected with the land, and have Martello Towers on them.   On St. Patrick's there are the ruins of a chapel.   Between Red and Colts Islands there is a boat passage, and between St. Patrick's and Colts one deep enough for small sailing craft.

There are several outlying dangers.   A reef extends 600yds. in a southerly direction, and Cross Rock, nearly dry at low-water, lies on the outer edge of a reef extending N. of Red Island, and is in the way of rounding closely for the harbour.

Rockabill is two miles and a half E. ½ S. from St. Patrick's Island. Two granite rocks rise abruptly 30ft. above the water from a depth of eight fathoms, with fourteen fathoms between them and St. Patrick's. On the higher of the rocks is the lighthouse.

Rockabill Light.—From a circular gray tower, 105ft. high, a flashing light is shown at an elevation of 148ft. above high-water, flashing every 12sec. It shows white seaward between the bearings of N. 80deg. W. through W. to S. 31deg. W., and red landward of these bearings, visible eighteen miles.

From the Skerries to **Rogerstown Inlet** the coast is indented. Rush is a village, on a rocky point, with a Martello Tower and a little dry pier harbour N. of it.

Tides.—It is high-water, full and change, at the Skerries at 11hr. 0min. Springs rise 13ft.; neaps, 10ft. The stream between the islands turns 1hr. before it does in the offing. The ebb sets down 1hr. earlier than in the offing and runs 7½hrs. Between **Rush** and the **Skerries** is a little fishing cove, called **Lough Shinny**, exposed to the E., with a ruined pier.

Rogerstown Inlet goes in some way. The bar nearly dries at low-water, and with a channel in which there are from 3ft. to 9ft. at low-water inside. The entrance is divided by a bank, which dries out, and has only 7ft. on it at high-water. It is a difficult place to get into, and dreary enough when you are there. On the S. point there is a conspicuous tower.

Lambay Island lies opposite this point. The passage between is one mile and a half wide, and is safe for average-sized craft. The island is about one mile and a quarter long, and is a conspicuous object all down the coast, as **Knockhaun**, its highest part, is 405ft. high, and the **Nose**, at the E. end, 180ft. The W. side is low and rocky, with some dangerous rocks lying off. The other sides are bold and steep-to. There is a pier harbour, dry at low-water, and liable to a heavy scend in E. gales. At 180yds. N. of the harbour is a rock which has less than 6ft. over it at low-water. The highest land of the island, kept open between the pier-heads, leads S. of it.

Burrin Rocks uncover at the last quarter of the ebb. They are marked by a beacon, and are 400yds. from the W. point of the island.   **Burge Bar** extends three-quarters of a mile N.W. by W. from them, with only 17ft. least water at 400yds. distance from the beacon, but with four fathoms and three quarters at its extremity.

Taylor Rocks are marked by a beacon, and lie 300yds. N. of Scotch Point on the N. side of the island.   The other patches have from three fathoms and a half to four fathoms and a half on them.

Vessels may anchor off the harbour with W. winds, and with winds from W.N.W. to S.E. in **Swallow Cove,** on the **N. side** of the island.

From **Rogerstown Inlet** the shore sweeps S.W. to the entrance of **Malahide Inlet,** which, like Rogerstown, has a shifting bar. The S. channel is marked by a **buoy,** which is to be left on the port when entering.   The bar nearly dries, but there is a channel inside with from 10ft to 16ft. at low-water, very narrow, being hardly 100yds. wide, and running along the S. side of the inlet up to the railway bridge.   Malahide Chapel, in line with the N. side of the hotel, leads through the S. channel.   When **Swords Church** comes in line with a solitary tree N. of Malahide, then steer for it, and anchor when Malahide Church comes in line with a conspicuous terrace.   There are here 14ft. at low-water.

The channel on the bar is divided into two, but the S. is the better.   This is a difficult place for strangers.

From **Malahide Inlet** to **Howth** the coast is low and fronted by a sandy beach, with moderately decreasing depth up to it.

Baldoyle Creek almost dries out, and the entrance is close against the **W. pier of Howth Harbour,** and the ebb-tide sets strongly across the mouth towards the E. pier, and leaves a deposit at the entrance.

Howth Harbour.—This harbour, if it only had a little more room at low-water, would be a far better place than Kings-town.   As it is, the space where there are from one fathom and a quarter to one fathom and a half at low-water is very limited, being practically confined to a small pool on the W. side, just within the entrance.   Easterly gales send a heavy sea across outside, but beyond the swell coming round the pier-heads there is no danger when once inside. Two piers run out towards **Ireland's Eye,** leaving an entrance of 100yds. between the pier-heads. Two-thirds of the harbour uncover at low-water and the rest is shallow. On the E. side a rocky foreshore extends to **Murr Rock,** which uncovers at low-water, and lies 100yds. from the W. pier at a distance of 200yds. from the harbour mouth. The W. corner of the harbour is the only place where vessels can take the ground. With off-shore winds there is safe anchorage between Ireland's Eye and **Baldoyle Sands,** at the N.W. side of the island.

Tides.—It is high-water, full and change, at Howth at 11hr. 9min. Springs rise 13ft.; neaps, 10ft. The stream turns 1½hrs. sooner between Ireland's Eye and the land than in the offing, and runs at the rate of two knots an hour. To the E. of Ireland's Eye the stream runs 9hrs. to the N., but only at the distance of one cable and a half from the shore.

Ireland's Eye lies one mile and a quarter N. of the **Nose of Howth,** and is steep-to on its N. side, rising to the height of 316ft., with a Martello Tower on its N.W. point, but slopes to the S., with ledges covering only at high-water as far as **Thulla,** an islet at its S. end. S. and S.W. of this, distant 300yds. and 400yds., are some heads of rocks, which uncover, called the Rowans. Howth Church open S. of the lighthouse on the E. pier-head, bearing W. by S., clears these. On the N.W. side, 100yds. from the N.W. point, is a patch which dries 6ft. at low-water, and 250yds. from the S.E. point is Flat Rock. In the middle of Howth Sound there is about 10ft. of water at low-water.

Light.—The lighthouse on the E. pier shows a **fixed red light,** visible eleven miles.

Dublin Bay is a fine expanse of water, but **fully exposed to the E.** Half of the bay also is occupied with the extensive banks which sweep round from **Black Rock** to the **Hill of Howth.** In the centre of the bay the **Liffey** discharges its waters, the channel being deepened and confined by **extensive works** running out to the edge of the sands, fully four miles from Dublin, at the extremity of which is Poolbeg Lighthouse on the S. wall, exhibiting a fixed white light from an elevation of 66ft. above high-water, visible twelve miles.

N. Bull Wall exhibits a white occulting light, bright for 40sec., obscured for 4sec. There are other lights up the river, but as the Liffey is not suited for cruising purposes they need not be described in detail.

The Hill of Howth is a very conspicuous sea-mark, being bold seawards and connected with the land by a low sandy neck, over which Ireland's Eye is seen from Dublin Bay. At its S.E. point is the Bailey Lighthouse.

Dublin Bay Lights—Howth Head Bailey Light.—From a white tower, 42ft. high, a fixed white light is shown at an elevation of 134ft. above high-water, visible fifteen miles.

Fog-signal.—A siren gives a blast of 5sec. every minute.

Kish Light-vessel.—The Kish Light-ship is moored in thirteen fathoms, one mile and a quarter N.E. from the N. end of the Kish Bank, and exhibits at an elevation of 36ft. a revolving white light, attaining its greatest brilliancy every minute.

She carries three masts, is painted black with a white stripe, and carries a ball at the mainmast head.

Bearings and distances from the Kish Light-ship.—Wicklow Head Light bears from the Kish Light-ship S.S.W. ½ W., distant twenty-one miles and a half. Poolbeg Light, N.W. by W. ⅞ W., eight miles and a half. Carlingford Lough, N. by E. easterly, forty-two miles. St. John's Point, Dundrum Bay, N.N.E. ½ E. easterly, fifty-five miles. Mull of Galloway, N.E., eighty-seven miles. Chicken Rock Light, Isle of Man, N.E. by E. ½ E., fifty-seven miles. Wyre Light, Fleetwood, E., one hundred and nine miles. Skerries, Holyhead, E. by S. southerly, forty-seven miles and a half. S. Stack, E.S.E., forty-four miles. S. Bishop Light, S. ¾ W., ninety miles and a half. Smalls, S. by W. ¼ W. westerly, ninety-seven miles.

Kingstown.—On the E. pier-head from a granite tower, 41ft. high, an alternately red and white revolving light is shown 41ft. above high-water, obscured when bearing N. of N. 39deg. W. over Muglins Rocks.

2 B

On the W. pier a fixed red light is shown, 36ft. above high-water, in a tower 29ft. high.

There are no outlying dangers in Dublin Bay itself, except the Bull Sands and the rocky foreshore between Kingstown and Bullock Harbour. Burford Bank is outside the bay, and has 15ft. least water. Rosbeg Bank, close to the Bailey, has 15ft. least water on it also.

Kingstown Harbour is a magnificent artificial shelter, but during E. gales a heavy swell comes in, and the central and W. side of the harbour are then uncomfortable, if not dangerous, berths. The E. side is the snuggest part, but that is kept for ships of war, the Irish light-ships, and the traffic of the mail steamers. One yacht alone has the privilege of this snuggest berth in all the harbour, and, perhaps, by judicious management a berth could be picked up also by others, for before I left another yacht was taken over there from alongside where I was lying, as a choppy swell was coming in, causing everyone to roll uncomfortably.

Off the Traders' Wharf, in Dunleary Harbour, at the W. corner there is 12ft. at low-water, and there is shelter enough, but a certain amount of traffic interferes with comfort and tranquility.

Although there is a good deal of room in Kingstown Harbour it requires judgment to pick out a snug place when it is crowded, as it mostly is during the yachting season after the Cowes week is over, especially if one is a stranger.

The coast from Kingstown to Dalkey is rocky, but from Bullock Harbour to Dalkey it is clear of dangers. Dalkey Island extends in a reef N. to Maiden Rock, with ledges on each side. The W. side is mostly steep-to. The Sound is quite navigable, with from three fathoms and a half to seven fathoms, and 200yds. wide. The land side is preferable to that of Dalkey.

The Muglins are a group of rocks, 20ft. high, lying 600yds. E. of Dalkey. They are steep-to on all sides except the W., where a rock dries 3ft. at low-water, 100yds. from the beacon. Muglins Beacon is a white conical stone edifice, painted white

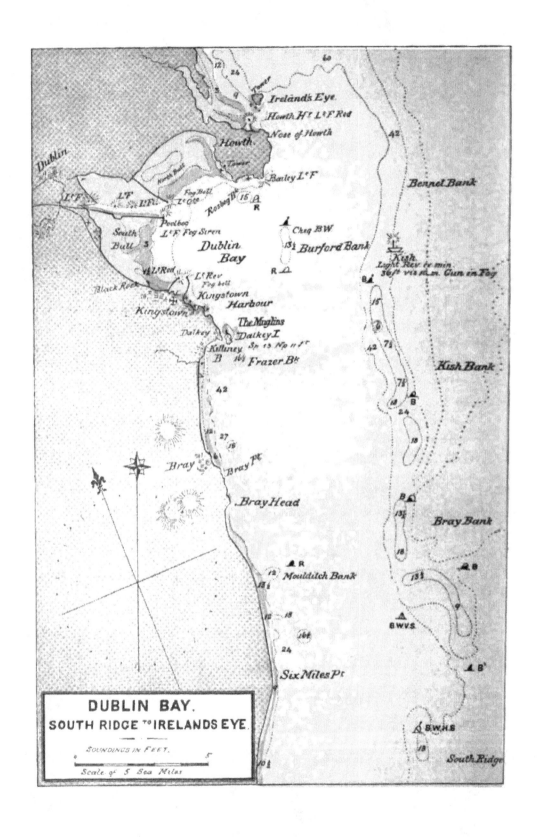

DUBLIN BAY.
SOUTH RIDGE TO IRELANDS EYE.

SOUNDINGS IN FEET.

Scale of 5 Sea Miles

with a red band round it.   It is quite safe to pass between Muglins and Dalkey, but Dalkey Sound is the safer.

Outlying Banks.—**Rosbeg Bank,** half a mile from the Hill of Howth, has 15ft. least water on it, is of small extent, and is of fine sand.   A red can buoy marks its S.E. side.   **Burford Bank** is a narrow ridge of hard sand, one mile and two-thirds long, in a N.N.E. and S.S.W. direction, with 15ft. least water on it, about half a mile from its N. end.   The sea breaks over this bank in easterly gales.   It is marked by two buoys. **N. Burford** lies in six fathoms, and is **a conical black and white chequered buoy, with staff and globe.   S. Burford is a conical red buoy,** lying in four fathoms and a half.

From **Dalkey Island** to **Bray Head** the low-water margin from being steep-to close under the N. side of Killiney Bay increases to 200yds. from the shore, about half-way.   At Bray coasting-vessels cross the bar of the Dargle River, and lie alongside the bank inside.

Killiney Hill is conspicuous from its shape, as well as from the Mapas Obelisk on the summit.   This obelisk open N. of Dalkey Tower leads clear of the N. Kish Buoy.

Frazer Bank, 1400yds. S. of **Dalkey Island,** has 19ft. least water over it.

Bray Head is a fine feature in the coast scenery; it is 780ft. high, with the railway running along its face.   Off its S. side is **Cable Rock,** which uncovers at half-tide.   It lies 200yds. from the shore, with other heads near it, but Mapas Obelisk kept in sight clears it.

The coast gradually decreases in height from **Bray Head** to **Greystones,** which is a conspicuous village on the shore, with a pier.   About a mile S. of it **Moulditch Bank** stretches out for nearly a mile from the shore.   There is 15ft. least water over it, but it consists of large stones and gravel.   Tide rips are usually to be seen over the bank.   A red can buoy, marked "Moulditch," lies in six fathoms four cables E. of it.

From here the coast continues low, with the fine range of the Wicklow Mountains behind, the highest summits rising from 2473ft. to 3029ft.

Six Miles Point is five miles and a quarter N. of Wicklow. The coast continues flat, with moderate depths, **Breaches Shoal**, with 17ft. least water, lying one mile and a quarter off the shore, where the Breaches, a tidal lagoon N. of Six Miles Point, breaks the low coast line. A railway bridge crosses the opening, and is a mark for the shoal. From here to Wicklow the coast sweeps in a wide curve to Wicklow Head, **Wicklow** itself standing at the estuary of the Broadwater, a long lagoon skirting the shore. The harbour has been much improved. A breakwater now shelters fifteen acres of water, with a depth of 17ft. at low-water springs alongside the quays. The river inside is being deepened to allow a depth of 8ft. in the channel at low-water springs.

Wicklow Lights.—On the head from a white tower, 46ft. high, an occulting white light is shown at an elevation of 121ft. above high-water, visible sixteen miles. It is bright for 10sec., eclipsed for 3sec. On the head there are two other towers N. 67deg. W. from the lighthouse.

Wicklow Harbour.—At the end of the pier is a fixed **red and white light**—red seaward; white in the harbour from N. 45deg. W. through N. to S. 22deg. E.

Off Six Miles Point, distant eleven miles, is the **Codling Bank Light-vessel.** She is moored in nine fathoms, four miles S.E. $\frac{1}{2}$ S. from the four fathoms S. edge of the Codling Bank. A **revolving red light**, attaining its greatest brilliancy every 20sec., is shown from a height of 39ft. above the sea, visible nine miles. She has three masts, and carries a **globe surmounted by a half globe** at her mainmast.

From here Wicklow Head bears W. $\frac{3}{4}$ S., distant eleven miles; Arklow Bank N. Light-vessel, S.W. $\frac{1}{8}$ S., ten miles and a half; and **Kish Light-vessel**, N., seventeen miles.

Fog-signal.—A fog siren gives three blasts of 1$\frac{3}{4}$sec. every 2min., with intervals of 5sec. silence after the first and second blasts, and 10sec. after the third blast.

Kish and Codling Banks.—The Kish Bank, including Bray Bank, with from 6ft. to 10ft. of water at low-tide over a good part of it, is a long, narrow ridge of sand, over rocky boulders, stretching nearly ten miles N. by E. ¼ E. and S. by W. ¼ W., at an average distance of seven miles from the coast. **Codling Bank** curves round S.E. from the S. end of Bray Bank, from which it is separated by a channel three-quarters of a mile wide, and with seven fathoms in it. The tide sets through here in a N.E. and S.W. direction. The least water on the Codling Bank is 9ft.

The three banks are buoyed as one danger. Kish Bank No. 1 lies in six fathoms off the N. end of the bank. It is black conical, with staff and globe. The shallowest part of the bank lies S. by W. of this, distant one mile and a half. No. 2 lies half a mile E. of the bank, in eighteen fathoms. No. 3 lies on the E. side, two miles and a half from the S. end, in seventeen fathoms. No. 4 lies, in eight fathoms, off the N.E. end of **Codling Bank.** No. 5, in seven fathoms, off the S. All these are black can buoys. No. 6 is a vertically striped black conical buoy, in fifteen fathoms, at the S.W. edge of the bank.

South Ridge and India Bank.—Between **Six Miles Point** and **Wicklow Head,** distant about seven miles from the shore, lie these banks, a southern continuation of the other banks; the least depth is 12ft. on the India Bank. A black conical buoy painted in black and white rings, with staff and globe, is moored, in eight fathoms, at the N. end of the S. ridge; and a similarly painted conical buoy lies off the S. end of the India Bank, in eight fathoms.

The tides set obliquely over these banks, and there are strong tide rips at the N. and E. edges. The tide inside the banks turns about 1½hrs. earlier than outside.

CHAPTER XXXV.

THE COAST AND OBJECTS OF INTEREST VISIBLE FROM THE SEA BETWEEN CARLINGFORD LOUGH AND WICKLOW.

WITH regret the anchor is weighed, and the peaceful beauty of Rostrevor begins to fade away behind Killowen Point. The coast has little to offer after this until Dublin Bay is opened and the Wicklow Mountains come in view.

The shores are far away as a yacht passes on her course, for Dundalk offers few attractions to overcome the difficulties of the entrance. A good deal of trade goes on, however, and a steamer leaves for Liverpool every other day.

It was at Dundalk that the last Irish king was crowned and kept his court in the island, and it was here Edward Bruce was attacked and defeated by the English, losing life and crown on the hill of Forghard, near the town. In 1689 Marshal Schomberg took the place without assault, the memory of Drogheda's dreadful massacre no doubt helping to bring about a speedy surrender.

As Dunany Point is left behind the coast becomes less and less pronounced, and only the slim Maiden Tower on the sand hills at the mouth of the Boyne indicates the shallow estuary of that historic river.

When I put in here I was assured I should have plenty of water. The evening was perfectly quiet. There had been a gentle northerly breeze all day, but towards sunset it fell, and as I was close in to the Boyne I thought I would see what it was like. The tide was high, with about half an hour more to run. I steered for the perches which mark the entrance. By the time I came abreast of the second stone beacon from the sand hills on the N. shore the breeze had died away, and the tide was running out. There was nothing for it but to anchor or let her go out again. As I was afraid the ebb would set me over the submerged sea-wall on the S. side, and I was told there was 6ft. at least on the bar, I anchored, for it was neap tides and I thought I should lie afloat. Presently the tide began to come out, and when the Boyne is letting itself out it does not waste time over it. The water simply sluiced past us, but I watched it comfortably, for I had sounded and found, if the information I had received was correct, that I should certainly float. Still the water ran out. Beacons, retaining walls—all gone to ruin, by the way, on the N. side—sands, all uncovered. Still the water ran out, rushing furiously past the stem, and making the chain gurgle and strain to the weight.

It was a lovely evening, and my faith was childlike. I took no further heed of the rushing water, when suddenly there came a grinding noise, followed by a fearful lurch, and the landscape whirled violently round. The little craft shook as if struck by an earthquake, the water dashed and seethed against her broadside, and then she lay down right across the stream, which sluiced against her bilge and went foaming away in wild rapids at stem and stern.

The anchor had been pulled home at the first shock, and only the strength of the old craft saved her. For one moment I verily believed she would have been rolled over and over and swept out to sea. As there was nothing to be done I went ashore and walked the dreariest walk I have ever taken, along a sandy tract alternating with mud and sand hills, the Boyne rushing beside me in its muddy ditch. I came to a collection of hovels, and then, since first I landed in Ireland, I recognised the truth of the description of the peasants' cabins; a dirtier, more wretched place than Queenborough I have never seen. When I got back the tide was beginning to rise ; by ten we were all afloat. There was no wind, and the tide seemed to come in nearly as fiercely as it ran out. By two in the morning I was able to weigh anchor and stand out. The old tub had suffered no harm as far as I could see, and when I laid her ashore after her cruise was over I found she had escaped scot free. It was a wonder.

Drogheda does a large trade in various goods, and is a flourishing place ; but it is not a yachting resort, nor likely to become one.

Of all the cold, bloody, ghastly massacres which civil wars have caused, the massacre of **Drogheda** is perhaps the worst. The Royalists had fought magnificently. Twice Cromwell had been repulsed ; the third assault, led by the resolute general, succeeded. Then followed a fearful scene. All the garrison, to the number of over 2000 men, were put to the sword. No pity was shown to anyone—gentle or simple, old or young—all were passed under the edge of the sword, " The sword of the Lord and of Gideon."

Truly Ireland has seen some bloodshedding. The bitterness of this treatment is partly to be accounted for by the terror and horror excited in England by the Irish rebellion of eight years before.

The panic caused by that massacre resembled that great cry of anguish and wrath which went up from England when the details of the Cawnpore massacre were known, and in 1641 it was all the more terrible because Ireland was but a day's sail from England, and Irish adventurers were already largely recruiting the royal troops. It is this fact which explains the merciless treatment dealt to the prisoners at Conway Castle when Archbishop Williams and General Mytton assisted at the *noyades* of the Irish mercenaries taken in the garrison, and looked on tranquilly while the poor wretches were tied back to back and hurled over the ramparts into the river below.

At **Drogheda** the slaughter was the more awful, that it was deliberately performed. The Cavaliers were not slain in the heat of the assault, but after two days' respite they were all put to death. Cromwell wrote a long account of the matter, the pith of his excuse being "That this bitterness will save much effusion of blood."

For the time it may have done, but the memory of that bloody day rankled in Irish minds for centuries, and when the United Irishmen at Bannow Bridge, in 1798, lifted their Protestant victims on the points of their pikes and hurled them into Wexford Bay, who knows whether the blood of those shed by Oliver Cromwell was not crying for a retribution too long delayed.

The innocent suffer for the guilty oftentimes, and who can tell if, in the mystery of existence, this may not be the greatest punishment of all for those who have ceased to exist on this planet.

There was plenty of time to think while sitting on deck in the starlight waiting for the tide to flow. Only seven miles from where I was listening to the rush of the tide as it seethed past the chain that battle was fought which decided the Protestant supremacy, and—what was of greater importance, perhaps —secured the liberties of England from the vicious despotism of a weak and bigoted race. The Stewarts, as Voltaire has remarked, were an unfortunate family, and not only were they themselves unlucky, but they involved all those who stood by them in their own mishaps.

I need not describe the battle of the Boyne. A more blundering battle seems hardly possible. The wonder is that with such mixed elements any order could have been preserved at all. French were fighting against French, English against English, Irish against Irish, Scotch against Scotch, and the Dutch were the only troops there who did not meet a regiment of their own countrymen opposed to them; and that might well have happened, for the United States of the Netherlands were bound by treaty to supply two regiments for the Great Monarch's service, only they had lately thought better of it.

Great names, too, were in command on each side. The Duke of Berwick, son of James II. and nephew of the great

Duke of Marlborough, was opposed by Schomberg, the veteran Marshal of France, whom royal bigotry had driven from his country—an English general commanding the French, and a French general commanding the English.

The heroic spirit of the defender of Derry fought side by side with that other hero of a persecuted people, who, simple peasant that he was, dictated terms to his own monarch, the proudest king France has ever seen, and wrested from the only French general who could attempt to oppose Marlborough conditions honourable alike to the Camisards and to Marshal Villars, and who now lies peacefully at rest in Chelsea Parish Church.

It was a battle of surprises, too. William of Orange escaped as it were by a miracle, for the guns were well masked which Tyrconnel trained on the little group of staff officers only some 500yds. before him. The death of the aged Schomberg was another piece of haphazard blundering. He rode alone to call up some fresh troops, when a party of Irish horse swooped down on him, and after they retired the warrior, who had fought in every part of Europe, was on the ground. James alone of all the well-known names met by that muddy Irish stream to fight for bigotry or liberty of conscience, for despotism or freedom, ran no risk.

It is refreshing to listen to Lady Tyrconnel, as she retorts to the royal fugitive, at all times ungracious, at all times selfish, complaining of the way the Irish ran, that in this as in all other respects His Majesty surpassed his subjects, for he "had won the race!"

An obelisk marks the spot where William passed the river. It was erected forty-six years after the battle by the Duke of Dorset.

Certainly, Rockabill is a curious set of twins. Those two peaks sticking up out of the sea so far from land, with deep water in between and all round them, are strange freaks of nature. I like to imagine how they would appear when there "is no more sea." In days before the lighthouse was built those two fangs must have devoured many lives.

Lambay is a fine-looking island. By the way, it should be spelt Lambey, as Ireland's Eye is really Irelandsey, the "ey" or "ea" being the Saxon for island, as Selsey, Guernsey, Chelsea, Mersea.

Swords, however, is much more interesting. There is a round tower, 73ft. high, and the ancient town is full of old-world memories, with its old castle hard by.

To those acquainted with the place Malahide Inlet is a commodious haven, as the right phrase hath it. Malahide Castle is a grand example of the feudal castle still used as a dwelling-place, although not much of the original fortress remains as it was when the first Talbot built it in the twelfth century. The **hall** and the **oak chamber** are the show bits of the castle, and there are some good pictures on the walls. Portraits by Vandyke and Lely, and a Nativity by Albert Durer, which Charles II. gave to the fascinating Bretonne, whose ancestral house is near Brest. The picture is said to have cost her royal lover £2000—a large sum for a painting in those days. Malahide Abbey, too, is worth a visit. There is an altar tomb in the ruins, which contains the remains of a lady who was on the same day "maid, wife, and widow." Her husband, Lord Galtrim, was hastily summoned to repel an attack on the very day he was married, and was killed in the engagement. Lady Galtrim subsequently married Sir Richard Talbot, and so came to be buried here.

The Talbots of Malahide came over with Strongbow, and are one of the most ancient families existing in Ireland.

Howth Hill is coming very close. If the wind were strong from the S.W. I should put into Howth rather than pound round the corner by the Bailey Light. Howth Castle is another ancient home of an old, old house. The very name, Armoric Tristram de Valence, conjures up a world of romance. There is a De Valence lying cross-legged on his altar tomb in Westminster Abbey, with his shield still bearing the blazon of his lineage in wonderfully fresh tincts.

The castle was re-built by Christopher, twentieth Lord Howth, in the sixteenth century. His tomb is still existing in the Abbey

of Howth, which overlooks the harbour, where it was removed
from Ireland's Eye, the original site of St. Nessan's Foundation.

On the whole, one might do worse than turn into this little
neglected harbour, which used to be the port for Dublin before
Dunleary became Kingstown. The walk round to the Bailey is
a breezy one, and the view from the top of the hill magnificent.

And so here we are in the Bay of Dublin, and what a beautiful
bay it is; but to describe Dublin City only is beyond the limits
of this book.

Let the amateur put into Kingstown and enjoy the hospitalities
of the place, as Dublin is easily visited from there.

The Royal St. George and the Royal Irish Yacht Clubs are
both most generous in welcoming visitors, and their club-houses
are as remarkable for comfort as are those who have to do with
the management of them for courtesy and kindly attention.

They certainly know how to handle craft here, I must say. It
was a pleasure to watch the way in which the yachts came in
at evening, and crowded as the harbour was—with a playful,
fitful breeze to bother a skipper—they all picked up their moorings
neatly, and I never saw a miss or a foul anywhere.

Those of my readers who come to Kingstown will have plenty
to do to amuse themselves without reading up the history of the
place, so I will just pass on and wait for them at the other side
of the bay.

What a beautiful sail it is all down this Wicklow coast. The
mountains are most lovely in their shapes and outlines. When
first I sailed along it I had crossed from Wales, and expected
to find Ireland tame. The surprise, therefore, was great when
at sunrise I was greeted by a succession of peaks, rosy with
the early dawn, looming above a misty sea.

The Sugar Loaf and Dunrain Hill, backed by the higher
summits of Kippure Talbot Mountain and Lugnaquilla, were
every bit as beautiful as Snowdonia and the much-vaunted
Rivals (Yr Eifl).

Bray Head, too, is a grand promontory. It is a pity there is
no harbour at Bray, for the watering-place is charming, and
the excursions round full of interest. Glendalough, Powerscourt,

and Dargle Glen are each delightful in their way; indeed, the variety of trips among the Wicklow mountains seems endless.

From Six Miles Point the scenery becomes tamer, but Wicklow Bay is a fine expanse of clear water, bounded by the headland with its three towers at the S.

Wicklow Harbour has been immensely improved, but there is nothing much to see in the town.

The cruise is now nearly at an end. Wicklow is the last convenient harbour on the E. coast. There is little to take one farther S., for Wexford Harbour is a broad and shallow mere. Here, then, I will end the cruise, only giving such further suggestions as will take the adventurous skipper back to home waters.

With regret one leaves Ireland. To my mind, the cruising over on that side of the Irish Channel is a long way to be preferred to the western coast; and, as for the Irish people, it is refreshing to meet them after a cruise in Scotland or Wales.

CHAPTER XXXVI.

WICKLOW TO MILFORD HAVEN AND THE LONGSHIPS.

Bearings and distances from Wicklow Head Light.—The Bailey Light bears from Wicklow Head N. by E. ¼ E. easterly, distant twenty-four miles. The Kish Light-ship, N.N.E. ¼ E., twenty-one miles and a half. The Skerries, Holyhead, E. ¾ N., fifty-seven miles. Bardsey Island, S.E. ¾ E., forty-six miles. The S. Bishop, S. ¼ W. westerly, seventy miles and a quarter. The Smalls Light, S. by W. westerly, seventy-six miles. S. Arklow Light-ship, S. by W. ¼ W., sixteen miles and a half. Tuskar Rock, S.S.W. ¼ W. westerly, forty-six miles.

Arklow Bank lies directly in the course from Wicklow Head to the Smalls. This bank has less depth of water on it than any of the dangerous outlying banks on the Irish coast. In the northern half there are several spots with less than 2ft. on them. Wrecks are said either to sink into the sand or are driven over it into deep water. This danger lies from four to six miles off the coast, and is ten miles long but hardly 600yds. wide, with seventeen to eighteen fathoms on each side.

It is marked by five red buoys. No. 1 or N. buoy is conical, with staff and globe. No. 5 is the S. buoy, and is also conical; all the rest are can buoys, and lie along the E. edge of the sands. The tides only rise 3½ft. at springs, but the currents run at one knot and a half at springs, and one knot at neaps.

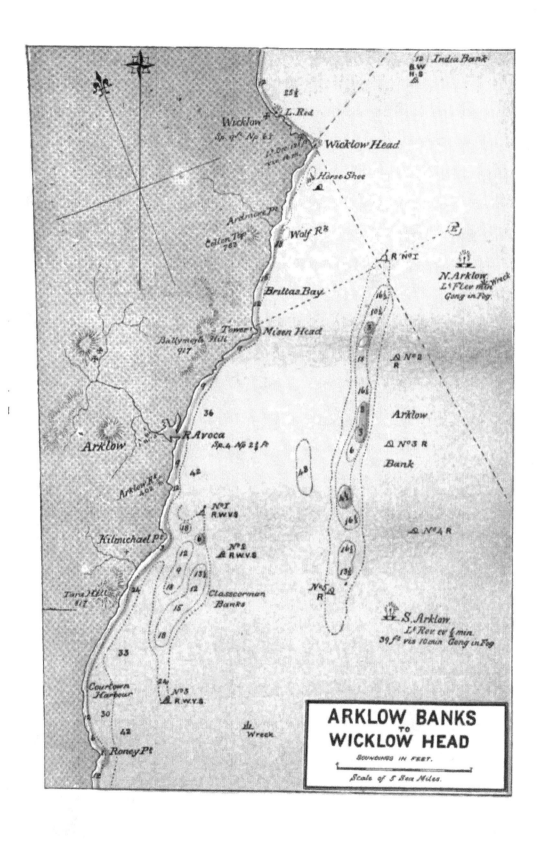

ARKLOW BANKS
TO
WICKLOW HEAD

SOUNDINGS IN FEET.

Scale of 5 Sea Miles.

The N.E. stream sets over the bank for 7hrs. and the S.W. for 5hrs.   There are two light-ships, one at each end of the bank.

Arklow N. Light-ship lies, in eighteen fathoms, S. 64deg. E., three miles and a quarter distant from the N. buoy.   It shows a flashing white light, giving two flashes in quick succession for 15sec. followed by 45sec. of darkness, visible ten miles.   The vessel carries one mast, and a jigger mast with ball.

Arklow S. Light-ship lies in twenty-six fathoms, two from the S. end of the bank.   It shows a revolving white light, taking half a minute to complete its revolution, visible ten miles. The vessel carries three masts, with a half-globe over a globe on the mainmast.   Both vessels are black with a white stripe, and the name painted on them in white letters.

In case of bad weather from the S.W. a yacht might make for Rosslare Bay, and if necessary go into Wexford, with help. New harbour works are near completion at Rosslare, in the S. part of south bay, and there is shelter with all winds except from the N.E.

The Lucifer Light-ship, lying two miles S. of Blackwater Bank, is a guide to Wexford.   It shows a fixed red light, visible eight miles, and carries three masts, with ball at the mainmast-head.   Between it and the S. Arklow is the Black Water Light-ship, exhibiting a fixed white light, visible ten miles.   She carries three masts, with two globes on the mainmast.   Both are painted as above in the usual way.

The Tuskar Rock lies five miles in a S.E. direction from Carnsore Point.   The rock is 15ft. above water, with smaller rocks on its N., S., and W. sides, extending altogether to about 300yds.   From a cylindrical white tower, 113ft. high, an alternately white and red revolving light is exhibited, taking 1min. to complete its revolution, visible nineteen miles.

Fog-signal.—An explosive rocket is discharged every 5min.

Bearings and distances from the Tuskar Rock.—From the Tuskar Rock the S. Bishop bears S.E. ¾ S. southerly, thirty-six miles.   The Smalls, S. by E. ¼ E., thirty-five miles.   The Longships, S. by W. westerly, one hundred and twenty-nine miles.   S. Arklow Light-ship, N.E. ½ N., thirty-one miles.

Codling Light-ship, N.E. ½ N. northerly, fifty-four miles. Mull of Galloway, same bearing, one hundred and fifty-four miles. Skerries Light, N.E. by E. ¼ E., ninety-three miles and a half. S. Stack, Holyhead, same bearing, eighty-six miles. Bardsey Island, E. by N. northerly, sixty-one miles. **Cardigan Bay Light-ship**, E. ¼ S. southerly, forty-six miles. As to whether the skipper will go for the **Smalls** or the **S. Bishop** must depend on the wind, and the time he is likely to get there. **On no account**, unless **very well acquainted** with the **locality**, should the passage inside the Bishop Rock be attempted by night.

For my part, I should be inclined to make for the **Smalls** and then shape a course for St. Anne's Head.

From **St. Anne's Head** to Cape Cornwall the course and distance are **S.W. by S. southerly, ninety-five miles.** From the **Smalls** the **Longships** bear S.S.W. southerly, ninety-nine miles.

Once the Longships are rounded the skipper is in home waters, and has nothing more to do than shape a course up channel after he is clear of the **Rundlestone.** (See Page 12).

And so the long cruise is over. As I look back at the gray tower on the black rock, keeping watchful guard over the entrance to the two channels, where the roaring Atlantic hurls itself over the defiant granite, before the steep cliff of Guethenbras hides it from my view, thoughts of the coasts far away in the N. pass rapidly before me.

Of all the many ports and inlets I have explored only four present themselves with perfectly comfortable memories. Two of those were in Ireland and two in Wales.

Of these four Lough Carlingford is a long way pre-eminent. Not only is the scenery lovely, the sailing easy, and the navigation rendered as safe as can be by the excellent system of lights and buoys, but the comforts ashore are so great.

Rostrevor would be a perfect place if only there were a decent landing jetty and a little more water. For large yachts there is no anchorage nearer than a mile, but for all drawing only 6ft. and under there is plenty of room within half that distance.

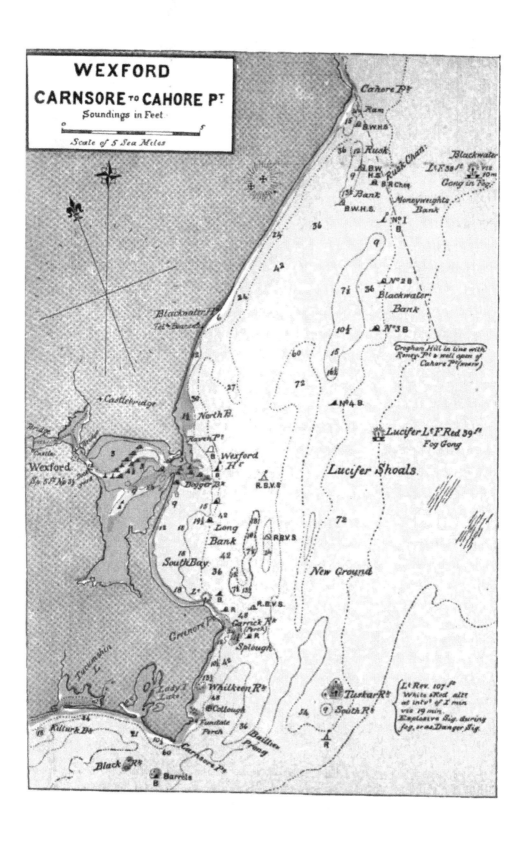

The anchorage at **Milford Haven** in the Cleddau comes next, and **Conway** third. Both these places have so much interest in their surroundings, but neither are places from which one can go just for a morning sail and back again; the attention which the navigation demands and the strength of the tides precludes that. Both are places where, when once a good berth has been picked up, a skipper will wish to remain until he weighs anchor for good. At Carlingford, in the Lough, there is plenty of room for going and coming when and how one likes. It is essentially a happy place, where one may cast dull care aside. I class Carlingford with Falmouth in its suitability for easy yachting.

Last of the four comes **Audley Roads**, Lough Strangford. If it were not for the very formidable strength of the tides this would be a delightful place; but here, if anywhere, the tides have to be considered. They are a very strong master.

It seems to me, as I look back, that the western coasts of England more especially are suited either for **large craft** of from fifty tons upwards, or else for **canoes** that can go from cove to cove and be hauled up for the night. In this way, by watching one's opportunity, a great deal could be done, more especially in the north, round the shores of Lancashire, Westmoreland, Cumberland, and the S. coast of Scotland. With a 6hrs. tide one can cover a good deal of distance. The worst of this way of exploring the coast is, that the navigator has to put up at a village inn, if one can be found, unless the adventurer carries a tent with him and camps out.

For large yachts, in all this extent of coast, there are really only six good harbours: Milford Haven, the Menai Straits, Holyhead, The Mersey, Barrow, and Silloth Roads, and these latter are not places yachts care to go to. On the Irish side there is a much better choice, and Douglas and Ramsay Bay, in the Isle of Man, are both largely frequented in the summer as places of call by vessels passing up and down channel, but they are not by any means first-class harbours, although both could be made so.

For cruising purposes the Irish coast offers the greatest attractions; indeed, it is admirably fitted for it. The weather is milder, there are fewer gales registered than anywhere else in the United Kingdom, and the prevailing winds are off shore. There are harbours or shelters of some kind every twenty miles or so, up or down, and some of them are absolutely safe in all winds. There is much less wet, too, on the E. of Ireland than there is on the W. of England and Wales. The tidal currents also are less violent; in fact, in one place there is no current at all, although the water rises and falls.

I strongly recommend all who can afford the time, and like an easy-going happy cruise, to cross at once to Irish waters and coast from Wicklow to Lough Larne. From there a passage to Scotch waters is easy, and having got as far it would be a pity not to sail amongst the Western Isles.

By the way, how very flat and tame the S. coast does look as one sails up channel after the glorious peaks of Wales and Ireland; but it has its pleasures, this English Channel, and not the least is that it is bringing the good ship home.

THE END.

INDEX.

···· YACHTING. ····

As the result of many years' application to the production of

HIGH-CLASS COMESTIBLES,

I have great pleasure in submitting the following list, chosen from among the many unique and *recherché* specialities always to be found in readiness, and which can be relied upon for excellence of quality and preparation:

READY FOR USE.

- Faisans ou Perdreaux truffes à la gelée.
- Poulets, Faisans ou Perdreaux rôtis au jus.
- Cailles ou Mauviettes à la gelée.
- Filet de Bœuf au jus.
- Selle de pré-salé au jus.
- Gigot de Chevreuil rôti.
- Rouelle de Veau braisée au jus.
- Pâté de Strasbourg en croûte.
- Pâté de foie gras aux truffes.
- Braised Beef à la gelée.
- Ox tongue à l'Epicure.
- Roast Beef au jus.
- Rillettes de Tours.
- Saucisses Parisiennes.
- Saucisses truffées.
- Caviar d'Astrachan.
- Sardines à l'huile.
- Anchois au sel, ou à l'huile.
- Harengs marinés.
- Saumon à l'huile.
- Saumon mariné.
- Homard au naturel.
- Ecrevisses à la marinade, &c.

TO BE HEATED UP.

- Salmis de Bécasses, Faisans, ou Cailles aux truffes ou Champignons.
- Poulet sauté, aux truffes, ou tomates.
- Canetons aux petits pois.
- Ragoût de Volaille à la Financière.
- Ragoût de Mouton aux Carottes.
- Poulet au Curry.
- Curry de Mouton à l'Indienne.
- Filet de bœuf braisé.
- Selle de Mouton.
- Quartier de Chevreuil, sauce poivrade.
- Ris de Veau aux Champignons.
- Civet de Lièvre.
- Tête de Veau en tortue.
- Extrait de Viande.
- Pigeons en Compote.
- Filets de Soles à la Bourguignonne.
- Saumon fumé.
- Homard au Curry.
- Homard à l'Americaine.
- Ecrevisses Bordelaise.
- Thick and Clear Soups of all kinds, &c.

Truffes du Perigord and all kinds of Preserved Vegetables.

Special Lists of Wines and Groceries on application.

Purveyor to the Principal Yachts, the P. and O., Cunard, Orient, White Star, Pacific, and other Steamship Lines.

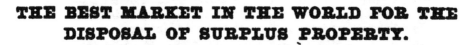

Catalogue of Practical Handbooks Published by L. Upcott Gill, 170, Strand, London, W.C.

American Dainties, and How to Prepare Them. By an AMERICAN LADY *In paper, price 1s., by post 1s. 2d.*

Angler, Book of the All-Round. A Comprehensive Treatise on Angling in both Fresh and Salt Water. In Four Divisions as named below. By JOHN BICKERDYKE. With over 220 Engravings. *In cloth, price 5s. 6d., by post 5s. 10d.*

    Angling for Coarse Fish. Bottom Fishing, according to the Methods in use on the Thames, Trent, Norfolk Broads, and elsewhere. Illustrated. *In paper, price 1s., by post 1s. 2d.*

    Angling for Pike. The most approved Methods of Fishing for Pike or Jack. New Edition, revised and enlarged. Profusely Illustrated. *In paper, price 1s., by post 1s. 2d.; cloth, 2s. (uncut), by post 2s. 3d.*

    Angling for Game Fish. The Various Methods of Fishing for Salmon; Moorland, Chalk-stream, and Thames Trout; Grayling and Char. Well Illustrated. *In paper, price 1s. 6d., by post 1s. 9d.*

    Angling in Salt Water. Sea Fishing with Rod and Line, from the Shore, Piers, Jetties, Rocks, and from Boats; together with Some Account of Hand-Lining. Over 50 Engravings. *In paper, price 1s., by post, 1s. 2d.; cloth, 2s. (uncut), by post 2s. 3d.*

Angler, The Modern. A Practical Handbook on all Kinds of Angling. By "OTTER." Well illustrated. New Edition. *In cloth, price 2s. 6d., by post 2s. 9d.*

Aquaria, Book of. A Practical Guide to the Construction, Arrangement, and Management of Freshwater and Marine Aquaria; containing Full Information as to the Plants, Weeds, Fish, Molluscs, Insects, &c., How and Where to Obtain Them, and How to Keep Them in Health. Illustrated. By REV. GREGORY C. BATEMAN, A.K.C., and REGINALD A. R. BENNETT, B.A. *In cloth gilt, price 5s. 6d., by post 5s. 10d.*

Aquaria, Freshwater: Their Construction, Arrangement, Stocking, and Management. Fully Illustrated. By REV. G. C. BATEMAN, A.K.C. *In cloth gilt, price 3s. 6d., by post 3s. 10d.*

Aquaria, Marine: Their Construction, Arrangement, and Management. Fully Illustrated. By R. A. R. BENNETT, B.A. *In cloth gilt, price 2s. 6d., by post 2s. 9d.*

Australia, Shall I Try? A Guide to the Australian Colonies for the Emigrant Settler and Business Man. With two Illustrations. By GEORGE LACON JAMES. *In cloth gilt, price 3s. 6d., by post 3s. 10d.*

Autograph Collecting: A Practical Manual for Amateurs and Historical Students, containing ample information on the Selection and Arrangement of Autographs, the Detection of Forged Specimens, &c., &c., to which are added numerous Facsimiles for Study and Reference, and an extensive Valuation Table of Autographs worth Collecting. By HENRY T. SCOTT, M.D., L.R.C.P., &c. *In leatherette gilt, price 7s. 6d. nett, by post 7s. 10d.*

Bazaars and Fancy Fairs: Their Organization and Management. A Secretary's *Vade Mecum.* By JOHN MUIR. *In paper, price 1s., by post 1s. 2d.*

Bees and Bee-Keeping: Scientific and Practical. By F. R. CHESHIRE, F.L.S., F.R.M.S., Lecturer on Apiculture at South Kensington. *In two vols., cloth gilt, price 16s., by post 16s. 6d.*

    Vol. I., Scientific. A complete Treatise on the Anatomy and Physiology of the Hive Bee. *In cloth gilt, price 7s. 6d., by post 7s. 10d.*

    Vol. II., Practical Management of Bees. An Exhaustive Treatise on Advanced Bee Culture. *In cloth gilt, price 8s. 6d., by post 8s. 11d.*

Bee-Keeping, Book of. A very practical and Complete Manual on the Proper Management of Bees, especially written for Beginners and Amateurs who have but a few Hives. Fully Illustrated. By W. B. WEBSTER, First-class Expert, B.B.K.A. *In paper, price 1s., by post 1 2d.; cloth, 1s. 6d., by post 1s. 8d.*

Begonia Culture, for Amateurs and Professionals. Containing Full Directions for the Successful Cultivation of the Begonia, under Glass and in the Open Air. Illustrated. By B. C. RAVENSCROFT. *In paper, price* 1s., *by post* 1s. 2d.

Bent Iron Work: A Practical Manual of Instruction for Amateurs in the Art and Craft of Making and Ornamenting Light Articles in imitation of the beautiful Mediæval and Italian Wrought Iron Work. By F. J. ERSKINE. Illustrated. *In paper, price* 1s., *by post* 1s. 2d.

Birds, British, for the Cage and Aviary. Illustrated. By DR. W. T. GREENE. *[In the press.*

Boat Building and Sailing, Practical. Containing Full Instructions for Designing and Building Punts, Skiffs, Canoes, Sailing Boats, &c. Particulars of the most suitable Sailing Boats and Yachts for Amateurs, and Instructions for their Proper Handling. Fully Illustrated with Designs and Working Diagrams. By ADRIAN NEISON, C.E., DIXON KEMP, A.I.N.A., and G. CHRISTOPHER DAVIES. *In one vol., cloth gilt, price* 7s. 6d., *by post* 7s. 10d.

Boat Building for Amateurs, Practical. Containing Full Instructions for Designing and Building Punts, Skiffs, Canoes, Sailing Boats, &c. Fully Illustrated with Working Diagrams. By ADRIAN NEISON, C.E. Second Edition, Revised and Enlarged by DIXON KEMP, Author of "Yacht Designing," "A Manual of Yacht and Boat Sailing," &c. *In cloth gilt, price* 2s. 6d. *by post* 2s. 9d.

Boat Sailing for Amateurs, Practical. Containing Particulars of the most Suitable Sailing Boats and Yachts for Amateurs, and Instructions for their Proper Handling, &c. Illustrated with numerous Diagrams. By G. CHRISTOPHER DAVIES. Second Edition, Revised and Enlarged, and with several New Plans of Yachts. *In cloth gilt, price* 5s., *by post* 5s. 4d.

Bookbinding for Amateurs: Being Descriptions of the various Tools and Appliances Required, and Minute Instructions for their Effective Use. By W. J. E. CRANE. Illustrated with 156 Engravings. *In cloth gilt, price* 2s. 6d., *by post* 2s. 9d.

Bulb Culture, Popular. A Practical and Handy Guide to the Successful Cultivation of Bulbous Plants, both in the Open and under Glass. By W. D. DRURY. Fully Illustrated. *In paper, price* 1s., *by post* 1s. 2d.

Bunkum Entertainments: A Collection of Original Laughable Skits on Conjuring, Physiognomy, Juggling, Performing Fleas, Waxworks, Panorama, Phrenology, Phonograph, Second Sight, Lightning Calculators, Ventriloquism, Spiritualism, &c., to which are added Humorous Sketches, Whimsical Recitals, and Drawing-room Comedies. *In cloth, price* 2s. 6d., *by post* 2s. 9d.

Butterflies, The Book of British: A Practical Manual for Collectors and Naturalists. Splendidly Illustrated throughout with very accurate Engravings of the Caterpillars, Chrysalids, and Butterflies, both upper and under sides, from drawings by the Author or direct from Nature. By W. J. LUCAS, B.A. *Price* 3s. 6d., *by post* 3s. 9d.

Butterfly and Moth Collecting: Where to Search, and What to Do. By G. E. SIMMS. Illustrated. *In paper, price* 1s., *by post* 1s. 2d.

Cabinet Making for Amateurs. Being clear Directions How to Construct many Useful Articles, such as Brackets, Sideboard, Tables, Cupboards, and other Furniture. Illustrated. *In cloth gilt, price* 2s. 6d., *by post* 2s. 9d.

Cactus Culture for Amateurs: Being Descriptions of the various Cactuses grown in this country; with Full and Practical Instructions for their Successful Cultivation. By W. WATSON, Assistant Curator of the Royal Botanic Gardens, Kew. Profusely Illustrated. *In cloth, gilt, price* 5s. *nett, by post* 5s. 4d.

Cage Birds, Diseases of: Their Causes, Symptoms, and Treatment. A Handbook for everyone who keeps a Bird. By DR. W. T. GREENE, F.Z.S. *In paper, price* 1s., *by post* 1s. 2d.

Canary Book. The Breeding, Rearing, and Management of all Varieties of Canaries and Canary Mules, and all other matters connected with this Fancy. By ROBERT L. WALLACE. Third Edition. *In cloth gilt, price* 5s., *by post* 5s. 4d. ; *with COLOURED PLATES,* 6s. 6d., *by post* 6s. 10d.

　　General Management of Canaries. Cages and Cage-making, Breeding, Managing, Mule Breeding, Diseases and their Treatment, Moulting, Pests, &c. Illustrated. *In cloth, price* 2s. 6d., *by post* 2s. 9d.

　　Exhibition Canaries. Full Particulars of all the different Varieties, their Points of Excellence, Preparing Birds for Exhibition, Formation and Management of Canary Societies and Exhibitions. Illustrated. *In cloth, price* 2s. 6d., *by post* 2s. 9d.

Cane Basket Work: A Practical Manual on Weaving Useful and Fancy Baskets By ANNIE FIRTH. Illustrated. *In cloth gilt, price 1s. 6d., by post 1s. 8d.*

Card Conjuring: Being Tricks with Cards, and How to Perform Them By PROF. ELLIS STANYON. Illustrated, and in Coloured Wrapper. *Price 1s. by post 1s. 2d*

Card Tricks, Book of, for Drawing-room and Stage Entertainments by Amateurs; with an exposure of Tricks as practised by Card Sharpers and Swindlers. Numerous Illustrations. By PROF. R. KUNARD. *In illustrated wrapper, price 2s. 6d., by post 2s. 9d.*

Carnation Culture, for Amateurs. The Culture of Carnations and Picotees of all Classes in the Open Ground and in Pots. Illustrated. By B. C. RAVENS- CROFT. *In paper, price 1s., by post 1s. 2d.*

Cats, Domestic or Fancy: A Practical Treatise on their Antiquity, Domesti- cation, Varieties, Breeding, Management, Diseases and Remedies, Exhibition and Judging. By JOHN JENNINGS. Illustrated. *In cloth, price 2s. 6d., by post 2s. 9d.*

Chrysanthemum Culture, for Amateurs and Professionals. Containing Full Directions for the Successful Cultivation of the Chrysanthemum for Exhibition and the Market. By B. C. RAVENSCROFT. New Edition. Illustrated. *In paper, price 1s., by post 1s. 2d.*

Chrysanthemum, The Show, and Its Cultivation. By C. SCOTT, of the Sheffield Chrysanthemum Society. *In paper, price 6d., by post 7d.*

Coins, a Guide to English Pattern, in Gold, Silver, Copper, and Pewter, from Edward I. to Victoria, with their Value. By the REV. G. F. CROWTHER, M.A. Illustrated. *In silver cloth, with gilt facsimiles of Coins, price 5s., by post 5s. 3d.*

Coins of Great Britain and Ireland, a Guide to the, in Gold, Silver, and Copper, from the Earliest Period to the Present Time, with their Value. By the late COLONEL W. STEWART THORBURN. Third Edition. Revised and Enlarged, by H. A. GRUEBER, F.S.A. Illustrated. *In cloth gilt, price 10s. 6d. net, by post 10s. 10d.*

Cold Meat Cookery. A Handy Guide to making really tasty and much appreciated Dishes from Cold Meat. By MRS. J. E. DAVIDSON. *In paper, price 1s., by post 1s. 2d.*

Collie, The. Its History, Points, and Breeding. By HUGH DALZIEL. Illus- trated with Coloured Frontispiece and Plates. *In paper, price 1s., by post 1s. 2d. ; cloth, 2s., by post 2s 3d.*

Collie Stud Book. Edited by HUGH DALZIEL. *Price 3s. 6d. each, by post 3s. 9d. each.*

> *Vol. I.,* containing Pedigrees of 1308 of the best-known Dogs, traced to their most remote known ancestors ; Show Record to Feb., 1890, &c.
> *Vol. II.* Pedigrees of 795 Dogs, Show Record, &c.
> *Vol. III.* Pedigrees of 786 Dogs, Show Record, &c.

Columbarium, Moore's. Reprinted Verbatim from the original Edition of 1735, with a Brief Notice of the Author. By W. B. TEGETMEIER, F.Z.S. Member of the British Ornithologists' Union. *Price 1s., by post 1s. 2d.*

Conjuring, Book of Modern. A Practical Guide to Drawing-room and Stage Magic for Amateurs. By PROFESSOR R. KUNARD. Illustrated. *In illustrated wrapper, price 2s. 6d., by post 2s. 9d.*

Conjuring for Amateurs. A Practical Handbook on How to Perform a Number of Amusing Tricks. By PROF. ELLIS STANYON. *In paper, price 1s., by post 1s. 2d.*

Cookery, The Encyclopædia of Practical. A complete Dictionary of all pertaining to the Art of Cookery and Table Service. Edited by THEO. FRANCIS GARRETT, assisted by eminent Chefs de Cuisine and Confectioners. Profusely Illustrated with Coloured Plates and Engravings by HAROLD FURNESS, GEO. CRUIKSHANK, W. MUNN ANDREW, and others. *In 2 vols., demy 4to., half bound, cushion edges, £3 3s.; carriage free, £3 5s.*

Cookery for Amateurs; or, French Dishes for English Homes of all Classes. Includes Simple Cookery, Middle-class Cookery, Superior Cookery, Cookery for Invalids, and Breakfast and Luncheon Cookery. By MADAME VALÉRIE. Second Edition. *In paper, price 1s., by post 1s. 2d.*

Cucumber Culture for Amateurs. Including also Melons, Vegetable Marrows, and Gourds. Illustrated. By W. J. MAY. *In paper, price 1s., by post 1s. 2d.*

Cyclist's Route Map of England and Wales. Shows clearly all the Main, and most of the Cross, Roads, Railroads, and the Distances between the Chief Towns, as well as the Mileage from London. In addition to this, Routes of *Thirty of the Most Interesting Tours* are printed in red. Fourth Edition, thoroughly revised. The map is printed on specially prepared vellum paper, and is the fullest, handiest, and best up-to-date tourist's map in the market. *In cloth, price* 1s., *by post* 1s. 2d.

Designing, Harmonic and Keyboard. Explaining a System whereby an endless Variety of Most Beautiful Designs suited to numberless Manufactures may be obtained by Unskilled Persons from any Printed Music. Illustrated by Numerous Explanatory Diagrams and Illustrative Examples. By C. H. WILKINSON. *Demy 4to, price* £2 2s. *nett.*

Dogs, Breaking and Training: Being Concise Directions for the proper education of Dogs, both for the Field and for Companions. Second Edition. By "PATHFINDER." With Chapters by HUGH DALZIEL. Illustrated. *In cloth gilt, price* 6s. 6d., *by post* 6s. 10d.

Dogs, British, Ancient and Modern: Their Varieties, History, and Characteristics. By HUGH DALZIEL, assisted by Eminent Fanciers. Beautifully Illustrated with COLOURED PLATES and full-page Engravings of Dogs of the Day, with numerous smaller illustrations in the text. This is the fullest work on the various breeds of dogs kept in England. In three volumes, *demy 8vo, cloth gilt, price* 10s. 6d. *each, by post* 11s. *each.*
    Vol. I. Dogs Used in Field Sports.
    Vol. II. Dogs Useful to Man in other Work than Field Sports; House and Toy Dogs.
    Vol. III. Practical Kennel Management: A Complete Treatise on all Matters relating to the Proper Management of Dogs whether kept for the Show Bench, for the Field, or for Companions.

Dogs, Diseases of: Their Causes, Symptoms, and Treatment; Modes of Administering Medicines; Treatment in cases of Poisoning, &c. For the use of Amateurs. By HUGH DALZIEL. Fourth Edition. Entirely Re-written and brought up to Date. *In paper, price* 1s., *by post* 1s. 2d. ; *in cloth gilt,* 2s., *by post* 2s. 3d.

Dog-Keeping, Popular: Being a Handy Guide to the General Management and Training of all Kinds of Dogs for Companions and Pets. By J. MAXTEE. Illustrated. *In paper, price* 1s., *by post* 1s. 2d.

Engravings and their Value. Containing a Dictionary of all the Greatest Engravers and their Works. By J. H. SLATER. New Edition, Revised and brought up to date, with latest Prices at Auction. *In cloth gilt, price* 15s. *nett, by post,* 15s. 5d.

Entertainments, Amateur, for Charitable and other Objects: How to Organise and Work them with Profit and Success. By ROBERT GANTHONY. *In coloured cover, price* 1s., *by post* 1s. 2d.

Fancy Work Series, Artistic. A Series of Illustrated Manuals on Artistic and Popular Fancy Work of various kinds. Each number is complete in itself, and issued at the uniform *price of* 6d., *by post* 7d. Now ready—(1) MACRAMÉ LACE (Second Edition); (2) PATCHWORK ; (3) TATTING ; (4) CREWEL WORK ; (5) APPLIQUÉ ; (6) FANCY NETTING.

Feathered Friends, Old and New. Being the Experience of many years' Observation of the Habits of British and Foreign Cage Birds. By DR. W. T. GREENE. Illustrated. *In cloth gilt, price* 5s., *by post* 5s. 4d.

Ferns, The Book of Choice: for the Garden, Conservatory, and Stove. Describing the best and most striking Ferns and Selaginellas, and giving explicit directions for their Cultivation, the formation of Rockeries, the arrangement of Ferneries, &c. By GEORGE SCHNEIDER. With numerous Coloured Plates and other Illustrations. *In 3 vols., large post 4to. Cloth gilt, price* £3 3s. *nett, by post* £3 5s.

Ferns, Choice British. Descriptive of the most beautiful Variations from the common forms, and their Culture. By C. T. DRUERY, F.L.S. Very accurate PLATES, and other Illustrations. *In cloth gilt, price* 2s. 6d., *by post* 2s. 9d.

Ferrets and Ferreting. Containing Instructions for the Breeding, Management, and Working of Ferrets. Second Edition, Re-written and greatly Enlarged. Illustrated. *In paper, price* 6d., *by post* 7d.

Fertility of Eggs Certificate. These are Forms of Guarantee given by the Sellers to the Buyers of Eggs for Hatching, undertaking to refund value of any unfertile eggs, or to replace them with good ones. Very valuable to sellers of eggs, as they induce purchases. *In books, with counterfoils, price* 6d., *by post* 7d.

Firework Making for Amateurs. A complete, accurate, and easily-understood work on Making Simple and High-class Fireworks. By DR. W. H. BROWNE, M.A. *In coloured wrapper, price 2s 6d., by post 2s. 9d.*

Fisherman, The Practical. Dealing with the Natural History, the Legendary Lore, the Capture of British Fresh-Water Fish, and Tackle and Tackle-making. By J. H. KEENE. *In cloth gilt, price 7s. 6d., by post 7s. 10d.*

Fish, Flesh, and Fowl When in Season, How to Select, Cook, and Serve. By MARY BARRETT BROWN. *In coloured wrapper, price 1s., by post 1s. 3d.*

Foreign Birds, Favourite, for Cages and Aviaries. How to Keep them in Health. Fully Illustrated. By W. T. GREENE, M.A., M.D., F.Z.S., &c. *In cloth, price 2s. 6d., by post 2s. 9d.*

Fox Terrier, The. Its History, Points, Breeding, Rearing, Preparing for Exhibition, and Coursing. By HUGH DALZIEL. Illustrated with Coloured Frontispiece and Plates. *In paper, price 1s., by post 1s. 2d.; cloth, 2s., by post 2s. 3d.*

Fox Terrier Stud Book. Edited by HUGH DALZIEL. *Price 3s. 6d. each, by post 3s. 9d. each.*
　　Vol. I., containing Pedigrees of over 1400 of the best-known Dogs, traced to their most remote known ancestors.
　　Vol. II. Pedigrees of 1544 Dogs, Show Record, &c.
　　Vol. III. Pedigrees of 1214 Dogs, Show Record, &c.
　　Vol. IV. Pedigrees of 1168 Dogs, Show Record, &c.
　　Vol. V. Pedigrees of 1662 Dogs, Show Record, &c.

Fretwork and Marquetry. A Practical Manual of Instructions in the Art of Fret-cutting and Marquetry Work. Profusely Illustrated. By D. DENNING. *In cloth, price 2s. 6d., by post 2s. 9d.*

Friesland Meres, A Cruise on the. By ERNEST R. SUFFLING. Illustrated. *In paper, price 1s., by post 1s. 2d.*

Fruit Culture for Amateurs. By S. T. WRIGHT. With Chapters on Insect and other Fruit Pests by W. D. DRURY. Illustrated. *In cloth gilt, price 3s. 6d., by post 3s. 9d.*

Game Preserving, Practical. Containing the fullest Directions for Rearing and Preserving both Winged and Ground Game, and Destroying Vermin; with other Information of Value to the Game Preserver. By W. CARNEGIE. Illustrated. *In cloth gilt, demy 8vo, price 21s., by post 21s. 5d.*

Games, the Book of a Hundred. By MARY WHITE. These Games are for Adults, and will be found extremely serviceable for Parlour Entertainment. They are Clearly Explained, are Ingenious, Clever, Amusing, and exceedingly Novel. *In stiff boards, price 2s. 6d. by post 2s. 9d.*

Gardening, Dictionary of. A Practical Encyclopædia of Horticulture, for Amateurs and Professionals. Illustrated with 2440 Engravings. Edited by G. NICHOLSON, Curator of the Royal Botanic Gardens, Kew; assisted by Prof. Trail, M.D., Rev. P. W. Myles, B.A., F.L.S., W. Watson, J. Garrett, and other Specialists. *In 4 vols., large post 4to. In cloth gilt, price £3, by post £3 2s.*

Gardening in Egypt. A Handbook of Gardening for Lower Egypt. With a Calendar of Work for the different Months of the Year. By WALTER DRAPER. *In cloth, price 3s. 6d., by post 3s. 9d.*

Gardening, Home. A Manual for the Amateur, Containing Instructions for the Laying Out, Stocking, Cultivation, and Management of Small Gardens—Flower, Fruit, and Vegetable. By W. D. DRURY, F.R.H.S. Illustrated. *In coloured wrapper, price 1s., by post 1s. 2d.*

Goat, Book of the. Containing Full Particulars of the Various Breeds of Goats, and their Profitable Management. With many Plates. By H. STEPHEN HOLMES PEGLER. Third Edition, with Engravings and Coloured Frontispiece. *In cloth gilt, price 4s. 6d., by post 4s. 10d.*

Goat-Keeping for Amateurs: Being the Practical Management of Goats for Milking Purposes. Abridged from "The Book of the Goat." Illustrated. *In paper, price 1s., by post 1s. 2d.*

Grape Growing for Amateurs. A Thoroughly Practical Book on Successful Vine Culture. By E. MOLYNEUX. Illustrated. *In paper, price 1s., by post 1s. 2d.*

Greenhouse Management for Amateurs. The Best Greenhouses and Frames, and How to Build and Heat them, Illustrated Descriptions of the most suitable Plants, with general and Special Cultural Directions, and all necessary information for the Guidance of the Amateur. Second Edition, Revised and Enlarged. Magnificently Illustrated. By W. J. MAY. *In cloth gilt, price 5s., by post 5s. 4d.*

Greyhound, The: Its History, Points, Breeding, Rearing, Training, and Running. By HUGH DALZIEL. With Coloured Frontispiece. *In cloth gilt, demy 8vo., price 2s. 6d., by post 2s. 9d.*

Guinea Pig, The, for Food, Fur, and Fancy. Its Varieties and its Management. By C. CUMBERLAND, F.Z.S. Illustrated. *In coloured wrapper, price 1s., by post 1s. 2d. In cloth gilt, with coloured frontispiece, price 2s. 6d., by post 2s. 9d.*

Handwriting, Character Indicated by. With Illustrations in Support of the Theories advanced, taken from Autograph Letters, of Statesmen, Lawyers, Soldiers, Ecclesiastics, Authors, Poets, Musicians, Actors, and the persons. Second Edition. By R. BAUGHAN. *In cloth gilt, price 2s 6d., by post 2s. 9d.*

Hardy Perennials and Old-fashioned Garden Flowers. Descriptions, alphabetically arranged, of the most desirable Plants for Borders, Rockeries, and Shrubberies, including Foliage as well as Flowering Plants. By J. WOOD. Profusely Illustrated. *In cloth, price 3s. 6d., by post 3s. 9d.*

Hawk Moths, Book of British. A Popular and Practical Manual for all Lepidopterists. Copiously illustrated in black and white from the Author's own exquisite Drawings from Nature. By W. J. LUCAS, B.A. *In cloth, price 3s. 6d., by post 3s. 9d.*

Home Medicine and Surgery: A Dictionary of Diseases and Accidents, and their proper Home Treatment. For Family Use. By W. J. MACKENZIE, M.D. Illustrated. *In cloth, price 2s. 6d., by post 2s, 9d.*

Horse-Keeper, The Practical. By GEORGE FLEMING, C.B., LL.D., F.R.C.V.S.. late Principal Veterinary Surgeon to the British Army, and Ex-President of the Royal College of Veterinary Surgeons. *In cloth, price 3s. 6d., by post 3s. 10d.*

Horse-Keeping for Amateurs. A Practical Manual on the Management of Horses, for the guidance of those who keep one or two for their personal use. By FOX RUSSELL. *In paper, price 1s., by post 1s. 2d. ; cloth 2s., by post 2s. 3d.*

Horses, Diseases of: Their Causes, Symptoms, and Treatment. For the use of Amateurs. By HUGH DALZIEL. *In paper, price 1s., by post 1s. 2 ; cloth 2s., by post 2s. 3d.*

Incubators and their Management. By J. H. SUTCLIFFE. New Edition, Revised and Enlarged. Illustrated. *In paper, price 1s., by post 1s. 2d.*

Inland Watering Places. A Description of the Spas of Great Britain and Ireland, their Mineral Waters, and their Medicinal Value, and the attractions which they offer to Invalids and other Visitors. Profusely Illustrated. A Companion Volume to "Seaside Watering Places." *In cloth, price 2s. 6d., by post 2s. 10d.*

Jack All Alone. Being a Collection of Descriptive Yachting Reminiscences By FRANK COWPER, B.A., Author of "Sailing Tours." Illustrated. *In cloth gilt, price 3s. 6d., by post 3s. 10d.*

Journalism, Practical: How to Enter Thereon and Succeed. A book for all who think of "writing for the Press." By JOHN DAWSON. *In cloth gilt, price 2s. 6d., by post 2s. 9d.*

Laying Hens, How to Keep and to Rear Chickens in Large or Small Numbers, in Absolute Confinement, with Perfect Success. By MAJOR G. F. MORANT. *In paper, price 6d., by post 7d.*

Library Manual, The. A Guide to the Formation of a Library, and the Values of Rare and Standard Books. By J. H. SLATER, Barrister-at-Law. Third Edition. Revised and Greatly Enlarged. *In cloth gilt, price 7s. 6d. nett, by post 7s. 10d.*

Magic Lanterns, Modern. A Guide to the Management of the Optical Lantern, for the Use of Entertainers, Lecturers, Photographers, Teachers, and others. By R. CHILD BAYLEY. *In paper, price 1s., by post 1s. 2d.*

Mice, Fancy: Their Varieties, Management, and Breeding. Third Edition, with additional matter and Illustrations. *In coloured wrapper representing different varieties, price 1s., by post 1s. 2d.*

Millinery, Handbook of. A Practical Manual of Instruction for Ladies. Illustrated. By MME. ROSÉE, Court Milliner, Principal of the School of Millinery. *In paper, price 1s., by post 1s. 2d.*

Model Yachts and Boats: Their Designing, Making, and Sailing. Illustrated with 118 Designs and Working Diagrams. By J. DU V. GROSVENOR. *In leatherette, price 5s., by post 5s. 3d.*

Monkeys, Pet, and How to Manage Them. Illustrated. By ARTHUR PATTERSON. *In cloth gilt, price 2s. 6d., by post 2s. 9d.*

Mountaineering, Welsh. A Complete and Handy Guide to all the Best Roads and Bye-Paths by which the Tourist should Ascend the Welsh Mountains. By A. W. PERRY. With numerous Maps. *In cloth gilt, price 2s. 6d., by post 2s. 9d.*

Mushroom Culture for Amateurs. With Full Directions for Successful Growth in Houses, Sheds, Cellars, and Pots, on Shelves, and Out of Doors. Illustrated. By W. J. MAY. *In paper, price 1s., by post 1s. 2d.*

Natural History Sketches among the Carnivora—Wild and Domesticated ; with Observations on their Habits and Mental Faculties. By ARTHUR NICOLS, F.G.S., F.R.G.S. Illustrated. *In cloth gilt, price 2s. 6d., by post 2s. 9d.*

Naturalist's Directory, The, for 1898 (fourth year of issue). Invaluable to all Students and Collectors. *In paper, price 1s., by post 1s. 1d.*

Needlework, Dictionary of. An Encyclopædia of Artistic, Plain, and Fancy Needlework ; Plain, practical, complete, and magnificently Illustrated. By S. F. A. CAULFEILD and B. C. SAWARD. *In demy 4to, 528pp, 829 Illustrations, extra cloth gilt, plain edges, cushioned bevelled boards, price 21s. nett, by post 21s. 9d. ; with COLOURED PLATES, elegant satin brocade cloth binding, and coloured edges, 31s. 6d. nett, by post 32s.*

Orchids: Their Culture and Management, with Descriptions of all the Kinds in General Cultivation. Illustrated by Coloured Plates and Engravings. By W. WATSON, Assistant-Curator, Royal Botanic Gardens, Kew; Assisted by W. BEAN, Foreman, Royal Gardens, Kew. Second Edition, Revised and with Extra Plates *In cloth gilt and gilt edges, price £1 1s. nett, by post £1 1s. 6d.*

Painters and Their Works. A Work of the Greatest Value to Collectors and such as are interested in the Art, as it gives, besides Biographical Sketches of all the Artists of Repute (not now living) from the 13th Century to the present date, the Market Value of the Principal Works Painted by Them, with Full Descriptions of Same. *In 3 vols., cloth, price 15s. nett per vol., by post 15s. 5d., or 37s. 6d. nett the set of 3, by post 38s. 3d.*

Painting, Decorative. A practical Handbook on Painting and Etching upon Textiles, Pottery, Porcelain, Paper, Vellum, Leather, Glass, Wood, Stone, Metals, and Plaster. for the Decoration of our Homes. By B. C. SAWARD. *In cloth gilt, price 3s. 6d., by post 3s. 9d.*

Parcel Post Dispatch Book (registered). An invaluable book for all who send parcels by post. Provides Address Labels, Certificate of Posting, and Record of Parcels Dispatched. By the use of this book parcels are insured against loss or damage to the extent of £2. Authorised by the Post Office. *Price 1s., by post 1s. 2d., for 100 parcels ; larger sizes if required.*

Parrakeets, Popular. How to Keep and Breed Them. By DR. W. T. GREENE, M.D., M.A., F.Z.S., &c. *In coloured wrapper, price 1s., by post, 1s. 2d.*

Parrot, The Grey, and How to Treat it. By W. T. GREENE, M.D., M.A., F.Z.S., &c. *In coloured wrapper, price 1s., by post 1s. 2d.*

Parrots, the Speaking. The Art of Keeping and Breeding the principal Talking Parrots in Confinement. By DR. KARL RUSS. Illustrated with COLOURED PLATES and Engravings. *In cloth gilt, price 5s., by post 5s. 4d.*

Patience, Games of, for one or more Players. How to Play 142 different Games of Patience. By M. WHITMORE JONES. Illustrated. Series I., 39 games ; Series II., 34 games ; Series III., 33 games ; Series IV., 37 games. Each 1s., by post 1s. 2d. *The four bound together in cloth gilt, price 5s., by post 5s. 4d.*

Perspective, The Essentials of. With numerous Illustrations drawn by the Author. By L. W. MILLER, Principal of the School of Industrial Art of the Pennsylvania Museum, Philadelphia. *Price 6s. 6d., by post 6s. 10d.*

Pheasant-Keeping for Amateurs. A Practical Handbook on the Breeding, Rearing, and General Management of Fancy Pheasants in Confinement. By GEO. HORNE. Fully Illustrated. *In cloth gilt, price 3s. 6d., by post 3s. 9d.*

Photographic Printing Processes, Popular. A Practical Guide to Printing with Gelatino-Chloride, Artigue, Platinotype, Carbon, Bromide, Collodio-Chloride, Bichromated Gum, and other Sensitised Papers. Illustrated. By H. MACLEAN, F.R.P.S. *Price 2s. 6d., by post 2s. 10d.*

Photography (Modern) for Amateurs. New and Revised Edition. By J. EATON FEARN. *In paper, price 1s., by post 1s. 2d.*

Pianofortes, Tuning and Repairing. The Amateur's Guide to the Practical Management of a Piano without the intervention of a Professional. By CHARLES BABBINGTON. *In paper, price 6d., by post 6½d.*

Picture-Frame Making for Amateurs. Being Practical Instructions in the Making of various kinds of Frames for Paintings, Drawings, Photographs, and Engravings. Illustrated. By the REV. J. LUKIN. *In paper, price 1s., by post 1s 2d.*

Pig, Book of the. The Selection, Breeding, Feeding, and Management of the Pig; the Treatment of its Diseases; the Curing and Preserving of Hams, Bacon, and other Pork Foods; and other information appertaining to Pork Farming. By PROFESSOR JAMES LONG. Fully Illustrated with Portraits of Prize Pigs, Plans of Model Piggeries, &c. *In cloth gilt, price 10s. 6d., by post 10s. 11d.*

Pig-Keeping, Practical: A Manual for Amateurs, based on personal Experience in Breeding, Feeding, and Fattening; also in Buying and Selling Pigs at Market Prices. By R. D. GARRATT. *In paper, price 1s., by post 1s. 2d.*

Pigeons, Fancy. Containing full Directions for the Breeding and Management of Fancy Pigeons, and Descriptions of every known Variety, together with all other information of interest or use to Pigeon Fanciers. Third Edition. 18 COLOURED PLATES, and 22 other full-page Illustrations. By J. C. LYELL. *In cloth gilt, price 10s. 6d., by post 10s. 10d.*

Pigeon-Keeping for Amateurs. A Complete Guide to the Amateur Breeder of Domestic and Fancy Pigeons. By J. C. LYELL. Illustrated. *In cloth, price 2s. 6d., by post 2s. 9d.*

Polishes and Stains for Wood: A Complete Guide to Polishing Woodwork, with Directions for Staining, and Full Information for Making the Stains, Polishes, &c., in the simplest and most satisfactory manner. By DAVID DENNING. *In paper, 1s., by post 1s. 2d.*

Pool, Games of. Describing Various English and American Pool Games, and giving the Rules in full. Illustrated *In paper, price 1s., by post 1s. 2d.*

Postage Stamps, and their Collection. A Practical Handbook for Collectors of Postal Stamps, Envelopes, Wrappers, and Cards. By OLIVER FIRTH, Member of the Philatelic Societies of London, Leeds, and Bradford. Profusely Illustrated. *In cloth gilt, price 3s. 6d., by post 3s. 10d.*

Postage Stamps of Europe, The Adhesive: A Practical Guide to their Collection, Identification, and Classification. Especially designed for the use of those commencing the Study. By W. A. S. WESTOBY. Beautifully Illustrated. *In Parts, 1s. each, by post 1s. 2d.*

Postmarks, History of British. With 350 Illustrations and a List of Numbers used in Obliterations. By J. H. DANIELS. *In cloth, price 2s. 6d., by post 2s. 9d.*

Pottery and Porcelain, English. A Guide for Collectors. Handsomely Illustrated with Engravings of Specimen Pieces and the Marks used by the different Makers. New Edition, Revised and Enlarged. By the REV. E. A. DOWNMAN. *In cloth gilt, price 5s., by post 5s. 3d.*

Poultry-Farming, Profitable. Describing in Detail the Methods that Give the Best Results, and pointing out the Mistakes to be Avoided. Illustrated. By J. H. SUTCLIFFE. *Price 1s., by post 1s. 2d.*

Poultry-Keeping, Popular. A Practical and Complete Guide to Breeding and Keeping Poultry for Eggs or for the Table. By F. A. MACKENZIE. Illustrated. *In paper, price 1s., by post 1s. 2d.*

Poultry and Pigeon Diseases Their Causes, Symptoms, and Treatment. A Practical Manual for all Fanciers. By QUINTIN CRAIG and JAMES LYELL. *In paper, price 1s., by post 1s. 2d.*

Poultry for Prizes and Profit. Contains: Breeding Poultry for Prizes, Exhibition Poultry and Management of the Poultry Yard. Handsomely Illustrated. Second Edition. By PROF. JAMES LONG. *In cloth gilt, price 2s. 6d., by post 2s. 10d.*

Rabbit, Book of The. A Complete Work on Breeding and Rearing all Varieties of Fancy Rabbits, giving their History, Variations, Uses, Points, Selection, Mating, Management, &c., &c. SECOND EDITION. Edited by KEMPSTER W. KNIGHT. Illustrated with Coloured and other Plates. *In cloth gilt, price 10s. 6d., by post 10s. 11d.*

Rabbits, Diseases of: Their Causes, Symptoms, and Cure. With a Chapter on THE DISEASES OF CAVIES. Reprinted from "The Book of the Rabbit" and "The Guinea Pig for Food, Fur and Fancy." *In paper, price 1s., by post 1s. 2d.*

Rabbits for Prizes and Profit. The Proper Management of Fancy Rabbits in Health and Disease, for Pets or the Market, and Descriptions of every known Variety, with Instructions for Breeding Good Specimens. Illustrated. By CHARLES RAYSON. *In cloth gilt, price 2s. 6d., by post 2s. 9d.* Also in Sections, as follows:

General Management of Rabbits. Including Hutches, Breeding, Feeding, Diseases and their Treatment, Rabbit Courts, &c. Fully Illustrated. *In paper, price 1s., by post 1s. 2d.*

Exhibition Rabbits. Being descriptions of all Varieties of Fancy Rabbits, their Points of Excellence, and how to obtain them. Illustrated. *In paper, price 1s., by post 1s. 2d.*

Road Charts (Registered). For Army Men, Volunteers, Cyclists, and other Road Users. By S. W. H. DIXON and A. B. H. CLERKE. No. 1.—London to Brighton. *Price 2d., by post 2½d.*

Roses for Amateurs. A Practical Guide to the Selection and Cultivation of the best Roses. Illustrated. By the REV. J. HONYWOOD D'OMBRAIN, Hon. Sec. Nat. Rose Soc. *In paper, price 1s., by post 1s. 2d.*

Sailing Guide to the Solent and Poole Harbour, with Practical Hints as to Living and Cooking on, and Working a Small Yacht. By LIEUT.-COL. T. G. CUTHELL. Illustrated with Coloured Charts. *In cloth gilt, price 2s. 6d., by post 2s. 2d.*

Sailing Tours. The Yachtman's Guide to the Cruising Waters of the English and Adjacent Coasts. With Descriptions of every Creek, Harbour, and Roadstead on the Course. With numerous Charts printed in Colours, showing Deep water, Shoals, and Sands exposed at low water, with sounding. *In Crown 8vo., cloth gilt.* By FRANK COWPER, B.A.

Vol. I., the Coasts of Essex and Suffolk, from the Thames to Aldborough. Six Charts. *Price 5s., by post 5s. 3d.*

Vol. II. The South Coast, from the Thames to the Scilly Islands, twenty-five Charts. *Price 7s. 6d., by post 7s. 10d.*

Vol. III. The Coast of Brittany, from L'Abervrach to St. Nazaire, and an Account of the Loire. Twelve Charts. *Price 7s. 6d., by post 7s. 10d.*

Vol. IV. The West Coast, from Land's End to Mull of Galloway, including the East Coast of Ireland. Thirty Charts. *Price 10s. 6d., by post 10s. 10d.*

Vol. V. The Coasts of Scotland and the N.E. of England down to Aldborough. Forty Charts. *Price 10s. 6d., by post 10s. 10d.*

St. Bernard, The. Its History, Points, Breeding, and Rearing. By HUGH DALZIEL. Illustrated with Coloured Frontispiece and Plates. *In cloth, price 2s 6d., by post 2s. 9d.*

St. Bernard Stud Book. Edited by HUGH DALZIEL. *Price 3s. 6d. each, by post 3s. 9d. each.*

Vol. I. Pedigrees of 1278 of the best known Dogs traced to their most remote known ancestors, Show Record, &c.

Vol. II. Pedigrees of 564 Dogs, Show Record, &c.

Sea-Fishing for Amateurs. Practical Instructions to Visitors at Seaside Places for Catching Sea-Fish from Pier-heads, Shore, or Boats, principally by means of Hand Lines, with a very useful List of Fishing Stations, the Fish to be caught there, and the Best Seasons. By FRANK HUDSON. Illustrated. *In paper, price 1s., by post 1s. 2d.*

Sea-Fishing on the English Coast. The Art of Making and Using Sea-Tackle, with a full account of the methods in vogue during each month of the year, and a Detailed Guide for Sea-Fishermen to all the most Popular Watering Places on the English Coast. By F. G. AFLALO. Illustrated. *In cloth gilt, price 2s. 6d., by post 2s. 9d.*

Sea-Life, Realities of. Describing the Duties, Prospects, and Pleasures of a Young Sailor in the Mercantile Marine. By H. E. ACRAMAN COATE. With a Preface by J. R. DIGGLE, M.A., M.L.S.B. *In cloth, price 3s. 6d., by post 3s. 10d.*

Seaside Watering Places. A Description of the Holiday Resorts on the Coasts of England and Wales, the Channel Islands, and the Isle of Man, giving full particulars of them and their attractions, and all information likely to assist persons in selecting places in which to spend their Holidays according to their individual tastes. Illustrated. Twenty-second Year of Issue. Ready in May. *In cloth, price 2s. 6d., by post 2s. 10d.*

Sea Terms, a Dictionary of. For the use of Yachtsmen, Amateur Boatmen, and Beginners. By A. Ansted. Fully Illustrated. *Cloth gilt, price 7s. 6d. net, by post 7s. 11d.*

Shadow Entertainments, and How to Work them : being Something about Shadows, and the way to make them Profitable and Funny. By A. Patterson. *In paper, price 1s., by post 1s. 2d.*

Shave, An Easy : The Mysteries, Secrets, and Whole Art of, laid bare for 1s., by post 1s. 2d. Edited by Joseph Morton.

Sheet Metal, Working in : Being Practical Instructions for Making and Mending Small Articles in Tin, Copper, Iron, Zinc, and Brass. Illustrated. Third Edition. By the Rev. J. Lukin, B.A. *In paper, price 1s., by post 1s. 1d.*

Shorthand, on Gurney's System (Improved), LESSONS IN : Being Instructions in the Art of Shorthand Writing as used in the Service of the two Houses of Parliament. By R. E. Miller. *In paper, price 1s., by post 1s. 2d.*

Shorthand, Exercises in, for Daily Half Hours, on a Newly-devised and Simple Method, free from the Labour of Learning. Illustrated. Being Part II. of "Lessons in Shorthand on Gurney's System (Improved)." By R. E. Miller. *In paper, price 9d., by post 10d.*

Skating Cards : An Easy Method of Learning Figure Skating, as the Cards *can be used on the Ice. In cloth case, 2s. 6d., by post 2s. 9d.; leather, 3s. 6d., by post 3s. 9d.* A cheap form is issued printed on paper and made up as a small book, 1s., by post 1s. 1d.

Sleight of Hand. A Practical Manual of Legerdemain for Amateurs and Others. New Edition, Revised and Enlarged Profusely Illustrated. By E. Sachs. *In cloth gilt, price 6s. 6d., by post 6s. 10d.*

Snakes, Marsupials, and Birds. A Charming Book of Anecdotes, Adventures, and Zoological Notes. A capital Book for Boys. By Arthur Nicols, F.G.S., F.R.G.S., &c. Illustrated. *In cloth gilt, price 3s. 6d., by post 3s. 10d.*

Taxidermy, Practical. A Manual of Instruction to the Amateur in Collecting, Preserving, and Setting-up Natural History Specimens of all kinds. With Examples and Working Diagrams. By Montagu Browne, F.Z.S., Curator of Leicester Museum. Second Edition. *In cloth gilt, price 7s. 6d., by post 7s. 10d.*

Thames Guide Book. From Lechlade to Richmond. For Boating Men, Anglers, Picnic Parties, and all Pleasure-seekers on the River. Arranged on an entirely new plan. Second Edition, profusely Illustrated. *In cloth, price 1s. 6d., by post 1s. 9d.*

Tomato and Fruit Growing as an Industry for Women. Lectures given at the Forestry Exhibition, Earl's Court, during July and August, 1893. By Grace Harriman, Practical Fruit Grower and County Council Lecturer. *In paper, price 1s., by post 1s. 1d.*

Tomato Culture for Amateurs. A Practical and very Complete Manual on the subject. By B. C. Ravenscroft. Illustrated. *In paper, price 1s., by post 1s. 1d.*

Trapping, Practical : Being some Papers on Traps and Trapping for Vermin, with a Chapter on General Bird Trapping and Snaring. By W. Carnegie. *In paper, price 1s., by post 1s. 2d.*

Turning for Amateurs : Being Descriptions of the Lathe and its Attachments and Tools, with minute Instructions for their Effective Use on Wood, Metal, Ivory, and other Materials. Second Edition, Revised and Enlarged. By James Lukin, B.A. Illustrated with 144 Engravings. *In cloth gilt, price 2s. 6d., by post 2s. 9d.*

Turning Lathes. A Manual for Technical Schools and Apprentices. A Guide to Turning, Screw-cutting, Metal-spinning, &c. Edited by James Lukin, B.A. Third Edition. With 194 Illustrations. *In cloth gilt, price 3s., by post 3s. 3d.*

Vamp, How to. A Practical Guide to the Accompaniment of Songs by the Unskilled Musician. With Examples. *In paper, price 9d., by post 10d.*

Vegetable Culture for Amateurs. Containing Concise Directions for the Cultivation of Vegetables in small Gardens so as to insure Good Crops. With Lists of the Best Varieties of each Sort. By W. J. May Illustrated. *In paper, price 1s., by post 1s. 2d.*

Ventriloquism, Practical. A thoroughly reliable Guide to the Art of Voice Throwing and Vocal Mimicry, Vocal Instrumentation, Ventriloquial Figures, Entertaining, &c. By ROBERT GANTHONY. Numerous Illustrations. *In cloth gilt, price 2s. 6d., by post 2s. 9d.*

Violins (Old) and their Makers: Including some References to those of Modern Times. By JAMES M. FLEMING. Illustrated with Facsimiles of Tickets, Sound-Holes, &c. *In cloth gilt, price 6s. 6d. nett, by post 6s. 10d.*

Violin School, Practical, for Home Students. Instructions and Exercises in Violin Playing, for the use of Amateurs, Self-learners, Teachers, and others. With a Supplement on "Easy Legato Studies for the Violin." By J. M. FLEMING. *Demy 4to, cloth gilt, price 9s. 6d., by post 10s. 2d.* Without Supplement, *price 7s. 6d., by post 8s.*

Vivarium, The. Being a Full Description of the most Interesting Snakes, Lizards, and other Reptiles, and How to Keep Them Satisfactorily in Confinement. By REV. G. C. BATEMAN. Beautifully Illustrated. *In cloth gilt, price 7s. 6d. nett, by post 8s.*

War Medals and Decorations. A Manual for Collectors, with some account of Civil Rewards for Valour. Beautifully Illustrated. By D. HASTINGS IRWIN. *In cloth gilt, price 7s. 6d., by post 7s. 10d.*

Whippet and Race-Dog, The: How to Breed, Rear, Train, Race, and Exhibit the Whippet, the Management of Race Meetings, and Original Plans of Courses. By FREEMAN LLOYD. *In cloth gilt, price 3s. 6d., by post 3s. 10d.*

Whist, Modern Scientific. A Practical Manual on new Lines, and with Illustrative Hands, printed in Colour. By C. J. MELROSE. *In cloth gilt, price 6s., by post 6s. 6d.*

Wildfowling, Practical: A Book on Wildfowl in Wildfowl Shooting. By HY. SHARP. The result of 25 years' experience Wildfowl Shooting under all sorts of conditions of locality as well as circumstances. Profusely Illustrated. *Demy 8vo, cloth gilt, price 12s. 6d. nett, by post 12s. 10d.*

Wild Sports in Ireland. Being Picturesque and Entertaining Descriptions of several visits paid to Ireland, with Practical Hints likely to be of service to the Angler, Wildfowler, and Yachtsman. By JOHN BICKERDYKE, Author of "The Book of the All-Round Angler," &c. Beautifully Illustrated from Photographs taken by the Author. *In cloth gilt, price 6s., by post 6s. 4d.*

Window Ticket Writing. Containing full Instructions on the Method of Mixing and Using the Various Inks, &c., required, Hints on Stencilling as applied to Ticket Writing, together with Lessons on Glass Writing, Japanning on Tin, &c. Especially written for the use of Learners and Shop Assistants. By WM. C. SCOTT. *In paper, price 1s., by post 1s. 2d.*

Wire and Sheet Gauges of the World. Compared and Compiled by C. A. B. PFEILSCHMIDT, of Sheffield. *In paper, price 1s., by post 1s. 1d.*

Wood Carving for Amateurs. Full Instructions for producing all the different varieties of Carvings. SECOND EDITION. Edited by D. DENNING. *In paper, price 1s., by post 1s. 2d.*

Workshop Makeshifts. Being a Collection of Practical Hints and Suggestions for the use of Amateur Workers in Wood and Metal. Fully Illustrated. By H. J. S. CASSALL. *In cloth gilt, price 2s. 6d., by post 2s. 9d.*

FICTION LIBRARY.

Decameron of a Hypnotist. Tales of Dread. By E. SUFFLING, Author of "The Story Hunter," &c. With Illustrations. *Cloth gilt, 3s. 6d., by post 3s. 10d.*

CLASSIFICATION INDEX.

Hair Preserved and Beautified.

The only article which really affords nourishment to the hair and resembles the oily matter which nature provides for its preservation is

ROWLAND'S MACASSAR OIL.

Without it the hair becomes dry and weak. It prevents the hair failing off, or turning grey, nourishes, preserves, and strengthens it more effectually than any other preparation; feeds the hair, removes scurf and harshness, and produces a strong and healthy growth. It is the best tonic and dressing for ladies' hair, and should always be used for children, as it forms the basis of a luxuriant growth. Also sold in Golden colour for fair and golden-haired ladies and children. Bottles, 3/6, 7/-, 10/6.

ROWLAND'S ODONTO
is the finest dentifrice. Removes all impurities from the teeth, imparts to them a brilliant polish, prevents and arrests decay, strengthens the gums, and sweetens the breath, 2/9.

ROWLAND'S KALYDOR
is the most perfect emollient preparation for beautifying the complexion and preserving it in all weathers. Allays all irritability of the skin, removes freckles, tan, redness, roughness, &c.; cures and heals all cutaneous eruptions, imparts a matchless beauty to the complexion and a softness and whiteness to the neck, hands, and arms unattainable by any other means. Sizes, 2/3 and 4/6.

ROWLAND'S EUKONIA
Is a pure, harmless, and non-metallic toilet powder in three tints—White, Rose, and Cream. Boxes, 1/- and 2/6. A certificate of Purity is attached to each box.

ROWLAND'S ESSENCE OF TYRE
Produces a perfect change in Red or Grey Hair to a beautiful and permanent Brown or Black, which colour remains so durable that neither washing nor perspiration can remove it. 4/- per box.

Ask Stores and Chemists for Rowland's Articles of Hatton Garden, London, and avoid spurious imitations.

The TESTIMONY of "DAGONET'S" DOGS.

12. *Clarence Terrace,*
Regents Park
N.W

May 1st, 1897.

Messrs. Spratts, Limited.

We, the undersigned Dogs, in common council assembled at opposite the Ducks' Villa, desire to express our high approval of "Spratts." We have lived on them all our lives, and when we ask for them we see that we get them.

(Signed) LADY GODIVA,
SANDOW, SAMSON,
BILLY GREET, BARNEY BARNATO,
PEDLAR PALMER, ALFRED SEWELL,
PRINNIE, FRIZZIE.

Their ✗ *mark.*

Witness to signatures of above, GEO. R. SIMS.

Photo. by G. & R. Lavis.　　　*Eastbourne.*

MR. GEORGE R. SIMS.